Memoirs
of a
Stuka Pilot

Memoirs
of a
Stuka Pilot

Helmut Mahlke

Translated by

John Weal

Frontline Books
London

Memoirs of a Stuka Pilot

This edition published in 2013 by Frontline Books,
an imprint of Pen & Sword Books Ltd,
47 Church Street, Barnsley, S. Yorkshire, S70 2AS
www.frontline-books.com

Copyright © E.S. Mittler & Sohn GmbH, 1993
Translation © Frontline Books, 2013

ISBN: 978-1-84832-664-4

First published in German as *Stuka. Angriff: Sturzflug*
by E.S. Mittler & Sohn GmbH, in 1993

CIP data records for this title are available from the British Library

For more information on our books, please visit
www.frontline-books.com, email info@frontline-books.com
or write to us at the above address.

Printed and bound in India by Replika Press Pvt. Ltd.

Typeset in 10.7/13.7 pt Arno Pro

Frontispiece: Hauptmann Helmut Mahlke at Dubovo-South airfield on 27 June 1941.
After a forced landing, Mahlke had just spent three days behind Soviet lines and
clearly shows signs of the strain involved.

Contents

Plates

All illustrations are from the author's collection. The colour plates are taken from the sketchbook of official war artist Hans Liska, also in the author's collection.

Foreword

I slept and dreamed
That life was joy.
I woke and saw
That life was duty.
I acted and lo –
Duty was joy!
                    Rabindranath Tagore

'How could you have let Adolf Hitler come to power? . . . How could you have gone along with everything?' These are the sort of questions that younger people have often asked me and others of my generation. I strongly suspect that most of them regard the answers we try to give them as unsatisfactory. Even we 'old ones' now find the events of the 1930s hard to comprehend. They can only be understood if looked at in the light of the situation in Germany at the time: the bitter economic plight of the masses and the almost total lack of hope for the future, both of which arose from the country's defeat in the First World War and the subsequent impositions of the detested Treaty of Versailles. But for the youth of today, who have – thank God – grown up in conditions of relative prosperity, and with much more freedom of thought and movement, such circumstances are hard to imagine.

   We of the older generation have learned the lessons of our past, lessons which lead us to hope that such catastrophes can be avoided in the future. But the realities of today are giving rise to doubts that those lessons will continue to be heeded. This is one of the reasons why I decided it might be beneficial to put my memories of those times down on paper – so that the future might be not just different, but better.

   This book does not want to glorify war. But what it *does* want to do is to use this portrayal of one young man's experiences of war to bring about a deeper understanding of the past and, at the same time, record those human values – the courage, comradeship and selflessness – that should be safeguarded today to ensure the future.

More specifically, it tells the story of one Stuka Gruppe in time of war. I. Träger-Stuka 186, as we knew it, was activated at Kiel-Holtenau in 1939 as a naval dive-bomber Gruppe, originally intended for service aboard the aircraft carrier *Graf Zeppelin*. Upon the outbreak of war it was transferred to the Luftwaffe and attached to Stukageschwader 1, being officially incorporated into that unit as III./StG 1 after the fall of France. In the autumn of 1943 the Gruppe was again redesignated, this time to become III./SG 1. It subsequently converted from Ju 87s to single-seat Fw 190 ground-attack fighters, which it flew until the end of the war.

As regular soldiers of the then Weimar Republic we were not entitled to take part in general elections. So not one of us actually voted for Adolf Hitler. Our task was to perform our military duties to the best of our ability – carrying out the orders of a regime voted into power by the German people. During the Second World War the Stukas did this by putting their lives on the line, and achieving successes beyond all expectations in the firm belief that they were serving a worthy cause: fighting for the survival of their homeland and freeing it from the oppressive shackles of the Versailles Treaty.

Our opponents may have feared the Stukas, but they respected their fighting qualities.

I dedicate my story to the Stukas in recognition of their many achievements and in honoured memory of my fallen comrades.

Helmut Mahlke
Heikendorf, autumn 1993

Foreword to the English Edition

In the nearly seven decades that have passed since the end of the Second World War the memoirs of numerous Luftwaffe fighter aces have appeared in the English language. But this is only the second major autobiography to be written by a German dive-bomber pilot since Hans Ulrich Rudel's classic *Stuka Pilot* was first published in English (in Dublin) in the early 1950s.

This present work, however, is no mere imitation of that earlier book – rather, it complements it. For whereas Rudel's narrative deals almost exclusively with the fighting on the Eastern Front post-June 1941, Helmut Mahlke served as a Stuka commander during the opening months and years of the war when the crank-winged Junkers Ju 87 was arguably the most feared and fearsome weapon in the Luftwaffe's armoury.

What follows is therefore a unique and gripping first-hand, Stuka pilot's eye view of some of the most historic air battles of the Second World War: the campaigns in Poland and France, Dunkirk, the Battle of Britain, the bombing of Malta, North Africa, Crete and Operation Barbarossa, the invasion of the Soviet Union.

With the exception of one or two very brief passages of a socio-political nature, which have been omitted as being of little relevance to the English-speaking reader, this is a true representation of the original text. A few historical inaccuracies have been corrected, but the benefit of hindsight has been studiously avoided. The claims made and beliefs (however abhorrent) expressed in these pages are exactly as the author set them down, even if – in some instances – more modern research may cast doubt on their veracity.

One addition has been made to the German original. Helmut Mahlke ends his story with his admission into hospital after being shot down for a third time in Russia. But he retained a keen interest in 'his' Gruppe, as he called it. For the benefit of an English-speaking readership it has therefore been decided to add a short 'afterword' chronicling the Gruppe's activities during the remainder of the war and describing what later befell some of the personalities his narrative brings so vividly to life.

It has been assumed that the reader has a working knowledge of Luftwaffe ranks, unit designations, organizational framework and the like. The German terms relating to such have only been explained or elaborated upon in the more unfamiliar cases. Lastly, in keeping with the period covered, place names have, wherever possible, been given in the form common at the time.

John Weal
Cookham, summer 2012

Chapter 1
Childhood

Born in Berlin-Lankwitz in August 1913, my very first recollection of soldiers dates back to the days of the First World War. My father, a local government senior planning officer in Berlin, was a Hauptmann der Reserve (captain in the reserve) and commander of a railway engineer company that saw service in both France and Russia.

During one brief spell of home duty he had ridden 'tall in the saddle' at the head of his company as it marched through the streets of our neighbourhood. We cheered and waved from the pavement. Although I was only a tiny little fellow, my father gestured for me to be lifted up to him. He sat me in front of him on the horse's broad back and let me ride along for part of the way.

It naturally made a huge impression on me. These were real . . . *daten* – my infant tongue couldn't manage all three syllables of the word '*Soldaten*', the German for 'soldiers' – and it was my very own father who was leading them! Young as I was, I can still clearly recall how proud I felt of him, and for days afterwards I could talk of nothing but the . . . *daten*.

As I was the youngest of her three children, my loving mother lavished special care and affection on me. Times were hard and food was short. Mother was able to rent a small plot of land close to our flat, and this she cultivated so successfully that we had the basic necessities to survive. Being the daughter of a country vicar and having grown up in a rural parish, she knew how to grow things. I was allowed to help her, but I suspect that my early attempts at weeding did a lot more harm than good. It soon taught me, however, that – even when times were bad – it was always possible to keep one's head above water with a little initiative and the use of one's own hands.

The First World War ended in revolution. Father returned home to a Berlin that was full of unrest. At night he would go out on patrol as a member of a volunteer security force charged with maintaining law and order on the streets. Mother was greatly concerned for his safety. But quiet finally descended on the city again and life got back to some semblance of normality – if the mere absence of immediate danger to life or limb can be described as normal!

The situation remained desperate, however. The whole nation was suffering under the yoke of the Treaty of Versailles. As a child I only ever heard the treaty referred to as the 'disgraceful *Diktat*'. It was apparently the cause of all our woes and, together with the lies about our war guilt, had wounded the country's pride deeply. It was the subject of endless discussion among the grown-ups.

And then came inflation. The value of money fell so catastrophically from one day to the next that on one occasion father came home from work with four packets of typing paper. They had swallowed his entire week's civil service salary. Mother was furious! How was she supposed to feed her family on four thousand sheets of paper? Father tried to pacify her by pointing out that the same amount of money wouldn't even be enough to buy a single loaf of bread the following day. Besides, he was lucky to have got the paper just before the shop shut. He needed it for the reports he had to write in his part-time job as a municipal dry-rot inspector. And somehow or other mother managed to cope, no doubt by dipping into the small stock of produce harvested from the tiny allotment that she still tended.

These were very hard times for all Germans – and the 'disgraceful *Diktat*' was seen as the root cause of everything. But in response there was a surge of national pride in the hearts of the nation's menfolk. With a growing sense of confidence and self-assurance, our fathers began to regard themselves as responsible citizens of their Fatherland once more.

I give just one small example to illustrate my point: as a young boy, whenever my parents entertained guests I would be invited into the 'salon', where the ladies were drinking mocha, and allowed to serve them with milk and sugar. Afterwards I would pass around the cigars and offer lights to the gentlemen gathered in the smoking room. There they would stand – professors, engineers, bankers, teachers and clergymen – their chests swelling with pride and with iron watch-chains dangling from their waistcoats. These chains were inscribed with the words: 'I gave gold for iron.' Their owners were fond of boasting about the amount of tax that they had paid . . . and the larger the amount, the prouder they were! They saw their contributions to the nation's coffers as both an expression and a measure of their civic worth.

Who could imagine anything of the like happening among a similar group today? If the subject of tax came up at all, the conversation would no doubt revolve around the different sorts of dodges that could be employed to 'save' on one's tax bill. But back then the tax system, and the voting system, were both very different. Even so, we could still learn a thing or two from our fathers, one being that it is not always right simply to make demands and expect the state to provide. Instead, it should be the responsibility of every citizen to support the state to the best of his own particular ability.

As a ten-year old I was permitted to type out father's reports and thus earn myself a modest amount of pocket money. I am still amazed to this day at the unending patience my father displayed as he slowly and carefully dictated his shorthand notes to me. At first he would often have to spell out unfamiliar words letter by letter. But I was full of enthusiasm and felt that I was helping the family and being very grown up, especially when I received my first 'wages' – the very first few *Pfennigs* that I had ever earned in my life, and which I naturally looked after with great care!

Father continued to let me earn my pocket money in this way right up until my *Abitur*, my final school exams. At first I got ten *Pfennigs* for every mistake-free page of typing that I produced. Later this was increased to twenty *Pfennigs*, and by the time I reached the sixth form it had risen to the princely sum of fifty *Pfennigs* per sheet. This allowed me to finance my hobbies. My first purchase was an ancient linen-covered canoe that was only held together and kept watertight by the numerous coats of paint applied by its many previous owners. But I loved messing about in that canoe and on hot summer days I was the scourge of Berlin's Wannsee. Later I was even able to treat myself to a ten-hour course of riding lessons.

The world of politics meant little to us children. That was something for the grown-ups. Nor were we subjected to any overt political pressure at school. All our free time was spent playing games, hiking and in sporting activities of every kind. We realised, of course, that our parents were very conservative and rigid adherents of the German National People's Party. They were firmly convinced that our country was still being unfairly shackled by the terms of the Versailles Treaty.

My parents felt this particularly keenly, as they had spent their first years of married life in the German colony of Tsingtao on the coast of China. Here at the turn of the century my father, in his role as government building supervisor, had overseen the construction of various official buildings. My parents had many interesting tales to tell of the big wide world. But Germany's overseas colonies had also been lost as a result of the Treaty of Versailles. Admittedly, conditions at home had gradually improved over the course of the intervening years, but the blame for all the difficulties that remained was – as always – still placed fairly and squarely at the doors of the 'disgraceful *Diktat*'. The older generation had to struggle on burdened by the knowledge that, for the foreseeable future, no matter how hard they worked or how many sacrifices they made, it would not alter the fact that the Fatherland lay helpless and humbled.

It was against this background that in 1931 – aged seventeen and just having passed my *Abitur* – I volunteered my services to the Reichsmarine as an officer-cadet. By so doing I genuinely believed that I would be making my own small contribution to the development of our nation. At the same time, of course, I also hoped that it would give me the opportunity to experience at first hand those far-off places and peoples that my parents had spoken of, and which I read about in the books by scientists and famous explorers that I devoured whenever I could get my hands on them.

But to my great disappointment I was turned down. The reason given was '6kg underweight'. True, as a child brought up in the big city during the lean wartime and post-war years, I was not very sturdily built; in fact, when it came to trials of strength in gymnastics or sports I was a total washout. But I could more than hold my own when stamina and endurance were called for, and so I didn't abandon my aims straight away.

I therefore decided instead to study marine engineering and aeronautical design at the renowned Technische Hochschule in Berlin-Charlottenburg, my reasoning being that this could only be of benefit to me in ultimately achieving the profession of my dreams. In the meantime I continued to call in on the city's naval recruiting officer at regular three-monthly intervals in order to find out whether, and in what other ways, I could improve my chances of a military career.

I must have made the poor man's life a misery with all my inane questions: demanding to know, for example, if the Navy really did go shopping for its officer-cadets on the basis of bodyweight alone? It was meant light-heartedly. But, just to be on the safe side, I thought I should perhaps eat a bowl of oatmeal porridge every day in an effort to put on those missing pounds. (This was a decision not taken lightly, as back then porridge oats were not the tasty treat that they are today. They were full of coarse grains that stuck in one's gullet and it required several hard swallows to get each mouthful down.)

I also described to the recruiting officer the steps I was taking to prepare myself as far as possible for my hoped-for naval career, including the studies at Charlottenburg and my enrolling for a sailing course with the Hanseatic Yacht Club Neustadt up on the Baltic coast. I added that I would also like to learn to fly, but that unfortunately my parents couldn't afford the tuition fees. He must have made a note of this latter snippet, for during the second visit of my renewed round of applications for the following year's intake, things finally started to happen.

After the usual medical examination I was asked to attend a two-day 'psycho-technical aptitude test', at the end of which I was required to come back again the following day. It was all terribly secretive. A jovial gentleman of advanced years welcomed me in a very friendly manner. Then he began to ask me a lot of questions. I couldn't for the life of me see where all this was heading. I was worried that he wanted to trip me up somehow. For example, he showed me a silhouette and asked, 'What's that?' – 'It's a silhouette,' I replied – 'Yes, but what does it *show*?' – 'A hare sitting up on its hind legs in a field.' – 'And can you picture the hare hopping away across the field?' – 'No.' – 'Why not?' – 'Because it's not really a hare, just a silhouette.'

For a good hour I kept asking myself what was the point behind all this question and answer business. But at last came the question that explained everything: 'Do you, in fact, know why you are here?' – 'Because I have volunteered to join the Navy.' – 'True, but I'm actually a doctor of aviation medicine and my job here today is to assess your suitability for pilot training.' This was absolute music to my ears! In the highest of spirits I sailed through the rest of the examination – and this time with success.

A few weeks later the naval recruiting officer telephoned to arrange a visit to my parents. I took the precaution of preparing them beforehand: 'If he should ask whether you consent to my being trained as a pilot, there's only one possible answer: "Yes!"' But mother was naturally concerned. She quoted the old proverb about not trusting oneself to the water, before adding, '. . . and as if that's not bad enough, now you want to go up in the air as well?' In the end, however, my parents gave me their blessing. I nonetheless received yet another deferment from the Navy, although in the same post I got my enrolment forms for the Deutsche Verkehrsfliegerschule [German Commercial Pilot's School] at Warnemünde.

On 1 April 1932 I was one of eighteen hopeful naval officer-candidates who presented themselves for final selection at Warnemünde, a small town on the Baltic coast north of Rostock. Twelve of us would be taught to fly here. The other six would depart to join the Navy's normal sea officer's training course. This was the last hurdle!

Proceedings began with yet another aircrew medical examination. The doctor's female assistant led off with the usual: 'If you would please strip, gentlemen.' This brought a prompt rejoinder from our Roderich Küppers: 'After you, miss!' And that set the tone. The whole affair was very informal and relaxed (although the doctor's assistant had sadly declined Roderich's invitation). When it came to my turn the doctor asked, 'How come you have such rosy lips? Do you use make-up?' That's something you probably know more about than I do, I thought, and so I answered in a similarly light-hearted vein, 'Naturally – but only the very best 4711 Eau de Cologne, of course!' His answering grin showed that he had a sense of humour and that we understood each other.

Later we were taken up for a test flight – a first for all of us – during which we were allowed to 'stir the stick around a little bit' to determine whether or not we possessed a natural 'feel' for flying. It's a funny thing: either you 'have it' – in which case you can be taught to fly – or you don't. And if you don't, you'll never master the art of flying however hard you try. Nobody knows where it comes from. The 'Old Eagles' of the First World War used to say that a natural flyer is born with it in the seat of his pants. And that's as good a place as any until some scientist investigates further and comes up with an alternative answer – or can perhaps suggest a different part of the anatomy!

At the end of the examination the doctor delivered his verdict on each of us. In my case, after appearing to ponder for a while, he announced: 'Well, he may have the complexion of a young girl, but he goes at things like a terrier after a rat!' – which was his somewhat unorthodox way of saying that I was in, one of the twelve 'new boys' who would be joining the Warnemünde German Commercial Pilot's School. I felt as if I had just won the lottery! Firstly, I had been one of only ninety naval officer-candidates selected from over 2,000 applicants. And then, of those ninety, I was one of just twelve who had been chosen for flying training! What I had only dared to hope for in my wildest dreams was now about to become reality.

Chapter 2
Training to be a Naval Pilot

We spent the first four weeks attending a course at the Hanseatic Yacht Club at Neustadt in Holstein, where we were introduced to the basic rules of seamanship; in other words, everything that we needed to know in order to be able to manoeuvre small boats (and later also floatplanes) about on the water without danger to ourselves or to others.

Then we moved along the coast to Warnemünde to begin flying training proper. The aircraft we flew were Udet U 12a Flamingos, the same type of machine that the ex-First World War fighter ace, Ernst Udet himself, was currently using at air shows up and down the country to thrill the crowds with displays of his flying ability and aerobatic artistry.

The Flamingo was an open cockpit, two-seater biplane – primitive in the extreme by today's standards – but 'fully aerobatic' nonetheless. The instructor sat in the front seat, the pupil behind him. Details of each flight had to be finalized before take-off, for once the engine was running there was no means of communication between the two occupants, as the machine had neither radio nor intercom.

To get the engine to start it had to be hand-cranked by a member of the ground crew. This was not an altogether safe occupation. Before the ignition was switched on the propeller needed to be swung a few times and then – with the ignition now on – the mechanic had to give one last almighty 'heave' while, at the same time, leaping smartly out of the way as the engine sprang into life. If he was not quick enough he ran the risk of being injured, or even killed by the whirling blades. Safety was therefore always of paramount importance during this procedure.

There weren't many controls in the Flamingo, just the petrol cock to regulate the supply of fuel to the engine, the ignition lock and key, the throttle, the elevator trimming wheel (rudder trim could only be adjusted on the ground by means of the trim tabs) and, finally, the control column and rudder pedals. This meant there wasn't a lot that could be forgotten or overlooked, and consequently rapid progress was made during our early training flights. These always began with the instructor doing everything first, while the pupil simply rested his hands and feet lightly on the controls to 'get the feel of things' before he then replicated the instructor's movements.

Initially we concentrated on 'circuits and bumps'. This was to teach us how to take off and land. After only a few lessons the instructors began to place both hands in plain sight on the cockpit sill, which meant that the pupil was expected to perform the take-off 'on his own'. Landings were much harder, however, as the trainee had to learn how to judge and coordinate his height, course, angle of approach and landing speed correctly in order to touch down alongside the landing cross.

This was important at Warnemünde where, in those days, the landing ground was little more than a tiny patch of grass. If you came in too fast or too high you would invariably overshoot and have to go round again. Anyone forced to fly this extra circuit, known as the 'lap of honour', was sure to be the butt of some good-natured ragging from his comrades when he eventually got down.

And if a pilot came in too high and with too little speed the resulting heavy landing – a 'boomps landing' as it was then commonly called – would inevitably bend the mainwheel axle so badly that it had to be straightened out before the machine could take off again.

But this was not as serious as it sounds. A couple of mechanics would be called across from the workshops – if they weren't already on their way, that is; they seemed to possess some sort of sixth sense as to when their services were going to be needed! Armed with a large iron crowbar apiece, they would advance on the machine with the weary measured tread of the true mechanic, shove a crowbar into each end of the axle – which was itself just a hollow iron tube – and, at the command 'Both together now!' each would lean his whole bodyweight against his crowbar. The axle was straight. The aircraft could take off again. The mechanics would be assured of their 'due' crate of beer (paid for by the offending pilot) and the incident was over and forgotten.

I had flown a good number of circuits, each of some two to four minutes' duration, when my instructor, 'Fritze' Festner, put both hands on the cockpit sill just as we were coming in to land. His message was clear: 'You are to carry out the landing on your own' or, in today's parlance: 'You have control.' And after this, once we had a sufficient number of normal landings under our belt, it was time to tackle the problem of precision landings. At a height of some 300 metres above the landing cross the throttle would be pulled back to idle. It was then up to the pupil to ease the machine into a gentle left-hand gliding turn and put it down as close to the landing cross as possible. This manoeuvre was practised from several different directions of approach.

To prepare us for an emergency landing in the event of engine failure, the instructor next switched the ignition off altogether. This was always done close to the airfield, enabling the pupil to glide in with a dead engine. Again, the object of the exercise was to come to a stop as close as one could to the landing cross. This was the last thing that had to be mastered before we were allowed to go solo, something we were all looking forward to with great excitement.

After I had completed about eighty training flights the big day finally arrived. We had landed and taxied back to the take-off point when 'Fritze' Festner climbed out of his cockpit and said, 'Cleared for your first solo flight!'

This is the moment of truth for every pilot. One he will never forget. And one he finds it quite impossible to describe to anybody who has not experienced it for himself: suddenly, and out of a clear blue sky (funny how the skies are always blue for first solo flights) the pilot finds himself, quite literally, on his own – the responsibility for what is about to follow is his and his alone. He has been taught everything that he needs to know, but now his concentration is absolute. He is desperate not to make the smallest error: full throttle, start to roll, hold the stick forward until the tailskid lifts off the ground, let the speed build up, keep her steady, pull the stick back gently, the bumping of the wheels across the grass ceases and *I am flying!*

Climb, ease off the throttle slightly, maintain height, now a gentle left-hand circuit of the field. I can see my instructor standing there below watching my progress. How tiny he looks now! Everybody down there looks tiny – or, at least, that's how they appear to me. I am the only one who is the same size as he was before – in fact, I imagine myself to be even bigger than before. I am beyond the reach of all those midgets clustered below; my whole being is filled with a sense of freedom such as I have never felt before.

But I have got a job to do. I have been ordered to fly a normal circuit. Nothing would give me greater pleasure, but perhaps I might be allowed to stretch it out a fraction further than is strictly necessary? The heady experience of flying through the heavens completely on one's own needs to be savoured just a little. All too soon I spot another aircraft in the landing pattern ahead of me. Be sure to keep a safe distance!

That was, without doubt, the longest and most enjoyable circuit I ever flew in the Flamingo. But my instructor raised no objections. It was enough that I had 'flown myself in'. Although it reflected none of the excitement of the occasion, this was the somewhat uninspiring expression generally used to denote a first solo successfully completed. Many of my course comrades also 'flew themselves in' on the same day, so we had ample reason to celebrate that evening!

After this milestone we rarely flew with an instructor in the front cockpit again; only on special occasions, such as a cross-country familiarization flight, or the first practice emergency landing in open country. Mostly we flew alone. On longer cross-country flights, however, the second cockpit was usually occupied by another trainee, who would be taking the opportunity to improve his map-reading skills.

Our flying training was backed up by ground tuition, particularly on days when the weather was bad. During such sessions we were introduced to the science of aircraft and engine design, the theory of aerodynamics, meteorology and 'What action to take in cases of emergency' – in short, all the things that would help us to become more competent and proficient pilots.

Well armed with this theoretical knowledge, our next step was aerobatic training. My aerobatics instructor, one Olaf Bielenstein, was brief and to the point:

> First, I'll demonstrate each figure separately. You keep a light hand on the controls, get the feel of what I've just done, and then fly the same manoeuvre. At the end, I'll go through the whole programme once again, and then you do the landing.

Off we went. At first I found it all rather tame: climb to a height of 2,000 metres – a loop – right-hand turn – left-hand turn – a roll to the right – a roll to the left.

I copied each of his movements to the best of my ability. He made me practise the rolls several times over. Finally satisfied, Olaf went through the entire programme again as promised . . . and then some! He hurled the aircraft about with such wild abandon that I scarcely knew what was up and what was down. He ended the performance with a terrifying spin before handing the controls over to me for the landing. But I made a complete pig's ear of it, misjudging my height so badly that Olaf had to grab the stick back again and ram the throttle forwards to prevent my committing the father and mother of all 'boomps landings'.

White as a sheet, I clambered unsteadily out of my seat. My stomach hadn't finished its own aerobatics yet and was still performing turns and rolls. While Olaf was patiently explaining to me the points I would have to watch, my breakfast fell out of my face. This made not the slightest impression on Olaf Bielenstein. He was clearly used to it and simply carried on talking. By now I was 'all ears' again and paying attention to what my instructor was telling me. What it boiled down to was: 'Right, I've shown you how to do it. So now climb back in and fly the whole programme again by yourself!'

This is going to be fun, I thought, as I struggled back into my seat, still pale as death and reeking of vomit. A final few words of advice from Olaf as I strapped myself in and then I was taxiing back out to the start line. 'Cleared for take-off!' – throttle to the gate – and suddenly I began to feel much more at ease. In fact, as I worked my way through the aerobatic programme I had never felt better. My stomach now knew where it was going, because I was doing the flying. And for the first time – with a feeling akin to intoxication – I was experiencing the joy of pure flight as I threw the aircraft about the sky enveloped in a wonderful sense of release and freedom!

At first, of course, our aerobatic figures were not all that successful. It took quite a number of practice flights before we could perform them properly and cleanly. But after a total of five-and-a-quarter hours in the air, our aerobatic training came to a close with an examination, in which we were required to fly the complete aerobatic programme before rounding off with a precision deadstick landing.

I now had my A-1 (Land) and K-1 (Aerobatic) pilot's certificates, but still no vehicle driving licence. But did I really need one? It would be a long time before I could afford to buy a car. As trainee pilots we earned little more than pocket money, and not very generous pocket money at that. We certainly couldn't do a lot with it. But, at eighteen or nineteen years of age, it meant that we were the 'keepers of our own purses'. This was very important to me. The feeling of financial independence boosted my self-confidence enormously. It must have been a great relief to my parents too. They had enough problems as it was. What with the expenses entailed in building their own house and financing my two elder sisters' studies, they were already having to live very economically.

We trainee pilots also led a simple and frugal life. We were housed in two rooms of the old airfield building: six of us to a room – three two-tier bunk beds in each – a small clothes locker with built-in wash basin apiece, a table, and six chairs. There was hardly enough space to turn round, let alone move about. We ate in the nearby mess hut, which was also furnished in a very Spartan-like manner with just the bare essentials. But we accepted it all with good grace. After all, we were learning to *fly*!

All our waking thoughts were concentrated on this one aim. We simply didn't have the time to worry about what we might be missing out on, or to wish for things to be any different. What little free time we *did* have was more than taken care of with such odd jobs as cleaning the aircraft's engines or 'pumping out floats'. We were frequently called upon to perform this latter chore. Whenever a seaplane took off or landed, a certain amount of water inevitably got into its floats. The thinking was, presumably, that as budding seaplane pilots ourselves, it was in our own best interests to make sure that the floats of the school's aircraft were kept as dry and buoyant as possible.

We also found ourselves involved in more than our fair share of involuntary physical training during our off-duty hours. This was thanks almost entirely to the Director of the DVS Warnemünde and the so-called 'Schnatermanns' that he handed out so liberally. Perhaps a word of explanation might be in order here. The process began with the morning parade: if a pupil was not turned out in strictly regulation manner, or had not shaved properly, he would simply be told:

'You've got a Schnatermann.' And so it would go on throughout the whole day, with Schnatermanns being awarded left, right and centre for the slightest misdemeanour.

After duty every unfortunate transgressor would be required to change into sports gear and report to the landing stage on the banks of the Breitling – the large body of inland water formed by the River Warnow just before it emptied into the Baltic – that the Warnemünde school used for its seaplane operations.

We would then be ferried by crash tender across to the far shore of the Breitling. Here, set among the trees, was a large forestry lodge and restaurant – the eponymous 'Schnatermann's'. It was a popular destination for holidaymakers and hikers alike. But less so for us. We were simply unloaded there and then had to run all the way back around the Breitling to the airfield. Although there was no set pace, hunger and the prospect of the evening meal meant that we seldom wasted any time. It soon became routine, and turned us all into useful long-distance runners into the bargain!

After supper we would often sit together listening to the sounds of our 'house band'. This was the brainchild of our musical genius, Storp junior – better known as 'Struppke' – who played a mean jazz trumpet and almost any other instrument he could lay his hands on. Kowalewski, 'Ko' for short, was a dab hand on the tango-harmonica and piano. Jochen Fehling, 'Tubby', accompanied them on the flute and Roderich Küppers – the 'darling of all unattached ladies' – was usually to be found on percussion, although we all had a go on the drums at one time or another.

We didn't have any sheet music; it wasn't needed. Nor did it matter, for Struppke couldn't read music in those days anyway. But he could produce some really swinging tunes and coax the catchiest melodies out of whatever instrument he happened to be playing. Turning to Ko on the piano, he would simply say: 'A-major', stamp his foot on the floor two or three times to establish the beat, and off they would go. Each in his own fashion, but blending so harmoniously as a whole that you would think they had been playing together for years.

The more excited Struppke got, the more frequently he would jump from one instrument to the next, amazing us with an intricately improvised solo passage skilfully interwoven with the melody of a popular hit of the day, before then soaring off on yet another new flight of fancy of his own making. Ko always seemed to be on the same musical wavelength. His piano accompaniments provided the perfect backing. And when Struppke sat down beside him at the keyboard they would immediately start to play four-handed, without a moment's break and each inspiring the other to even greater heights.

The music that we made and enjoyed during those evenings together was so original, spontaneous and full of spirit that we couldn't get enough of it. I have never experienced anything like it since. This was due in no small measure to our more gifted comrades being able to express their exuberance in music. It was a feeling we all shared in common: the exuberance of *flying*! For us, mankind's oldest dream had become a reality.

In 1932 aviation in Germany was still in its infancy – another result of the Treaty of Versailles, by the way – and was regarded by most people as something rather special. It was a world open to very few. But to those few the air meant freedom. Airspace was not as congested as it is today, and strict air traffic control not yet a necessity. Back then flight safety consisted of little more than a controller's making a note prior to an aircraft's departure, and ticking it off again when a phone call was received from its point of destination to say that it had arrived safely. It was only when no such message came in, or if the pilot hadn't phoned to say that he had had to make a forced landing somewhere en route, that a search and rescue operation would be set in motion.

In those early 1930s flying was a far more romantic affair than it is today. This applied just as much to those actually involved in it, whose shared passion for aviation created a special bond of comradeship. The aura of flying was shrouded in such secrecy that the ordinary man in the street looked upon a pilot as some sort of heroic adventurer. But flying was not as dangerous as most people thought. Nor had it been for a long time. Our generation had, to a large extent, assimilated the collective lessons learnt at such high cost by our predecessors, the 'Old Eagles' of the Great War. Nevertheless, once aloft a pilot had to be entirely self-reliant. He alone was the one who had to deal with any unforeseen emergencies. And, truth be told, there were enough of those – just as there always will be as long as man continues to take to the air.

Which is why, perhaps, we were more than a little proud of the fact that we could (already!) fly. At weekends, whenever a group of us strutted along the promenade at Warnemünde in our smart blue jackets sporting the DVS flying school badge in our lapels, we were convinced that everyone saw us as 'conquerors of the skies'. We felt all-powerful – not in any arrogant way – but simply as young men full of the joys of living.

By this stage we had also begun seaplane training on the Heinkel He 42. This presented us with one or two new problems to think about and to master: above all, how to manoeuvre on the water while taxiing and during take-offs and landings. The He 42 was fitted with two large plywood floats, the undersides of which were reinforced by wooden strakes. At about two-thirds of the way along their length the floats were 'stepped'. When moving through the water at speed this step produced a powerful wake, which gradually lifted the rear third of the float clear of the surface and allowed the aircraft to take off. Without the step, the back of the float would simply have dug itself deeper and deeper into the water like the stern of a fast-moving speedboat.

But the Heinkel's floats did not have any auxiliary rudders to help steer it through the water. The machine's design, combined with its inherent drag, meant that it always turned its nose into the wind. If he wanted to go in any other direction, the pilot had to make judicious use of the aircraft's control surfaces and engine power. This could be a tricky business, especially in a strong wind. And if the machine's own rudder forces proved insufficient, the only way of avoiding an obstacle in the water ahead was to pour on full throttle – little wonder that we were required to spend a considerable time skating about on the surface of the Breitling perfecting our taxiing skills before finally being allowed to perform a take-off.

In the air a seaplane is slightly more cumbersome, of course, because of its floats. But flying such a machine poses no particular difficulties for the beginner. Extra demands are only placed on a naval pilot when visibility is poor. Under these conditions he has no clear horizon. The same applies when the surface of the water beneath him is perfectly smooth, for this means he will be unable to judge his height accurately.

But the greatest danger facing any inexperienced pilot is an exaggerated sense of his own abilities. Under the motto: 'He who places himself in unnecessary danger won't survive to tell the tale!' the most important rules of flying a seaplane were hammered into us time and time again: 'Always fly around rain showers!' – 'Never fly into a thunderstorm unless there is compelling reason!' – 'Always fly *around* a thunderstorm!' – 'Avoid flying into fog!' – 'If in doubt, turn back in good time or seek an alternative or emergency landing place!' In other words, leave flying in poor visibility to those properly trained in blind flying and piloting an aircraft fully instrumented for the purpose. And for us that goal was still a long, long way away.

In our quieter moments we naturally reflected on the fact that we were not being taught to fly purely and solely for our own enjoyment. The purpose behind all our training was that, if things got serious, we would be available for duty as fully operational naval pilots. But back in those days the combat and reconnaissance aircraft then equipping the Navy, or about to enter service, were not exactly confidence-inspiring. All our current seaplane types were so slow and unwieldy that it was hard to imagine their being able to survive any kind of enemy action.

One thing *was* clear, however: if push ever did come to shove, an awful lot was going to be asked of us naval flyers. But the likelihood of such a situation arising seemed so absurdly remote that we managed to convince ourselves that future advances in aircraft design and development would by then have more than redressed the balance.

Who, in 1932, could have imagined that we would be facing another war in so short a time? None of us had the slightest inkling, nor did we even consider it possible. True, we didn't concern ourselves over much with politics. We managed to keep more or less abreast of the main political events, but this didn't mean a great deal as we were not allowed to vote – firstly on account of our age, and secondly due to the fact that we were members of the armed forces. Not that this mattered to us in the least. We had more than enough on our plates learning everything we needed to know to be able to follow our chosen profession. We wanted to become proficient flyers, able to perform the duties that the nation expected of us – perhaps one day might even be forced to demand of us.

It was around this time that Jochen Fehling and I were given permission to fly to Berlin-Tempelhof in an Udet Flamingo to visit our parents. Officially, the trip was to help us gain cross-country experience. I was to pilot us to Berlin – Jochen would fly us back. Any sort of aerobatics over our parents' houses was strictly forbidden, of course. More than one young pilot had bitten the dust showing off to friends and relations. It was out of the question for us anyway, as both sets of parents lived in the centre of the capital, an area where low flying was banned for safety reasons. As a safeguard in the event of engine failure, we had therefore been ordered to approach Berlin with sufficient height in hand to enable us to glide to a suitable emergency landing ground outside the city limits.

I was to be forcefully reminded of this shortly before arriving at Berlin. The capital was already in sight when the engine suddenly said blip-blip-blip and came to a dead stop. I fumbled about with the few levers and switches that might have persuaded it back into life again – but without success. So there was no option but to find a suitable spot for an emergency landing before reaching the outskirts. Fortunately, I quickly spotted a large field of stubble that looked promising and was well within gliding distance.

Shi . . . shame, I thought to myself, that's the visit to our relations down the drain. Our parents will have travelled to Tempelhof to meet us, and all for nothing. The stubble field was growing larger. I prepared to land and was on the point of levelling out when, just before the wheels touched the ground, the engine sprang back into life, revs all normal, like a well-behaved sewing machine.

I had immediately pushed the throttle forward and was beginning to climb away when Jochen looked back over his shoulder at me with a broad grin on his face. And then the penny dropped – he'd switched the engine off! The ignition key was located in the front cockpit where the instructor normally sat, but which was now occupied by Jochen. Full of high spirits – it was a glorious summer's day and the flight was proving a pure delight – he had decided to liven things up a bit by playing a trick on me. He'd certainly given me one hell of a fright.

I couldn't stay annoyed at him for long. I chalked the experience up as an extra bit of useful training. But that didn't stop me from tackling him about it after we had landed: 'You might have switched that ignition back on a bit earlier – not every engine starts up again straight away!' He gave a casual shrug, 'Where's the problem – ours did! Besides, you've got to have a bit of fun now and again.' And, of course, he was right.

Every young pilot is tempted to bend the rules slightly at some time or another, during his first low-level practice flights, for example, when the sensation of speed can be almost overpowering. I was always fascinated by the sight of cows galloping away across the fields in front of my machine's nose – until one day, that is, when I learned that the sight and sound of a low-flying aircraft caused the terrified beasts a great deal of suffering. I felt ashamed that I had not thought of this myself and stopped tormenting the poor creatures from then on.

Like many of my comrades, another temptation that I couldn't at first resist – despite its being expressly forbidden – was to make the most of the occasional unsupervised moment by performing aerobatics over one of the many nearby beaches to impress the young girls sunbathing below. Again, until one day when I asked myself: just who is it exactly you are trying to impress? Nobody down there has the slightest clue as to the identity of the 'intrepid birdman' showing off up here for their benefit. In fact, most people are probably complaining, 'Who is that idiot disturbing our peace and quiet?' I must confess it was this thought, rather than any official ban, that persuaded me to give up this practice too.

In Tempelhof there was a joyous reunion with our families. Jochen and I were naturally proud to have flown here all by ourselves for the very first time, even though our little Flamingo was all but lost in the vast expanse of the airport. We all had lots to talk about. At home that evening the conversation turned to politics. More and more was being heard of the 'Nazis' and their activities. My parents didn't think a great deal of National Socialism. 'But why ever not?' I asked them, 'Much of what the Nazis are proposing seems perfectly reasonable. And, if I understand father's rather conservative beliefs correctly, some of their ideas even seem to reflect his own national hopes and desires.'

They admitted that this was indeed so. But it did nothing to dispel their general uneasiness and pessimistic attitude towards the future. On the other hand, they were unable to explain why they felt this way. They could offer no evidence, or give any concrete reasons for their innate mistrust of National Socialism. It didn't help, of course, that there was little objective political information available to allow them – and millions like them – to form a balanced judgement. Mother simply said: 'You mark my words, it'll all end badly with the Nazis.' It was just an instinctive feeling that she had. All in all, our trip to Berlin did little to improve my sketchy grasp of the current political situation. But what did that matter? As a serving member of the armed forces I was not allowed by law to play an active part in politics anyway.

Chapter 3:
Naval Officer's Basic Training

On 26 July 1932 we at Warnemünde heard the terrible news that the Navy's sail training ship *Niobe* had capsized and sunk after being hit by a freak squall off the Baltic island of Fehmarn. She had taken with her a large part of the 1932 intake, our fellow cadets who were on board undergoing seamanship training while we fortunate dozen were learning to fly. It was an enormous blow, not just for the immediate families and friends of those lost, but for the whole Navy, indeed the entire nation. It was a tragic reminder of the perils faced by those whose chosen professions pitted them against the forces of nature.

The Navy now had to fill the gaps that the *Niobe* disaster had ripped in the ranks of the 1932 intake. One of the first measures taken was to call on the reserve intake pool. Meanwhile, the twelve of us at Warnemünde were ordered to complete our training for the B-1 (Seaplane) pilot's certificate as quickly as possible. Once this had been added to our A-1 (Land) and K-1 (Aerobatics) certificates, our course was to be terminated. A dozen new naval officer cadets would be posted to Warnemünde to be taught to fly in our stead, while we were to join the remaining survivors and reserves of the 1932 intake to commence naval officer training.

The month of August was therefore fully taken up in completing our now sadly truncated course of flying training. One small consolation was that the Director of the DVS Warnemünde (he of 'Schnatermann' fame) had promised us all a champagne breakfast if we got through it without crashing any of his precious aircraft. There *had* been one minor incident, ending with a machine standing on its nose. During a cross-country Wilhelm Brockmann, known to all and sundry as 'Wil', had suffered engine failure: a seized piston. He had made an emergency landing in a field of oilseed rape, but as he ploughed across it the rape began to wind itself ever tighter around the machine's axle until the wheels became fully jammed. Just before coming to a halt, the aircraft tipped gently forward on to its nose, snapping off the propeller blades.

A commission of enquiry subsequently found that Wil had selected the most suitable field available for his emergency landing and had done everything that could possibly have been expected of him under the circumstances. As a result the incident was written off as an Act of Providence, Wil was exonerated, and we were given our champagne passing-out party as promised. But it was tinged with no little sadness, all the same, for we knew that we were bidding farewell to our days of flying for a long time to come. What that meant to a young pilot can hardly be imagined by anyone who is not – or who was not once – a flyer himself.

On 28 August 1932 we arrived on the Dänholm, a small island linked by bridge to the Baltic port of Stralsund. The *Niobe* reserve cadre had begun their basic naval infantry training here two weeks earlier, and so we twelve had a lot of catching up to do. The squad leader whose job it would be to make sure that we did just that – and fast! – was one Bootsmannsmaat Roth, a no-nonsense, powerfully built petty officer who enjoyed something of a reputation as a martinet and strict disciplinarian, and who was feared far and wide as the 'Lion of Dänholm'.

His speech of welcome was succinct and to the point. It went something along the lines of: 'In fourteen days' time this intake will parade to take the oath of allegiance under arms. And God help you if my squad isn't up to scratch and judged unfit to take part. But if you work hard and *do* make it, then we'll get along just fine together!'

After that it was straight down to business. The Lion of Dänholm drove us to the very limits of physical endurance. We soon realised, however, that everything he demanded of us had some sort of sense or purpose to it – although this was not always immediately apparent. When for the umpteenth time, for example, he gave the order: 'To the banana and back, quick march!' (the banana being a straggly little bush on the far side of the parade ground) and then followed this up in rapid succession with: 'Down!' – 'On your feet!' – 'Quick march!' – 'Down!' – 'On your feet again, march!' we did begin to wonder what good it was supposed to be doing us.

But then, just when we were about all in, he would bark another 'Down!' and this time he would allow us a short breather to give us a chance to recover. Our instructor was the archetypal naval petty officer, with a very keen sense of just how far he needed to go to ensure that the youngsters in his charge were properly trained. In his own inimitable way he showed us exactly what we were capable of. He chased us. He tormented us. But in such an adroit manner that we always felt we could detect a hint of human warmth and comradely goodwill behind all the yelling and shouting. The incomparable team spirit that we twelve had already developed during our recent flying training made our present situation much easier to bear. The stronger among us helped the weaker. I, of course, numbered among the latter.

On the first Sunday morning our instructor then amazed us all by waking us with a brilliant trumpet solo! He really was one of a kind, our Bootsmannsmaat

Roth, and this was his unique way of demonstrating it to us. Under the tough exterior of the much-feared Lion of Dänholm there really did beat a soft heart.

And so, under his guidance, we were able to participate in the official swearing-in ceremony after all, parading to take the oath of allegiance under arms with the rest of the intake. The days of dashing about all over the Dänholm were drawing to a close for squad leader and squad alike. As a well-oiled team we clocked the fastest time over the assault course; the secret of our success was that the smaller among our ranks were simply heaved, or hurled bodily over the obstacles by the larger! Everything had gone like clockwork – and we had learned an awful lot in the process. In the space of just six short weeks the Lion of Dänholm had turned a bunch of trainee pilots into a group of really worthwhile soldiers.

Following this we were posted to the naval school at Flensburg-Mürwik for four weeks' further training in seamanship. Then, on 5 November 1932, we boarded the cruiser *Köln*. The ship was in the throes of preparing for a twelve-month overseas training cruise and each day was a frantic round of activity. After being divided into watches and assigned our battle stations, we found ourselves involved in taking on ammunition, cleaning and painting ship, and a myriad other duties.

We were inspected by the ship's commander, Kapitän-zur-See Schniewind, and a number of other senior officers. Konteradmiral [Rear-Admiral] Schulze, the Navy's Inspector of Training, Education and Cultural Affairs, wished us well for the coming voyage and exhorted us to 'help restore the name of Germany to its former glory wherever you go'. Next to come on board was the Commander-in-Chief Baltic, Vizeadmiral Albrecht, who expressed similar good wishes and also urged us to be worthy ambassadors of our nation at our various foreign ports of call. After brief shore leave we rejoined the *Köln*, which was now berthed at Wilhelmshaven, and helped carry out the final preparations for the forthcoming twelve-month cruise – taking on stores and provisioning ship.

8 December 1932: the day of departure! As we negotiated Wilhelmshaven lock we were addressed by Vizeadmiral Foerster, the Commander-in-Chief North Sea, who repeated his Baltic counterpart's previous good wishes and exhortations. At the end of his speech we gave three rousing cheers for the Fatherland and for the Reich President. Then it was 'Let go all lines!' To the strains of the German national anthem the *Köln* slowly and majestically gathered way. The great voyage had begun.

Chapter 4

Foreign Training Cruise

The cruise was to take us to Spain, Sicily, Egypt, Australia, the South Seas, Japan, China, India, the Netherlands East Indies, Ceylon, Egypt, Crete, Corfu, Italy and finally Spain again before, on 10 December 1933, the pilot would come on board close to the Weser lightship to guide us back into Wilhelmshaven and home.

We were to see a lot of the world during the voyage: ancient monuments erected by alien cultures, sites and shrines dedicated to foreign religions, and many other impressive sights and places of interest. Above all, there were the many unforgettable personal experiences gained during our numerous contacts with peoples of other creeds and races that I can still vividly recall to this day.

Of course, it wasn't purely a pleasure trip or educational jaunt organized solely for our benefit. Our instructors made sure of that by keeping us cadets hard at it. This would be particularly noticeable after we had spent an enjoyable or interesting day in some foreign port or other. Returning on board, we would immediately be put to work – often more rigorously than was strictly necessary, we felt – by instructors whose sole aim, as they put it, was to 'get our weary bones moving again'. This treatment robbed us of some of our youthful illusions. But it also taught us how to cope with rapidly changing situations. Although I did not realize it at the time, this was to stand me in good stead during my later years, as indeed did the entire cruise. In fact, the memories of the many and varied experiences that marked those twelve months have remained with me ever since.

As we did not stay very long in any of the ports that we visited, most of the impressions we gained were admittedly somewhat superficial. But they were more than enough to give us a broader view and better understanding of world events, something that was denied those at home where the media were now being employed more and more to manipulate and misrepresent.

The stark contrast between our trips ashore, where – as 'ambassadors of the German Navy' – we were naturally expected to conduct ourselves in an exemplary manner at all times, and the treatment meted out to us on board as lowly sea cadets often resulted in some extreme situations. But this was something else that we simply had to get used to. It was another important lesson in life: if you could take all the knocks and insults that were heaped upon you without breaking, you emerged all the better for it.

Obermaat Kurz, the chief petty officer and number one gun layer in turret '*Cäsar*', always found some particularly choice phrases to express the esteem in which we were held: 'Idiot cadets,' he would roar, 'a pile of crap, the lot of you. If you were as tall as you are stupid, you'd have to bend over to kiss the moon! You could guzzle a whole chemist's shop full of clever pills and still be no smarter!' – or, if his imagination failed him, we might simply be told with a resigned sigh: 'You've got the brains of a sparrow.'

On one occasion we returned on board after attending an official reception at some English-speaking port of call. In our guise as 'representatives of the German Navy' we had been treated with due respect at the formal function and then warmly invited to a private party afterwards. Our stumbling attempts at intelligent conversation in English had clearly won over a number of elderly female hearts at the reception, and we conquered several other younger ones while flirting on the dance floor during the party that followed – altogether a most successful evening.

But as we climbed up the gangway to report our return to the petty officer of the watch one of our little group reminded us in a low voice: 'Time to switch back, comrades.' During the course of the voyage we learned to flick this mental switch between our shore-going and our shipboard selves. It was just one more lesson. This one taught us not to take ourselves too seriously or be too full of self-importance; just be natural.

We were involved in all sorts of extreme situations, some more bizarre than others. Like most of the cadets, I was assigned to a week of ship's cleaning duties; more specifically, I was detailed for the post of 'lavatory attendant'. This was not a pleasant job, but a very necessary one. The *Köln*'s designers had ingeniously arranged the waste pipes in the ship's heads to minimize the less than fragrant odours that emanated from this particular part of the vessel. But the bends in the pipes also meant that they were subject to frequent blockages. There were no special implements to deal with the situation – the unfortunate 'attendant' had to insert the full length of his arm into the pipe and clear the blockage by hand!

One day we were lying in harbour and I was looking forward to coming off duty when someone reported two pipes blocked. I reached in, my arm up to the shoulder in the accumulated mess, and fumbled around until everything was flowing freely again. Then – all within the space of the next fifteen minutes – it was a thorough lathering, a quick hop under the shower, straight into walking-out uniform, and report on deck ready to be ferried ashore for another official reception.

Forty-five minutes later still and that same arm was around the waist of a beautiful blonde in an elegant ball gown as we glided together across the polished parquet floor of a grand chandelier-lit salon. I couldn't help thinking that if this vision of loveliness only knew what I had been doing an hour ago, she would probably wrinkle up her pretty little nose in disgust and leave me flat. But, on reflection, I like to think that my spell of duty in the ship's heads did me no harm. In fact, it might even have made a better man of me.

We cadets may have had our faults, but we were not the only ones to make mistakes. To err is human, and our superiors occasionally slipped up too. Several of us were witness to one event that might be described as a 'crisis of confidence'. We were at anchor in a bay. As it was ideal bathing weather, the order was given: 'Cadet division into swimming trunks and report to the forecastle.' To demonstrate our courage, we were then required to dive into the sea far below. A section officer and a boatswain, Bootsmann Hahne, both resplendent in their summer whites and peaked caps, stood beside the diving platform. In alphabetical order the cadets were called forward one by one and their dives noted down.

The style of dive was optional. The platform was a considerable distance above the surface of the water and most of us had never dived from such a height before. But dive we did. The majority performed a straightforward header – with varying degrees of success – but there were also one or two spectacular 'belly flops'.

Everything was going according to the book. Then it was Franzke's turn. He stepped forward, hesitated for a moment, and then blurted out: 'I can't, Herr Leutnant!' – 'You will dive as ordered, Franzke!' – 'But I can't swim, Herr Leutnant!' (How on earth was that possible, we asked ourselves, every aspiring naval officer cadet has to be able to swim? But Franzke had joined our intake as a serving petty officer and the question of whether he could swim or not had simply never arisen before.)

Despite this, the section officer repeated his order: 'Franzke, you will dive!' His words hit us like a bombshell. The atmosphere was electric. Nobody moved a muscle. Franzke stood on the diving platform and peered down at the water with an anxious look on his face. We all stood absolutely still, as if turned to stone.

Only Boatswain Hahne made a move. He took off his wrist watch and handed it, together with his cap, to the cadet standing beside him, stepped up on to the platform pushing Franzke to one side and – in full uniform – executed a perfect swallow dive into the water below. Hardly had he resurfaced before he called up to Franzke: 'Now it's your turn! I'll get you back on board!' And so Franzke dived. Hahne grabbed hold of him the moment he reappeared above the surface, swam to the ship's side and the pair climbed back up the gangway on to the forecastle as if nothing untoward had happened. The bosun had saved the day. And all credit to him.

From that moment on Boatswain Hahne could do no wrong in our eyes. But we had lost all respect for the section officer. It was the sort of situation that you never forgot. A superior officer who couldn't see that he had clearly made a mistake and didn't take immediate steps to rectify it, but who instead persisted in exercising his authority, right or wrong, had had his chance as far as we were concerned. As the old saying goes: 'He who has won the heart of his subordinate has won the whole man as well' – but the reverse was equally true.

This glaring error of judgement was very much the exception rather than the rule, however. Generally speaking, the ship's officers and instructors took great pains to give orders that made sense and – however tough the training might be – to ensure that their subordinates were treated in as reasonable and considerate a manner as possible. Nonetheless, as the twelve months of the voyage unfolded, the cramped conditions and close proximity in which the crew had to live on board ship made it almost inevitable that we became ever more conscious of the slightest injustice or perceived act of unfairness that came our way.

The mental image we had formed of the perfect superior officer may well have been unrealistic. We were certainly sensitive to any behaviour on their part that failed to live up to our expectations. Of course, if one of our own number slipped up or began to show signs of irritability, we naturally blamed it on the unaccustomed tropical climate and the pressures that we were under. But we weren't quite so understanding or forgiving when it came to our officers. Little wonder then, as the weeks went by, that our perception of the 'ideal superior' began to take a few knocks.

In fact, by the time we neared the end of the voyage and put in to Vigo in northern Spain, our illusions had sunk to rock bottom. It was while in Vigo that we were to take our midshipman's exams. These would decide whether we stayed in the Navy or would need to seek alternative employment elsewhere. But by then most of us were at such a low ebb that we went into the exams not caring a jot one way or the other. The general feeling was that if they didn't want us we'd draw a line under the whole business, put a tick against our time in the Navy, label it 'done that', and go on to pastures new with little, if any, regret.

To remove any temptation for last-minute revision, we spent all our off-duty hours ashore in Vigo. In the evenings we would eat a leisurely meal in a small Spanish restaurant and not return on board until 'darken ship'. As a result none of us suffered any pre-examination nerves and we all cleared this latest hurdle with flying colours.

Compared to some of the others, our section leader was the very epitome of fairness and 'correctness'. The ship's cadet division was divided into six sections in all. And we of the 'First' were particularly fortunate to have as our leader none other than the now Oberbootsmannsmaat Roth, the 'Lion of Dänholm'. Here on board ship, our new chief petty officer proved to be the same exemplary leader of men. The master of every situation, he never lost his composure, no matter what was going on around him. He stood like a rock in a raging torrent, displaying a natural 'feel' for combining authority with justice. His keen sense of responsibility also meant that he was always prepared to intervene in person to protect those in his charge.

On one occasion, for example, we had returned exhausted from a lengthy and gruelling session at the oars of the ship's cutter in some foreign harbour. We came alongside. The falls were lowered and the hooks secured ready to hoist the heavy cutter back on board. We were about to clamber wearily up the Jacob's ladder, when the officer in charge gave the order: 'Cutter crew to board ship via the lifelines!'

Chief Petty Officer Roth stood in the stern of the cutter ready to spring into action – a 'lion' indeed! – for he knew full well that not one of us was in a fit state even to hold fast to a lifeline, let alone shin up it. But somehow or other, using our last reserves of strength, shin up them we did. Once at the top, however, we then had to swing hand over hand along a wire rope to get to the ship's railing.

And this is when the inevitable happened: Heitmann, one of the burliest and heaviest of our number, could no longer keep his grip. He fell from quite a height back down into the cutter. But Roth was even quicker. Leaping forward, he managed to break Heitmann's fall. The pair crashed to the bottom of the cutter in a tangle of arms and legs, but neither was hurt. Our section leader had saved his subordinate from serious injury. Little wonder that we felt safe in his hands.

The crew of any warship sailing in distant waters is naturally very interested in every scrap of news from home. This was especially so in our case as it was during the very period of our voyage that political events in Germany began to gather momentum – a process that was being watched with some 'considerable attention' by the rest of the world.

Looking back in hindsight over the intervening years, it is very difficult for anyone to describe with any objectivity exactly how he felt at that time. Whether intentional or otherwise, his impressions of those far-off days would inevitably be coloured by what came after. But the Navy, in its infinite wisdom, had decreed that while on board ship we cadets were to keep 'logbooks'. These were, in effect, private diaries of our on- and off-duty hours. Fortunately, I still have the logbook from my time in the *Köln*. The following extracts from it thus provide an accurate record of how one nineteen-year-old naval cadet on the other side of the world saw and 'experienced' the political developments in Germany during that momentous year of 1933:

31.1.1933 at sea: . . . News from the homeland causing quite a stir. The leaders of the national parties have got together to form a government. This must mean that an agreement has been reached. We are eagerly awaiting further news as to what steps the new government will now take.

3.2.1933 at sea: . . . At noon we encountered the German steamer *Uckermark* of the Hapag Line and the Norddeutschen Lloyd steamer *Trier*. We fell in on the forecastle and as we passed the *Trier* its band struck up 'Deutschland über Alles'. Although it was not being played terribly well, the strains of our national anthem floating across the water moved me deeply. Heard in these far distant seas it really brought home to me for the first time just how proud I was to be German. Love for the Fatherland, for the homeland, seems to grow stronger the more one sees of the outside world, however undeniably beautiful much of that world might be.

My father later added his own comment in the margin of my diary at this point: 'Yes, that's exactly how I felt in December 1902 when I passed three German warships moored in the Yangtze off Shanghai. *Father*.'

6.3.1933 at sea – Sunda Strait: Events at home have again proved of special interest today. In the general election the Nazis have gained 281 seats, and these – together with the German Nationalist Party's 59 seats – mean that they now have an absolute majority in the Reichstag. We all hope that this change at the top will also bode well for the future of the Navy.

16.3.1933 Fremantle (Australia): . . . The Navy's new black–white–red national ensign was hoisted for the first time today. It met with universal approval. But what does it mean for us? In my opinion, it is not merely a reminder of the proud times that once were. It also shows that the Fatherland has found the strength of will to rid itself of all feelings of shame and humiliation and transform itself back into the 'old' Germany once more.

21.3.1933 at sea: . . . A holiday! The opening of the Reichstag. After cleaning ship there is a church parade. Then the captain says a few words about the new ensign. He describes it as an expression of the homeland's avowed intention to win back the position Germany once occupied on the world stage. At the end of his speech a full salute is fired. It is a big moment, for this salute heralds a new era – an era of national thinking, purpose and action. The masthead flag is also flying and this too shows that the rebuilding of a new national Germany has begun . . .

12.5.1933 in Sydney: At a private party hosted by a prominent Australian family the eldest son, a chemist, says to me: 'We need a Hitler in Australia too!'

28.6.1933 at sea: . . . Versailles! The flag is at half-mast. Fourteen years ago today 'the world' signed the treaty that turned Germany into a political nonentity – an impoverished, famished country full of internal unrest and discontent. Nationalist circles longed for another Bismarck, a man with the ability to rouse the nation out of its turmoil of inner strife and hatred and to lead it in unity towards those two great goals: freedom and equality of rights.

When I first expressed a desire to join the Navy, people would ask me: 'Why on earth do you want to do that?' Quite apart from the attraction of life at sea itself, it was the wish to play my part in restoring Germany to its former eminence. The fulfilment of such a wish, however, seemed to lie impossibly far in the future.

Then along came Hitler with his rallying cry of 'Germany awake!' and things began to happen. People suddenly started to take notice, and election results showed how unbelievably rapidly his Nationalist Socialist Party was growing. At first it was just one party among many. But soon it was simply 'The Party'. During our foreign cruise we awaited each daily news bulletin with eager anticipation, for it was clear that a 'fresh breeze' was blowing at home. Now there were men at the helm who – in stark contrast to the previous government – knew how to say 'No!'

29.6.1933 Kobe (Japan): . . . Mail! In general the news from home shows just how long we have been away. It would be all too easy for us to get a false impression of the political goings-on back in Germany, for we aren't experiencing the latest developments at first hand, but rather as outside observers. It's only on days like today, when we receive letters fresh from home, describing the excitement and the enthusiasm, that we can begin to get a taste of it ourselves. But it rarely lasts long and all too soon we are back in the routine of daily shipboard duties.

13.8.1933 Shanghai: . . . Quickly into a taxi and off to the cinema where the film *Germany Awakes* is being shown. Our ship's band is part of the programme, and very good they are too. An altogether excellent show. It makes quite a big impact and is extremely well received.

Here I must resort to my still very vivid memories of our visit to Shanghai to add one or two things that didn't get noted down in my diary simply due to lack of time – if every day of the cruise had been as eventful as those spent in Shanghai, I would have had to stay up half the night furiously scribbling away under the dim emergency lighting simply to keep my 'logbook' up to date.

In the cosmopolitan city of Shanghai, one of the most important trading centres in the Far East at that time, I was most surprised to find a company of SA men. They were German businessmen, dressed in the brown uniform of the Nazi Party, who were mingling with the motley crowds of the International Settlement without – as far as I could see – causing any offence whatsoever. Admittedly, they were only a small group among what was the largest German 'colony' we visited on our voyage, but it gave me pause for thought nonetheless.

Either these men were employees of some international German company who were so secure in their jobs that they could afford to indulge in such behaviour without fear of the consequences, or the people here were on the whole sympathetic to events in the homeland. Personally, I thought the latter more likely, and this was confirmed by the showing of the film *Germany Awakes*. The German colony had invited many of the settlement's dignitaries to the première in Shanghai's largest and most luxurious cinema and every seat of the theatre was taken.

An impressive spectacle met the guests' eyes the moment they entered the magnificent domed auditorium. The whole place was in semi-darkness, illuminated only by the subdued coloured lighting reflecting indirectly off the huge shimmering blocks of ice that had been strategically placed in large bowls along the aisles to keep the temperature down. In the gloom a broad swathe of white stretched across the hall from one side to the other. This was the off-duty watch of the *Köln* in their dress uniforms, sitting together in a group and occupying five or six rows of seats.

The curtains parted. And there in the centre of the stage, bathed in the sudden glare of the spotlights, was our ship's band, their instruments polished and gleaming. In front of them were arrayed four ceremonial trumpeters, standing like statues, legs wide apart, trumpets resting on their right thighs. You could have heard a pin drop. The bandmaster raised his baton. As one, the four trumpeters lifted their instruments to their lips and a majestic fanfare reverberated throughout the auditorium.

Perhaps it was the excellent acoustics, but the sound seemed to fill my whole being. I could feel the hairs rising on the back of my neck – the only time in my life that I have ever experienced such a sensation – as the entire audience burst into a spontaneous and thunderous round of applause.

And then came the first half of the film. We watched in amazement as we finally saw for ourselves the developments that had taken place at home during the nine months of our absence, developments that we would not have thought possible – certainly not in such a short space of time. Another stirring fanfare – the second part of the film – and yet more applause. It could not fail to make an impact on a

German citizen in a foreign land. But it seemed to have had the same effect on every single member of the distinguished international audience as well. I looked around me and could not see one person who was 'holding back' and not joining in the general acclaim.

> *15.10.1933 at sea: . . .* Still half asleep, I hear someone saying excitedly: 'Germany has withdrawn from the League of Nations! Parliament has been dissolved!' 'It's too early in the morning, I don't believe it,' I mumble as I try to go back to sleep. But I can't get the thought out of my head. Can it really be true? It's the sort of move our new leaders would certainly be capable of. Then the radio announces it officially. A heated debate ensues. How will the other nations react? We weigh up the various possibilities: France and Poland are sure to be against. And it's a safe bet that Italy will come down on our side. The Italians are becoming increasingly worried about France's growing strength in the Mediterranean and they have already demonstrated their friendship towards us on a number of occasions, not just during this present voyage but also, for example, by Marshal Balbo's earlier visit to Warnemünde.
>
> That leaves just the question of England – what is her position likely to be? We are of the opinion that France is also getting too strong for England's liking. If her previous foreign policy is anything to go by, England would no doubt prefer to see two powers of equal strength maintaining a balance in continental Europe, which would allow her a free hand to pursue her own foreign and colonial political affairs undisturbed. This leads us to suspect that, while England might not align herself actively alongside Germany – which is hardly to be expected – she will at least remain neutral.
>
> Our discussion of these suddenly tremendously important matters is brought to a close by the call to clean ship and then fall in for captain's inspection. It is not a full inspection, however. The captain simply strides along the front rank before congratulating our newly made-up boatswain's mates on their promotion. Then the officer in command of cadets gives a brief outline of the latest developments and, in closing, the captain addresses all hands.
>
> He describes Germany's situation over the past few years and the present turn of events, which have been brought about by 'the emergence at long last of a unified German people under a new, focussed and determined leadership.' And what of the likely consequences? An interesting question. We should have our answer in the next few days when we are scheduled to pass through the Suez Canal. Will things have come to such a head by then that difficulties are placed in our way?'

In the event, our passage through the canal passed off completely without incident.

11.11.1933 Corfu: . . . Armistice Day! Germany's fate was sealed fifteen years ago to the day. The enemy still celebrates the event each year, but for us too this day has now begun to assume a different meaning from that associated with it hitherto. We no longer remember the humiliation and poverty that it brought in its wake. Now we see it as a signpost towards the future: a call to set Germany free from the shackles of the Versailles Treaty. It has become a tradition that no German warship remains in a foreign port on this date. In the early hours we leave harbour for the open sea and battle drill . . .

And that was how, as a nineteen-year-old naval cadet, I saw and recorded the tumultuous events that took place in the homeland during 1933 from the distant vantage point of a naval cruiser sailing to the far side of the world. I should perhaps add that nowhere on our voyage did we experience any negative attitudes or consequences arising from these events.

On 10 December 1933, after a totally trouble-free cruise, we entered the home waters of the Jade Bight and dropped anchor in the Schillig Roads off Wilhelmshaven. We could see the familiar low-lying green strip of homeland coast and impatiently awaited the moment we could set foot on German soil again.

But first there were any number of procedures and formalities to be gone through. In quick succession a whole host of top brass arrived on board to welcome ship and crew home and prepare us for a visit from the Führer. It seems that Hitler could not deny himself the pleasure of greeting us in person – in recompense, perhaps, for the fact that we had only been able to follow events leading up to his 'seizure of power' from afar. As far as we were concerned, however, the extent of the preparations required for his visit, and the time we had to spend on them, were nothing but an unnecessary delay to our getting ashore.

As to the actual 'Führer visit', most of us – including myself – found it something of a letdown. We were paraded on deck, called to attention and given the 'Eyes right!' Hitler came on board. We cadets were quite some distance away from him. Even so, I remember thinking how grim and serious he looked. But that is about all I *do* remember of the occasion. I can't even recall whether Hitler addressed us, or if a formal speech of welcome was dispensed with as there was not enough space for the whole crew to be fallen in on deck to hear it. (My logbook-cum-diary entries had ended a couple of days earlier.)

But one odd little thing has stuck in my mind, something quite trivial and unimportant. While in Australia the crew had been presented with a young wallaby as a mascot. In honour of the Führer's visit the ship's tailor had made the animal a small sailor's suit to wear. As the great man stepped on board the wallaby was squatting alongside the party gathered at the head of the gangway. But Hitler took absolutely no notice of this strange apparition. He strode straight past it without the slightest flicker of an expression on his face.

Our initial reaction was: 'What a completely humourless character.' It was a disappointment, to say the least, for experience had taught us to regard all superior officers who lacked a sense of humour with a healthy dose of scepticism. But this in no way diminished the respect we felt for what the Nazis, under this man's leadership – and without any serious opposition from the rest of the world – had done for the German nation.

Then, finally, we were able to put in to Wilhelmshaven. Even before the lines were fully secured, the 'guests' began to pour on board. A throng of parents, siblings and other family members soon packed the cadets' mess. And suddenly, amidst the crush and all the hubbub, there stood my parents. They had travelled up from Berlin to welcome me home. And what a welcome it was! Twelve months before they had waved goodbye to a callow youth. Now – to my mind at least – they were hugging a grown man.

When I stepped ashore after so long an absence, the first thing to strike me was that the beggars had disappeared from the streets. Everything gave the impression of being clean and orderly, just as I remembered it of old. The new provision of employment programme was clearly already bearing fruit. To my eyes the people in the streets appeared happy and contented.

I freely admit that everything I had heard, seen and experienced of National Socialism to that date seemed thoroughly positive. Like the overwhelming majority of the German population, I had found nothing that could be considered in any way objectionable. But who of us in those early days of the regime could have seen the signs, could have had any idea of the terrible and tragic developments that were to come in the years ahead?

After a short home leave we were bundled through all the Navy's various midshipman's training courses in the space of just six months: the infantry course, torpedo course, signals course, anti-aircraft machine-gun course and boom defence course. After these came the final part of a naval officer's training: the nine-month finishing course at the Flensburg-Mürwik Naval Academy. It was while we were at Flensburg, in March 1935, that Hitler introduced general military conscription. We saw this measure, which brushed aside one of the last remaining military restrictions of Versailles by greatly increasing the size of our nation's armed forces, as another step towards Germany's attaining her equality of rights. I need hardly describe the enthusiasm with which this declaration was greeted in our midshipmen's mess!

But then, on 18 April 1935, we erstwhile pilots on the Flensburg course – having passed our final naval officer's exams and been made up to Oberfähnriche zur See, or senior midshipmen – were unexpectedly discharged from the Navy and transferred to the newly established Luftwaffe!

Our course leader, or 'father of the midshipmen' as he was known, chose to say a few words expressing his regret. After all the time, trouble and labour it had gone to, the Navy had apparently grown quite fond of us. And now we – the fruits of that labour – were being cruelly snatched away. (The in-fighting that had been going on between Admiral Raeder of the Navy and Luftwaffe chief Hermann Göring for overall control of Germany's maritime aviation units is another story altogether.)

And so, on 30 April 1935, after another brief spell of leave, we were ordered to report back to Warnemünde – the cradle of our naval flying careers – but this time as serving members of the Luftwaffe.

We got the distinct impression that the Navy was not at all happy about sacrificing its flying arm 'just to give the new Luftwaffe a birthday present'. But we flyers were merely pawns in the game. Nobody had asked for our opinion. And why should they? Such a move had been on the cards for years. As far as we were concerned, our yearning to fly had been held on ice for long enough – just let us get back into the air!

Thus were we removed from the custody and care of the Navy, with understandable feelings of regret, but with our comrades' warm wishes for continued success in our resurrected flying careers 'under new management' ringing in our ears.

Chapter 5
Transferred to the Luftwaffe

Now in our new guise as senior midshipmen transferred to the Luftwaffe, we reported to Warnemünde on 30 April 1935. The earlier Commercial Pilot's School (DVS), where we had undergone our initial flying training, had in the meantime been transformed into Fliegerschulen 1 (Flugzeugführer) and 2 (Beobachter) – Flying Schools 1 and 2 for pilots and observer/navigators respectively. We were welcomed by our group leader, Hauptmann Schalke, whose somewhat unusual nickname, we soon discovered, was 'Null-Acht-Fünfzehn' ['Zero-eight-fifteen'], or 'By the book.'

He began by reading out the course curriculum to us: three to five hours of W/T (wireless-telegraphy) instruction each day, plus several hours of navigation, engineering and the like. We listened open-mouthed, not believing what we were hearing. 'Why does a pilot require so much W/T training?' we asked. 'Who said anything about pilots?' he replied frostily, 'You're here to train as observers!'

This was a huge blow and a bitter disappointment. We had been enormously excited at the prospect of getting back into the air again, but had naturally assumed that it would be as pilots. The fact was, however, that at that time it was the rule in maritime aviation that aircraft were commanded by the observer. Rather than playing first fiddle in the back seat we would, of course, much preferred to have been sitting in the front cockpit 'stirring the stick' for ourselves.

But it was not to be. Every attempt to get this decision overturned met with failure and we were duly trained as observers. All other ambitions had to be put back on hold for the time being, although each of us secretly nursed the hope that fate might smile more kindly upon us at some point in the future and allow us to attain the one thing that we wanted above all else: to be pilots.

And so it was as a result of reluctantly obeying orders – rather than from any personal desire, or even inclination on our part – that we slowly amassed the skills needed to turn us into competent aircraft commanders. We learned how to send and receive Morse at the required speed and without mistakes. Navigation became routine. We were taught how to use the Lotfe bombsight to drop our bombs in level flight and from a considerable height – although not with any great deal of accuracy, it must be said – but achieved better results with the rear-cockpit machine gun against targets both in the air and on the ground.

Such was the rapid rate of expansion in the armed forces that even before we had completed our maritime observer's course, we ourselves were already being employed as quasi-instructors to teach petty officers to become auxiliary observers. Then, when our course did finish, we were all immediately posted away to other units and schools. All but me, that is. I was fated to remain at Warnemünde, being appointed to the staff of Maritime Training and Reserve Command, which shared the base with the two flying schools. My assignment was to formulate and develop an integrated training programme. And Haupt-mann Kannengiesser, senior maritime representative at Training Command HQ in Berlin, clearly had his sights on me from the word go.

I had hardly reported for duty before he sent me a teleprint ordering me to prepare draft guidelines for the training of maritime pilots, observer/navigators, auxiliary observers, wireless-operators and wireless-operator/rear gunners, all of which were to be submitted to Berlin for approval in just four weeks' time! Prior to this not a single sheet of paper had been written on the subject. Up until now what passed as training programmes had been more or less dependent on the initiative and improvisational skills of individual instructors. I could foresee a mountain of paperwork coming my way and so set about ways of trying to tackle it. The first step was to despatch a teleprint back to Berlin requesting a two-month extension to the deadline. This was promptly granted.

The next thing was to take stock and seek the views of the instructors at the various training establishments. Their comments and suggestions were many and varied, but all, without exception, were most helpful and more than willing to assist me in my endeavours. So each day I held discussions and gathered together documentation, and every night I would sit up into the early hours working on my guideline proposals. It finally got to the stage where I was even dreaming at night about what I had to write the following day. I had neither the time nor the mind for anything else. I simply had to get this job off my plate!

And, wouldn't you know it, just as things were becoming really hectic, my parents decided to come to Warnemünde for a couple of weeks. They had booked into a small hotel nearby and naturally thought that I would be able to spend the evenings with them. But I proved to be very poor company. They had never known me to be so monosyllabic. I was like a stranger even to myself. My thoughts kept returning to my work. For the first time in my life, for the first time in my chosen profession, I was confronted by a task that demanded my full and undivided attention.

My parents were of course very disappointed. They wondered just how important the assignment could possibly be if it was being entrusted to a mere senior midshipman. But they consoled themselves with the fact that their son seemed to be progressing well in his career. It didn't help matters when I failed to turn up two nights in a row and had to phone to say that I could not make it until the following evening. To make amends I invited them to dinner at Hübner's Hotel on the promenade at Warnemünde. I also had to promise not to think about work, but to concentrate solely on celebrating the occasion with them – after all, it *was* my twenty-first birthday!

We had put on our glad rags and were sitting at a table on the hotel veranda. Dinner had already been ordered and we were looking forward to a splendid meal when mother suddenly spotted two familiar faces among the throng of summer holidaymakers strolling past outside: 'Why, there are the Vogts!' she exclaimed in surprise. The Vogts had also seen us and were coming in to say hello.

Mother just had time to whisper to me that the Vogts were old friends from student days and that they had a very nice daughter. I hissed back that I was now a very old man, with a beard down to here – I held my hand against my chest – and that I didn't have any time for little girls at present and therefore wasn't interested. Then the Vogts were approaching our table and we rose to greet them.

Smiles and handshakes all round as we were introduced. 'Well, isn't it a small world!' – 'Do you have any plans?' – 'None?' – 'Then won't you please join us, we've just ordered.' – 'We'd be delighted to, thank you.' We sat down again, I with my back to the room. The conversation became animated; as conversations tend to do when old friends suddenly and unexpectedly bump into one another after any length of time. While they chatted away nineteen to the dozen, I found my thoughts drifting back to the work piled up on my desk awaiting attention. Idly I turned and glanced around the room . . . and something quite extraordinary happened.

A young lady had just made her way through the revolving doors. I gazed transfixed at this vision of grace, charm and beauty. She wasn't very tall, but she carried herself with a natural nobility of poise and elegance. Her eyes sparkled and her flawless skin was lightly tanned by the August sun. In short, a perfect picture of healthy young womanhood. But was this picture real, or was it all in my mind's eye? What was it I had just said to mother – a beard down to here? – not interested? Yes, but a moment ago I had had no idea that such a vision as I now beheld could possibly exist.

Slowly, with an air of composure that belied her youthful years, she moved across the room in our direction. Which table was she making for, I wondered, as she disappeared from my view. Somehow I resisted the temptation to crane my neck and watch her progress. I squinted to the left, expecting her to reappear, but then realized that she had stopped at our table and was saying hello to her mother and father!

After exchanging a few words with my parents, she was then introduced to me. The first thing she asked me was whether I knew Senior Midshipman Wolf Luckhardt? Did I know Wolf Luckhardt – of course I did. What a lucky dog, I thought, for I had heard that he was engaged and that his fiancée was spending her holidays in Warnemünde. Not long afterwards the man himself arrived and joined our little group. We chatted amiably enough, but my head was in a complete spin. For an 'old man with a beard down to here' I had been well and truly smitten! If this wasn't a classic case of love at first sight, I didn't know what was. I found it hard to hide my true feelings and not encroach upon my comrade's preserves.

Then, three days later, everything changed. Wolf Luckhardt had asked me: 'Do you want to come dancing with us?' 'If your fiancée has travelled all this way to spend her holidays with you, she won't want me tagging along,' I had replied. 'What on earth are you talking about? She's not my fiancée,' he explained, 'she's my fiancée's cousin – and she'd be delighted if you joined us.' The penny dropped. 'You stupid great ox,' I yelled, giving him a hefty thump on the shoulder, 'why didn't you tell me that to start with? Of course I'll come with you!' And suddenly the world had become a much brighter and more beautiful place.

I immediately decided that I could catch up with my work at night while everybody else was asleep. The love of my life wasn't going to be in Warnemünde for much longer and I had to make every day count. For although my feelings for her were all-consuming, she clearly didn't feel the same way about me. Not surprisingly, she had a wide circle of friends and was sweet and charming to them all. Vivacious and full of innocent fun, she was not averse to a little mild flirting, but knew instinctively where to draw the line. Her enjoyment of life made every moment in her company a moment of pure pleasure.

Of one thing I was sure: this was the girl I wanted to spend the rest of my life with. *Her* initial attitude, on the other hand, was more along the lines of: Mmh, a nice enough boy, perhaps we could meet again some time. I wasn't her only suitor, of course. That was to be expected. And in fact, as an insignificant little senior midshipman, my chances didn't look all that good. In those days a young naval officer had to obtain the permission of his superiors before he could get married, and that permission was rarely, if ever, granted to anyone under the age of twenty-five. In my case that was still a very long way off. But, undeterred and full of hope,

I set out to pursue my dream until the day should come when I could make her mine.

With renewed vigour I threw myself headlong back into my work. On the very last day of the three months allowed me, I went to Berlin to submit my draft plans for the training of all maritime flying personnel. And they were actually approved and put into force! From then on every school and training establishment had to follow the guidelines as laid down in the published directives. They weren't all that keen on the idea at first, as it deprived them of the freedom of choice they had previously enjoyed when formulating their individual programmes. But they readily admitted that such a move had been long overdue, for it would standardize training throughout the command and greatly increase effectiveness.

The fact that I would now be required to attend frequent meetings with the commanders and instructors of the five maritime flying training schools at Warnemünde, Pütnitz, Parow, Bug auf Rügen and Stettin gave fresh impetus to my dormant, but far from forgotten ambition to be a pilot. The flying control officers at Warnemünde flatly rejected my request to be allowed to resume pilot training. The reason: I was now a fully qualified observer and that was enough. They themselves, I was pointedly informed, had only been given one bite at the training cherry.

I was in the fortunate position, however, of already having my A-1 (Land) and B-1 (Sea) pilot's certificates. And as the representative of Headquarters Training Command I was also entitled to have an aircraft placed at my disposal. This was made ready for me whenever I was required to carry out an official visit to one or more of the other flying schools. I was therefore able to utilize these flights to continue my pilot training off my own bat. To gain the obligatory high-altitude flying experience, for example, I would take a barograph along in the aircraft with me and get flying control at Warnemünde to certify the readings upon my return.

If the machine happened to be a type I had not flown before, Leutnant Zunker, one of the school's instructors, would take me up early in the morning prior to going on duty and quickly show me the ropes. With the basics under my belt, the rest took care of itself during the course of the subsequent flight. Thus, without too much fuss or bother, my pilot training progressed at a fairly rapid rate. It also made my current desk job quite bearable.

On 1 October 1935 we senior midshipmen were promoted to Luftwaffe Leutnants. I was, of course, the youngest member of the permanent staff at Warnemünde and, as such, started referring to myself as the 'Duty two-majors'. This was a barbed reference to the fact that, according to the establishment scale, the work

I was doing should have been handled by two majors – but we simply didn't have the requisite two majors on strength.

My superior was Oberst Ritter, whose twin passions – hunting and sailing – took up nearly all of his time. He was the ideal commanding officer. Rarely disturbing us at work, his official activities were confined in the main to acknowledging the end results of our labours, which he always did with an air of jovial benevolence. He could be relied upon to sign any piece of paper placed in front of him. Although he may have left something to be desired as a role model where hard work was concerned, he never failed to be friendly and interesting company.

By contrast, his adjutants – such was the composition of the Luftwaffe in its formative years – were ex-Army. The first of them was a Hauptmann Hoffmann, who had previously commanded an armed motorcyclist unit and was very spit-and-polish. He was later followed by Hauptmann Henning Wilke. Initially, both were clearly of the opinion that part of their duties should consist of instilling some semblance of military bearing into us young naval types. But thanks to the Navy's superiority in numbers at Warnemünde, the outcome was quite the reverse. During the course of several convivial evenings in the mess we 'promoted' them to the rank of 'Supernumerary Boatswain's Mate of the Reserve' and presented each with a bosun's whistle!

The rest of the officers on the staff actually *were* reservists, that is ex-regulars of the old school who had been called back to the colours, bringing with them a vast amount of invaluable specialist knowledge. As I had been given an almost completely free hand as far as my own job was concerned, I was thus able to draw upon a wealth of expert support whenever it was needed. Despite the ever-accelerating rate of expansion of the Luftwaffe and the highly complex nature of our duties, our small team performed smoothly and efficiently.

To my good fortune, it was at this time that off-duty weekend flying was officially introduced. Its intended purpose was to enable those staff officers who had a pilot's certificate, but who were currently desk-bound, to keep their hands in. The only condition attached was that a distance of at least 1,000km had to be flown between the Saturday morning and Sunday evening. Needless to say, I made full use of this new concession, carefully planning my routes so that I would arrive in Magdeburg-South on Saturday afternoons with a good three-quarters of the necessary 1,000km already behind me. This then left just the remaining 250km or so back to Warnemünde to cover the following evening.

The reason that my weekend flights invariably ended at Magdeburg-South is easily explained. The love of my life – the girl I had met at Warnemünde – was the daughter of the owner of the Lignose Explosives Factory at nearby Schönebeck/Elbe. The family lived in neighbouring Bad Salzelmen, and I was always assured of a lift there from the airfield.

But on the first occasion that I made this trip it resulted not only in a joyful reunion with the girl of my dreams, it also – totally unexpectedly – brought down on my unsuspecting head the wrath of her father.

I had announced my coming. Flying alone in a Focke-Wulf Stieglitz, an open cockpit two-seater biplane, I decided to fly past the factory to see where my beloved lived. I had half hoped that she might appear at a window to wave at me, but nothing of the kind happened. I turned steeply and flew back low along the road leading to the factory. As I passed what I took to be the main office block, I noticed a large Buick saloon parked in front of it. The chauffeur was waving up at me enthusiastically, but there were no other signs of life.

And so I banked away and headed for Magdeburg-South, which lay only some 12km distant. After landing I reported to flying control, anchored my aircraft, stowed my parachute and one or two loose items away, and had just made myself presentable for the weekend, when the object of my affections arrived in the car to pick me up. It was a warm welcome, to put it mildly! But it didn't last long. After a moment she burst out: 'Father is appalled! What on earth possessed you to fly between the chimneys of his factory?'

'Who says that I did?' I replied hotly, 'I'm not that tired of life!' – 'Yes, and then you flew so low along the road that our chauffeur could even see the red upholstery in your aeroplane!' – 'That just shows you! My aircraft doesn't have any upholstery! He's imagining things!' – 'Well, that's what they said!'

What mindless stupidity, I thought to myself. Fancy telling the owner of an explosives factory, whose sole concerns in life are the happiness of his daughter, the well-being of his workers and the safety of his business, that there's a young suitor buzzing around his factory's chimneys. It must have given the good Herr Direktor quite a shock! He probably had visions of my aircraft being blown to smithereens and taking his precious factory with it. What a mess! The people below had doubtless meant no harm with their exaggerated tales of my flying activities, but I could not imagine a worse way of re-acquainting myself with my prospective father-in-law.

There was nothing to be gained from arguing my case, however objective and factual I tried to be. In the old boy's eyes I was now clearly an irresponsible young idiot. But after giving vent to his initial displeasure in no uncertain terms, he was a big enough man never to refer to the matter again. So, although I had begun my first weekend in Bad Salzelmen under an enormous black cloud, the skies soon turned sunny again. Just to be on the safe side though, I always made it a policy in the future to give the factory at Schönebeck a very wide berth indeed.

1936 was proving to be another eventful year. On 7 March German forces had reoccupied the demilitarized zone of the Rhineland. In the summer the Olympic Games were held in Berlin. They were a triumph of organization and sporting achievement that was acclaimed by all, spectator and participant, German and foreign alike. And in Spain a civil war had broken out. Despite the strictest secrecy, word began to leak out as time went by that units of the Luftwaffe – operating under the title of the Legion Condor – were participating in the conflict. Fighting on the side of General Franco's Nationalists, they were gaining combat experience with the latest German weaponry.

At Warnemünde and everywhere else training was in full swing and we had our work more than cut out keeping abreast of the accelerating rate of expansion as one new operational unit after the other was brought into being. Even so, I nonetheless managed – alongside my official duties – to complete my do-it-yourself flying training and successfully apply for my advanced pilot's certificate/land and sea. This allowed me to fly single- and multi-engined land and seaplanes of all classes. The only thing I was unable to achieve was my blind-flying certificate. Officially, this would have required my attending a lengthy course, something for which I simply didn't have the time. And unfortunately it was not something that I could organize and carry out on the quiet, as there were no such courses available in our immediate command area.

While on the subject, it might perhaps be of interest to point out how relatively few training flights were made in the company of an instructor back in those days. In my own case, from first flight to obtaining my advanced pilot's certificate had entailed 187 accompanied training flights – a total flying time of 15 hours and 45 minutes in all – on eighteen different aircraft types. Admittedly this was not the norm, due to my self-help approach during the later stages, but even pupils going through the official training programmes did not put in a great deal more time than this under the direct supervision of an instructor.

On 1 April 1937 I was promoted to the rank of Oberleutnant. This may not have been a huge step up the ladder, but I regarded it as sufficient to risk asking my prospective father-in-law for his daughter's hand in marriage. He, no doubt, would have preferred to have seen a much more serious and financially secure suitor for his one and only, dearly loved and tenderly cosseted daughter! His opinion of me was summed up by a question he once put to his wife: 'What *is* he exactly?'

But she, to her credit and my eternal gratitude, saw me in a more intuitive light. I was by then already in her good books. I was even permitted to sit on the cushions of the sofa, which were normally there for decorative purpose only (that's how people actually behaved in those days!) – and she had replied: 'Just be patient, he's going to make something of himself!'

And because it was his daughter's wish, the old gentleman gave us his blessing. On 2 May 1937 we celebrated our engagement.

Chapter 6
Shipboard Aviator

On 1 March 1938 I was posted as an observer to Bordfliegerstaffel (Shipboard squadron) 1./196. Based at Wilhelmshaven, this Staffel provided the aircraft and crews that were carried aboard the Navy's three new pocket battleships.

My pilot was to be Leutnant Köder – popularly known as 'Kuddel-Köder' – and shortly after I joined the Staffel our He 60 floatplane was hoisted aboard the pocket battleship *Admiral Scheer*, which was about to sail for Spanish waters and beyond, into the Mediterranean. The ship was commanded by Kapitän-zur-See Ciliax, who was an outstanding naval officer but with a reputation as a very strict disciplinarian. The entire crew was more than a little in awe of him – and with good reason – as we were to discover on our very first day on board.

Not long after leaving Wilhelmshaven we were sent off on an aerial reconnaissance exercise. The captain wanted to reassure himself that everything between ship and aircraft was functioning properly. Catapult launch! Kuddel-Köder allowed a few moments for the He 60 to build up sufficient speed and then hauled the machine around in a tight right-hand turn back over the *Scheer*'s forward turret directly in front of the bridge. I was standing up in the rear cockpit and waved casually but perfectly affably down at the bridge personnel as we roared past just in front of their noses. Then we climbed away and proceeded to carry out our mission as ordered.

When it was completed we landed back alongside. The ship's crane operator lowered the hook; I slackened it off and attached it to the lifting eye. The He 60 was hoisted out of the water, placed back upon the catapult and secured. All straightforward and strictly according to the book. I was just climbing out of my cockpit when the bridge messenger appeared on the catapult: 'The Herr Oberleutnant is to report to the captain at once!' 'I'll be right there,' I told him, 'I've got to report my return on board anyway.'

But when I presented myself to the captain I was in for a shock. He immediately let fly at me at the top of his voice: 'I will not tolerate such dangerous flying – turning sharply straight after launch like that and flying back across the foredeck!' 'Herr Kapitän,' I replied, 'there was nothing dangerous about it. My pilot executed a perfectly clean turn. He was in full control of the aircraft at all times and there was no possibility whatsoever of anything untoward happening.'

At this he lost his composure completely. In front of all those present on the bridge he ranted and bellowed at me loud and long. It was quite a performance. But I was not unduly impressed as it quickly became clear to me that he was no expert on the subject of flying and didn't really know what he was talking about. Under the circumstances I therefore decided that it was wiser to say no more but simply listen in silence until the storm had abated. The tirade finally ended with a curt: 'Dismiss!'

As I was leaving the bridge I noticed the captain's flag lieutenant, Oberleutnant Mengersen, standing behind me. In passing, I whispered to him: 'Have you got a moment?' 'Yes, of course, what is it?' We went out on to the signal deck and I explained that he could perhaps do me a service if ever he had occasion to speak to the captain in private. This happened quite often, he told me. I therefore asked him to suggest to the captain that he not pontificate too loudly about aviation matters in front of his officers and men. He obviously knew less about the subject than we did and it didn't make a very good impression – and it certainly cut no ice with us however loud the lecture.

About an hour later I happened to bump into Mengersen on the upper deck. 'I passed your comments on to the captain word for word,' he informed me. The next day, when we were crossing the Biscay, I was ordered to report to the captain once again. I found him sitting in front of a pile of paperwork. 'Have you seen the report from the crew of the aircraft aboard the *Deutschland*?' he asked me. 'No, Herr Kapitän.' 'Here, read this page.' I took the proffered sheet and scanned the paragraph indicated. It stated that night flying trials had not been carried out over the Atlantic due to the difficulty of obtaining spare parts while abroad. In the margin alongside these words someone at Naval High Command had scrawled a terse comment: 'No excuse!'

The captain's next question was: 'Have you been given any instructions to undertake night flying trials while we are in the Atlantic?' 'Not as yet, Herr Kapitän.' 'Has anybody ever done so?' 'No, Herr Kapitän.' 'Are you quite sure of that?' 'Yes, Herr Kapitän, quite sure.' 'Would you be able to carry out such trials?' 'If one or two provisions can be made and the sea is reasonably calm, yes, Herr Kapitän.' 'What is it that you require?' 'Some lights along the port rail that can be dimmed if necessary so that we are not blinded.' 'Very well, give the torpedo officer details of everything you need. The first trial will be flown tonight!'

By that evening lighting had been strung along the rail on the port side of the ship. As we had requested, it could be set to three strengths: bright, medium and dim. We had been briefed to fly a night gunnery co-operation exercise. I was ordered to remain in visual contact with the ship and to switch the aircraft's navigation lights on and off as and when instructed. This was to test the target acquisition capabilities of a brand new and highly secret item of equipment that had just been fitted to the *Scheer*: 'Freya' radar.

We were catapulted into the night at 22.00 hours. Visibility was good, the horizon stood out clearly and everything went without a hitch. We flew the exercise exactly as ordered. I stoically manned the navigation lights switch: On–Off– On–Off–On–Off. It soon became evident that once the ship could no longer see us, it was having great difficulty in keeping track of us by radar. After an hour we were instructed to land back alongside.

The rail lights were switched on. In the blackness of the night their combined glare was like a battery of searchlights! I ordered them to be dimmed. They were still much too bright, but it was too late to do anything about it now. We prepared to land. A light wind had started to blow. Kuddel-Köder held the He 60 ten metres above the gentle swell as we approached the *Scheer* from astern. He had throttled right back, but it was impossible to tell how far away we were from the ship. The rail lights provided the sole source of illumination in the inky darkness and there were no other points of reference to enable us to judge our distance.

Suddenly we found ourselves abeam of the ship. Kuddel immediately chopped the throttle. We touched down but shot straight past the *Scheer* before coming to a stop some distance ahead of her. As I climbed out of my seat and freed the lifting eye ready for us to be hoisted back on board, I could hear the commands being given by the captain on the bridge: 'Both engines full ahead – Port twenty – Both engines stop! – Midships! – Both engines full astern – Both engines full astern – Both engines stop!'

The pocket battleship lay alongside us. The hook of the crane was lowered and attached. We were plucked neatly out of the water and placed back on the catapult. The whole manoeuvre had lasted no more than twenty seconds longer than the time it usually took us by day, thanks to the captain's superlative seamanship. We were full of admiration at the way he had handled his huge vessel. He too was clearly pleased that things had gone so smoothly. It was obvious that new ideas appealed to him. More importantly – and unlike the vast majority of the older generation, old school of naval officers – he was quick to grasp their potential. He could now see that a shipboard aircraft offered him hitherto untold operational possibilities – possibilities that he was eager to exploit to the full.

His attitude towards us had undergone a complete about-turn since our first rather unfortunate encounter and we were frequently sent out on lengthy reconnaissance flights. From a navigational point of view alone, these missions could be quite fraught undertakings. For, after spending anything up to four hours patrolling the empty wastes of the ocean, it then became necessary to find our way back to our floating home. And to do so we had to rely entirely on dead reckoning.

We had no radio direction-finding equipment in the He 60. We were rarely in sight of land, coastal marker buoys or other such aids to navigation, and all too often found ourselves flying in poor conditions with visibility down to little more than two or three nautical miles. I really had to have my wits about me the whole time. Never in my life before or since have I checked wind strengths, directions and drift as frequently and as assiduously as I did during those flights!

When, after those four long hours – and with dwindling reserves of fuel – we finally approached the designated rendezvous point with the *Admiral Scheer*, it was always an enormous relief actually to find her there. The alternatives didn't bear thinking about. The open ocean was generally so rough that, had we been forced to make an emergency landing, there would have been little chance of our getting away with it in one piece.

In order to put down safely we usually had to ask the *Scheer* for the 'duck-pond.' This she would produce by performing a sharp 30-degree turn to port; the turbulence of her wake would smother the heavy swell to create a relatively calm patch of water within her turning circle. And if the duck-pond wasn't sufficient, we had to resort to the landing mat. As its name suggests, the landing mat was just that: a small rectangular mat of reinforced canvas that would be paid out from a swinging boom on the port side of the ship forward and streamed on the surface of the water close alongside.

For a pilot, landing on the mat was the ultimate test. It was so narrow that he could not afford to be more than a metre off the centre line if the aircraft was to be recovered intact. A few more centimetres to the right and the starboard wingtip would be smashed against the side of the ship. A few more centimetres to the left and the port float would miss the landing mat and the machine might be lost altogether. Kuddel-Köder, however, always seemed to achieve the impossible with his usual air of casual aplomb.

On one occasion weather conditions had turned extreme by the time we got back to the ship. Kuddel managed to put the He 60 down in the middle of a rather lively duck-pond, but then had to yank it smartly back up again and make a couple of large hops in order to clear the crests of two oncoming waves. A moment later and there we were: sitting high, dry – and whole – on the landing mat! And not just on it, but also neatly centred – albeit with the nose of the Heinkel only a hair's breadth from the projecting boom.

The captain was mightily impressed. 'Quite a landing!' he said admiringly. 'That's what I'd like to see you do every time!' Kuddel and I exchanged glances. If he only knew how easily things could have gone horribly wrong. But we had been fortunate. We had pushed our luck, without overdoing it, and had got away with it. It was another boost to our growing self-confidence.

While in harbour we flyers were more or less free to come and go as we pleased. Our naval brethren weren't at all happy about this arrangement, as they had to oversee cleaning ship, scrubbing decks and other such domestic chores whenever we were in port or at anchor. When the first lieutenant tried to add our names to the ship cleaning rota, I defended our position as Luftwaffe officers by quoting the official orders concerning our 'shipboard duties', which stated that these were confined exclusively to the care and maintenance of the aircraft. Any additional duties or responsibilities could only be undertaken upon the direct orders of the captain.

But in the interests of inter-service harmony – not to mention the opportunity of adding to the fund of knowledge that might prove useful to my future career – I said that I was more than willing to stand watch on the bridge when not flying. This offer was accepted with alacrity and so there was I, an Oberleutnant of the Luftwaffe, putting in time as a trainee officer of the watch on the bridge of the pocket-battleship *Admiral Scheer*! Under the able tutelage of the senior watch officer, Kapitänleutnant Kals, I found it to be both stimulating and rewarding – a fascinating experience that didn't come the way of many Luftwaffe officers.

In April 1938 we headed for Italy. By the 14th we were lying off Gaeta, to the north of Naples. It was the time of the referendum on Austria's becoming part of the German Reich and we had ballot boxes set up on board. Those German and Austrian nationals living in the Rome area who were eligible to vote were ferried out to the ship, which legitimately enabled them to cast their ballots on German sovereign territory. It was an historic event and the overwhelming 'yes' vote was welcomed as a positive step not only by all of Germany, but also by the great majority of the Austrian population as well.

29 May 1938, my fiancée's birthday, was the date we had originally fixed for our wedding. But on that day I was still serving aboard the *Admiral Scheer* in Spanish waters. I therefore decided to send her a MAPRIFU [*Marine-Privat-Funkspruch*, or 'Naval private wireless message'] saying: 'With loving regards on our intended wedding day. Your would-be husband.' Such MAPRIFUs had to be authorized by the commanding officer. I was duly sent for. I couldn't word it like that, I was told; it would compromise my fiancée. 'In what way?' I enquired, 'I'd be there if I could – or perhaps you can grant me immediate compassionate leave to get married?' As that was out of the question, the captain simply said: 'Very well then, send your message as it stands.'

And so it was on 9 July 1938, a few days after my return to the homeland, that we celebrated our wedding in Bad Salzelmen and Magdeburg. My parents-in-law had spared no expense. With loving kindness they had made all the arrangements both for the *Polterabend*, the customary festivities on the eve of the wedding, as well as for the great day itself. And everything was done so beautifully that not only did we – the happy young couple – feel as if we were experiencing something straight out of a fairy-tale, but all the guests said the occasion would be a memory they would long treasure. In addition to family and friends, my old flying comrades from the intake of 1932 had also been invited and all those who were able to obtain leave duly turned up. It made for quite a party.

Only my mother was a little downcast, as I had not paid her a farewell visit beforehand. I couldn't understand her attitude. After all, I had only just got back from Spain and knew that I would be seeing her at the wedding. Besides, what was all this business about 'farewell'? I would still be her son. But there was no consoling her. I had apparently done something unforgivable.

She reminded me of the fact that I had disappointed her like this once before. It was at the time of my *Abitur*, the school-leaving examination. One morning when she woke me I had declared that I wasn't going to go to school any more. 'But Helmut, darling,' she had said, 'you can't give up your studies at the last moment.' 'It's not that, but I'm still not going to go to school any more – yesterday was the last day of our *Abitur* exams!' 'And you didn't tell me?' 'What for, you would only have got all worked up about it and quite unnecessarily!' But such youthful consideration on my part had not been appreciated in the least. And she was quite right, of course. Mothers feel an inherent need to be involved in such matters. But this was something I only came to understand in later life.

We had originally planned to spend our honeymoon in Venice. The tickets had already been booked, but I was unable to get leave. In my own humble opinion the government's current political manoeuvrings were giving no particular cause for alarm, but my Staffelkapitän – or maybe those above him – begged to differ. Our honeymoon destination had to be changed to the Baltic coast so that, in the event of an emergency, he could send a floatplane at short notice to have me picked up from the beach. I protested that the young Oberleutnant Mahlke surely couldn't be *that* important. But there the matter rested.

And so we spent our honeymoon blissfully happy, and quite undisturbed, in the picturesque resort of Bansin on the island of Usedom. Afterwards we moved into our first very own little nest together in Wilhelmshaven. Once again we had my wife's parents to thank for their generosity. They had furnished the apartment with such loving care and forethought that we wanted for nothing. My father-in-law even topped up my rather meagre Oberleutnant's pay so that there was something left at the end of each month. When my wife asked if we could afford to go to the cinema, I was always able to say yes.

We were happy and content with our lot. Not even my frequent spells of duty on board ship could spoil our idyll, for they were spent in home waters and usually only lasted for a few days. Brief as they were, homecoming was always a joy. We would be catapulted off to fly back to Wilhelmshaven ahead of the ship. Swooping in low over the rooftops, the first thing we did after landing was to phone all the wives and girlfriends – the '*Muttis*', or 'mummies' as we called them – to let them know what time the *Admiral Scheer* would be entering Wilhelmshaven lock. These flights quickly became standard procedure. They ensured that there was always a big crowd waiting to cheer the ship's arrival – and they had the added advantage of allowing us to get home before everyone else!

On 30 September 1938 Chamberlain, Daladier, Hitler and Mussolini signed the Munich Agreement ceding the Sudeten territories of Czechoslovakia to Germany. On 3 October German forces marched into the Sudetenland. Five months later, on 15 March 1939, Germany occupied the rest of Czechoslovakia. Bohemia and Moravia were declared a joint protectorate the following day, while Slovakia – having announced her independence – voluntarily placed herself under German protection.

The Luftwaffe staged a flypast over Prague on 17 March 1939. Just prior to this I had been temporarily posted to a long-range reconnaissance Staffel that had been activated for service in the event of Czech resistance. But we were not called upon. The Staffel was disbanded again after the bloodless seizure of Czecho-slovakia, and its members, myself included, were returned to their original units.

In mid-March 1939 Lithuania offered to return the Memel-land region, which it had controlled as an 'autonomous territory' since 1923, to the German Reich. On the morning of 23 March 1939, the day of the official hand-over, units of the Luftwaffe circled for an hour above the town of Memel. That same afternoon a more formal flypast took place. The pocket battleship *Admiral Scheer* was also standing off the Memel-land on this date and we were launched to fly a sixty-minute patrol along the area's beautiful coastline as our own symbolic 'Welcome home to the Reich' greeting.

I must admit to having had some misgivings about the occupation of Czechoslovakia. Was this really justified in an historical context, I had asked myself? But I had no such qualms about the reintegration of the Memel-land. I was more than happy that the status quo had been restored with the territory's return to the Reich, and could only hope that the inhabitants of the region felt the same way after their sixteen-year separation.

On 1 May 1939, in Wilhelmshaven's naval clinic, my darling wife presented me with our first-born. Coincidentally, it was the 'Day of German Labour' – the Nazi Party's equivalent of May Day! At the time, to the sound of massed military bands, I had been marching through the streets of the town at the head of a company from the naval air station as part of the celebrations. But, as an anxious father-to-be, the moment the parade was over I had driven at top speed to the clinic. There my wife, exhausted but beaming with happiness, introduced me to a healthy, robust little boy – our son! We were overwhelmed with feelings of pride, relief and joy. In addition to my service duties, the weeks that followed were, needless to say, fully taken up in our mutual care and concern for the new arrival. The care part was, I fully admit, handled almost exclusively by my wife with all the natural instincts of a young mother. I restricted myself to the role of devoted spectator and quickly came to realize that, from the birth of our first son onwards, my wife was – and still is to this day – by far the stronger of the two of us.

I soon had to return on board ship for fleet exercises in the Skagerrak. These involved a series of practice attacks and defensive counter-measures between a group of capital ships and a flotilla of U-boats. While the U-boats were carrying out their attacks on the ships of the fleet, the latter's' floatplanes were to be launched one after the other to fly anti-submarine reconnaissance and protection patrols.

When it came to our turn I was fortunate to spot an attacking U-boat almost immediately after leaving the *Admiral Scheer*'s catapult. We circled above the submerged boat, reporting our sighting to the vessels of the fleet by every available means at our disposal – visual and wireless – so that they could take the necessary avoiding action and initiate defensive measures in good time. Then I grabbed my aerial-reconnaissance camera from its mounting and took a few quick shots of the submerged U-boat.

This sighting of the U-boat from the air, and the photographs I took of it, were to feature prominently in the subsequent post-exercise debriefing in Wilhelmshaven. More than that: for me they resulted in a completely unexpected but decisive career change from observer to pilot. And this is how it all came about . . .

When the subject of the U-boat sighting from the air was raised during the Wilhelmshaven debriefing, the U-boat commanders were frankly sceptical. Impossible, they muttered – with their new camouflage finish our boats can no longer be seen from the air – the captain must have been handling his boat like a novice. And more along the same lines. The officer commanding therefore suggested: 'Let's hear first of all what the observer involved has to say.'

I could only state that the captain of the U-boat in question had made a flawless approach. He had manoeuvred into the perfect position from which to launch a torpedo attack on his chosen target. It had been impossible to detect his periscope in the choppy seas. Yet from one particular spot in the sky, at fairly low altitude and with the sun at my back, the entire length of the boat had been clearly visible to me.

The refraction of light at this shallow angle had obviously been a contributory factor in allowing me to see the U-boat beneath the surface of the water. And when doubts continued to be expressed about my claim, I was able to produce the photographs that I had taken – which luckily had by this time been developed and printed – suggesting that perhaps if the gentlemen cared to look at them they might be convinced by the evidence of their own eyes. The officer commanding then called a brief halt to the proceedings to allow the prints to be scrutinized.

During this short pause Kapitän Coeler, the chief of staff of the F.d.Luft (C-in-C Naval Aviation) came over to have a word with me: 'I see that you are wearing an observer's badge, but tell me, do you have any pilot's certificates?' 'Jawohl, Herr Kapitän, all except that for blind-flying.' 'So you could fly small aircraft as well?' 'Jawohl, better than the larger ones, in fact.'

It wasn't until the following day that I found out where these questions had been leading. We were back on board the *Admiral Scheer* and were making our way through the Kiel Canal to carry out torpedo-firing practice in Eckernförder Bay. When we reached the Kiel-Holtenau locks at the eastern end of the canal I was given twenty-four hours leave of absence. The regatta that was held every year during the famous 'Kiel Week' festival of sail happened to be taking place and I had arranged to be 'deckhand' on the 50 square-metre cruising yacht that our Wilhelmshaven naval base had entered in one of the races.

Arriving at the yacht basin at about six in the morning, somewhat bleary-eyed and still unshaven, I was greeted by my crewmate Rudolf Rücker, who was serving on the staff of the F.d.Luft: 'Hello, Helmut,' he said cheerily, 'letting your dive-brakes grow already?' 'What's that supposed to mean?' I asked. 'I mean your beard. It was only yesterday evening that I was told to put your name forward for Stuka training as a potential Staffelkapitän.' 'It's too early in the morning for jokes. Just tell me what's going on?'

'It's no joke. We've had a request for three officers to be sent for dive-bombing training as prospective Staffelkapitäne for service aboard the aircraft carrier. The moment Kapitän Coeler got back from the exercise debriefing yesterday he instructed me to include your name as one of the three.' 'That's fantastic news! Thanks for letting me know.'

I could think of nothing else throughout the whole of the regatta. With my mind elsewhere, we were last past the starting buoy. To make up for it we had to take a chance by separating ourselves from the pack in the hope of finding a 'private' gust of wind to help us along. We were lucky. Backed by a stiff breeze we were ahead when rounding the first marker and some judicious luffing on the home stretch enabled us to hold on to the lead and take first place.

Of the approximately 2,000 applicants for the German Naval Officer's Training Course of 1932,
the twelve 'Starfish' – the dozen selected for flying training – won the jackpot.
With every reason to look happy they are, from the left: Storp jun., Brockmann, Hielscher,
Luckhardt, Mahlke, Kowalewski, Rücker, Fehling, Sander, Küppers, Gude and Bohn;
Neustadt in Holstein, April 1932.

Basic flying training at the Deutsche Verkehrsfliegerschule (DVS) Warnemünde.
A line-up of Udet Flamingos, summer 1932.

The author does a stint as duty clerk, logging take-off and landing times.

Our Udet Flamingo at Berlin-Tempelhof, 15 August 1932.

The twelve 'Starfish' (plus one) in more formal attire. From left: Mahlke, Hielscher, Bohn, Rücker, Gude, Storp jun., Luckhardt, Cormann (instructor), Kowalewski, Sander, Küppers, Brockmann and Fehling.

Heinkel He 42: the floatplane used for B-1 (Sea) naval flying training.

Left: The German Navy's sail training ship *Niobe* foundered in a Baltic storm with heavy loss of life among the 1932 intake.

Right: Catapult launch of a Heinkel He 60.

The cruiser *Köln*, which took the author to Australia and the Far East.

The *Admiral Scheer* (background) off the coast of Spain.

He 60 landing alongside in calm water - no need for the landing mat.

A choppier sea, but the He 60 is safely aboard the landing mat and about to be hooked up.

Aircrew of Carrier Stuka Gruppe I./186 [I.(St)/186(T)] at Wertheim 1939–40
(author second row, seventh from right).

The aircraft carrier *Graf Zeppelin* at an advanced stage of fitting out in the Deutsche Werke
shipyards at Kiel; 21 June 1940.

Leaving church after marrying Annemarie Vogt ('Amei') at Bad
Salzelmen near Schönebeck/Elbe, 9 July 1938.

It had been a good day for me. And the best part of all was the likelihood of a posting to dive-bombers. I tried to work out how it had all come about. That initial U-boat sighting had been nothing out of the ordinary. It was part and parcel of the job for a shipboard flyer. Any one of my comrades would have done exactly the same thing had they been in my place at the time. But, as chance would have it, on this occasion the chief of staff of the F.d.Luft had been shown the request for three naval Stuka pilots immediately prior to his attending the fleet exercise debriefing.

I could almost follow his train of thought as he sat listening to the proceedings: 'One of the primary duties of the Stukas on board the aircraft carrier will be to protect the vessel itself from enemy attack, particularly from U-boat attack. And to achieve that they must, above all, find the attacker before he launches his assault – which is exactly what one observer has just done during these exercises. There's every hope, therefore, that he could do the same if flying an anti U-boat patrol in time of war.' Hence, perhaps, his asking me whether I could fly small aircraft as well. Now I began to understand, although I did wonder for a moment how small he imagined a Stuka to be when compared to the He 60 floatplane.

When, a few days later, a posting arrived ordering me to report to the Stuka School at Kitzingen on 1 July 1939 to commence training as a dive-bomber pilot, I was like the cat that had swallowed the cream. That's just the sort of luck a soldier needs, I said to myself: to be minding his own business, going about his everyday duties, and then to come to the attention of a superior officer at the precise moment when that officer happens to be looking for someone to fill a specific role.

This posting meant a great deal to me in a number of ways. It wasn't simply the fact that at this time in the naval air arm there were dozens of elderly officers chasing every Staffelkapitän's vacancy, and that I was fortunate enough to be one of the first three young Oberleutnants to be handed such a prize. I was delighted to have been chosen, of course, but even this honour paled into insignificance against my change of role from observer to pilot. The old dream of actually being an operational pilot in my own right was now at long last about to become reality.

And not just any pilot either, but a dive-bomber pilot, part of an arm of the German Luftwaffe that had already gained quite a reputation for itself. Given the technology of the time, it was the only arm capable of hitting a pinpoint target with any degree of accuracy. On top of that a Stuka pilot had to possess a certain reckless courage, for the chances of his surviving the combined fire of the enemy's defences at low level were not rated as being particularly good.

The question of the operational risks involved had been a significant factor in the development of the Stuka dive-bomber. All the experts were agreed that the only way of knocking out a small target effectively and at relatively little cost was by dive-bombing. In those days there were no suitable bombsights available that would allow a high-altitude bomber to carry out an attack with anything like the same precision. It was for this reason that the Technical Office of the German Air Ministry had issued specifications for a dedicated dive-bomber. But doubts were then expressed as to whether man and machine would be capable of withstanding the strain of dive-bombing operations for any length of time.

Ironically, the one person above all others who had been convinced that the dive-bomber stood no chance of surviving enemy fire at altitudes of less than 1,000 metres was Oberst Wolfram Freiherr von Richthofen, the then head of the Development Department at the Technical Office. But bomb release heights of no more than 500 metres were essential if the required accuracy was to be achieved. This had led to Richthofen signing an order, dated 9 June 1936, stating that: 'Further development of the Ju 87 is to be suspended . . .'!

Just twenty-four hours later Oberst Ernst Udet took over as chief of the Technical Office. One of Germany's most successful fighter pilots of the First World War and an internationally acclaimed post-war aerobatic flyer, Udet had been a staunch advocate of the dive-bomber for many years. In the autumn of 1936, after a fly-off between the Ju 87, the He 118 and several other designs, he decreed that: 'The dive-bomber units of the German Luftwaffe are to be equipped with the Ju 87.' The decision had been taken and the question of the risks inherent in dive-bombing, if not resolved, was at least no longer a subject for discussion.

Not that this mattered a great deal to me. As naval flyers, and shipboard ones at that, we were already familiar with the dangers of low-level flying, even in peacetime. And if hostilities *did* break out, we were only too well aware that every type of seaplane currently in service would be just as vulnerable to enemy fire – if not more so – than any dive-bomber. Although this was a situation beyond our control, my views on the subject had almost got me into hot water when General Geisler, the AOC Naval Air Command, paid an official visit to our Staffel.

Seated next to him at lunch, I rather foolishly asked the general why our maritime units couldn't be equipped with land-based aircraft, which were altogether faster, more manoeuvrable, more powerful and more heavily armed – and thus stood a far better chance of surviving in combat – than our present lame-duck seaplanes. But the general was having none of it. He flatly rejected any such idea, giving as his reason the seaplane's ability to put down on water in the event of an emergency, something he regarded as an indispensable safety measure in maritime operations.

I expressed my doubts about this, saying that if they came down in the water a crew usually ended up in a dinghy anyway, irrespective of whether they had been flying a seaplane or a landplane. I explained that only shipboard Staffeln such as ourselves were wholly dependent on seaplanes. And I was certain in my own mind that if we were to become involved in a naval engagement on the high seas our chances of getting back on board our ship would be slim. It was far more likely that we would have to attempt an emergency landing on open water, and even for us the floats would then be of questionable value as they were unable to stand up to anything rougher than sea strength three.

My poor opinion of the safety value of floats on an aircraft clearly did not go down at all well. That very same evening every naval air unit was in receipt of a teleprint from the F.d.Luft, which, if I remember rightly, read something along the lines of: 'With immediate effect, I forbid any discussion whatsoever among the commissioned ranks regarding the deployment of land aircraft over the sea. *Geisler.*'

Little more than three months later I heard that the F.d.Luft had been ordered by Luftwaffe C-in-C Hermann Göring in person to train a number of land-based bomber units for maritime operations. I regarded this as a necessary and sensible decision, for in those days – as indeed now – seaplanes were only required for missions where take-offs and landings on water were unavoidable.

Chapter 7
Training to be a Stuka Pilot

Happy beyond words at the prospect of getting back into the pilot's seat and holding the stick in my own hands again, I reported to the Stuka school on 1 July 1939. The two other Staffelkapitän candidates, Hauptmann Helmut Bode, and my old comrade from the intake of 1932, Oberleutnant Roderich Küppers, arrived at the same time, as did a number of other trainee Stuka pilots.

Together with the theoretical side of the training, the course included familiarization on the Henschel Hs 123 and Junkers Ju 87, formation flying, dogfighting practice on the Hs 123, aerial gunnery against ground targets and dive-bombing practice on the Ju 87. For the dogfighting exercises I was always paired with Roderich Küppers. They began with our flying towards each other on opposing courses. Once we were level, each had to turn in towards the other and try to get into a favourable firing position on the tail of his 'opponent' as quickly as possible.

Needless to say, neither one of us wanted to concede an inch to the other, and things invariably degenerated into a wild free-for-all as we threw the Henschels about the sky. The turns would grow tighter and tighter until often the mist descended. The 'mist' – or 'veil' – was our term for what we experienced when centrifugal forces became so strong that they interfered with the blood supply to the main optic nerve. This condition first became noticeable when the forces reached some four or five times a pilot's bodyweight (4–5 g). His field of vision would become ever more limited until, finally, he was totally blind. Now was the time to ease off the stick and reduce the g forces, otherwise there was the very real danger of his losing consciousness altogether.

After a few seconds the veil would lift and vision return. As soon as the 'enemy' was sighted battle was rejoined. Climb – dive – a steep turn – climb through a dazzling white heap of fair weather cumulus – dive again. For someone with a passion for flying these dummy dogfights were a pure delight. At the same time, we were fully aware of the fact that the training programme had not been organized solely for our personal enjoyment and so we made every effort to prepare ourselves as far as possible for the sort of operations we might be expected to fly should hostilities break out – what we didn't realize, however, was just how close those hostilities actually were.

The most important part of our training was, of course, precision dive-bombing practice. To ensure the necessary accuracy, the Stuka had to dive at an angle of at least 70–80 degrees. At first, an angle of 70 degrees seemed to me to be impossibly steep, but it soon became routine. What I found much more difficult was estimating the correct height at which to release the bomb. The altimeter couldn't unwind fast enough when the Stuka was in a near-vertical dive and always lagged a little behind the machine's actual height. The pilot therefore had to rely mainly on his own judgement as to his altitude – or lack thereof!

The g forces during the recovery didn't affect me unduly. Again, it was to a large extent very much in the pilot's own hands to make sure that he didn't pull the aircraft out of its dive any more sharply than was humanly bearable. This also meant that the airframe itself wasn't subjected to excessive loads. In the light of all the hair-raising stories I had heard to date, I soon came to the conclusion that the Stuka arm was doing a very good job in selling itself to the general public. In my opinion, much of what it was called upon to do was portrayed as being far more dangerous than it actually was in peacetime practice.

I won't deny that individual dive-bomber pilots may have had different perceptions of the physical demands made upon them. For some, perhaps, those demands may even have been close to the limits of their endurance. But, speaking personally, the only problem I ever experienced when diving from any great height was an occasional and unpleasant build-up of pressure in my ears. This was caused by the rapid increase in external air pressure and could usually be alleviated by the act of swallowing. A slight popping of the eardrums would then indicate that the correct balance of pressure had been restored. However, even the slightest of head colds could cause real problems, leading to an extremely painful accumulation of pressure in the ears – and this at the very moment of greatest concentration, when the pilot was committed to the dive and focussing all his attention on the point of bomb release. The pain was admittedly severe, but it didn't last long and so even this could be endured.

The demands made upon the gunner sitting in the rear cockpit of the Stuka were far greater than those required of the pilot. Facing rearwards, monitoring the airspace behind the machine and ready to let fly at any attacking fighter approaching from astern, he would often be forced to his knees by some of the pilot's more violent defensive manoeuvres. Yet I never once heard a single word of complaint from any of our gunners. They did their job with commendable courage and resilience.

It was commonly believed that the near vertical dive to earth was in itself an enormous strain on a Stuka crew. Many of those who asked me how I could possibly stand it were amazed when I told them that a vertical dive was not all that different from normal horizontal flight. This was due to the fact that, with the underwing dive brakes extended, the speed during the machine's descent was kept very much to a constant and there was little or no g effect. This only became apparent when the pilot pulled out of the dive and the crew were pressed down in their seats by some 3–5 g. But, as already explained, it was very much up to the pilot to judge his recovery. Most came out of the dive at about 3 g, which the body could tolerate quite comfortably.

During one of our early practice missions, however, it was another situation entirely that was very nearly my undoing. As part of our training we had been ordered to fly back from the bombing range to our airfield as low as possible. As we snaked along the valley of the River Main, my old naval aviator's instincts came to the fore. The best place to fly at zero altitude, I thought to myself, is over water. There'll be no obstacles along the river apart from the occasional barge, which will be clearly visible from a distance and quite easy to avoid. And so – all unsuspecting – I took us down until we were racing along little more than a metre above the surface of the Main.

Suddenly I spotted a thick ferry cable stretched across the river immediately ahead and just above me! With no time to climb, I had no choice but to fly straight under it. It scared the daylights out of me. My heart was hammering madly and I could only thank my lucky stars that I had been obeying orders to the letter and was flying as low as possible. This time I had got away with it by the skin of my teeth. But it had taught me a valuable lesson. In those days there were no air safety regulations requiring overhead wires or cables to carry high-visibility, bright orange warning markers. And so, from then on, whenever I flew low along a valley or followed the course of a river, I always kept a sharp eye open – not only for shipping, but also for any masts or riverside pylons indicating the presence of power cables and similar such obstacles.

On 15 August 1939 the infant Stuka arm suffered a terrible tragedy. Thirteen crews from I./StG 76 lost their lives on the Neuhammer troop training ground. A thick ground mist had been covering the area and they had all dived straight into the ground. We could hardly take in this shattering news. How could such a thing have happened? Details were sketchy at first, but over the next few days we gradually pieced together the course of events. Two Stukagruppen, I./StG 76 under Hauptmann Sigel and I./StG 2 'Immelmann' commanded by Hauptmann Hitschhold, had been briefed to stage a demonstration dive-bombing attack at Neuhammer in front of some top Army and Luftwaffe brass. Among those watching would be Generals von Manstein, von Richthofen, Sperrle and Loerzer.

Prior to take-off Hauptmann Sigel had been handed a weather report. This forecast seven-tenths cloud at an altitude of 900 metres above the target area at the appointed time of the demonstration, but stated that good visibility could be expected below that height. Armed with this information, Sigel had made his plans accordingly. His three Staffeln were to dive through the forecast cloud layer and release their smoke bombs at an altitude of 300 metres.

But by the time Hauptmann Sigel and his I./StG 76 arrived over the target area sixty minutes later a thick ground mist had formed. This crucial piece of information was not passed on to the Gruppe. And they themselves – approaching from above the upper layer of cloud – remained totally unaware of this insidious change in the weather conditions below. The Kommandeur consequently led his three Staffeln down into the cloud as planned.

Sigel recognized the danger at the last split-second. He managed to wrench his own machine out of its dive with barely a metre to spare, yelling a desperate warning to his men as he did so. But it was too late for the leading Staffel immediately behind him. Thirteen Stukas slammed into the ground in quick succession or were smashed to pieces in the woods bordering the training ground.

In the enquiry following the disaster no blame was attached to Hauptmann Sigel. The cause of the tragedy, according to what we heard, was the misleading weather report.

It wasn't until much later that the day's events were described to me first-hand by Major Friedrich Lang. At the time Lang had been a Leutnant serving with I./StG 2 'Immelmann', the other Stuka Gruppe taking part in the Neuhammer demonstration. He told me that he had been flying as left-hand wingman to the Gruppenkommandeur, Hauptmann Hitschhold:

> We took off from Cottbus. There wasn't a cloud in the sky and visibility was very good. Between Cottbus and Neuhammer a ground mist began to gather and was identified as such by our Gruppe. It stretched away in a solid white blanket to the eastern horizon, its lightly ruffled upper surfaces bathed in the most glorious late summer sunshine.
>
> Some two to three kilometres off to the right ahead of us the other Gruppe was flying at an altitude of about 3,000 metres. Because of the ground mist I was fully expecting the formation leader to abort the exercise. But when I next happened to glance in their direction I was horrified to see huge columns of dark smoke climbing out of the mist. I knew at once that something terrible had happened. We circled above the area and then flew back to Cottbus. The news of the deaths of so many of our comrades did not take long to reach us.

Lang went on with his story:

About half an hour after we had landed we received the order to return to Neuhammer and carry out the demonstration at low level; the mist had meanwhile lifted to a height of about 150 metres. At the time we thought that this order – which had come down from General von Richthofen, who was attending the demonstration in the company of Manstein – was both callous and senseless. But he presumably wanted to show the Army general just what hard stuff his Stuka crews were made of.

Although not all details of the Neuhammer disaster had been made known to us at the time, it was a salutary lesson for me, for it brought home just how great a burden of responsibility for all the aircraft and crews under his command the leader of a Stuka unit had to bear. With a massed Stuka attack requiring every crew to follow the leading machine down into the dive in close formation and without a moment's hesitation, it was essential that the unit commander think not just for himself, but for every single man he was taking into action with him. His primary concern was, of course, to ensure that he carried out his mission in such a way as to achieve optimum results – but of almost equal importance was the safe return to base of all his crews.

These thoughts were still uppermost in my mind when, towards the end of August 1939 and after the completion of our Stuka training, Bode, Küppers and I were ordered to Berlin. There we reported to an Oberst Weygold, who informed us of our new appointments. The maritime Staffeln intended for service aboard the as-yet-unfinished aircraft carrier *Graf Zeppelin* were to be activated at Kiel-Holtenau and we three were instructed to proceed there forthwith.

The Kommandeur of the ship's embryonic Stukagruppe, I.(St)/186(T), was Major Walter Hagen, an experienced First World War naval pilot whose flying career had continued into the post-war era. A modest individual, he was a superb pilot who had played a pivotal role in the earliest days of naval aviation. He was also an incomparable leader of men who treated those under his command with respect, consideration and absolute fairness. We could not have wished for a better commanding officer.

The Gruppe's first Staffel, 1.(St)/186(T), was to be set up by Hauptmann Helmut Bode. I was to be similarly responsible for activating the second – 2.(St)/186(T) – while the third was created by the simple expedient of redesignating Hauptmann Blattner's already extant and operational 4./186 to become 3.(St)/186(T).

At the same time Roderich Küppers was tasked with setting up a Staffel of single-engined fighters. Like our Stukas, these were also initially earmarked for service on board the *Graf Zeppelin*. Although the vessel was still under construction, and would clearly remain so for a long time to come, we were under orders to press ahead at full speed with the activation of our respective Staffeln so that they could be declared operational at the earliest possible opportunity.

Armed with these instructions and directives we arrived at Kiel-Holtenau at the end of August 1939. We were totally ignorant of the imminent attack on Poland. Nor, of course, were we aware that back in March 1939 Hitler, as Supreme Commander of the Wehrmacht – an office he had assumed on 4 February 1938 – had ordered the German High Command to draw up plans for 'Case White', his intended invasion of Poland, which were to be ready for implementation at any time from August 1939 onwards. Admittedly, we realized that the situation was tense. That was only too clear from the political manoeuvrings of the European nations, whose activities had been making headlines throughout the year:

31 March 1939: Great Britain guarantees Poland's independence.

7 April 1939: Italy annexes Albania.

15 April 1939: US President Roosevelt sends a message of peace to Hitler and Mussolini.

27 April 1939: Great Britain introduces general conscription.

28 April 1939: Germany revokes the Anglo-German naval treaty of 1935 and the German–Polish treaty of 1933.

22 May 1939: The German–Italian pact forming the Rome–Berlin 'Axis' is signed in Berlin.

22 June 1939: Diplomatic discussions aimed at persuading the Soviet Union to join the Western nations' 'Peace Front' open in Moscow.

10 August 1939: Military talks between the Western Allies and the Soviet Union.

23 August 1939: German–Soviet non-aggression pact signed in Moscow.

25 August 1939: Signing of the Anglo-Polish military alliance.

26 August 1939: Germany pledges to respect the neutrality of Belgium, Denmark, Holland, Luxembourg and Switzerland. German propaganda reports border violations along the German–Polish frontier.

From the above it must have been apparent even to the most politically blinkered observer that Germany's leaders were making every effort to get rid of the 'Polish Corridor'. Created by the Versailles Treaty, this strip of territory, which gave Poland access to the Baltic Sea, was a particular thorn in the side of the German nation, for it effectively cut the province of East Prussia off from the rest of the Reich. But even at this late stage, we still did not believe that the German government would risk going to war to achieve its ends. After all, what was it that Hermann Göring, the then Reich's Commissioner for Aviation, had said on 30 January 1933 when announcing the setting up of the German Luftwaffe:

> I will carry on this struggle for Germany's equality of rights with all the passion and tenacity for which we National Socialists are renowned until I can be sure that the safety of the German nation has been secured.

And later, as Reich's Minister of Aviation and Commander-in-Chief of the Luftwaffe:

> The German Luftwaffe is just as passionately imbued with the will to defend the Fatherland to the last bullet, as it is convinced that never will it be employed in such a way as to threaten the peace of other nations.

Having taken up our duties in Holtenau, we immediately set about the task of activating our Staffeln. The first drafts of naval personnel had already arrived. More turned up every day; their posting to the Gruppe also resulting in their automatic transfer from the Navy to the Luftwaffe. We began to take delivery of stores and equipment. There were even a few old He 50s, which were to be used for training purposes until our specially modified Ju 87Bs came off the production lines.

The only operational Staffel within our Gruppe – the one commanded by Hauptmann Blattner – was already fully equipped with Ju 87s. It had left Holtenau a day or two earlier, ostensibly on an exercise, and was currently based at Stolp-West in Pomerania. Those of us still in Kiel didn't have the slightest inkling of the real reason behind its sudden departure.

The news of 1 September 1939 hit us like a bolt from the blue! *War!* At 04.45 hours, and without a declaration of war, German forces had invaded Poland! Now how would it all end?

Under the circumstances, our daily routine of grappling with all the minutiae and other odd jobs that inevitably surrounded the setting up of a new Staffel suddenly seemed so unimportant and insignificant that we felt almost embarrassed about it. We nonetheless resolved to press on with the task and have it completed as soon as possible. But every spare moment was spent glued to the wireless to keep ourselves abreast of developments and get the very latest news from the fighting fronts:

> *1 September 1939:* As Germany advances into Poland, Italy declares itself a non-belligerent. Great Britain and France demand the immediate cessation of hostilities in Poland and the withdrawal of German troops back behind the Reich's borders.

2 September 1939: The German advance gains ground. The Jablunka Pass is taken. Units of the 10. Armee under General von Reichenau reach the River Warthe north of Tschenstochau [Czestochowa].

3 September 1939: Britain, France, Australia, New Zealand and India declare war on Germany. The High Command of the German Navy begins the submarine campaign against enemy shipping with seventeen U-boats.

4 September 1939: General von Küchler's 3. Armee advancing out of East Prussia makes contact with the 4. Armee of General von Kluge operating out of Pomerania and thereby restores the land connection between East Prussia and the Reich. German troops reach Kulm. Heavy fighting in the Tucheler Heath area.

5 September 1939: Polish fortresses at Graudenz [Grudziadz] and Mlawa captured. First British air raids on Cuxhaven and Wilhelmshaven. The USA declares its neutrality. Slovakia enters the war against Poland.

6 September 1939: All of the Polish industrial region of Upper Silesia back in German hands. Limited French offensives in the Saarbrücken area. The Union of South Africa declares war on Germany.

7 September 1939: German motorized units reach the River Narew. 14. Armee under General List advances out of Slovakia into West Galicia. Cracow surrenders without a fight. A spearhead of General von Reichenau's 10. Armee is heading towards Warsaw.

8 September 1939: The Polish defenders of Fortress 'Westerplatte' surrender after an heroic struggle. Attacks by units of a German armoured corps against the southwestern suburbs of Warsaw driven back by Polish forces. Start of the 'cauldron battle' of Radom.

9 September 1939: Pursuit of the routed Polish armies, whose retreat behind the River Weichsel [Vistula] is being blocked by German forces. Capture of Lódz and Radom.

10 September 1939: Attempts at a break-out by General Bortnowski's encircled Polish Posen-Armee [Poznan Army] are thwarted. German armoured break-through between Sandomierz and Kutno reaches the River Weichsel. Canada declares war on Germany.

12 September 1939: Start of the Battle of Kutno in the great bend of the Weichsel.

13 September 1939: The 'cauldron battle' near Radom ends with the capture of some 60,000 Polish prisoners.

15 September 1939: Gdingen [Gdynia] in German hands. Polish attempts to break through at Jutno beaten back. Warsaw rejects German demands for its surrender.

17 September 1939: Kutno and Brest-Litovsk in German hands. Soviet army groups advance into eastern Poland without a declaration of war. The Polish government escapes into Romania and is interned there.

18 September 1939: The British aircraft carrier *Courageous* is sunk by *U-29* commanded by Kapitänleutnant Schuhart.

19 September 1939: End of the Battle of Bzura in the bend of the Weichsel. Polish troops lay down their arms. Around 170,000 Poles taken into captivity.

20 September 1939: German forces begin to withdraw behind the demarcation line agreed with the Soviet High Command.

21 September 1939: Surrender of the Polish armies under General Langner engaged against Soviet forces in the Lemberg [Lwów] area. Some 217,000 prisoners-of-war.

25 September 1939: Major assault on Warsaw. Heavy raids by German Luftwaffe. Under the command of General von Richthofen a total of 1,177 aircraft attack military targets in the Polish capital almost without pause. As a result of the destructive and sustained effects of these raids the OKW (High Command of the German Armed Forces) refrains from further attacks on Warsaw.

26 September 1939: One million leaflets dropped on Warsaw demanding the surrender of the city. In the afternoon the military commander of Warsaw offers the unconditional surrender of the city.

27 September 1939: Upon completion of surrender negotiations a cease-fire comes into effect from 14.00 hours.

28 September 1939: German–Soviet Treaty of Friendship establishes new demarcation line partitioning Polish territory. The Soviet government acquires military bases in Estonia.

29 September 1939: Surrender of the Polish fortress at Modlin (around 35,000 prisoners taken).

30 September 1939: Formation in France of a Polish government-in-exile under General Sikorski.

1 October 1939: German troops enter Warsaw. Surrender of the Polish naval base at Hela [Hel].

3 October 1939: French forward troops retire behind the Maginot Line.

5 October 1939: The Soviet Union acquires military bases in Latvia via a mutual aid pact.

6 October 1939: The last of Poland's regular forces lay down their arms at Kock and Lublin (17,000 men). In his speech to the Reichstag assembly Hitler offers peace to the Western powers. Britain and France reject his proposals and increase the pace of their rearmament and mobilization programmes . . .

. . . and thus the final threshold leading up to the Second World War was crossed. Havoc and disaster had been unleashed and were now free to take their course.

The third Staffel of our Gruppe commanded by Hauptmann Blattner – still operating under its original designation as 4./186 – had returned to Kiel-Holtenau on 28 September after its successful participation in the campaign against Poland. The unit had suffered the loss of two of its crews. Unteroffiziere Czuprina and Meinhardt had been brought down by ground fire while dive-bombing the Polish submarine base at Hela on 3 September. The Thuringian Oberleutnant Rummel and his gunner, Oberfunkmaat Blunck, had failed to return on 14 September after attacking a 40mm Flak battery. These losses had cast a pall over the entire Staffel and the returning crews seemed to derive little pleasure from the otherwise remarkable successes they had achieved during the short-lived campaign.

We, on the other hand, were naturally keen to learn all we could about the combat experiences of the first of our comrades to have seen front-line action. Although they were somewhat reticent about what they had just been through, we were gradually able to build up bit by bit an accurate picture of the Staffel's operations against the Poles.

4./186 – or 3.(St)/186(T) as it should now more accurately be called – had attacked the Polish naval and submarine base at Hela on 1 September 1939, the opening day of the campaign. It mounted two further attacks on the same target on 3 September. In the course of these raids a number of enemy vessels had been sunk, among them the 2,250-ton minelayer *Gryf*, the largest and most modern ship of the Polish fleet. Also sunk were the 1,540-ton destroyer *Wicher*, which took a direct hit amidships from Oberfeldwebel Lion, the tender *Smok* and the patrol boat *MB*. In addition, a munitions dump was hit and a 40mm gun battery put out of action.

Operating out of Brüsterort and Lauenburg, the Staffel then supported the ground fighting, dive-bombing and strafing enemy troops during the battle for the Oxhöfter Kämpe positions and knocking out another Flak battery near Pagorsch. Continuing in their ground-support role, they flew four missions each on both 12 and 13 September. They attacked enemy positions at Kasimir and Eichenberg, destroyed an armoured train near Gdingen, silenced a Flak battery at Kielau and machine-gun nests at Sagorsch, before intervening yet again in the fighting for the Oxhöfter Kämpe where they successfully neutralized enemy command posts and machine-gun emplacements. During a dive-bombing raid on the goods yard at Gdingen they destroyed an ammunition train and tore up large sections of track.

Two raids on the harbour at Heisternest on 14 September resulted in the sinking of more Polish ships: the 200-ton survey vessel *Pomorzanin*, the 280-ton tender *Lech*, the 183-ton minesweeper *Jaskolka* and the small mine-clearance vessel *M9*. Another minesweeper, the *Czapla*, was severely damaged. On the same day the Staffel scored five hits on a field battery near Neu-Oblusch, effectively putting it out of action, and blew up an ammunition depot at Ostrowgrund. Further ground-support missions targeting enemy troops were flown until the Polish defenders of the Oxhöfter Kämpe finally capitulated on 19 September.

Transferred to Danzig three days later, the Staffel carried out attacks on the Hela Peninsula on 23 and 25 September, cutting the railway line in several places. From 26 to 28 September the Staffel had been based at Radom, south of Warsaw, where it was temporarily subordinated to Stukageschwader 77. No missions were flown during this time, however, and on 28 September 1939 Hauptmann Blattner and his men returned to their home base at Kiel-Holtenau.

In their raids on heavily defended targets our comrades of 3. Staffel had developed a healthy respect for the density and accuracy of fire thrown up at them by the Polish Flak batteries. Two gallant crews had fallen victim to the enemy's anti-aircraft gunners. In contrast, they had not encountered a single Polish fighter, thanks to the Luftwaffe's opening air strikes of the campaign, which had quickly achieved absolute air superiority.

We also asked the Staffelkapitän, Hauptmann Blattner, what effect his Stukas had had when attacking troops on the ground. He hesitated before answering, 'Bombing and strafing marching columns and troop assembly areas are entirely different from normal dive-bombing,' he said thoughtfully:

> When you fly at low level back along a road packed with troops you've just been attacking, it's a scene of such utter chaos and indescribable horror that you can't get it out of your mind for a very long time. In fact, I'm not sure if the sort of carnage we have witnessed can ever be forgotten.

We all fell silent at his words. The full reality of war had suddenly been brought home to us and each was alone with his thoughts.

While our 3. Staffel comrades had been fighting in Poland, we had begun working up with our own Staffeln in the homeland. At first we had had to make do with the old He 50s, two-seater open-cockpit biplanes powered by air-cooled radial engines. During practice dives in these antiquated old crates the engines vibrated so badly that we were worried they would shake themselves right out of their mountings. Oil sprayed out of every joint and seam. At the end of each exercise we climbed out of our cockpits covered in the stuff and looking like a tribe of blackamoors. It wasn't until mid-September that we were able to collect the special Ju 87Bs intended for our Staffel and flying training on our new mounts could begin in earnest. By the end of October 1939 the process of activation was complete. The Staffel was fully 'flown-in' and ready for operations.

In the meantime there had been a slight thaw in relations between the high commands of the Luftwaffe and the Navy regarding both our own Stukagruppe and our companion Jagdgruppe. As carrier-based units we would be tactically subordinated to the Navy. Our personnel had come exclusively from the ranks of the Navy before being transferred to the Luftwaffe. But because it was not known at this juncture just how long it would be before our aircraft carrier, the *Graf Zeppelin*, entered service – which, in the event, she never did – the Luftwaffe was demanding that, in the interim, our Gruppe should be placed under the control of its own Luftflotte [Air Fleet] 2.

The Navy's opposition to this demand – made mainly as a matter of prestige, I suspect – was put to the OKW, which came down firmly on the side of the Luftwaffe. Naturally, we knew nothing of these goings-on at our lowly level. We were simply surprised and delighted when, at the beginning of November 1939, we received orders to transfer to Wertheim, near Würzburg, for service under Luftflotte 2.

On 8 November 1939 we landed at Wertheim, thereby taking our place as a tactical unit on the Luftwaffe's operational order of battle alongside all its other Stukagruppen. The move was very welcome from a flying point of view, but it did pose a number of problems for our ground staff, which would continue to plague the Gruppe for a long time to come. Still nominally a carrier-based unit, we had been furnished with very little transport of our own. The Gruppe itself had been allocated a single Ju 52 transport aircraft, while the HQ and each Staffel was provided with one 3-ton lorry, one small car and one motorcycle for use while lying in harbour.

Obviously, this was totally inadequate for a normal Stuka unit's day-to-day operations, let alone for a rapid transfer from one airfield to another. We were constantly bringing this deficiency to the attention of the authorities responsible, but to absolutely no effect. We were still down on their books as a carrier Gruppe and, as such, we were not entitled to a regular establishment of vehicles. Bureaucracy had a field day and the bumph blossomed. We were informed that our transport requirements would be met by whatever airbase we happened to be stationed on at the time, and by our attached FBK [Airfield Servicing Company]. But such units were equipped only with sufficient vehicles for their own purposes and would have few, if any, to spare.

When it came to transferring from one airfield to another, a limited amount of air transport capacity would be placed at our disposal, while road convoys would handle the bulk of our ground equipment. But these latter would have to be brought in from elsewhere. This was always a lengthy business and meant, in practice, that they never arrived on schedule.

At first, this highly unsatisfactory state of affairs merely hampered the everyday running of the Gruppe. Later however, during the campaign in France, it was to have such a detrimental effect on our operational efficiency that we were forced to resort to self-help. By gathering together a motley collection of captured enemy vehicles and by repairing anything on wheels that we found abandoned by the roadside, we were finally able to make ourselves as independently mobile as all the other Stukagruppen had been from the start.

Admittedly, our ground convoys during the later stages of the French campaign were something of a sorry spectacle. Made up of civilian and military vehicles of assorted French, British and German manufacture, they must have looked to the casual observer more like a band of nomads on the move rather than the ground echelon of what was, in reality, a highly disciplined Stuka unit. But their external appearance didn't worry us unduly. In fact, it may even have provided good camouflage. The important thing was that our vehicles, whatever their pedigree, were serving their purpose: the Gruppe had the mobility to meet its operational commitments.

In Wertheim, as 1939 neared its close, we continued to press ahead with our formation-flying practice whenever the wintry weather allowed. All the while we were expecting to get some word from on high evaluating the Stuka units' performance in the recent Polish campaign and setting out the latest guidelines on their future deployment. But we waited in vain. It appeared that the basic tactical principles had proven essentially sound, although there was little evidence available as to the Stuka's vulnerability, or otherwise, to enemy fighter attack. The rapid establishment of total air superiority meant that very few Stuka crews had encountered opposition from Polish fighters. All in all, what we learned from official sources was not much more than could be gleaned from the daily press and was known to the general public.

Basically, what this amounted to was that the German Luftwaffe had played a vital role in the campaign against Poland, both by securing early superiority in the air and by targeting enemy road and rail supply networks. Above all, its disruption of the enemy's communications meant that the Polish armies had been rendered largely leaderless by being cut off from their higher commands.

The one element in the campaign that came as a total surprise not only to the Poles, but also to our own High Command, was the effect achieved by the close collaboration between the Stukas (and the Luftwaffe's sole Hs 123-equipped ground-attack Gruppe) and the fast armoured units on the ground. Their combined striking power had completely demoralized the enemy and proved to be the decisive factor in bringing the campaign to a swift and successful conclusion – so much so, that a special word was coined to describe this new kind of mobile, hard-hitting warfare: *Blitzkrieg*.

The one officer responsible above all others for the development of *Blitzkrieg* tactics was General Manfred Freiherr von Richthofen who, as the 'Fliegerführer z.b.V.' [AOC Special Purposes], had commanded the Luftwaffe's close-support forces in Poland. Based upon his experiences during the Spanish Civil War, Richthofen employed his seven Stukagruppen and single ground-attack Gruppe to devastating effect by providing direct support to the ground forces at every critical point and decisive phase in the fighting.

In the absence of any official information we naturally made every effort to contact the crews of those Stuka units that had been involved in the Polish campaign to learn from their experiences and to prepare ourselves for what lay ahead. Personal accounts by those of our comrades who had been in the thick of the action were of especial interest to us, and often very instructive too. Among those accounts are some that could well still be of historical value today, for they throw fresh light on events that have not been dealt with – or, at least, not with total accuracy – in any post-war literature. One such, for example, concerns the first Stuka attack of the war, which was also the very first Luftwaffe operation of all in the campaign against Poland: the bombing of the bridge at Dirschau.

One of the major priorities of the German High Command at the very outset was the capture intact of the bridge at Dirschau, which carried the main Berlin–Königsberg [Kaliningrad] railway line across the Weichsel on the eastern edge of the Polish Corridor. This operation was planned down to the minutest detail, as may be gathered from these extracts from the war diary of the then Chief of the Army General Staff, Generaloberst Halder, which was published in 1962:

> 17 August 1939: Discussion with Gen. Jeschonnek: 'Dirschau'. Luftwaffe participation essential.
> 19 August 1939: 'Dirschau'. SS: 12 men recruited locally (familiar with area). Luftwaffe: 3 Staffeln = 1 Stukagruppe: 3 x 9 (exc. HQ machines) = 27. Time: X-Day, preferably *before* X-Hour.
>> Execution:
>> a) 1 Coy. of assault engineers in mufti aboard goods train (approaching from Marienburg); behind that, armoured train; behind that, motorized Group Medem: remainder of assault engineer battalion, anti-tank platoon, mobile heavy field howitzer battery, 1 MGK [armoured reconnaissance troop]. Luftwaffe to bomb: barracks, power station, railway station.
>> b) Alternatives: Cooperation with SS. Advance at night.

c) If rail traffic crippled, only operation a) in civilian trucks. Rail traffic must be maintained. (Special Commando Dirschau tasked with capturing bridges intact; units of the Army, SS and Luftwaffe to stand by in support.) . . .

22 August 1939: 3rd Dirschau: At dawn on Y-Day Stukagruppen to attack western end of bridge and town (barracks, power station, etc.) At same time train from Marienburg, followed by armoured train and remaining units of Medem.

1 September 1939: . . . 06.30 hours: Border crossed at all points; Dirschau air units taken off; Westerplatte landing force (Coy.); Fuhrer's proclamation to Wehrmacht.

08.00 hours: Dirschau reportedly unsuccessful. *Air attack apparently ineffective.* In Königsberg: Not successful, bridge demolished.

The Stuka unit involved in the Dirschau operation was the East Prussia-based I./StG 1. The most important part of their mission was to cut the demolition cable leading from the railway station out onto the bridge in order to prevent the latter being blown up by the Poles. The bridge itself was not, under any circumstances, to be damaged during their attack.

On the eve of the mission the Gruppe's aircraft had transferred singly up to Elbing, close to the eastern edge of the Polish Corridor. All machines arrived safely except for that of the Kommandeur, Major Rentsch, and his adjutant Leutnant Tichy. It was shortly before dusk when Tichy finally landed at Elbing. He informed the unit's senior Staffelkapitän, Oberleutnant Hozzel, that there had been an accident. The Gruppenkommandeur had fallen down the stairs in his quarters and was suffering from concussion. Luftwaffenkommando Ostpreussen, the Area Command, had therefore appointed him, Oberleutnant Hozzel, as acting Kommandeur of the Gruppe.

Weather conditions on the morning of 1 September 1939 were so poor that the bulk of the Luftwaffe units briefed to attack Poland were unable to take off. Despite this, the pilots of I./StG 1 had carried out their mission successfully. Oberleutnant Hozzel himself described this first air operation of the Second World War in the following words:

Those of us who had been selected to fly the mission had been able to get a good look at our intended targets a few weeks before the war began. Dressed in civilian clothes and travelling individually so as not to attract attention, each of us had made the journey by train across the Corridor and so knew exactly what we had to aim at. As I was to lead the attack, I had a lengthy discussion the night before with Oberst Medem, the commander of the engineer assault unit that was to take the bridge by storm immediately after our dive-bombing.

When we lifted off from Elbing the cloud base was down to fifty metres and visibility less than one kilometre. I had already despatched six machines under Oberleutnant Dilley. Painted in distinctive yellow markings and each carrying a single 500kg bomb, they had taken off at about two-minute intervals. Their job was to approach the target at low level and sever the demolition cable leading to the bridge.

Only moments before the attack was due to go in – at 04.42 hours – the weather cleared slightly. This was just enough to allow me to lead the main part of the Gruppe up to a height of 2,000 metres before starting the dive. A second or so before our bombs hit we spotted Dilley's six machines racing diagonally across the railway tracks below us. The bridge hadn't gone up. We'd done it!

I sent the Gruppe back separately to Griesleinen and remained on my own above the target area to see what would happen next. No explosion. But no signs of Medem and his two trains, one armoured and one troop train, anywhere near the bridge either. The ground force's attempt to take the enemy by surprise had obviously failed.

The Poles had blocked the line at the Marienburg bridgehead, brought their anti-tank guns into action and had shot the two locomotives to pieces. The fighting on the ground dragged on. The Poles had gained time and finally managed to blow the bridge – using makeshift equipment brought up by bicycle – four hours after our Stukas had done their work. Oberst i.G. Holle, the chief of staff of Luftwaffenkommando Ostpreussen, later told me that a commission of enquiry had confirmed that we had hit all the demolition ignition points and that the cable leading out to the bridge had been destroyed.

In fact, Oberst Medem had lost the element of surprise even before the operation began. The Poles had been warned by a laughable oversight on the part of a German railway employee on the Marienburg side of the border. After the last German express had gone through at two in the morning, he had neglected to wish his Polish counterpart the customary 'Goodnight'. As this was something he normally always did, the Polish railwayman attempted to ring him back. But the line was dead. His German colleague had switched it off.

The Poles grew suspicious. 'Why has he done that?' they asked themselves. As a precaution, they closed off the crossing point at the Marienburg bridgehead by barricading themselves behind a pile of rails and deploying their anti-tank guns. It was these weapons that had done the damage, knocking out the locomotives of the two trains as they came steaming towards them on parallel tracks just as dawn was breaking. And so Medem never did get to the bridge – or, at least, that's how the story goes.

This very first mission was thus a classic example of the fickle nature of war. A detailed and carefully planned operation brought to nothing by the most trivial of unforeseen circumstances! At the same time, the planning revealed the remarkable confidence that the military hierarchy apparently had in the bombing accuracy that could be achieved by the dive-bomber. And the success of the Stukas in carrying out their attack under particularly difficult conditions fully justified that confidence. It seems all the more pity, therefore, that General Halder was not aware of this at the time, as his diary entry dealing with the Dirschau episode reveals: 'Air attack apparently not effective.'

Sadly, his words are but one example of a phenomenon that – apart from a few honourable exceptions – runs like a thread throughout all the official Army reports of the time, as well as through much of the post-war literature on the subject. Only on very rare occasions do accounts by the Army contain any specific details concerning the actual extent and effectiveness of the support provided by the Luftwaffe to operations on the ground – not even the work of the Stukas and ground-attack aircraft, whose missions were often flown under the very noses of their own troops.

The effectiveness of air support was not always quantifiable, of course. But even in those cases where it was – such as, for example, when a Stuka attack so demoralized an enemy force that it surrendered to advancing German troops without a fight – reports of the incident, if any, would usually be made only by the Luftwaffe, who had learned of the results of their actions either from intercepted enemy radio traffic or from a grateful message of thanks sent by the Army unit with whom they had been cooperating.

This seeming reluctance on the part of the Army chiefs to acknowledge the part played by the Luftwaffe in many of their operations is all the more remarkable when one considers that, at the lowest levels, relations between the Stukas and the troops on the ground – in other words, those actually doing the fighting – were always very cordial and comradely; and especially so if the two groups had got to know each other well by working together over a longer period.

Admittedly, the basis for successful inter-service cooperation had first to be established. And much of the credit for this again has to go to General von Richthofen. As the Fliegerführer z.b.V. in Poland, he had sent members of his staff – the so-called Fliegerverbindungsoffiziere [Air liaison officers: 'Flivos' for short] – to the HQs of the armies in the field so that he could be kept fully informed of the latest developments. Also, his Fieseler Storch could frequently be found flying above the spearheads of the attacking forces where, often under heavy enemy fire, he could see for himself exactly what the situation was. In this way he could ensure that his Stuka, ground-attack and fighter units were being employed to the maximum effect immediately ahead of the 10. Armee's ground troops, thereby saving them a lot of time, effort and blood.

In the early days such cooperation did not always go smoothly, as is evident from these reports of the Fliegerführer z.b.V. dated 16–18 September 1939:

> *16.9.1939 situation report:* We fail to reach agreement between the 8. and 10. Armeen on the course of action to be taken against the strong Polish forces around Lowicz. Based upon the results of our recent cooperation, 10. Armee requests air support. 8. Armee, on the other hand, rejects any kind of support from the air simply because they are not used to it. As we have a clear overview of the situation, I override the opposition of 8. Armee and decide to deploy all units in a massed assault to smash the enemy forces between the Weichsel and Bzura rivers.
>
> *17.9.1939 situation report:* 8. Armee fails to achieve a decisive breakthrough into the enemy forces massed north of Lowicz. Since dawn 10. Armee on the Bzura has been offering strong resistance against enemy forces attacking from the west. Our armoured units unable to penetrate enemy positions. Something must be done to make progress and avert a crisis. Fliegerführer z.b.V. scrapes together all serviceable machines in an attempt finally to 'shred' the closely concentrated mass of enemy troops.

Since dawn all available air units had been harassing the long columns and massed formations of the Poles without let-up. The Bzura battlefield was being thoroughly ploughed up. Each air attack followed hard on the heels of the last. New targets were continually being assigned as the successes mounted. The aircraft of the Fliegerführer z.b.V. flew 820 individual sorties that day, dropping a total of 328,000kg of bombs in all.

From midday onward enemy activity began to slacken off. By the afternoon Polish troops were throwing down their weapons. Our ground forces were now facing a broken adversary. The commanders in the field therefore requested that air attacks on the defenceless mass of enemy troops be halted. But aircraft remained over the area until nightfall ready to deal with the slightest sign of any resistance. At the end of the day the Fliegerführer z.b.V. was able to report:

> Flying up to 4–5 missions each, units of the Fliegerführer z.b.V. have broken the morale of the enemy. Enemy threw down his arms in the afternoon. Signed: *Richthofen.*

This message was despatched to both Luftflotte 4 and to 10. Armee. Throughout the entire day only one Ju 87 had been lost; the result of a mid-air collision.

And finally, the 18 September situation report:

> 10. Armee now advancing into the Weichsel–Bzura triangle and no longer meeting any enemy resistance. One Stukagruppe held at readiness, all others stood down to conserve fuel and munitions for future operations . . .

Yet, despite all the above evidence, in his *Geschichte des Zweiten Weltkrieges* [*History of the Second World War*], first published in 1951, author Kurt von Tippelskirch does not devote a single word to the Luftwaffe's part in the Battle of the Bzura. Instead, he writes:

> . . . in the days from 9 to 11 September the 8. Armee had to fight bitter defensive battles to withstand the Poles, who were making repeated attempts to break through to the south. Gradually the ring encircling the enemy was tightened. On 16 September, near the town of Lowicz, the Poles launched one final desperate effort to break out of their encirclement, but then their strength was spent. Compressed into a small area of territory between the Weichsel (Vistula) and Bzura rivers, the remains of nineteen Polish divisions and three cavalry brigades, a total of 100,000 men in all, laid down their arms on 19 September. Among them was their Commander-in-Chief, General Botnowski. With their capture the last large group of enemy forces west of the Weichsel had been eliminated . . . and the one dangerous crisis of the entire campaign had been averted.

And in his summing up of the Polish campaign Tippelskirch goes on to say:

> . . . nor did [the military leadership] fail to recognize the true significance of the limited number of casualties suffered. Welcome as these were in themselves, they were an indication, not only of good training and leadership, but also proof that there had been but few hard-fought battles . . . The German nation had to mourn the deaths of 10,572 of its sons, while 30,322 had been wounded and 3,409 were missing. These relatively low casualty figures were received with great relief, even if those at home could hardly be expected to be able to interpret them correctly . . .

From what I recall of that period, the German people were simply happy that the Polish campaign had been brought to such a speedy and successful conclusion, so that they could now look forward to some sort of amends by the re-establishment of the old pre-1914 German border with Poland.

But the number of casualties that the campaign had cost weighed heavily, not just on those families directly affected, but also on the vast majority of the population. Not a few Germans – probably more than is generally realized, and especially among the mothers – also spared a thought for those of the defeated enemy who had bravely given their lives in battle. The misery and despair that had followed in the wake of the First World War was still too fresh in peoples' minds. The effects of that conflict were still being felt in this present war. A large proportion of the populace only saw the current hostilities as making any sense if they were being waged in order to win back those territories lost to Germany in 1914–18.

As for the 'great relief' cited by Tippelskirch, as far as I can remember that only applied for as long as the population continued to share in the common hope that the conclusion of the Polish campaign also meant the end of the war. The people yearned for nothing more than peace. But they saw their hopes fade after the Western Powers rejected the peace offer made by Hitler during his Reichstag speech of 6 October 1939 and events then took their inevitable course – events which filled many of them with dread:

> *14 October 1939:* Kapitänleutnant Prien of *U-47* sinks the British battleship *Royal Oak* in Scapa Flow.
>
> *7 November 1939:* An offer by the King of Belgium and the Queen of the Netherlands to mediate in peace negotiations is turned down by the warring nations Great Britain, France and Germany.
>
> *8 November 1939:* Attempt on Hitler's life in the Bürgerbräukeller in Munich.
>
> *13 November 1939:* Unsuccessful offer of mediation by King Carol of Romania.
>
> *30 November 1939:* After diplomatic relations are broken off by the Soviet Union, Russian troops invade Finland without a declaration of war. Soviet aircraft bomb Helsinki. Finland's president declares a state of hostilities against the Soviet Union.
>
> *13 December 1939:* Damaged in action against three British cruisers in the South Atlantic, the pocket battleship *Admiral Graf Spee* sails into the estuary of the River Plate.
>
> *17 December 1939: Graf Spee* scuttled in the estuary of the River Plate.

In the Luftwaffe a Staffel was among the lowest of the low on the organizational ladder of command and was not privy to high-level decision-making. We were completely unaware, for example, that on 23 November 1939 Hitler had informed his Wehrmacht chiefs that he was planning to violate Belgian and Dutch neutrality in his forthcoming attack on France. But from all the signs that *were* apparent, even to us, it was clear that German forces were preparing for some sort of an assault in the west.

On 13 January 1940 our Gruppe was transferred to Darmstadt. And when we were ordered back to Wertheim just five days later, we assumed it was because of the incident that was the subject of rumours currently going the rounds in Luftwaffe circles. It seems that on 10 January a Luftwaffe officer carrying important operational documents had lost his way while flying from Münster to Cologne. He had landed by mistake on Belgian territory and had been taken into custody before he was able to destroy the documents. Presumably the High Command needed some extra time to consider the possible consequences of this unfortunate mishap.

At Wertheim we resumed our normal flying training routine. Just how essential this constant training was had been forcefully brought home to us back in December when we had witnessed for ourselves the results of a tragic accident that had befallen 3. Staffel. At the time we had been unable to put in much flying training because of the adverse weather. But on 6 December 1939 conditions finally improved. While we were despatched to the ranges to carry out practice dives in close formation, 3. Staffel had been ordered to make individual dives over the airfield itself.

One of the unit's pilots, Unteroffizier Herbert Urbons, an East Prussian from the Tilsit region who had already distinguished himself in the Polish campaign, totally misjudged the height of his pull-out and flew straight through the roof of the station sick quarters. A tremendous explosion rent the air. A gruesome scene confronted the fire crews and members of base staff who rushed to the scene to help. Urbons and his gunner, Gefreiter Heinz-Günther Liebetrau, had been killed instantly and were beyond all human help. Their bodies could only be identified by the badges of rank on the flying overalls they had been wearing. The aircraft had been smashed into thousands of fragments and was scattered over a radius of many hundreds of metres across the surrounding fields. We had to bid farewell to two gallant comrades and there were some of us who pondered long and hard about what we could do to prevent such unnecessary losses in the future.

On the afternoon of 1 April 1940 our Gruppe was transferred up to Koblenz, only to be ordered back to Wertheim again the very next day. The tension was growing. But what was the reason behind all this hopping about? Was it for purposes of camouflage, to deceive the enemy about our true intentions, or was the High Command simply waiting for more favourable weather conditions? We had no answer to this. Nor did we expect one from higher up. We fully appreciated the importance of security and accepted the fact that every soldier was told just enough to permit him to carry out his given task, and no more. We were still in the dark – metaphorically speaking – when we landed back at Wertheim at around midday on 2 April 1940.

Another snippet of information that had been withheld from us was that on 14 December 1939 Hitler had ordered the start of preparations for the occupations of Denmark and Norway – although at that time he was still hoping to avoid an escalation of the war. It was this operation, code-named 'Weserübung', that was now on the point of being launched. We first learned of it from the news reports of 9 April 1940 stating that German troops had marched into Denmark and landed in Norway in the early hours of that morning. By the evening we heard that Denmark had been occupied almost without resistance and that, after some hard fighting, the important Norwegian coastal towns of Oslo, Kristiansand, Stavanger, Bergen, Trondheim and Narvik were all in German hands.

Oslo, the capital, had been captured in a daring operation from the air, with Junkers transport planes landing troops on Fornebu airfield in the face of heavy enemy fire. While negotiating the 110km-long Oslo Fjord the German cruiser *Blücher* had been sunk by torpedo. And off Kristiansand another cruiser, the *Karlsruhe*, had been torpedoed and sunk by a British submarine. Despite these losses, the first wave of invading troops – parts of three divisions, comprising some 10,000 men in all – had been successfully put ashore under the protection of strong air and sea cover. The Wehrmacht had beaten the British–French expeditionary force into Norway by a nose! Later we learned more of the background to these events:

> *28 March 1940:* The Allied war cabinet in London had taken the decision to begin mining Norwegian coastal waters on 5 April 1940 and to send a British brigade, including a contingent of French troops, to occupy the iron ore port of Narvik and to land other units at Stavanger, Bergen and Trondheim. The operations were subsequently postponed until 8 April 1940.
>
> *8 April 1940:* The Western Powers informed the Norwegian government of the mining of their waters at 05.30 hours, some thirty minutes after the first mines had already been laid in three locations.
>
> *9 April 1940:* In the early hours of the morning the German ambassadors in Oslo and Copenhagen handed similarly worded notes to the Norwegian and Danish governments giving as the reason for Germany's intervention 'the urgent necessity to protect the two nations' neutrality against the imminent Anglo-French landings'. The declared aim of the German government was to carry out a peaceful occupation. Any resistance, however, would be crushed without compunction and only lead to unnecessary bloodshed.

The Western Powers made strenuous efforts to drive German forces out of Norway. On 10 April 1940 British aircraft sank the cruiser *Königsberg* in Bergen harbour. Between 10 and 13 April ten German destroyers were sunk by superior British naval forces in Narvik Fjord. On 14 April British, French and Polish units landed at Harstadt in the Lofoten Islands off Narvik, and at Namsos to the north of Trondheim. On 17–18 April further Allied landings followed at Åndalsnes south of Trondheim. But in the meantime the German forces in those areas had received reinforcements by air. On 21 April land contact had been established between Oslo and Stavanger, via Kristiansand, and by 30 April this had been extended northwards as far as Trondheim.

The Luftwaffe had played a decisive part in the rapid occupation of Norway. After the initial air landings it had quickly succeeded in wresting air superiority from the enemy by constantly pushing its units forward with the utmost speed. This had secured the air corridors that were vital to keeping the ground forces supplied with equipment and reinforcements. At the same time, it had prevented the Allies' far superior naval forces from deploying their strength to the full.

Such was the effectiveness of the German air presence over Norway that the Allies had to call off their counter-invasion at the end of April and withdraw their troops from the two bridgeheads they had been holding to the north and south of Trondheim. Only around Narvik in the far north of the country did heavy fighting continue until late May. But then here too the Allies were forced to evacuate at the beginning of June, before all remaining Norwegian units finally ceased resistance on 8 June.

The only Stukagruppe involved in the Norwegian campaign had been Hauptmann Hozzel's I./StG 1. This unit was equipped with the Ju 87R, a special long-range variant of the Stuka, which was fitted with underwing fuel tanks to give it a much greater radius of action. Taking off from Kiel-Holtenau on 9 April 1940, the Gruppe had first attacked the fortresses guarding the approaches to Oslo. Before the day was out its 1. Staffel had transferred up to Trondheim, while the other two Staffeln had initially staged to Århus in Denmark, before then flying in to Stavanger-Sola on 10 April.

Until a makeshift runway could be laid at Trondheim-Vaernes airfield, 1./StG 1 operated from the frozen surface of nearby Lake Jonsvatnet. Later, the whole Gruppe was based at Trondheim-Vaernes, with temporary deployments being made to Hatfjeldal for operations over the Narvik region. Their missions included attacks on enemy troops in support of the ground fighting, raids on the Allied bridgeheads and on the British forces occupying the airfield at Bardufoss. The Stukas of I./StG 1 also chalked up considerable successes against Allied shipping at Narvik, Åndalsnes, in Mosjoe Fjord and off Namsos.

Meanwhile, on 11 April 1940, our Gruppe had been ordered to move yet again. But this time the transfer was to be made in such a way that it would not come to the attention of the enemy. Our destination was to be the small forward landing ground at Hennweiler, south of the River Moselle, where an advance party was already in place and awaiting our arrival. The aircraft flew singly, at low level and under strict radio silence to Hennweiler. Upon landing, each was immediately hidden in a well-prepared dispersal point in the woods bordering the field.

All the signs pointed to our Gruppe's being readied for imminent action. We were now part of Luftflotte 3, which was to operate in collaboration with General-oberst von Rundstedt's Heeresgruppe [Army Group] A. The organizational chain of command for our Gruppe was made up as follows:

Luftflottenkommando 3	Generaloberst Sperrle
Nahkampfführer	Generalmajor von Stutterheim
[AOC Close Air Support]	
Geschwaderkommodore StG 1	Oberst Baier
Gruppenkommandeur I.(St)/186(T)	Major Hagen
Staffelkapitäne:	1. Hauptmann Bode
	2. Hauptmann Mahlke
	3. Hauptmann Blattner

Our time at Hennweiler, however, was to stretch into weeks. The days seemed endless. For reasons of security we were not allowed to carry out our normal flying routines. The ground crews occupied themselves in checking and re-checking the machines. Bombs of all shapes and sizes lay ready nearby so that the aircraft could immediately be loaded with whatever ordnance was required for our first targets. We pilots and crews spent a lot of hours discussing that old favourite: 'Actions to be taken in cases of special emergency.'

This was a subject that had first been introduced during our flying training and such sessions always proved extremely useful. They helped a pilot to make snap, but correct decisions and to take the appropriate actions if he suddenly got into difficulties due, say, to some unexpected technical malfunction or other. We organized aircraft recognition sessions too – particularly of our own and the enemy's fighters. And the defensive measures to be employed against fighters and Flak, when flying either in formation or singly, were also hammered home so thoroughly that we felt well prepared to handle anything that our opponents were likely to throw at us.

Early in May General von Stutterheim, the AOC Close Air Support, made a one-day visit of inspection to our Gruppe. His verdict was that it was trained to a peak of operational readiness, was well disciplined and that morale was high. He also took the time and trouble to have a fairly lengthy, but informal chat with the Gruppenkommandeur and us three Staffelkapitäne.

Later in the evening he spoke to all the officers of the unit. They had gathered for the occasion in the officers' mess, which was simply an ordinary room designated as such in the one and only house situated on the edge of the field. During the course of the evening we again brought up the subject of our totally inadequate transport facilities, stressing the fact that whenever we were required to transfer from one base to another we could not move our ground echelon with the limited means at our own disposal, but had to rely on outside help.

The next topic of conversation was the question of fighter escorts for the Stuka units. Our Kommandeur had already raised this matter on numerous occasions during his discussions with higher authority. He argued that our machines, being slow and poorly armed for air combat, needed to be provided with at least a small force of fighters to fly close escort. He was fully supported in this by all the other Stuka Kommandeure. But the fighter pilots rejected the suggestion out of hand, and for very good reason – from their point of view. They were convinced that their *freie Jagd* tactics of free-ranging offensive sweeps would clear the airspace around us so effectively and so completely that no enemy machine would ever get anywhere near our formations.

And, as far as it went, they had a valid point. For only by flying *freie Jagd* sorties could they make full and unfettered use of their tactical manoeuvrability. This would naturally give them a far better chance of intercepting and destroying the enemy in the air than if they were rigidly bound as close escorts alongside a gaggle of Stukas. Hermann Göring, who had himself been a fighter pilot during the First World War, settled the argument: the fighters were to fly *freie Jagd* sweeps to clear the airspace above the immediate area of operations – in other words, no close escorts for the Stukas.

We still had grave misgivings, however, for we were not so sure that our fighters would always be able to keep the enemy well away from us by the use of *freie Jagd* tactics alone. But we appeared to be very much in the minority, and therefore had to work out how best to help ourselves. Clearly, while en route to the target the obvious thing to do was to fly in as tight a formation as possible. This would enable our gunners to combine their fire against any enemy attack from astern. It was not much of a deterrent, as each aircraft had only a single MG 15 flexible-mount rearward-firing machine gun – and one, moreover, whose arc of fire was severely restricted by the Stuka's large tail unit – but it was the best we had to offer.

Once we had completed our dive-bombing attack, we could change our tactics and then perhaps be able to bring our two fixed forward-firing wing machine-guns to bear. Although slow and not in the same league as a single-engined fighter, of course, the Stuka was nonetheless a fairly handy machine with good flying characteristics and we might just be able to outmanoeuvre the enemy and get in a shot or two. The only alternative was to form a defensive circle and beat a fighting retreat while guarding each other's tails.

Of one thing we were certain, however: the carrying out of our mission – the attack on the assigned target – had to take absolute precedence. This inevitably meant that our freedom of tactical movement while on the approach to the objective was almost nil. Only after the target had been bombed would the Gruppenkommandeure and Staffelkapitäne be able to manoeuvre their units as they best saw fit to protect them from attack by enemy fighters.

We Staffelkapitäne were always particularly concerned about what could be done for the machine bringing up the rear of the formation. This was the one most vulnerable, as the enemy usually launched his attacks from astern. But there was no obvious solution to this problem. The responsibility for the safety of all the unit's aircraft – and for every one of his crews – thus weighed heavily on the Staffelkapitän during every mission flown. In fact, it proved a far greater burden than any thoughts of what he himself might have to suffer in the line of duty.

Another of the evening's topics of conversation arose when General von Stutterheim began recounting some of his previous combat experiences. Shot down behind enemy lines on one occasion, he had overcome many hardships and difficulties to make his way back on foot to friendly territory. He had only been able to do this, he maintained, by resolving not to be captured alive, but to save the last bullet in his pistol for himself.

Rather than being inspired by this shining example, I said to the Herr General that – with the greatest respect – I considered such traditional concepts of honour to be outmoded and illogical in this modern day and age. Naturally, it went without saying that it was the duty of any crew shot down over enemy territory to do all in their power to get back to their own lines as quickly as they could. But an evader who opted to take his own life – even if he was down to his last bullet – was of no use to anyone. Quite the opposite, in fact, for by so doing he threw away all chances of reversing his situation. Even if he *were* captured, the possibility of escape could not be ruled out. But that possibility was gone for ever if he decided to put a bullet in his head.

This opinion voiced by one junior officer did not please the general at all. He regarded the ancient custom of saving the last bullet as providing very important moral guidance and support in the proper conduct of any officer of honour. When I nonetheless continued to plead my case that a soldier would be displaying far more courage by not sacrificing himself in this way, the discussion was brought to an abrupt end.

Remembering this conversation, I was more than a little moved to hear towards the end of the French campaign that General von Stutterheim had died of injuries sustained in a crash landing. As Geschwaderkommodore of KG 77 he had been aboard one of his unit's Do 17 bombers carrying out a reconnaissance mission when the machine received a direct hit from enemy Flak. Although the aircraft was barely controllable, the pilot managed to nurse it back over the German lines, where he suggested that the crew bail out as he would not be able to land the stricken bomber. The General overruled the pilot and demanded that he make an emergency landing, only to be severely injured in the resultant crash.

We were deeply saddened by this avoidable loss of a gallant soldier of the old school. The war itself had added a tragic and irreversible postscript to our last discussion.

Chapter 8
Staffelkapitän in the Campaign against France

On the eve of 10 May 1940 the Gruppe was briefed for its first operational mission against the west. In true *Blitzkrieg* style, the Luftwaffe's opening strikes were designed to neutralize the enemy's air power on the ground and in the air. Our Gruppe was to destroy the hangars and ground installations of the French air base and depot at Metz-Frescaty. Time of attack: 06.00 hours.

Details of the individual targets, including aerial photographs, were handed out to us. Each Kette of three aircraft was furnished with particulars of its own specific objective. The crews studied the documents carefully. Every pilot memorized the contents, imprinting the information in his mind so that he would be able to locate and identify his own target before committing himself to the dive. My Kette was fortunate in this respect. We had been assigned to attack Metz's old airship hangar, the largest and most easily identifiable structure on the field.

The designated time of take-off was 05.00 hours the following morning. After completing our mission we were to land at Ferschweiler, a small forward airstrip near Bitburg in the Eifel Hills. Here we were to come to operational readiness again as rapidly as possible, in case we were called upon to fly any further missions. But just how quickly we would be able to do so depended entirely on our ground echelon, which had been ordered to leave Hennweiler immediately after we had taken off and proceed with all despatch the 75km by road to Ferschweiler.

The preparations had been made. With nothing more to be done, we turned in early. But on this particular night it took me a very long while to get off to sleep. Thoughts of what tomorrow might bring were going round and round inside my head. Stage fright? I suppose it could be described as something of that sort. I would be responsible not only for my own aircraft, my own gunner – Unteroffizier Fritz 'Fritzchen' Baudisch – and myself, but for the entire Staffel. Had I done everything in my power to justify the responsibility placed on me? What was going to happen tomorrow, our first day in action? What did the future hold? What else could I have done – what else *must* I do – to make sure that all the crews entrusted to my care got 'home' safely? Questions that I had asked myself often enough in the past now filled my thoughts as never before, running through my mind over and over again like a continuous loop of film until Morpheus finally took pity on me and allowed me to drift off to sleep.

The first mission

It was still dark when, at 04.00 hours, the landing ground began to come to life. Very soon it was a hive of activity. The mechanics' shaded torches danced and skittered like fireflies along the edge of the woods bordering the field. The shrubs and saplings hiding the aircraft were quickly cleared away. The armourers yoked a 250kg bomb to the belly of each machine. The chief mechanics ran through the checklists. They knew their jobs and carried them out swiftly and surely even in the dim illumination that was all they had to work by.

Shortly before 05.00 hours the crews walked out to their machines. Brief 'Good mornings' were exchanged; the chiefs reported 'Aircraft all ready!' and the crews climbed up into their cockpits. The mechanics helped the pilots and gunners into their harnesses, pulling the straps tight, and then went to stand by the starting handles. At 05.00 hours precisely came the signal to start engines. The mechanics set to with a will. As they turned the handles the starter motors began to whine, at first with a deep sluggish drone, and then getting ever faster and shriller until sufficient revs had been built up. A yell from the mechanic up to the watching and waiting pilot: 'On!' The pilot switched the ignition on and suddenly the nocturnal quiet of Hennweiler was shattered by the thunderous roar of engines as thirty Ju 87s started up almost as one.

With their navigation lights on, the machines taxied down to the end of the field in strict order of take-off. In the lead was the Gruppenkommandeur, Major Walter Hagen. He was immediately followed by the other two aircraft of his Stabs-kette [HQ Flight], and then by the machines of 1., 2. and 3. Staffeln.

After lifting off, the Kommandeur flew a wide climbing turn to port above the field to enable the rest of us to close up behind him and get into a Gruppe 'vic', or arrowhead, formation. It was still so dark in the morning mist that we could only sort ourselves out by the navigation lights of the other machines around us. Once we had done so, the Gruppenkommandeur set course southwest towards the target. It was not long before we were nearing the French border. The navigation lights were switched off. We were still having a little difficulty keeping correct station within the formation. A hurried glance downwards; hardly any details could be made out. Like a delicate veil, the milky morning haze still shrouded the landscape below us. Nothing stirred. It was as if the whole countryside was deep in slumber.

The tension was growing by the minute. What would be waiting for us on the other side of the French frontier? Over the target area? Come to think of it, exactly how far had we flown already? No idea. But I'd been keeping a close eye on the Kommandeur's machine and he'd be sure to know how to get us to the target. This comforting thought had hardly crossed my mind when I got the shock of my life. The Kommandeur's voice over the R/T: 'Anton to all. What's our position?' Nobody answered. Not one of us knew for certain where we were!

There was nothing else for it; we'd have to fall back on the old naval art of dead reckoning. The Kommandeur had been holding a steady course. Given the time we'd been in the air, we should be over the target in about three minutes . . . if the course was correct.

There was still nothing to be seen on the ground ahead of us. In the growing light the River Moselle must surely be visible. Had we perhaps flown over it already? I continued to search the landscape sliding past and there, suddenly, I spotted the target off to the left diagonally beneath us. I flipped the R/T switch: 'Anton 2 to Anton: target on the port beam below!'

The Kommandeur ordered us into line-astern attack formation and began a wide left-hand turn, leading us on a 'lap of honour' around the target so that we would all be able to dive on our individual objectives against the wind, just as we had been taught on the bombing ranges.

In the meantime Metz's heavy Flak had opened fire on us. There wasn't a great deal of it at first, just a few grey puffs staining the sky off to one side in front of us. The height was not at all bad, but they were much too far away to pose any real threat. The leading Ketten of the formation were already beginning their dives exactly according to plan.

Then it was our turn. A brief check: bomb switches on, radiator flaps closed, dive brakes extended, close throttle, drop the left wing and put the machine into an 80-degree dive. And suddenly the large airship hangar that was my target – and which had drifted into my bombsight with such apparent slowness only a moment ago – now came rushing up to meet me at a terrifying rate. With the wind constant, the crosshairs of the bombsight remained firmly fixed on the centre of the hangar roof. It was growing larger by the second as our altitude unwound: 2,000 metres, 1,500 metres – is the enemy Flak still shooting at us? No time to worry about that now – 1,000 metres.

At a height of 500 metres I pressed the bomb button as briefed. There was a slight jolt as the bomb release fork swung down clear of the arc of the propeller and then the bomb was on its way. As we pulled out of the dive into a climbing left-hand turn, we watched it strike almost dead centre near the front of the hangar roof. My two wingmen also scored direct hits.

Three bombs had gone straight through the roof of the huge airship shed. So what happens now? – Nothing? – Were all three duds? The armourers had set the fuzes to delay, but that meant they would detonate only about half a second after impact at most. They must have exploded by now, surely? We continued to weave slightly to throw the Flak gunners off their aim, but kept our eyes glued on the hangar, which was still standing there as if nothing had happened. Every second seemed an eternity. It was inconceivable that all three bombs should have failed to go off.

But then, at last, we detected definite movement in the sides of the shed. They had begun to bulge as if the whole building was being inflated. Cracks appeared and grew into large fissures. The ruptured walls could no longer support the hangar roof and the entire structure collapsed in on itself. This all happened so slowly that it was like watching a film in slow motion. The blast from the three 250kg HE bombs exploding within the cavernous interior of the airship shed had only just sufficed to bring the whole lot crashing down. The smoking ruins of the depot's other installations showed that the other Ketten had also hit their targets.

We began to get back into loose formation again. The enemy's Flak gunners were now banging away with much more enthusiasm, but were unable to follow our erratic defensive weaving. Only very few salvoes came close enough to persuade us that they actually *were* aiming at us. The experience didn't seem as dangerous as we had been led to expect, but we were under no illusions and knew full well that we would not always escape as lightly as we had done today.

Once we were safely beyond the range of the Flak we tightened up into 'close Gruppe formation' and at 06.40 hours we touched down on our new forward landing ground at Ferschweiler.

For the crews this first mission had been a total success. They had undergone their baptism of fire and had done exactly what had been asked of them. It gave a huge boost to their self-confidence. Some expressed surprise that everything had gone so precisely according to plan and that the enemy's defences had hardly bothered us at all. But we put the latter down to the fact that the timing of our attack had caught our opponents well and truly on the hop. The general feeling was that we had given them a very nasty 'wake-up call'.

It was at this point, however, that the Gruppe was to suffer its first major setback. We had landed at Ferschweiler as ordered. But now we were stuck fast. True, the Gruppe was able to report: 'Mission accomplished. Targets at Metz-Frescaty destroyed. No losses.' But then it was forced to add: 'Ground echelon not yet arrived. Not yet possible to resume operational readiness.'

It was just as we had feared: the column of transport that was supposed to convey our ground echelon from Hennweiler to Ferschweiler had not turned up on time. When it finally did arrive at Hennweiler, our stores and equipment were loaded with all possible speed. But by then it was too late – every road to the west was choked with advancing Army units and the convoy could not get through. At Ferschweiler we spent the rest of the day fretting and fuming, waiting in vain for our missing ground crews to appear. Without them we were unable to carry out the follow-up missions that we had been scheduled to fly. In the evening we were therefore ordered to make the short hop to nearby Dockendorf. This was the temporary home of another Stukagruppe, with whose assistance we would hopefully be able to operate the following day.

Hardly had we touched down at Dockendorf, however – by then it must have been about 21.30 hours – than we were instructed to return to Ferschweiler at first light next morning. Our ground echelon had apparently got through at last.

This opening day of the campaign in the West had taught us a salutary lesson. Henceforth, whenever we had to transfer from one field to another – providing the move did not involve an operational mission en route, such as that we had just flown against Metz – every machine's chief mechanic would squeeze into the rear cockpit alongside the gunner. In addition, a crate containing a few essential tools would be attached to the aircraft's under-fuselage ETC weapons rack. Assuming that the airfield or landing ground that we were making for already held stocks of fuel and ammunition, this meant that we could always come to operational readiness on our new base in fairly short order.

Admittedly, this practice breached official safety regulations, but the good old Iolanthe, as the Ju 87 was known throughout the Luftwaffe, was a willing work-horse and there was actually little risk involved. In fact, with the authorities turning a blind eye, this prime example of do-it-yourself soon became standard operating procedure among all Stuka units.

11 May 1940: our second day in action. The armoured units of Generaloberst List's 12. Armee were already surging westwards towards the River Meuse at Sedan. We had landed back at Ferschweiler at 05.30 hours. While the aircraft were quickly being refuelled and re-armed, the Gruppe's crews gathered for a briefing. We were to attack enemy troop movements and artillery positions in the Sedan area. Our task was to prevent the French from bringing up reinforcements against our armoured spearheads. We took off at 06.30 hours. My Staffel had been ordered to bomb French columns reported to be moving up the Mouzon–Carignan road to the southeast of Sedan. We successfully completed the mission in the face of some fairly weak ground fire. One or two of our machines had collected a few minor small-calibre bullet holes from the enemy's infantry, but this damage was soon made good by the ground crews after our return to Ferschweiler.

The news from 3. Staffel was not so good, however. Two of their aircraft had failed to return. Those proven stalwarts of the Polish campaign, Staffelkapitän

Hauptmann Erich Blattner from Konstanz and his gunner, Feldwebel Karl Fernholz from Gelsenkirchen, had both been killed. Their machine had been brought down by ground fire during a low-level attack and had exploded on impact. Another crew, pilot Unteroffizier Heinz Ullrich and gunner Feldwebel Werner Bornemann, were still missing, fate unknown.

These losses were a serious blow, not just for 3. Staffel, but for the whole Gruppe. Our military training had, to some extent, prepared us to come to terms with the inevitability of losses in combat. We had all accepted the fact that Stuka operations were not going to be a picnic. But these sudden deaths of our close comrades had really brought home to us just how thin the thread of survival actually was – just how quickly and easily each and every one of us might also be called upon to make the ultimate sacrifice. Naturally, we all tried to suppress such thoughts. It was not the sort of thing we liked to dwell on.

Of one thing I was sure, however: not one of those young men, so healthy and full of life, had deliberately sought a hero's early death. With unflinching courage, they had simply flown the mission as ordered as if there had been no risks involved whatsoever. This made me all the more determined to lead my own Staffel in such a way as to enable it to carry out every assignment it was given, while – at the same time – doing everything in my power to ensure that all my men returned safely. I found myself spending every free moment mulling over in my mind just how I could achieve this. But now was not the time for brooding or philosophising. There was a new campaign to be won.

3. Staffel's senior Oberleutnant, Ulrich Heinze from Halle-on-the-Saale, re-placed the fallen Erich Blattner as Kapitän. In the afternoon the Gruppe took off again for another mission against enemy troop dispositions in the same areas as the morning's attacks. This time everything went smoothly and after successfully engaging a number of French columns all aircraft returned to base without incident.

By 12 May the leading elements of three armoured divisions of the Panzerkorps Guderian had reached the Meuse on either side of Sedan, and had taken the town itself, which lay on the river's eastern bank. The next day they were to force a crossing. Initially, however, the Army had only a limited number of heavy artillery pieces far enough forward to support the attempt. The Luftwaffe was therefore ordered to concentrate all its efforts here. We were, in effect, to be employed as 'flying artillery' to lay down preliminary bombardments and cover the crossings.

On 13 May we thus flew four missions against the fortresses around Sedan and against enemy artillery emplacements and field fortifications immediately to the front of the planned crossing sites. Protected by this aerial umbrella put up by the Luftwaffe, shock troops of the Army crossed the river in assault boats and rubber dinghies. By the evening the Army had breached the river defences of the Maginot Line and established two small bridgeheads to either side of Sedan. Our Gruppe had played its due part in the day's action, accomplishing all its missions successfully and without loss. Everything, in fact, had gone without a hitch.

So far we had not been bothered by enemy fighters. But some other Stuka units had not been so lucky, for our own fighters were not always able to keep clear the airspace around them. Stuka formations were still being denied a close fighter escort. As a result, our Gruppe received instructions from the AOC Close Support Forces to the effect that: 'In the event of contact with enemy fighters, abort mission and return to base.'

I couldn't believe what I was hearing when Major Hagen, our Kommandeur, read this out to us. What on earth were 'those upstairs' thinking of? Didn't they know that the fighters were twice as fast as us? We couldn't just turn tail and slink off home, even if we wanted to. And if a mission could be abandoned simply because some enemy fighters were buzzing around in the neighbourhood, then why mount it in the first place? No – an order such as this was totally wrong! I felt it was a blatant but futile attempt by our discomfited leaders to evade their responsibilities. Others were of the same opinion and we made our feelings very clear to Major Hagen. He was not only an experienced pilot, but also a very understanding superior officer who was always prepared to listen to the cares and concerns of those under his command. I suspect he shared our views, for on this occasion – most unusually for him – he brought our protests to an abrupt halt by stating flatly: 'Those are now our orders!'

And we had to get to grips with the problems posed by these new orders on the very next day, 14 May. Reconnaissance had reported enemy armour approaching our still relatively weak Meuse bridgeheads from the south. It was already late in the afternoon when we were briefed to attack French tanks in the Brieulles region.

We took off at 18.43 hours. For the approach to the target area we closed up into a Gruppe arrowhead formation, with the aircraft of each of the three Staffeln that formed the 'vic' flying in line astern. We were nearing our objective east of Sedan – I was leading my Staffel on the left flank of the formation – and had just flown over Florenville, when one of the pilots to the rear reported over the R/T: 'Enemy fighters approaching!' Upon my signal the Ketten behind me tucked themselves in even tighter. This was to give our gunners a chance to coordinate and concentrate the fire of their single machine guns against the attackers.

A flight of four French Morane fighters came barrelling in fast. Obviously aware of the limited traverse of the Stuka's rearward-firing armament, they attacked our Staffel from behind and below, letting fly with everything they had. Our rearmost

Kette was blown apart. The three machines dived away from the formation, a couple of them already trailing thin banners of smoke. The Kommandeur's voice sounded over the R/T: 'Abort mission! Return to base!'

Suiting the action to his words, the Kommandeur went into a wide right-hand turn. But by this time a second group of enemy fighters was bearing down fast on what remained of my Staffel out on the exposed left-hand flank. We were already over the scene of the ground fighting going on below and it was now that something entirely unexpected happened. Behind the Staffel, between us and the rapidly approaching fighters, a few bursts from the enemy's heavy Flak guns suddenly speckled the evening sky. The fighters immediately broke off their attack. Climbing away, they quickly disappeared from sight.

What to do now? We were only three minutes or so away from our assigned target: the enemy tanks that were threatening our troops holding the Meuse bridgehead. The Staffel had been reduced to only six aircraft. But perhaps those six aircraft might just make all the difference. The thoughts chased each other through my mind. The enemy fighters were no longer around. Decision time: keep going! With my little band of Stukas behind me, I headed for the target. Just under three minutes to go. I prayed we wouldn't be spotted by any more fighters. With nerves stretched almost to breaking point we anxiously scanned the airspace around us. It's incredible how long three minutes can be in a situation like this. The responsibility was weighing heavily on me and I could feel the sweat gathering under my flying helmet.

And then – at last – the target came into view. Enemy tanks on the road leading north out of Brieulles. There weren't many of them, just a small detachment. Almost automatically I went through the motions preparatory to the attack. At my signal the pilots took up combat formation in close line astern. Ready to dive. Dive!

The smaller the target, the lower we had to go to be sure of a hit. So down we hurtled, the enemy tanks growing ever larger in our sights. We pulled out just above ground level. As we climbed away again on course for home we observed the results of our attack. The target had been well and truly plastered. Several of the aircraft behind me had also scored direct hits. That's one troop of tanks that won't be bothering our comrades defending the bridgehead. The Staffel had quickly reformed and was now well on the way back to base. We were no longer likely to be pestered by enemy fighters, but the one big worry still remained: what had become of the three machines that had dropped out of formation after the French fighters' opening pass?

We touched down at Ferschweiler at 20.02 hours. Nobody had seen what had happened to our rearmost Kette: no crashes had been observed, no forced landings, no parachutes – nothing. I hurried across to make my report to the Gruppenkommandeur: '2. Staffel returned from mission. Three aircraft and crews missing after first fighter attack. Remainder of Staffel continued on to target after enemy fighters broke away. Individual tanks of a small enemy armoured unit on the road north of Brieulles destroyed.'

Major Hagen simply acknowledged the report. He said not a word about my ignoring his order to abort the mission. Like the rest of us, he was in a very sombre mood due to the heavy losses the Gruppe had suffered in its first clash with enemy fighters. No fewer than eight aircraft and crews had failed to return.

Later that evening and during the course of the night, thank God, three crews reported back safe and sound. They had been damaged by fighters and had been forced to make emergency landings. Among them were the leader of my missing Kette, Oberleutnant Günter Skambraks, and his gunner. Skambraks, who hailed from Tilsit, was turning the air blue. His forthright comments on the performance of our fighters, expressed in the broadest of East Prussian dialects, didn't bear repeating.

Early the following morning another of my pilots, Unteroffizier Otto Reuss, also turned up. Despite being badly wounded and suffering from severe burns, he had commandeered an Army truck to drive him back to base. He was determined to make his report, and it was more than a little moving to see him trying to hide the obvious pain he was in from his comrades as he did so. The moment he was finished he was rushed off to hospital. (Unteroffizier Reuss would return to the unit fully recovered from his injuries and fit for duty again some eleven weeks later on 29 July 1940.)

This 14 May 1940 had been a black day indeed for our Gruppe. A total of eight aircraft had been lost and nine crewmen killed. No part of the Gruppe had been spared:

> The Gruppenstab had lost Adjutant Oberleutnant Hanfried Heyden from Düsseldorf and his gunner, Leutnant der Reserve Helmut Cords from Stettin. Their machine had been shot down by fighters and was seen to crash near Florenville.
>
> 1. Staffel's all-Unteroffizier crew of pilot Fritz Hemken and gunner Otto Kopania were killed when their aircraft came down 10km east of Sedan after being attacked by fighters.
>
> From my 2. Staffel, Feldwebel Walter Strehler and his gunner, Gefreiter Heinrich Hüsch, were shot down by fighters over Florenville and later found dead in the wreckage of their machine some 12km to the east of Sedan. Gunner Unteroffizier Ernst Hecht from Berlin (crewman of the wounded Unteroffizier Reuss) had been killed in action against fighters over Florenville.

Finally, 3. Staffel lost Oberfähnrich Hans-Jürgen Ellerlage from Kiel and his gunner, Unteroffizier Alfred Froese from Regau, both shot down by fighters east of Florenville.

It was a crushing blow. Our sympathies went out to the loved ones of our fallen comrades. At the same time, it made me realize just how quickly our little unit – the Staffel – had grown from a motley collection of individuals, thrown together by circumstances, into a close-knit community. It had developed an amazing inner strength and forged human ties that had bonded it into what was, in effect, almost a small family. And today the war had claimed its first victims from among the members of that family. The Staffel felt their loss more keenly than any of the others suffered in this war to date. Things had suddenly become much more personal – or, to paraphrase a few words from the famous old ballad about true comrades, it was 'As if we'd lost a part of ourselves.'

I was perhaps most deeply affected because I held myself personally responsible for the men of my Staffel. And those men, each in his own way, now did their best to help me come to terms with my cares and woes. The members of most military units seem to have some sort of sixth sense about what is going on in their commander's mind. This was certainly the case in my Staffel. Individual pilots made it a point to offer a few words of consolation and try to raise my spirits. I'm sure they hadn't arranged this amongst themselves beforehand. It was a purely spontaneous reaction on their part. For example, whenever I wandered through the dispersal area where the ground crews were busy repairing the damage to our machines, one or other of the pilots would seek me out for a brief chat. I can still remember one such exchange:

'Well, at least we're still better off than the other Staffeln, Herr Hauptmann.' 'How do you make that out? We lost a whole Kette in that first fighter pass.' 'True enough, Herr Hauptmann, but then we went on to give those enemy tanks a good hard pasting. We completed the mission. The other Staffeln suffered losses too, but they had nothing to show for it. And that's even harder to take.' (Which is exactly why I had decided to carry on to the target, I thought to myself. But if things had gone wrong you'd be talking to my replacement by now.)

In everything that was said to me I detected a certain pride in the fact that we *had* gone on to complete the mission. This had also been apparent during the attack itself. Every single pilot of our depleted little band had dived on those enemy tanks with an aggression and determination that I had not witnessed before. It was almost as if they were putting in that extra bit for our missing comrades. Take Feldwebel Kurt Märgner from Karlsmarkt, for instance. 'Punkt' [or 'Dot'] as we called him on account of his diminutive size – had brought his machine back to base with its wings riddled with shrapnel holes and splattered with lumps of mud and clay the size of one's fist.

He had gone in so low and so close to the aircraft in front of him that when he pulled out of his dive he had thundered straight through the fountains of earth and steel thrown up by the explosions of his predecessor's bombs. It had given him one hell of a shock, but he had taken it all in his stride. He was quite a character, our Punkt. He was the smallest man in our Staffel (some even said in the entire Luftwaffe!), and at the same time one of the most reliable and popular. The nickname Punkt worried him not one jot. In fact, I rather suspect that he was quite proud of it. As he was fond of telling us with a cheeky grin: 'I'm so tiny, nobody's ever going to hit me!' (Happily to say, his confidence was to prove fully justified. After more than 600 missions on all fronts as both a Stuka and a ground-assault pilot, our Punkt – promoted in the meantime to the rank of Oberleutnant – returned home at the end of the war in one piece.)

The Gruppenkommandeur called his three Staffelkapitäne together to go over the day's events with us one more time. He told us that in his official report he had demanded that the question of fighter escorts for Stuka units be reconsidered. But apparently the orders were to stand, at least for the time being. We were all agreed that we needed the greatest possible freedom of tactical movement if we were to carry out our missions successfully. But we were also all convinced that during the approach flight – while we were still carrying our bombs, that is – our most effective method of defence, meagre though it was, was to remain in close formation. After the attack had been made and our bombs had been dropped, we would then try to utilize what manoeuvrability we had to improve our chances against enemy fighters. It was little enough, but what else could we do?

Necessity, however, is the mother of invention! In the course of the discussion Hauptmann Helmut Bode, the Kapitän of 1. Staffel, happened to remark in passing: 'During pre-war air shows we always used to throw rolls of toilet paper out of our aircraft. They'd unfurl and hang in the air for ages like great long paper snakes. It was quite a sight and the spectators would wonder what on earth was going on.'

'That's the best idea I've heard yet!' I exclaimed. 'Why don't we give it a go the next time we're attacked by enemy fighters? As long as they don't realize that it's only toilet paper, they might even show a bit of respect for our new defensive "wonder weapon!" It can't do any harm and it's certainly worth a try.'

So try it we did. From then on, whenever we flew on ops every gunner took a few rolls of toilet paper along with him in the rear cockpit. If enemy fighters were reported to be approaching from astern, the plan was for all the gunners – upon the word of command – to throw out all their toilet rolls simultaneously to form a 'barrage'. And, believe it or not, the ruse actually worked!

On two subsequent missions (unfortunately I failed to make a note of the exact dates and locations) enemy fighters were spotted closing in behind us. The order was given: 'Toilet paper – Throw!' and the sky between us and the fighters was suddenly alive with long writhing strips of paper. Faced with this extraordinary aerial curtain of noodles, the enemy pilots thought better of it. Scenting possible danger, they immediately shied away and we continued on to the target un-molested. But soon even this new 'weapon' was denied us. We ran out of toilet paper!

The admin officer was sent off in a 3-ton truck to find us a new load. But he was unlucky. By this time we had moved forward into France. And although he was able to requisition fresh supplies from a captured French store, the paper there came not in rolls but in packets of individual sheets. Our experiment was at an end. Nor was the trick ever repeated, for by the time we had been issued with the right sort of toilet paper again, the powers-that-be had finally seen the light and were providing Stuka formations with fighter escorts – which had been the proper military solution to our problems all along.

On 15 May 1940 the Gruppe was called upon to mount a maximum effort. We put every aircraft we had into the air. By making use of each Staffel's three reserve machines we very nearly had the full Gruppe complement of thirty aircraft. Our target was to the southwest of Rocroi, where enemy forces were blocking the path of the Panzerkorps Reinhardt, one of the two armoured corps that made up the Panzergruppe von Kleist. The mission itself went smoothly enough, but while taxiing back to dispersal after landing my machine was rammed by another aircraft. Fortunately the damage was only minor and was made good by some sterling work on the part of the ground crews during the night. After a brief air-test at first light, my trusty Ju 87B, 'J9+AK', was fully operational again and I was able to lead the Staffel in that day's attack on Oches.

17 May saw us transferred forward to Bastogne in Belgium. This move greatly reduced the time required to reach our targets. We were now subordinated to Stukageschwader 1, part of General Freiherr von Richthofen's VIII. Fliegerkorps. As successor to the close-support Fliegerführer z.b.V. of the Polish campaign, the Korps' present task was to support the armoured divisions of Generals von Kleist, Guderian and Reinhardt in their breakthroughs at Sedan and Charleville and subsequent advances across the River Oise to the English Channel. From Bastogne we attacked enemy tanks south of Stonne on 19 May and at Liez the following day.

By 21 May we were on the move again, this time to Guise, east of St-Quentin in France. The 150km-plus road journey that separated Bastogne from Guise, together with our chronic shortage of unit transport, meant that it was some time before we could report ourselves fully operational at our new base. We felt that enough was enough, and it was at this juncture that we decided to resort to a little self-help. As already described, small parties of mechanics were sent out into the surrounding area with orders to check over the many vehicles left abandoned by the roadside. Any that could be of use to us were to be repaired and brought back. We soon had enough to be fully mobile and were thus no longer dependent on others for our future moves.

During our time at Guise we flew as many as three missions nearly every day. In the main, our targets were troop concentrations, bridges and exit roads leading out of towns and villages. The purpose of this was to disrupt the flow of enemy movement and communications. In the case of those bridges that were to be preserved for subsequent use by our own advancing troops, our orders were to render the bridge approaches impassable, but to leave the structures themselves intact. On 21 May we attacked Valhuon, and on 22 May we bombed enemy forces north of Cambrai and at Lillers.

It was while returning from the latter mission, flown late in the afternoon, that we were again caught by enemy fighters. This time, unencumbered by bombs, we decided that attack might prove to be the best method of defence and so tried to mix it with the enemy, hoping to be able to bring our forward-firing wing machine guns to bear. A wild free-for-all soon developed. Naturally, we didn't succeed in shooting down any of the fighters. Their far superior speed and manoeuvrability made that impossible. One thing that did very quickly become apparent, however, was that, if we managed to turn in towards them in good time and 'show them our teeth' head-on, they would always break away before getting within firing range.

Could it possibly be that the *schnellen Leichten* ['fast lightweights'] – our favourite expression for enemy fighters at that time – found the sight of a large and aggressive Stuka coming straight at them a bit too intimidating? Were they perhaps thinking: 'If our two machines should touch, only one will still be flying afterwards – and it won't be mine!' Who knows? At all events, whenever we tried to take them on head to head, they would invariably turn away and attempt to get on our tails instead. This we had to prevent at all costs. It would have meant the end for us.

On the other hand, we did have one defensive trick up our sleeves if a fighter came in for a beam attack. We would wait until he was fully committed, in other words, on the point of opening fire on us, and then a hefty yank on the stick would send the faithful Iolanthe leaping upwards like a startled gazelle. It required a cool nerve and split-second timing, but if done properly the fighter's salvo of machine-gun bullets would pass harmlessly beneath us. So the watchword was: always be on the alert!

The mêlée northwest of Cambrai had lasted a good fifteen minutes. We arrived back at base with a large number of bullet holes to show for our endeavours. But, all in all, for an unescorted Stuka formation we had not received too savage a mauling.

Of my 2. Staffel, Feldwebel Walter Bartsch and his gunner, Unteroffizier Walter Philipp, were forced to make an emergency landing to the south of Arras after their machine had been damaged by the fighters. Bartsch's head had been creased by a bullet during the encounter, and both he and Philipp sustained further wounds and burns during their landing.

Leutnant der Reserve Otto Blumers of 3. Staffel had to crash-land his blazing aircraft between Arras and Agnetz. With a bullet lodged in his back and suffering first-degree burns, he was evacuated to a hospital in Germany. His gunner, Unteroffizier Gerhard Wenzel from Grünewald in Pomerania, had been killed during the aerial engagement. It proved impossible to retrieve his body and the burning Stuka became his funeral pyre.

Our three wounded comrades all returned to the unit fit for duty after fairly short stays in hospital: Unteroffizier Philipp on 11 June, Leutnant der Reserve Blumers on 14 July and Feldwebel Bartsch on 29 July.

Such casualties were nonetheless hard to bear, as indeed was any loss suffered. When I said that we had not received 'too savage' a mauling, I meant in comparison to our first disastrous encounter with fighters back on 14 May. This time we *had* escaped relatively lightly. And we had learned some valuable lessons in the process.

On 23 May we flew three missions, the first to block the exit roads leading out of Arras and the others against Rouvroy and Drocourt. The following day we sank a destroyer in Boulogne harbour. There was a considerable amount of Flak over the target area. Our Kommandeur, Major Hagen, suffered a near miss and had to make an emergency landing at St-Mour. Fortunately neither he nor his gunner had been wounded. The Kommandeur nursed his slightly damaged Iolanthe back to Guise, carefully bringing her in not long after the rest of the Gruppe had landed.

By this time Panzergruppe von Kleist had reached the Channel coast. On Hitler's express instructions Generaloberst von Rundstedt, GOC Heeresgruppe A, ordered the tanks to halt there. To prevent heavy ground losses, the Luftwaffe was being given the chance to force the surrender of the Allied troops surrounded at Dunkirk by air attack alone. And what were our thoughts on the subject when we learned of it? 'Hermann [Göring] has opened his mouth a bit too wide this time – he's bitten off slightly more than we can chew!'

On the morning of 25 May we were briefed to bomb the northern edge of a fairly large expanse of forest to the south of Amiens. This wasn't to our liking at all. The fact that our objective was situated very close to the southern flank of the Army's line of advance didn't bother us too much. But it was hardly the sort of target that required the pinpoint accuracy of a Stuka attack. Horizontal carpet-bombing by standard Kampfgruppen with their far greater bomb loads would be much more effective. True, for some days now we had been flying with both a single 250kg bomb slung below the fuselage *and* four 50kg bombs underwing. Our Stukas could easily cope with this load, even though – officially – they were only rated to carry either one 250kg bomb or four of the smaller 50kg bombs. Even so – a long stretch of forest's edge as a Stuka target? But those were our orders and there was no arguing with them.

By this time, too, our Gruppenkommandeur had introduced a system whereby each of the Staffeln took it in turns to lead the Gruppe on its missions. This was in order to get us – his Staffelkapitäne – used to handling Gruppe-sized formations. He himself, together with his Stabskette, would fly in a position somewhere within the main body of the formation, albeit one from which he could always quickly assume control again if necessary.

Today it was my turn to lead the Gruppe attack. I assigned each Staffel one third of the length of the forest edge that was to be our target. Bombing would be carried out singly, in line astern parallel to the edge of the trees. From above there was absolutely no sign of life within the forest. So we simply distributed our bombs as instructed along the forest's northern perimeter and flew back to base. Somewhat dissatisfied and without too much enthusiasm I made my report: 'Bombs unloaded on the edge of the forest as ordered.'

To my astonishment the Ia, or ops officer, was all smiles. 'Congratulations!' he said. 'How so, congratulations?' I replied, 'That was hardly a target for Stukas.' 'You may not have thought so. But two enemy tank regiments had been assembling in that forest and your Gruppe caught them just as they were about to launch a counter-attack. As it was, they surrendered without a fight. Your mission was a complete success.' 'Well, if that's the case, you're right – it *was* a target for our Stukas, even if we didn't see a thing. Thanks for letting me know.'

On 26 May the German armoured units that had been halted short of Dunkirk were given the go-ahead to resume their advance. In the morning we had flown a mission against the fortifications around Calais, which fell later that night.

Then, in the afternoon, we had taken off in brilliant sunshine for a second mission to attack enemy troops inside the Dunkirk perimeter near Armentières. Once again I was leading the formation at the head of my 2. Staffel. An extensive storm front covered the target area. There was no option: if we wanted to locate our target we would have to fly beneath the low-lying storm clouds. The countryside unrolled ahead of us as we neared our objective. We were sitting ducks for

Flak of every calibre, for at this low altitude even the enemy's light anti-aircraft guns could inflict considerable damage on us. We were already over enemy territory. But all remained eerily quiet.

Suddenly, a colossal firework display of concentrated Flak fire came shooting up at us from every direction. There was a tremendous bang, almost a small explosion, in the rear fuselage of my Iolanthe. The stick was flapping about loosely in my hand. The elevator controls must have been shot away! I called my gunner: 'What's happened back there? Are you wounded, Fritzchen?' 'No, but the control cables in the rear fuselage have been cut by Flak.' 'Can you reach them and do a makeshift splice job?' 'Very much doubt it, but I'll give it a try.'

The moment he started to inch back into the rear fuselage, however, the machine pointed its nose towards the sky. Without the use of my elevators I was powerless to halt the involuntary climb. 'Fritzchen, stop! Come back immediately, otherwise I won't be able to hold her!' The machine was climbing steeply into the low-hanging cloud base and rapidly losing speed. I turned the trimming wheel fully forward. The aircraft slowly levelled off until we were back on an even keel. But now we were in the thick of the storm clouds and being violently buffeted about by turbulence.

The ailerons were still working, but all I had in place of the useless elevators were the trim tabs. These were controlled by the trimming wheel, but could only be moved a degree or two up or down no matter how hard I spun the wheel. 'Prepare to bail out, Fritzchen! But wait until I give the word. It'll only be as a last resort. I'm trying to turn onto a southerly course. If I can keep her heading south for about seven minutes we should be out of this witches' brew and then we'll be able to fly below the cloud base and see where we're going.'

But that was easier said than done. We were still being tossed about like a child's plaything by the malevolent forces of nature. Soar upwards – turn the trimming wheel! Sink like a stone – turn the trimming wheel! Compass course? The magnetic compass was spinning like a top! We should have been given more blind-flying lessons, I found myself thinking as my hands struggled with the controls. Our knowledge and experience of flying on instruments was sketchy, to say the least. The only blind-flying instrument in our machines was a rudimentary sort of turn-and-bank indicator with a needle to show how far we were deviating to either left or right, and a small ball which, if we were flying straight and level, sat in the middle of a little curved glass tube.

But at the moment the needle was dancing backwards and forwards from left to right of the dial and the little ball was jumping about, first being pressed hard up against one end of the glass tube and then, a fraction of a second later, hard up against the other. Very well then, let's see how well the good old Iolanthe can cope on her own if I stop my demented fumbling about with the controls. I turned the trimming wheel to zero and took my hand off the stick. And it worked! Slowly the Ju 87's flight became smoother and more stable; even the turbulence seemed to be lessening. The compass had also settled down and was showing a steady course.

Very carefully I eased the machine round on to a southerly heading. After a few more minutes I tried trimming her slightly nose down. Gradually we started to lose height. It was growing appreciably lighter. Suddenly we burst out of the cloud and the countryside stretched ahead of us bathed in bright sunshine. No sign of any Flak activity. We both heaved a sigh of relief: made it! Now the only problem was how to get her down.

Juggling ailerons and trim I steered us back towards base. When Guise came in sight I said to my gunner, Fritz Baudisch: 'When we're over the field, Fritzchen, I want you to bail out and tell the ambulance and fire crews to stand by ready for any emergency.' His response was calm but firm: 'If the Herr Hauptmann intends trying to land, then I'm staying put – at least the machine won't be quite so nose-heavy then.' 'That's very game of you, Fritzchen – but if you stay it's entirely voluntary, you understand.' 'Jawohl!'

As we neared the landing ground we fired a red flare, the signal for an emergency. The ambulance and fire tender emerged from their camouflaged bays and drove out to the runway. We began the approach. With a little throttle and the trimming wheel turned fully to tail-heavy we floated down towards the landing cross. But I quickly realized that we were coming in just a bit too fast and a bit too high. The field wasn't big enough and we were going to overshoot! Nothing for it but to increase power gently and go round again. A 'lap of honour!' A tad demeaning for an experienced old Stuka hand like myself – but it couldn't be helped. In circumstances like these you made the best of a bad job and took whatever opportunities were on offer.

Lining up for a fresh approach – this time from a little further out. Even less throttle, the trimming wheel again hard up against the tail-heavy stop. Everything looked just right. Slightly nose-up and at a steady rate of descent we were pointed directly towards the landing cross. We were only 100 metres off the ground when the aircraft was suddenly and violently shaken by an extremely strong thermal gust. I could just about keep her level on the ailerons, but the nose had dropped like a stone. Full throttle! It wasn't enough to bring her back up. We were at an impossibly steep angle and heading straight for the ground!

Ignition off! Tuck in legs, arms crossed in front of face – we had both automatically adopted the crash position as we were forced against our seats. There was a terrible vibration, a rattling noise, an enormous bang – and then silence!

That can't be it, I thought to myself. I was just about to lift my head and risk a quick peep between my folded arms when there was another ear-splitting crash. Although still protected by my raised arms, my head flew uncontrollably backwards and forwards like an overripe plum clinging to a branch in a howling gale. I was dimly aware of a jet of flame in front of me – and then silence again!

I slammed my fist against the harness release. The straps of the safety belt fell loose – now out! Out as fast as you can! Fritzchen Baudisch had also scrambled from the burning machine. We ran a few paces to get away from the immediate area of danger. Amazed and hardly believing our luck, we realized that we had again both escaped in one piece. With a quick handshake we wished each other 'Happy birthday!' to celebrate our survival. But our trusty machine had well and truly had it – scattered in pieces back over 100 metres or more. The first impact had ripped off the undercarriage and one of the wings. The other wing was only hanging on by the rear-spar attachment bolt. The engine was a mass of flames. We'd had the devil's own luck in getting out of it alive.

We sat on the grass to await the arrival of the ambulance and fire crews. I lit a cigarette and inhaled a lungful of smoke with a sigh of relief – a pleasure denied Fritzchen who was a non-smoker. The first vehicle to reach us was a small van carrying our worried mechanics. As it squealed to a stop beside us, their obvious delight at finding us safe and sound was truly heart-warming. 'We can hardly believe you're still alive,' they shouted. 'All we saw was an enormous cloud of dust and then we heard two loud explosions, one after the other. We thought you were goners for sure!' With huge grins on their faces, every single one of them shook us by the hand. And then it was straight back to business as usual.

Major Hagen, who had flown on the mission with us, later jotted a terse note in the remarks column of his flying logbook: 'Flak! Whew!' Fortunately, however, my aircraft was the only one written off during the operation. As casualties went, it was relatively easy to accept.

The Armentières operation had been the fortieth combat mission for my gunner, Feldwebel Fritz Baudisch. For this achievement he became the first member of our Staffel to be awarded the Iron Cross, First Class.

On 27 May we flew two missions against Merville and Amiens. I first had to get used to my new aircraft. Every machine had its own 'individual' little foibles and characteristics – in the trim settings, for example, or in its response to rudder movements and the like – but you quickly got the feel of it. I did notice, however, that now, whenever I moved my left arm, I felt sharp stabbing pains in my left breast. Our Gruppe MO, Oberarzt Dr Hörner, wanted to take me into hospital for an examination. Fine, when I've got the time. At the moment we're still at almost permanent readiness.

The morning of 28 May saw us bombing Bailleul, just off the Lille–Dunkirk road. But after that the weather worsened and we were stood down. I took the opportunity to drive to the hospital with Dr Hörner – 'Strip to the waist!' – The doctor felt my chest. 'Lie on this table here,' he said, 'and close your eyes. Now breathe out, deeply – deeper! – deeper still!' I felt as if I hadn't an ounce of breath left in my body when, suddenly, he slapped a long piece of adhesive plaster at least 15cm wide diagonally across my chest. I gasped for air, but could hardly breathe. 'You're not supposed to,' the doctor explained with a cheerful smile. 'You've broken a couple of ribs. They've got to be kept immobile until they grow back together again.'

On 29 May we targeted the locks in Dunkirk harbour. We climbed up between snowy white banks of cumulus cloud to an altitude of 3,500 metres. If the weather allowed, we always preferred to make our approaches over hostile territory at this altitude. Up here we were beyond the range of the enemy's light and medium Flak, but not yet high enough to have to put on our oxygen masks, which could not always be relied upon to work properly.

In the thin air, with the summer's evening sun still beating hotly through the cockpit windows and with the large plaster stretched tight across my chest, I found myself panting like a thirsty dog after a long walk. But that was not so important. What *was* important was to keep a sharp look-out for the enemy in the skies around us.

Today, it seemed as if everybody who *was* anybody in the Luftwaffe was heading for Dunkirk. The airspace around us was crowded with German aircraft. And ahead of us it was full of flying lead too. The target area was already clearly visible in the far distance, marked by large fires and clouds of black smoke. The enemy's heavy Flak was not doing a bad job. Shortly before 20.00 hours we were over the target. Standing on our wings, we dived almost vertically into the attack. We saw our bombs explode close to the lock gates. That should have done the trick. The light and medium Flak was also letting fly at us now, but we all escaped serious damage and returned to base without loss.

By this time the British were sending every vessel – naval, merchant or civilian, which was capable of carrying troops – across the Channel in a desperate attempt to evacuate their expeditionary corps from Dunkirk. And on this particular day, 1 June, we had been ordered to attack this shipping off Dunkirk's beaches. We approached the target zone above a thin layer of cloud. In the harbour of Dunkirk itself a number of ships were lying half-submerged on the bottom. Our previous attack on the lock gates appeared to have been successful. Along the beaches the British had driven long lines of vehicles into the water, presumably to act as make-shift boarding stages.

Standing close inshore there was a mass of shipping of every conceivable kind. From our height it was difficult to make out which of the vessels had already been hit and which were still seaworthy. The Luftwaffe was up in force, with formations of aircraft attacking in waves one after the other. There was a tremendous amount of activity in the air from both friend and foe alike. But our fighters seemed to be keeping the other side in check. We arrived over the target area unmolested and split up into smaller formations to carry out our attacks.

I led my Staffel down against a fair-sized steamer that was getting under way just offshore. We scored several hits amidships and near the stern of the vessel. There were some heavy bursts of Flak to port, but as we couldn't hear the crump of the exploding shells, they were clearly too far off to be of any danger. Then more Flak to starboard. This time it was pearls of little red 'mice' chasing each other through the air, indicating tracer fire from light or medium weapons. We hurriedly jinked away – turning sometimes gently, sometimes sharply – until we were safely out of range.

As we flew back to base I couldn't get the horrific spectacle that was Dunkirk out of my mind. An absolute inferno! Those poor beggars down there desperately fighting for survival. Just as well that at our height we were spared the gory details. True, the enemy was also doing his utmost to shoot us down. Just how much lead had been aimed my way again today I dreaded to think. But those men down there, trying to escape but packed together so tightly on board their ships that they could hardly move, didn't stand a chance if set upon by Stukas. Why didn't they lay down their arms? They'd lost this battle. There could be no argument about that.

But I had to put such thoughts out of my mind. We were at war, and as soldiers we had to carry out our orders. And that we had done. In fact, we were more than a little proud to have performed our duty in the way expected of us. So it was best not to dwell too much on the drama being played out below. After nearly two hours in the air we all, without exception, landed safely back at Guise.

Two hours later, however, and we were taking to the air again. Same situation, same orders. Over the target area we saw the ship that we had attacked earlier lying dead in the water, listing badly and with its stern under the surface. For this present mission we had split up into separate Ketten and were searching for fresh targets a little further out to sea. Through the thin layer of cloud the shape of a larger ship came into view ahead of us. We started to dive. But as we broke through the cloud layer I could see that the vessel had already been hit and was partly under water.

Pull out of the dive – quickly look for a new target. Not far away a small transport of scarcely 2,000 tons was fleeing northwestwards at top speed. It wasn't long before I had it in my bombsight. We were already at a fairly low altitude, but with just enough height left to carry out an attack. Release bomb – recover – observe results: I had missed completely, but my wingmen more than made up for it with two direct hits on the vessel's afterdeck. The ship's sternpost disappeared beneath the waves as it slowly began to sink.

'Spitfires coming in from starboard astern,' Fritzchen Baudisch calmly reported. Get her round! Banking steeply we turned to meet the enemy. Let battle commence! This time, fortunately, only a handful of Spitfires had managed to penetrate our fighter screen and get close enough to attack us. Twisting and turning, we somehow succeeded in fending them off. There were several very nasty moments of course, but after a fraught ten minutes we were finally able to make a break for it and retire almost unscathed. We re-formed and returned to base in close formation – mission accomplished.

Another two hours and we were taking off again and heading for Dunkirk and the British evacuation shipping for a third time. Close inshore, all we could see were stranded and half-sunken vessels and floating wreckage. Further out to sea, about 10km from the coast, there was still a whole flotilla of little ships of every kind: coastal steamers, sailing boats, tugs towing barges, and much more. There were also one or two bigger ships amongst the throng. The leading Ketten were already selecting their targets. We spotted a tug struggling northwards with a large lighter in tow and I gave the signal to attack. As we dived through the thin but persistent layer of cloud Baudisch reported: 'Kette to port already diving on same target!' I levelled out and decided to look elsewhere.

Not far away I caught sight of a ship that had been hidden by cloud up until that moment. It was by no means huge – perhaps 1,000 to 2,000 tons – but big enough. So a quick change of target to starboard. Put her nose down – attack! Because of the abortive dive on the tug we were already below 500 metres, but I went even lower. Closer – now! My bomb hit the water immediately ahead of the ship's bow. As we started to climb away we kept our eyes glued to the vessel. Unable to take avoiding action in time, it was steaming straight through the widening circle of ripples that marked the point where the bomb had disappeared into the water. At that moment there was an almighty explosion immediately under the middle of the ship. It seemed to lift right out of the water and bits of wreckage were hurled a good fifty metres into the air. A fascinating sight – but a horrible one!

'Fighter to port!' Baudisch's voice sounded in my earphones. He loosed off a few rounds – but then his gun jammed. The Spitfire was curving in for a stern attack. I reefed my machine around in an effort to meet it. But the distance between us was far too small. Both still banking almost vertically, we flashed past each other no more than twenty metres apart. He turned in for another attack.

Again I dragged the Ju 87 around onto a collision course. And again we shot past each other with only metres to spare.

'Fighter on the right!' A second Spitfire was closing in fast from the other side and already getting dangerously close. No time to turn in towards this one. He's going to open fire at any moment now. I hauled back hard and sharp on the stick and the fine white strands of his machine-gun fire passed beneath us.

One of the Spitfires was coming in from astern again. Another steep 180-degree turn to meet this new threat. The enemy fighters made several more passes, but each time I was able to face them almost head-on. I didn't manage to get in a single shot at them, but my aggressive tactics were enough to put them off their aim as well. A Spitfire raced past me one last time before they finally broke away. They must have been running short of fuel and needed to get home. Then I noticed that one of the pair had curved in on my tail again and was slowly drawing level with me off to my right. He was presumably out of ammunition, for he showed no evil intent. He must also have realized that he had nothing to fear from Fritzchen in the rear cockpit, who was still struggling desperately to clear his stoppage.

When we were almost wingtip-to-wingtip, he looked across at us and raised his hand to his flying helmet in salute! Dumbfounded, I automatically returned the compliment. Then he banked away in a graceful arc and was quickly lost to sight. We were alone again – and out of danger. Throttling back to economical cruising speed, I gave my hard-worked engine a breather as we set off to follow our comrades back to base.

But I could not get that salute – given by a tough opponent at the end of a hard fight – out of my mind. It had almost been like a medieval knight raising his visor before leaving the field after an undecided jousting contest. Were we the modern knights of the air? That was undoubtedly overdoing things, far too naive and romantic a notion. But what would flying be without a touch of romanticism? That such a gesture was still possible – despite the severity of the air fighting, and despite the heavy losses on both sides – was surely evidence enough that there *was* such a thing as the brotherhood of the air. It had made me realize that those of us who shared the freedom of the skies, although having to do our duty on opposing sides in times of war, were nonetheless joined by a common bond.

How many soldiers fighting on the ground, I wondered, would be granted an opportunity of this kind to demonstrate their respect for a valiant opponent? And how many would have the wit to seize that opportunity should it arise? Not many, I'll wager. And so I mentally doff my hat! That unknown British pilot was a remarkable man. (Although I never did discover his identity, he still has my total respect to this day.)

In the meantime, however, the realities of the moment had reclaimed my attention. Our right wing had taken a few hits and a thin stream of some fluid or other was escaping from the trailing edge. Fuel? The fuel contents gauge was showing normal. So was the oil pressure gauge. Probably just some minor damage to one of the less important oil lines.

It was now that Baudisch told me: 'One of those fighters was only firing with his four starboard machine guns.' 'We've had the devil's own luck again then, Fritzchen. It could have been very nasty for us if all his guns had been working! But make sure you're tightly strapped in when we land. That burst that went under us was a bit too close for my liking. Our tyres may have caught a packet.'

When we got back to Guise I decided to be safe rather than sorry and tried to do what we called an 'egg-landing', in other words, to set the machine down as gently and carefully as possible. Even so, as we lost speed we heard a very suspicious thumping sound coming from the right wheel. Ignition off! Just before coming to a complete stop we executed a stately ground loop to the right. As I suspected, the starboard mainwheel tyre had been punctured by machine-gun fire. The ground crew had spotted the trouble as we came drifting in and were quickly on the scene with tools and a new tyre ready to help our lame bird back on to its feet. They also discovered that one of the oil lines in the right wing had been nicked by a bullet and was leaking slightly.

The other crews were already at debriefing. Reports were being collected together and the successes tallied up. The day's score for our 2. Staffel was four transports sunk, plus two other transports, one destroyer and one seagoing tug severely damaged. The final results of the latter actions had not been observed as the crews involved had been caught up in ferocious air battles almost immediately afterwards. The other Staffeln had enjoyed similar success, but our Gruppe had again had to suffer its share of losses on this 1 June:

Of the Gruppenstab, Oberleutnant Dietrich Troll from Rüstringen/ Oldenburg and his gunner, Feldwebel Walter Rampf from Freiburg-im-Breisgau, had been shot into the Channel by enemy fighters some 10 nautical miles north of Dunkirk.

3. Staffel's Leutnant Walter Stengel from Munich had been killed in action over Mardyck, just outside Dunkirk. His gunner, Unteroffizier Paul Horstmann from Werne, managed to bail out and returned to the unit slightly wounded.

A gunner from our 2. Staffel, Unteroffizier Julius Müller from Gimbweiler, had also been wounded in action against enemy fighters. But his injuries were more serious. Hit in the shoulder and in both legs, he was flown to Mannheim hospital by Ju 52. (He would report back to us fit for duty again on 19 August 1940.)

It was now 19.00 hours and the Staffel had finally been stood down. A few comrades of the 'black fraternity' – mechanics, that is, known as 'black men' from the colour of the overalls they wore – worked late into the night repairing the damage to our machines in order to have them serviceable again by morning.

The crews were relaxing outside their tents enjoying supper. Today there was even a nice drop of wine to go with it. They were swapping experiences and describing the day's events to the ground crews, who invariably flew the missions with us in their thoughts and were always keen to hear about what had actually happened after we got back. And today there was a lot to tell.

There had been so much going on in the skies above Dunkirk – and on the land and water below – that it was more than one pair of eyes could possibly take in. We could count ourselves lucky that we had at least been aware of the most important parts of the confused battle, those that directly affected us, and had always been able to react accordingly. But the overall picture of the sprawling drama that was Dunkirk – the innumerable separate combats, the personal tragedies, the individual fates that were being decided during every single minute of this momentous day – was simply too huge to grasp.

After a particularly hot day, in every sense of the word, it wasn't long before we retired into our tents. Although we were all dog-tired, our thoughts gave us no rest. Thoughts of our comrades who would not be returning, and of their grieving loved ones. But thoughts too of those countless numbers of our opponents who had undoubtedly fallen victim to our attacks, and of *their* next-of-kin. Perhaps I was more deeply moved than usual today because, as an ex-sailor, I had some idea of the traumas faced by defenceless men struggling for survival at sea. Or maybe it was that unknown British fighter pilot and his salute that had struck such a chord with me, awakening those normal human feelings that we tried so hard to suppress when in combat.

Whatever the case, it did no harm for a soldier to spare a thought for an honourable and worthy adversary. After all, those on the other side – like us – were not fighting this war for any personal motive. They – like us – were simply doing their duty: 'As the law demanded', to paraphrase a well-known German saying.

Something else struck me as thoughts of our recent operations continued to fill my mind: we wielded a truly fearsome weapon of war. We, the Stukas, were feared – and rightly so. For our task was always the same: to smash and destroy until the enemy's will to resist was broken. Our targets were invariably pinpoint military objectives – that is to say, small military targets such as bunkers, artillery emplacements, tanks, trucks, parked aircraft, ships, trains, road junctions, bridges, command posts – in short, all those things that the enemy was in a position to use, either directly or indirectly, to offer resistance to our ground troops.

Contrary to many wartime reports and post-war accounts, we never deliberately targeted civilians. Of course, the destructive power of our bombs inevitably resulted in human casualties among those who found themselves in, or in the immediate vicinity of, the areas that we were attacking. Just how many casualties, we didn't know. But what we did know, thanks to the accuracy of the Stuka, was that they were almost always enemy troops engaged in action against our own forces. Often they would be Flak gunners who, in turn, were doing their level best to shoot *us* out of the sky.

The height, and often the distance at which we operated made such matters easier for us to cope with. We rarely saw all the details of what was being played out on the ground. Combat for us was, to a large extent, a case of machine versus machine. The fact that those machines were being operated and served by human hand was something we tended not to think about. Another reason for our apparent lack of feelings was that our missions were carried out as a result of direct orders from above, and usually at very high risk to our own persons. This may also explain the overriding sense of pride whenever we successfully accomplished our given task, especially if it had been in the face of fierce enemy resistance.

Yes, perhaps this is what had made today different from all other days, what had prevented me from properly appreciating our undoubted successes: the knowledge that the ships we had sunk had been crowded with soldiers of an already beaten enemy army. They had barely escaped the inferno of Dunkirk only to find themselves defenceless and at the mercy of our bombs. Many of them had paid with their lives. But that too is war. A soldier has to come to terms with such situations. We had another saying that was trotted out whenever things got sticky: 'What doesn't finish us off can only make us harder!'

From 2 to 4 June 1940 our Gruppe flew no operations. VIII. Fliegerkorps was preparing for a new offensive to the south.

By 4 June Dunkirk was in German hands, and twenty-four hours later the Battle of France proper began. At first VIII. Fliegerkorps was tasked with supporting 6. Armee; more specifically, that army's Panzer units during their assault crossings of the River Somme at Peronne and Amiens. On the morning of 5 June we twice bombed enemy positions near Moreuil. In the afternoon we targeted Amiens. A machine of 3. Staffel was brought down by light Flak. The pilot, Feldwebel Heinz Idel, and aircraft mechanic Obergefreiter Heinz Dziallas, who was occupying the back seat, were both killed instantly when the Ju 87 hit the ground east of Amiens.

With the approach routes to our new targets now much shorter and with each mission lasting less than an hour, 6 June saw us fly a total of five operations: to Pertain, Rosières-en-Santerre, Roye, Marche-Allouarde and Meharicourt. All were directed against French forces and positions standing in the path of our own armoured spearheads. Supported by the Luftwaffe, the Army had little trouble in smashing through the so-called Weygand Line, which was still under construction.

The three missions of 7 June took us to Pierrepont, Chaussoy and Breteuil. They were followed by a day of rest for the Gruppe. But while we relaxed, the ground crews grabbed the opportunity to carry out some major servicing and overhaul work on the aircraft.

VIII. Fliegerkorps was by now supporting both 6. and 9. Armeen in their advance on Paris and drive to the east of the French capital, across the River Marne, in the direction of the upper Seine. On 9 June, during the breakthrough across the River Aisne, we attacked artillery and field emplacements at Jaulzy, east of Soissons. That same afternoon we flew two missions against Creil on the River Oise to the north of Paris. There were a number of bridges across the river in this area and our orders were to block the approaches to these traffic bottlenecks in order to impede the enemy's movements. 10 June then found us attacking targets at Nanteuil and Crépy-en-Valois. And on the morning of 11 June we were sent out against Reuilly-Sauvigny.

Upon our return from Reuilly-Sauvigny we were ordered to leave Guise and transfer southeast to the small landing ground at Buzancy. We touched down there at around 16.00 hours. This time our ground echelon had encountered no problems and by the evening we were fully operational on our new field.

On 12 June reconnaissance reported the presence of several trains loaded with tanks standing in the station at Esternay. We were immediately despatched to Esternay with orders to destroy them.

The weather forecast read: 'Sunny and bright, two-tenths cloud between 300 and 500 metres, increasing to five-tenths on the approach to the target, clear skies above 500 metres.' I was to lead the formation with my 2. Staffel. We took off in glorious summer sunshine, formed up and set course for Esternay. I wanted to get above the clouds before making my approach so that we wouldn't have to worry about light Flak while flying over enemy territory.

The gaps between the clouds were already getting smaller. I headed towards the largest one I could see and started to climb. We should soon reach the reported upper cloud limit of 500 metres. We continued to climb and were already well above the 500-metre mark, but the cloud was, if anything, getting even thicker. If I didn't want the formation to become hopelessly scattered there was only one option open to me: stick to my present course and keep climbing through the cloud. Without my urging, the Staffeln had already tucked in more tightly behind me. The damp grey blanket closed in around us. In the gloom it was just possible to make out the navigation lights and the wing of the neighbouring machine. I hoped and prayed we would soon be out of it. We carried on climbing steadily:

1,000 metres, 1,500 metres, 2,000 metres – and still it was like flying through a steam-filled Turkish bath. Then, at last, the sky around us began to show signs of lightening.

At 2,500 metres we finally broke through the top layer of cloud. Clear blue skies and radiant sunshine. My Staffel had stuck together like glue. But where were the other two? We looked around us with mounting anxiety. They *must* be visible against the layer of cloud below, which was no longer dirty grey but a dazzling white expanse bathed in bright sunlight. Tense minutes passed. Finally, way off to starboard, a collection of tiny black dots popped out of the cloud. It was one of our two missing Staffeln!

I led my Staffel towards them, wanting to get the formation back into shape again as quickly as possible. Then the other Staffel appeared out of the clouds as well – but a long way off to port. I turned to gather them in too. But then the realization hit me and my blood ran cold. The two Staffeln had exchanged places! We had entered the cloud base in a close arrowhead, but somewhere in that dim swirling cauldron they had unwittingly crossed over each other! Had they collided – which they might easily have done – the results would have been unimaginable. But thank the Lord we had all made it safely.

The Gruppe was back in formation. My only problem now was how to get it down again and, more importantly, how to lead it to the target. I studied my map. It showed a large area of forest to the east of Esternay. Cutting through the southern edge of the forest was a railway line. I traced its route westward and saw that it led to Esternay. That was the answer!

I had been keeping track of our position by dead reckoning. Because of the two large 'loops' I had been forced to make in order to gather in my errant Staffeln, my calculations may no longer have been absolutely accurate. But the expanse of forest was so huge that I was sure we would emerge from the clouds somewhere above it. Then all I would have to do was head south until I picked up the railway line, turn right, and follow it to the target. It was the only possible way.

I signalled to the Gruppe to take up close line-astern formation. With the machines tucked tightly one behind the other, this was the easiest formation for the pilots to fly and also the best way of keeping together while descending through the cloud. When we got to what I calculated to be the correct position, I eased back on the throttle and let myself sink slowly into the glaring white blanket of cloud. The altimeter began to retrace its steps: 2,000 metres – 1,500 metres – 1,000 metres – 500 metres.

I had lifted the nose of my machine slightly so that we would not emerge from the cloud base at too high a speed. I wanted to have a safety margin, as our altimeters always lagged a little behind our true height. Mine was now indicating

300 metres and still no sign of the earth below! A mental image of the Neuhammer tragedy flashed through my mind: that dreadful day on 15 August 1939 when thirteen crews of I./StG 76 had hurtled out of low cloud straight into the ground. That mustn't happen to us now! Very slowly and very grudgingly I relinquished more height. 250 metres – 200 metres – 150 metres – I could feel the sweat pearling on my forehead – 100 metres!

And there, finally – immediately below us – the tops of trees could just be made out between the last ragged wisps of cloud! At last! Hugging the treetops we headed southwards. I fervently hoped that this was the right forest; the one I had spotted on the map. We'd know when we reached the edge of it. There's the railway line! A sharp turn to the right, and then make use of one of the most basic methods of cross-country flying – 'left leg above right-hand rail' – to follow the tracks all the way to Esternay. This primitive form of navigation was known as 'flying the railway'.

The further west we flew, the more the landscape levelled out and the higher the cloud base began to lift. By the time Esternay station came into view we were at a comfortable 200 metres and the ground visibility had improved considerably. First I flew past the station in order to allow all crews to get a good look at the target, and also to enable them to spread out into attack formation as we made a wide sweeping turn to come back in again. There were several trains standing in the station. A number of flatbed wagons were still loaded with tanks. Prepare to attack! Widen the turn a fraction more for a flank approach. Let go bombs as low as possible. Recover, but remain at low level while re-forming for the flight back to base.

Our bombs had all gone down in and around the station yards. It was not the most accurate attack we had ever made, but considering the miserable weather conditions we had to be content with the fact that we found the target at all and had managed to inflict a fair amount of damage.

We headed home in open formation, flying just below the cloud base, which slowly rose from 200 to 300 metres. The risk of encountering enemy ground fire was one that had to be taken. Climbing back up through that soup again would be tempting fate just once too often. And in fact Oberfeldwebel Heinz Obermeier from Hamburg, our Kommandeur's regular gunner, *did* get hit by machine-gun fire from the ground some 5km north of Esternay. When we got back to base he had to be taken to the field hospital at Soissons with three bullet wounds in his arm. The rest of the Gruppe returned safely and without further incident.

After debriefing my crews and reporting to the Gruppenkommandeur, who had accompanied us to Esternay and was now mourning the temporary loss of his gunner – they had flown all their previous missions together – I returned to my

Staffel's dispersal area. As I strolled into the large black tent, which had been captured from the enemy and now served as our crew room, I heard Feldwebel Ebertz saying to the other pilots: 'Alright, so we hit a station, that I grant you – but it was never Esternay!'

'Really,' I asked, 'and why ever not?' A little taken aback by my sudden appearance, Ebertz turned to face me: 'I'll tell you why not. In all that filthy weather, and after having to stooge around in those clouds for so long, it just wasn't possible to find the right target.'

My response to that was:

> Listen to me everybody! I want every crew to make a sketch-map of the station we attacked today. Do it immediately and mark on it exactly where you saw your bombs fall. Once the Army has occupied the area and we have a half-day stand down, I'll organize a truck to drive you over there. Take your sketch-maps with you and check the positions of all the bomb craters . . . and don't forget to make a note of the name of the station.

It was a few days before the opportunity arose. I then sent all those crews who had flown the mission back by truck to Esternay. When they returned from their little excursion I asked them: 'Well, what did the station sign say?' 'Esternay, Herr Hauptmann,' they confessed. 'And did you check the positions of your bomb craters?' 'Jawohl, Herr Hauptmann!' They had taken it all in good part, however, and seemed to have been convinced by the evidence of their own eyes. I even got the impression that from then on – at least as far as navigation was concerned – they had fewer reservations about flying behind me!

Yes, that Feldwebel Hans Ebertz from Mühlheim was certainly one of a kind. Sturdily built, a butcher by trade before joining the Luftwaffe, he was the strongest man in the unit. It was said that he had nerves of steel. Nothing seemed to throw him. And yet I knew for a fact that when it came to flying a mission, he had to struggle far harder against his 'inner demons' than any of the rest of us. But he suppressed his fears and was as aggressive as the next man when diving to the attack. And that deserved respect.

Everybody was afraid when things got tough. That is only human and perfectly normal. A courageous soldier is one who conquers his fears and carries out his mission. And Ebertz was a courageous soldier. On the ground he was loud and assertive. He liked to think that he always knew better. Many's the time we returned to base without him because he was convinced in his own mind that we were on the wrong course for home. Whenever it was found that he wasn't amongst us, it would be a case of: 'Don't worry, he'll turn up shortly. He's landed somewhere else again.'

It was for this reason that I warned him: 'Ebertz, I don't like posting pilots away. But the next time I get a request for an experienced pilot to do a stint as an instructor back in the homeland, you're top of the list.' He was none too happy about this, but he accepted it without a grumble. On 26 June he was duly transferred to the VIII. Fliegerkorps' Ergänzungsstaffel [Operational Training Squadron] which was based at Lippstadt, to the east of the Ruhr. But after only two weeks there he sent me a plaintive letter: would I *please* request his return to the unit as a matter of some urgency. He wanted nothing more than to get back to his 'old mob' as soon as possible. I answered his plea and he was back with us in time to play his part in the Battle of Britain.

On 13 June we flew three missions against enemy troops and columns at Troyes/St-Parres, Chauchigny and le Bachot.

We attacked Troyes three more times on 14 June. That day's fourth mission was directed against the bridgeheads at Pont-sur-Yonne. Paris was declared an open city and German troops marched into the French capital unopposed. The government of France had decamped to Bordeaux.

On 15 June we again bombed columns of enemy troops near Troyes. Then we were called upon to fly a supply mission. We ferried bombs down to the forward landing ground that was being established at Villenauxe, ESE of Paris. Some of the remaining operations that day involved just single Staffeln as there was now felt to be little further likelihood of our encountering enemy fighters. My own Staffel flew two such missions: one against Chablis and the other targeting French columns in the Troyes area. In the evening the Gruppe transferred to Villenauxe.

While my Staffel was stood down on 16 June, 3. Staffel had to suffer yet more losses. Two of its aircraft crashed close to the railway station at Beaune, to the southwest of Dijon, victims either of enemy Flak or a mid-air collision. All four crew members, Feldwebel Richard Dietz from Burgsolms and his gunner, Unteroffizier Hans Kortenhaus from Herne, and Unteroffizier Heinz Ullrich from Schönebeck/Elbe and his gunner/mechanic Obergefreiter Heinz Heine from Struveshof, had lost their lives.

On 17 June my Staffel was ordered to bomb the exit road leading out of Châtillon-sur-Seine. The attack had been timed for 15.00 hours. I was already committed to the dive when I saw German troops feverishly laying out air recognition panels and German flags on the edge of the town. 'Abort! Abort! Do not release bombs! Friendly troops below!' I yelled. As we swooped low over the houses of the town I quickly assessed the situation. Everywhere I looked German soldiers were moving about the streets quite freely. In the main square a group of French prisoners were surrounded by German guards who were waving up at us.

Châtillon-sur-Seine was clearly in German hands. The fight for the town was over. I led the Staffel deeper into enemy territory. But there was nothing moving – not a living soul to be seen far and wide. After a fruitless search for an alternative target, we returned to base still carrying our bombs.

Relieved that we had not inadvertently bombed our own troops, I made my report to General Freiherr von Richthofen, the GOC VIII. Fliegerkorps, who just happened to be present in our ops room on a visit of inspection. He was plainly annoyed at the failure of our mission, complaining in an aggrieved tone: 'Will the Army *never* learn that they're supposed to stick to prearranged timetables like everybody else!' With all due respect to the leadership qualities of our general, I must admit that at first I was more than a little surprised at this reaction.

I cannot deny that the selfless personal courage displayed by the general in always leading from the front, and his insistence on close cooperation between the air and ground forces, had been major contributory factors in the success of the Wehrmacht's recent *Blitzkrieg* campaigns. We had also learned to appreciate the clear and concise nature of the orders that he issued to those of us commanding the flying units under his control. So why then, I wondered, did he regard it as such a 'failure' that we had returned to base without dropping our bombs – that on this occasion the ground troops had been able to take their objective earlier than planned, perhaps even without a fight, and certainly without the need of Stuka support? In any case, our bombing attacks were mostly intended simply to break enemy resistance in front of our advancing ground forces. In other words, to clear a path for our own troops and keep their losses to a minimum. And here the ground troops had, for once, achieved that aim without any help from us.

But on further reflection I came to realize that our general's anger had been fully justified. It was purely by chance that we had been able to break off our dive-bombing attack in the nick of time. From our normal operating height, details of what was happening on the ground were not all that easy to distinguish. It was usually impossible to tell friend from foe. Certainly, our commanders could not rely on our always being able to do so.

So what would have happened if we had attacked as ordered and at the time agreed with the Army? We would have bombed our own troops! It didn't bear thinking about! I could imagine the flap, the uproar on all sides – not to mention the inevitable court of enquiry, the search for a scapegoat. As it was, the commanders involved, and we ourselves, had been spared all that. It had been a matter of pure luck. And the luckiest of all had been those Army troops down there in Châtillon-sur-Seine. All in all, I decided, it had been a very satisfactory day . . . despite the general's displeasure.

Early on 19 June we transferred to the small forward landing ground at Auxerre. My Staffel was briefed for a mission later that afternoon. It was to be a *freier Kampf* – the Stuka equivalent to the fighters' *freie Jagd* – a free-ranging sweep against any enemy troop movements we could find in the Issoudun area. We spotted and attacked a moving goods train, scoring a number of hits. These immediately set off a chain reaction of violent explosions. They ripped along the length of the train until there was nothing left of it. It must have been carrying ammunition.

This was to be our last combat mission in the campaign against France. Late that same evening we were ordered back to Villenauxe.

20 June saw us being called upon to carry out a couple of supply missions, ferrying bombs down to Nevers for other Stuka units that were still flying ops. But we ourselves didn't take part in any further attacks. The enemy's resistance had been well and truly broken.

On 22 June 1940, in the same railway carriage in which France's Marshal Foch had received the German surrender of 1918, the German–French Armistice terms were presented and signed. It was not only the same railway carriage; it had also been taken to the very same spot in the Forest of Compiègne where the 1918 surrender – leading to the infamous Treaty of Versailles – had been signed. This symbolic gesture was not lost on Germany's older generation, those who had experienced the end of the First World War and particularly those who had fought in that conflict. It brought them great satisfaction; or at least that was the impression I got from one of my father's very infrequent letters, in which he expressed his feelings on the subject in the pithy and forthright manner to be expected from an old soldier.

The cease-fire in the West sounded on 25 June 1940. Our Gruppe was stood down at Villenauxe. We used the time to catch up on our paperwork and deal with all those myriad items that were so essential to the smooth running of Gruppe and Staffel affairs, but which had tended to be ignored during the recent days and weeks of constant readiness and frequent missions. While the fighting had been going on, all our attention had been fully focussed on operations. Now there was a whole pile of admin stuff to catch up on. But we also found time to draw up a brief balance sheet on our Staffel's performance:

2.(St)/186(T) in the campaign against France

The Staffel had flown a total of sixty combat missions against the enemy; fifty-nine of them had been carried out successfully, sometimes in the face of strong enemy fighter and Flak opposition, sometimes under the most difficult and adverse weather conditions. And among ourselves, we also counted the one mission that we didn't complete as ordered as being a particular success: we didn't bomb those troops occupying Châtillon-sur-Seine!

Those missions had cost us some good comrades: one pilot and two gunners killed in action (Unteroffiziere Strehler and Hecht, and Gefreiter Hüsch), plus two pilots and two gunners wounded (Feldwebel Bartsch and Unteroffiziere Reuss, Philipp and Müller, Julius). But compared to our earlier fears, and when measured against the losses sustained by some other Stuka units, we felt we had escaped very lightly indeed.

Our satisfaction at the defeat of France, the cause for which our comrades had suffered and died, helped us to come to terms with their loss. We were still labouring under the impression that the war would soon be won and that this was one step nearer to our returning home. Who at that time could possibly have known what the future still held in store? Wrapped up in the tight little world that was our Staffel, we certainly didn't!

Chapter 9
Operations over England as Gruppenkommandeur

VIII. Fliegerkorps was now preparing to attack British convoys in the Channel as well as targets along England's southern coast. On 30 June 1940 the Korps' flying units were transferred to the areas to the south and southeast of Cherbourg. Our Gruppe was assigned a landing ground near Falaise. To disguise the move the aircraft flew to the new base separately and at low level. They took their chief mechanics with them, crammed into the rear cockpit alongside the gunner.

As I was coming in to land I saw aircraft wreckage scattered along one edge of the field. After I had touched down the leader of our advance ground party confirmed my worst fears: Oberleutnant Wolf-Dietrich Herbst from Emmagrube had hit the ground while on his final approach. Herbst, the senior Oberleutnant of my Staffel, together with his gunner, Unteroffizier Franz Kollmitt from Tollack in East Prussia, and chief mechanic, Unteroffizier Erich Schug from Neuwied on the Rhine, had all been killed in the crash. The pilot must have tried to take the final curve too steeply, or with insufficient speed. The machine had stalled and gone straight in.

After all that they had been through with us during the recent operations and air battles in France, the loss of the Herbst crew – and their chief mechanic – hit us particularly hard because it had been so unnecessary and could have been so easily avoided. It just went to show how quickly the slightest lapse of concentration, even by the most experienced of pilots, could lead to disaster. It was a sombre gathering that paid its last respects to three good comrades as they were laid to rest in Falaise cemetery.

'Third Stuka One'

On 2 July 1940 there were sweeping personnel and organizational changes within our Gruppe. Initially activated for service aboard the aircraft carrier *Graf Zeppelin* and still bearing our original naval designation I.(St)/186(T), we were now to be officially incorporated into Stukageschwader 1 as that unit's III. Gruppe. Hence-

Portrait of a pilot.

A formation of Ju 87s flies over the ruins of Calais, 1940.

Ju 52 transports above a serpentine supply road in Greece, 1941.

An Indian soldier of the British forces in Greece captured by German paratroops, Corinth 1941.

A group of soldiers of the British expeditionary force captured in Greece, 1941.

A formation of Stukas returning to their airfield near Athens after an early morning raid on Crete.

A Soviet airfield after an attack by Ju 87 Stukas. The damage inflicted to the machines shown was the result of a single bomb. German aircraft were operating from this field just one day later.

Clearing the debris from a captured Soviet airfield as Ju 52s bring in supplies.

forth we would operate as III./StG 1 or, in the common parlance of the time: 'Third Stuka One'.

Our three component Staffeln were likewise redesignated accordingly. Hitherto known as 1., 2. and 3./186, they now became 7., 8. and 9./StG 1 respectively.

At the same time we lost our highly respected Gruppenkommandeur, Major Walter Hagen. To our great joy, however, his posting did not take him far. He was appointed to be the new Geschwaderkommodore of StG 1!

The long-serving Kapitän of our 1. Staffel, Hauptmann Helmut Bode, had already left us back on 11 June to take over as Gruppenkommandeur of III./StG 77.

All of this resulted in a certain amount of reshuffling in the ranks of what was now III./StG 1. The new Gruppenkommandeur was a certain Hauptmann Helmut Mahlke from Berlin-Lankwitz, and his three Staffelkapitäne were:

7. Staffel: Oberleutnant Hartmut Schairer from Nagold
8. Staffel: Oberleutnant Günter Skambraks from Tilsit
9. Staffel: Oberleutnant Ulrich Heinze from Halle (as heretofore)

For those involved, these appointments were undoubtedly an honour. But, at the same time, they brought with them a heavier burden of responsibility. As the Kommandeur of an operational Stukagruppe in time of war a great deal would be resting on my 26-year-old shoulders. But thanks both to the wisdom and foresight of Major Hagen – who had prepared us well by allowing each of his three former Staffelkapitäne to lead the Gruppe in combat – and to the fact that I was taking over our old crowd and not some new and unknown unit, I was quietly confident that I would be able to perform my soldierly duty and prove myself equal to the task that now faced me.

While we were establishing our new landing ground special emphasis had been placed on good camouflage. This was not solely in the hope of winning first prize in the 'camouflage competition' that the AOC VIII. Fliegerkorps had organized between all the Korps' flying units, but also – and undoubtedly more importantly – because it offered the best protection against enemy air attack.

Our field was particularly well suited to the purpose. The aircraft were easy to hide under the thick foliage that bordered it on all sides. Our vehicles and tented accommodation were also tucked away out of sight among the surrounding orchards and shrubbery. The field itself was precisely that: a large meadow whose length was just enough to allow us to take off and land.

The two grass runways ran parallel to a hedge that protruded out almost into the centre of the field. A light-coloured path ran diagonally right across the middle off the take-off and landing strips. It was perfectly flat and level with the grass around it. As an added touch, I had a lot of small branches stuck into the ground along one side of this path. In the summer sun they cast a strong shadow and from the air it looked for all the world as if the path was flanked by a deep drainage ditch. As a camouflage measure this 'obstacle' proved amazingly effective. So much so, in fact, that I regularly got the fright of my life when I unthinkingly taxied across it after landing!

Running the length of the field on one side there actually *was* a deep ditch that separated it from an adjoining orchard. Here, in line with the end of the landing strip, our service company constructed a wide wooden-planked bridge to provide a safety margin in case any machine came in too fast. From above the whole field appeared very rustic and innocent. And to heighten that impression we sometimes even had a Gefreiter working on it during the day, leisurely guiding a harrow back and forth behind a team of horses.

After only a few days in residence we received advance warning that General von Richthofen was flying around in his Fieseler Storch inspecting the various fields occupied by his units and checking personally on the effectiveness of their camouflage. Now things were about to get interesting! In our case, they turned into an absolute *Mords Gaudi* – or a hell of a lot of fun – as the Bavarians say!

The AOC's Fieseler Storch was spotted circling a field of stubble not far from us. Round and round it went without a break. 'Should we lay out a landing cross?' my men asked. 'No,' I replied, 'only if it's requested, or if we are suddenly called upon to fly a mission.' And still the Storch continued to circle. Eventually I ordered one of my men out of hiding, telling him to go out into the middle of the field where the landing cross would normally be displayed and 'send up a green'. A green flare indicated permission to land.

The Storch came bumbling in our direction and put down in another stubble field still some 400 metres away from us. I drove across and reported to the general: 'Third Stuka One on duty!' All I got in return was: 'Your field can be recognized from miles away by the vehicle tracks. You'll have to get rid of those for a start!' 'You didn't even *see* our field, Herr General, otherwise I imagine you would have landed on it!' 'Over there,' he pointed, 'in front of that patch of woods, are a lot of very deep tyre tracks.' 'Yes, but they're not ours, Herr General. They were made by an Army transport unit that was here before us and has long since departed. The Royal Air Force can dump as many bombs as it likes over there, it's a good thousand metres away from our field. May I show you our field, Herr General? It's in that direction.'

I chauffeured the general back to our landing ground. The camouflage clearly found favour. But all he said was: 'You're still not getting a prize though! You've got absolutely ideal conditions here. Other units have been finding it much tougher. They're right out in the open and have had one hell of a job getting themselves hidden away under camouflage netting and the like.' 'Thanks, but we've had our prize already, Herr General – your failure to find us!'

On the morning of 7 July we were moved up to Théville outside Cherbourg in preparation for an attack on British shipping in the Channel. But no vessels were reported in those sea areas within range of our Stukas and so in the evening we had to return to Falaise empty-handed.

Four days later, on 11 July, we were sent back up to Théville and there briefed for an operation against some ships said to be hugging the English coast. This time we were even provided with a fighter escort, which duly made rendezvous with us at the time and position specified in the briefing. Well protected, we set out across the Channel. I had given orders for the attack to be carried out in Staffel order, the dive to be steep, height of bomb release 400 metres. But when we reached the target area we found just one solitary vessel, close inshore, heading westwards.

I led the attack, tipping over onto one wing and diving into the wind. Everything seemed to be going smoothly when, suddenly, the target started to slide rapidly out of the crosshairs of my sights. At 1,000 metres the wind had changed direction and was now pushing me hard to one side. I corrected, turning into the wind again until the vessel had drifted back into the centre of my sights. But it refused to stay there, and *again* I was forced to correct. By now I was down to 400 metres and out of time. My aim was not perfect, but it would have to do. Release bombs – missed!

My two wingmen also failed to hit the target. 7. Staffel were coming down hard on our heels: same target, same results. One after the other, their bombs exploded harmlessly in the water around the ship. Next came 8. Staffel, and then 9. Staffel. All were aiming at the same target – they had to be, it was the only ship in sight. And although it was admittedly small – it couldn't even be described in all honesty as a 'worthwhile' target – every single one of their bombs missed! It hardly seemed credible – not one hit! What a shambles. And what a thing to happen to an 'old Stuka crowd' like us.

The cause of the fiasco was obvious. The unexpected and violent changes in wind direction at 1,000 metres and lower had thrown the pilots completely off their aim. None had been able to find the exact point of deviation and necessary angle of correction in the little time left available to them before bomb release. The wind had been the ship's saviour. After touching down at Théville thoroughly chastened, we were ordered back to Falaise. The mission may have been a total flop, but we had suffered no damage. All that was dented was our pride.

We mustn't let such a thing happen again. I talked with my Staffelkapitäne about how best we could avoid it in the future. As it was wartime, we couldn't always rely on getting precise forecasts of the winds at all altitudes in our target areas. It was therefore decided that, immediately prior to any future attacks on shipping, we would use the current weather forecast as a basis for determining our angles of dive, correction and sight, and the height of bomb release.

The first pilot to attack would stick rigidly to these criteria when diving on the target. The following aircraft would then observe the results, note where his bombs had hit, and correct accordingly. This procedure meant that such an attack would inevitably last a little longer than usual. It would therefore only be feasible if we had fighter protection to keep the enemy off our backs for a sufficient length of time.

Good news

On 21 July 1940 we heard the good news that our erstwhile Gruppenkommandeur Major Walter Hagen, now our Geschwaderkommodore, had been awarded the Knight's Cross and promoted to Oberstleutnant. All the members of his old Gruppe were delighted and felt it was an honour that he richly deserved. One newspaper report of 29 July had this to say about him:

> Major Hagen, who flew as the leader of Jagdstaffeln during the Polish campaign, has achieved decisive successes in the west as Gruppenkommandeur of a Stukagruppe. Under his personal leadership, the Gruppe Hagen's successes include the bombing of French airfields, attacks on enemy forces during the advance to Sedan and the Meuse crossings, the smashing of French armoured counter-attacks, support throughout the advance to the Channel coast, and the bombing of the Citadel and forts of Calais.
>
> At Dunkirk the unit destroyed two locks and sank a number of ships, both naval vessels and merchantmen. By repeated attacks on enemy columns the enemy's retreat was severely disrupted. At Cosne the bridge across the Loire was destroyed, and at Beaune important railway yards and a munitions train were also hit. Flying at its head, Major Hagen has led his Gruppe from success to success.

Yes, as a good soldier 'our' Oberstleutnant Walter Hagen had of course done all of that – and more. Although no longer in the first flush of youth he was still young at heart, an outstanding pilot, and a good comrade who was admired and respected by all those under his command as an exemplary superior. His flying career was, in fact, so unique that it warrants brief description here:

The son of a Kiel merchant, he had been born on 16 March 1897. In June 1915 he volunteered for service in the First World War. Posted to 1. Seefliegerabteilung [1st Naval Air Detachment] in November 1917, he had flown his first operational missions over Flanders in 1918. After the First World War he test-flew many new aircraft. In Kiel he was involved in the first aircraft catapult-launch trials and later served as a pilot aboard mail steamers, being launched by catapult to fly on ahead, his machine loaded with sacks of mail, as soon as the vessel came within aircraft range of its port of destination.

An article in his local newspaper, the *Kieler Nachrichten* – published to mark his winning the Knight's Cross – brought a nostalgic smile to his face when it reminded people at home that, for a while, he had also played in goal for KSV Holstein, the town's premier football team.

Walter Hagen would continue to lead Stukageschwader 1 until 30 March 1943. And those who were present when he handed over command to his successor, Oberstleutnant Gustav Pressler, swore that there were tears in his eyes. Truly an inspirational human being and genuine comrade.

On 25 July 1940 we again moved up to Théville in preparation for another attack on Channel shipping. We took off from there at 11.03 hours and, as on the previous occasion, our fighter escort again delivered us safely to the target area. This time the attack was much more successful. As we recovered from the dive we observed a number of direct hits on the vessels we had been aiming at. We were unable to see if any actually sank, for suddenly the enemy's fighters were upon us!

The British fighter pilots had long ago recognized when we were at our most vulnerable: the time between pulling out of our individual dives and before being able to get back into formation again. They knew that during this phase we were almost completely defenceless and that they had little to fear from the return fire from the single machine gun in each plane's rear cockpit. This was their chance and they grabbed it. The only response we had was to turn in towards our attackers as best we could. A wild free-for-all developed within a matter of seconds. All thoughts of re-forming were forgotten. The vital thing now was to keep a sharp watch-out. Watch out that no enemy fighter crept up on us unawares, giving us no time to react. Watch out that we didn't collide with one of our own aircraft. Watch out, and try wherever possible to help any of our comrades who seemed to be in real difficulty.

But after a few endless minutes our fighter escort came screaming down to join the fray. Their presence was felt immediately. The British fighters abruptly lost all interest in us – they had their own problems now. We landed back at Théville at 12.33 hours. None of our aircraft was missing, but all were showing signs of damage, some of it serious. Unfortunately, however, we had again suffered casualties. Obergefreiter Josef Stillinger from Pfarrkirchen in Bavaria, one of 8. Staffel's gunners, had been killed in the action and Unteroffizier Walter Meissner from Danzig, a 7. Staffel gunner, had been wounded during an enemy fighter attack 15km to the southwest of Portland Bill. He was taken to hospital at Potigny with the bullet still lodged in his thigh.

One thing was already abundantly clear: Britain's fighters were beginning to make our job ever more difficult and dangerous. Our clashes with them were growing harder and more fiercely fought. This time we had been able to carry out our mission and score a number of hits on the enemy's vessels. But to our sorrow we had lost another good comrade. By evening we were back in Falaise.

31 July again saw us transferred up to Théville in readiness for yet another attack on Britain's Channel shipping. But we spent the whole day in idleness. No vessels came within effective range of our Stukas. After many fruitless hours it was back to Falaise again that same evening.

The same process was repeated on both 2 and 3 August, although on these occasions our jumping-off point was not Théville but Picauville, another advance landing strip to the south of Cherbourg. Again, no ships were reported and no missions flown.

On the night of 8 August we received orders to stand by. At first light we flew up to Théville. During the night a British convoy had passed Dover heading west. It had been attacked by our motor torpedo boats during the hours of darkness and was in some disorder, but still holding its course westward. At 09.30 hours we took off with orders to find and attack this convoy.

With a strong fighter escort we set out across the Channel. The convoy was spotted some ten nautical miles to the southwest of the Isle of Wight. As the vessels had by this time closed up again, I decided that we would attack in Ketten. The wind was steady. The targets remained firmly fixed in our sights during the dive – and bombing results were consequently very good. Several direct hits had been scored on a number of ships, among them three fair-sized merchantmen, which were seen to be sinking. Others had been severely damaged by our bombs.

But then there was no more time to observe our handiwork, for once again enemy fighters had suddenly appeared on the scene. They had been lying in wait at low level and were upon us before I could gather the Gruppe back into formation. Within moments we were embroiled in another furious mêlée. I had the feeling that our opponents outnumbered us this time. Whether this was actually true or not, I couldn't say. But I do vividly recall at one point seeing no fewer than three enemy fighters bearing down on me from three different directions! I could only turn towards one of them. I would have to try to 'jump' the bullets from the other two when they opened fire on me. It was a good thing that my trusty Iolanthe was so responsive. She answered to my every heave and yank on the stick with childish ease.

And still the fighters continued with their attacks. It was absolutely impossible to keep track of them all. Time and again we turned in towards them, hoping to get in a few shots with our two forward machine guns, but it was no use. Our opponents were much too fast for us. They could choose where and when to launch each assault. They dictated the terms and the course of the fight. And if we *did* find ourselves in a position to meet them head-on, they always sheered away. They obviously didn't like confronting us face-to-face, even though they each had eight machine guns to our two.

This behaviour of theirs soon gave rise to a saying within the Gruppe: 'He who gets stuck in will see more of life!' In other words, take the fight to the enemy and your chances of survival will be that much the greater. 'Get stuck in!' – that was our best hope. The Stuka was our given weapon of war; it was up to us to make the most of what strengths it possessed.

Even so, on this occasion we were more than a little relieved when our fighters finally succeeded in driving the enemy away from us. We re-formed and set course for the French coast. Oberleutnant Klaus Ostmann of 8. Staffel had been seriously wounded. A bullet had shattered his right knee when his machine was attacked by a fighter ten nautical miles to the south of the Isle of Wight. He was still flying, but was so weakened by loss of blood that he was barely conscious. Trying every trick in the book to keep him awake, the other members of his Staffel found that he reacted instinctively if one of them pulled up sharply right in front of him. The shock of seeing another machine suddenly filling his windscreen seemed to put new life into him.

And so this is what they did; drawing ahead of Ostmann and popping up directly in front of him one after the other, and at ever shorter intervals, until they had got him back to our forward landing ground. After touching down the machine rolled to a stop at the end of the field. Ostmann was lifted unconscious from the cockpit and rushed to the hospital at Valognes near Cherbourg where he received emergency treatment. True comradeship had helped him get back to base with the last ounce of strength left in his body.

The 9. Staffel crew of pilot Unteroffizier Roland Reiter and gunner Ober-gefreiter Bernhard Renners were also wounded. Both had been hit in the shoulder and they too were immediately taken to Valognes hospital after landing. Two other crews of 9. Staffel were missing. Nothing had been seen or heard of pilot Feldwebel Herbert Torngrind and gunner Gefreiter Heinrich Bauer, or of Gefreiter Gottlob Walz and his gunner, Gefreiter Robert Schütz, since our clash with the enemy fighters southwest of the Isle of Wight. There seemed little hope that any of the four had survived.

The post-op debriefing revealed the extent of our success against the convoy: 18,000 tons [gross register tons: grt] of enemy merchant shipping sunk. Other vessels were hit and damaged, but no further details observed due to the ferocity of the attack by enemy fighters. Every one of our returning aircraft had suffered substantial combat damage. We were therefore sent back to Falaise, where our ground crews quickly got to work repairing the worst of it. Two hours later all serviceable machines were ordered to return to the advance landing ground at Picauville. In the interim the other Stukagruppen of VIII. Fliegerkorps had attacked the convoy. They too had been fiercely opposed by enemy fighters and had undergone much the same experience as ourselves.

In the afternoon we were to combine forces for another attack on the depleted convoy. We took off from Picauville at 16.30 hours. The mission was a repeat of the morning's proceedings. Our escorting fighters got us safely to the target area. We carried out our attack, scored another string of hits, but were unable to observe the results as we were once again pounced upon by enemy fighters. This time, however, our own fighters were quicker off the mark. It was thanks entirely to their intervention that we were able to disengage from the enemy with all our feathers seemingly intact.

It was only when we were heading back to base, and were about halfway across the Channel, that one of our aircraft began to pour black smoke. It dropped out of formation and veered off eastwards. He wouldn't get home if he insisted on going in that direction! I handed the Gruppe over to my deputy Kommandeur, Oberleutnant Karl-Hermann Lion, and set off after our wayward and clearly damaged Iolanthe. As I got closer to it I could see from the markings that it was the aircraft of the Kapitän of my 8. Staffel, Oberleutnant Günter Skambraks.

The glass of the cabin windows was black with oil. Skambraks had opened his canopy a fraction and was pressed motionless far back and high in his seat. Was he still conscious? Perhaps he was trying to peer ahead through the open slit in his cockpit roof? I carefully eased my own machine out to the left just in front of him and started to edge inwards, very slowly turning on to a southerly heading in the direction of Cherbourg. Yes! He was responding! Tucked in behind my right wing, he followed my every move as we completed the turn to starboard. His aircraft was still losing oil and dragging a dark banner through the sky in its wake. But the prop seemed to be holding its revs.

Cherbourg airfield came into view ahead. If his engine held out for just a few minutes more, Skambraks should be able to make it. Soon we reached the point where he would be able to glide the rest of the way if necessary. I signalled across to him to put down at Cherbourg. He waved in acknowledgement and started his descent. He had by this time switched off his engine to prevent its overheating from any further loss of oil. His near perfect deadstick landing on Cherbourg airfield was marred only by a final ground loop caused by a bullet-holed mainwheel tyre. The dipstick later showed that the oil tank was to all intents and purposes empty – it registered just one millimetre!

That evening Skambraks reported back to me at Falaise. He was his usual breezy, cheerful self. Laughingly, he showed me a tiny red mark on his calf where a few hairs had been singed away. He told me that a bullet had gone through the right leg of his flying overalls and uniform trousers and had grazed the flesh. It could hardly be called a wound.

The British convoy that we had attacked – 'C.W.9' – had been hit hard. The official British history of the war at sea would later have this to say on the subject:

> The seriousness of the enemy's effort lay in the fact that, at their peak, one ship in three in these convoys had been damaged or sunk. Such unattractive odds could, if continued, make it impossible to man the ships . . .

Later that same evening I called my Staffelkapitäne together to discuss the day's events. We went over our shared experiences and tried to work out what conclusions could be drawn from them. How could we improve upon our attack procedures and, above all, how could we prevent – or at least reduce – future losses? There was no discernible pattern to our casualties. Of today's two missing 9. Staffel pilots, one, Feldwebel Torngrind, was an *alter Hase* – a veteran with many ops already under his belt, while the other – Gefreiter Walz – had been on his first combat mission.

Yet it would be undeniably true to say that it was the inexperienced pilots who were at greatest risk in the sort of action we had just been through. With so much going on all around them, so much happening at the same time or within the space of a split second, they had not yet learned to separate the important from the unimportant. We had all been through this stage in the beginning: gripped, almost mesmerized, by scenes and events that we should have totally ignored. But, unlike poor Walz, we had been lucky. We had survived long enough to recognize the difference and concentrate solely on those things that immediately concerned us and which required a rapid response on our part. And even so, some of us had only just escaped the attentions of today's enemy fighters by the very skin of our teeth.

Nor could we expect future operations to be any different. We therefore decided that, as our top priority, we had to do more to help our novice crews get through their first few missions until they had gained the necessary amount of experience. This was easier said than done. But we definitely needed to put more conscious effort into keeping the enemy fighters off their backs than we had done to date. We would also talk to them during off-duty hours on the ground and try to explain to them what things they had to watch out for, and what they needn't worry about.

We decided that our method of attack also required altering. Most enemy merchant ships normally carried just two Flak guns: one at the bow and one on the stern. In future, irrespective of wind direction, we would *always* attack in Ketten from behind the target vessel. Diving to a height of 500 metres, we would then begin to pull out and – while still in a shallow dive – rake the ship with machine-gun fire, aiming first at the weapon on the stern (to throw the enemy gunners off their aim) and then continuing along its entire length until we saw our bullets striking the water in front of the bow. This was the moment to release our bombs, which should then hit the vessel aft of the bridge structure. Hopefully, it would also help to prevent their bouncing overboard, something that had happened more than once during previous attacks.

We would now be at low level. But with the bomb fuzes set to mV – '*mit Verzögerung*' ['with delay'] – it would be a few seconds before they exploded. This would allow time for the two wingmen of each Kette, following immediately on the heels of their leader, to drop their own bombs and be well clear before any debris started flying.

Next came the question of withdrawal from the target area, always the most vulnerable phase in any of our missions. Rather than climb away and re-form, as had been standard practice during the Battle of France, we decided that we would remain at wave top height and form into what we called a *Sauhaufen*. Literally a 'herd of boar', this could best be described as a kind of 'organized gaggle', in which we all stuck close together but which gave us a certain freedom of movement within the group as a whole. Not only would this prevent enemy fighters from attacking us from below, we also hoped that it would dissuade them from approaching us from behind.

I would be flying at the front of the gaggle, but keeping my speed deliberately low. Any aircraft to the rear that found itself threatened by a fighter from astern could thus pour on full throttle and move up into the middle of the gaggle for safety. If the enemy pilot persisted in his pursuit, he would find himself overtaking other Stukas that would, in turn, try to get on *his* tail – or at least loose off a few shots at him as he passed. From previous experience we doubted that any enemy fighter would want to place itself in that position. Hopefully, it would break away before having a chance to open fire.

Similarly, our newer and still inexperienced crews should, as far as possible, also be tucked well into the middle of the gaggle where they would be least likely to come under attack. We hoped that this change in tactics would enable us to cope better with the opposition. It should give us a greater chance of success at reduced risk to ourselves – or at least until the enemy got wise and came up with an effective counter-measure.

At first, however, all this planning remained purely theoretical. The large number of ships already lost to air attack had persuaded the British government to re-route their main Atlantic convoys northwards. Traffic through the Channel was now confined to small local convoys – and these sailed mostly under cover of darkness.

Adlertag

On the morning of 13 August 1940 all Stuka units were ordered to move up to their advance landing grounds closer to the Channel coast. For our Gruppe this meant Picauville again. The Geschwaderkommodores and Gruppenkommandeure had been summoned to Branville for a briefing. Here the High Command's intentions were revealed to us: *Adlertag* [Eagle Day] was to be a simultaneous assault by all units on the airfields situated along England's southern coast. Its purpose was to secure for Germany air superiority over that entire operational area.

The targets for the individual Gruppen were then announced. Major Sigel's I./StG 76, which was currently attached to our Geschwader, was to attack Portsmouth airfield and harbour. My Gruppe's main target was the airfield at Lee-on-Solent to the west of Portsmouth. We were also given the task of knocking out Ventnor radio station on the Isle of Wight, which was serving as a British fighter control HQ. Armed with this information we returned to our units all ready to go. But the weather over the target area was so bad that take-off had to be delayed.

We employed the time spent waiting by considering how best to carry out our missions. We in Stukageschwader 1 discussed the matter with our Kommodore, Oberstleutnant Hagen. Major Sigel of I./StG 76 outlined his plan of attack. After bombing Portsmouth he intended retiring out along the Solent, the stretch of water separating England's south coast from the Isle of Wight. I strongly advised against this. He'd be a sitting duck for every British naval Flak gunner in the area, and they – as we knew from past encounters – were exceptionally good shots. I explained that I was going to lead my Gruppe out at low-level straight across the Isle of Wight, and recommended that he do the same. The British would hardly be expecting us to take this exit route. It hadn't been done before and, in addition, we would be able to use the contours of the island as cover.

But Sigel would have none of it. He went even further, urging the Kommodore to order me to fly out along the Solent with his Gruppe. Hagen very wisely brought the discussion to a close by saying: 'Tactical decisions of this kind are a matter for the formation leaders in the air.' And quite right too. Only the formation leader can assess the true situation at any given moment during the course of an operation. And only he, to the best of his knowledge and experience, can decide what action to take.

We returned once more to our respective Gruppen, explained to our crews the purpose of the mission, briefed them on their specific targets and went to readiness to await the order to take off. But weather conditions over the whole of the target area remained so poor that eventually the attack had to be postponed until further notice. We flew back to Falaise, where we continued to wait for an improvement in the weather throughout all of 14 and 15 August.

It was not until the early hours of 16 August that we received orders to stand by. The weather was still murky and overcast when we took off at first light for Picauville. There I double-checked our availability figures for the coming operation. Two 7. Staffel aircraft were missing. Schairer, the Staffelkapitän, reported that he had issued a couple of his Leutnants with late passes to attend a theatre performance being put on by a troop entertainments company in Caen. They were supposed to have returned by 02.00 hours, but were still not back when the Staffel took off. I told him they were to report to me after the mission.

I went over the plan of attack with my Staffelkapitäne one last time. After making rendezvous with our fighter escort, we would first head for Ventnor on the Isle of Wight. Shortly after we had passed over the radio station Skambraks and his 8. Staffel were to peel off and dive on the station from north to south. This would allow them to dip below the cliffs immediately upon recovery and retire out to sea at low level. Hopefully, the clifftop Flak would be unable to depress their guns far enough to shoot at them.

Meanwhile, the rest of the Gruppe would continue on to Lee-on-Solent and carry out its attack on the various targets pinpointed there by our aerial reconnaissance. After bombing we would head south at low level, form ourselves into a *Sauhaufen* and then hedge-hop across the Isle of Wight. I stressed to Skambraks that his target was the fighter control and transmitter building: the 'heart' of the radio station. 'Any questions?' – 'All clear!' The Staffelkapitäne made their way back to the dispersal areas to impart these final details to their crews. Then they went to readiness to await the order to take off, which still hadn't come through yet.

A couple of Ju 87s suddenly appeared low over the horizon to the southeast. They obviously had 'all the stops out' and were approaching fast. It was the two missing 7. Staffel pilots. They landed and taxied to their dispersal area where they were hurriedly armed and refuelled. Now 7. Staffel was all present and correct as well.

The operation got the green light at last. We finally took off at 13.00 hours, climbed to the rendezvous point and joined up with the other Stuka units and our force of escorting fighters. Everyone was ready and in position at the appointed time – except for StG 2. Where on earth had they got to? Too late to worry about that now. The Stukas had taken up formation and were already heading north from the assembly point towards their assigned targets. Still no sign of Dinort and his StG 2. His fighter escort could not hang around any longer, otherwise they would start to run short of fuel. They therefore opted to attach themselves to our StG 1.

Protected by more fighters than we had ever seen before, we reached the target area without incident. We flew over Ventnor. As ordered, Skambraks and his Staffel turned away, diving steeply towards their target. The transmitting station disappeared in the explosions of their bombs. A huge cloud of smoke and debris climbed high into the sky behind them as the Stukas hugged the surface of the water, racing their shadows back out over the Channel.

Soon we too were over our objective: Lee-on-Solent. Attack! We also managed to place our bombs bang on target. After recovery I throttled back, gathering the Gruppe together again at low level as we set course southwards. We first had to cross a narrow stretch of water before reaching the Isle of Wight. A small warship, possibly a torpedo boat or coastal defence vessel, lay ahead of us off to starboard. It was hosing up an awful lot of Flak. The gunners' aim was good and their fire was getting much too close for comfort.

One of my Ju 87s broke away from the gaggle. It veered off to starboard and made straight for the warship, gaining a little height as it did so. Banking slightly, it flew directly across the vessel. There was a large explosion on the forecastle and the Flak fell silent. By this time we were over the Isle of Wight and were beginning to race low across the first fields. From their rear cockpits our gunners reported seeing the ship 'apparently sinking' in the water behind us.

How had this been possible? It later transpired that Oberleutnant Heinze, the Kapitän of 9. Staffel, had forgotten to arm his bombs prior to diving on Lee-on-Solent and they had thus failed to release. Then as we were retiring, he saw the chance to make amends by carrying out a solo bombing run on the enemy warship. It was successful and the Gruppe got away unscathed.

We encountered no further Flak as we flew across the Isle of Wight. In fact, there were no defensive measures of any kind. The farmers working in the fields waved up at us, naturally assuming that we were friendly. It was only as we passed close overhead that they recognized the crosses on our aircraft. We could almost see their joy turn to terror as they threw themselves under cover. But why bother to hide? We weren't going to do them any harm.

During the return flight across the Channel we saw a large formation of Ju 87s high above us heading towards England. Could that possibly be Dinort and his Geschwader? Surely not! Not now that the enemy had been fully alerted and had put every fighter he'd got into the air – while ours were already running out of fuel and having to make for home! But Dinort – if that's who it was – was sticking rigidly to his course, even though he was totally devoid of fighter cover. We could only hope that by the time he arrived 'over there' the enemy fighters would also be on the ground refuelling too.

We landed back at Falaise at 15.09 hours. 8. Staffel's machines had all touched down safely some time earlier. The Geschwaderkommodore, who had flown on the operation with us, was also back safe and sound. Mission accomplished! That was just the way we liked it.

But, unfortunately, not every Stuka unit had escaped as lightly as us. StG 2, in particular, had suffered disproportionately high losses. Because of a breakdown in communications, Dinort had based his entire operational plan on the wrong times for assembly and attack. His Geschwader had nonetheless managed to carry out a successful attack on its assigned targets, but had then become caught up in a series of ferocious and costly battles with enemy fighters. Sigel's I./StG 76 had also sustained casualties, two of his aircraft and crews having failed to return.

That evening Oberleutnant Skambraks came up to me, clicking his heels together as he stiffened to an exaggeratedly overdone position of attention:

Herr Hauptmann, beg to report that the whole of 8. Staffel has been shot down by the enemy!

'What sort of nonsense is this?' I asked. Skambrak's face creased into a grin as he explained:

I've just heard it from the radio intercept boys. The British have released details of the Stuka attack on Ventnor transmitting station. Apparently it was put out of action for a short while, but all the attacking aircraft were shot down! That trick of disappearing below the cliffs worked a treat. They didn't spot us climbing away and re-forming out to sea, so they must have assumed that we'd all gone into the drink!'

'In that case, may I offer my heartiest congratulations! It just goes to show – you've got to keep coming up with new ideas if you want to stay ahead in this game!'

The two Leutnants who had overstayed their late passes in Caen also reported to me. As our take-off from Picauville had been delayed by the weather, they had managed to catch up with us and fly the mission – and fly it well, in fact, as if by showing that little bit of extra dash and daring they could somehow make up for their earlier transgression. Now they stood before me, their guilty consciences written all over their faces. They knew that I was obliged to hand out some form of punishment. But was that *really* necessary?

Did I have to punish this exemplary young pair of Stuka pilots, who had always given of their best on every operation – men on whom I could depend, pilots I could rely upon to carry out every order I gave them – just because of one single lapse? I was fully conscious of my responsibilities for maintaining discipline within the Gruppe and for ensuring the proper behaviour of my officers. But I felt that I knew these two well enough to be able to come up with some sort of sensible solution. I reminded them of the fact that absence without leave when on operations was an automatic court martial offence (something they were all too aware of themselves). Then I dismissed them, saying that I would consider the facts carefully and decide whether their case could be dealt with as an internal disciplinary matter.

I left them to stew in their own juice for several days before ordering them to report to my office in service dress. 'I hope you have both thought long and hard about your misdemeanour over these past few days,' I said. They assured me that they had. 'Very well, in that case you can look upon the time thus spent as being "morally confined to quarters". You have therefore served your sentence and, as far as I am concerned, the matter is now over and forgotten. But if it happens again I'll nail your hides to the wall! Dismiss!' Freed from the weight on their shoulders, they couldn't get out of the door fast enough!

Seen against the background of a world at war, is this one minor incident worth mentioning? It had certainly caused me quite a headache at the time. My actions had not been correct, nor did they accord with accepted military procedure. They would not have been found anywhere within service regulations, no matter how liberally one chose to interpret those august pages. But I was convinced in my own mind that you could only get the utmost performance out of a body of men if they had the utmost confidence and trust in each other. And that trust started at the top. It presupposed that a commanding officer would, if it were at all within his power, take it upon himself to deal with any subordinate who transgressed. In other words, keep it in the family and – to use the rather coarse military expression common at the time – 'wipe his arse for him!'

And, on this occasion, it *had* been within my power. In fact, all infractions were handled within the Gruppe as far as possible. For example, each crew had its own particular aircraft, and if a pilot accidentally damaged his machine – through a moment's inattention while taxiing, say – then he would be 'punished' accordingly. After it had been repaired, he would have to let another crew, whose own aircraft was unserviceable for some reason, fly 'his' machine for one mission. Despite all the rigours and dangers associated with our operations, such measures proved remarkably effective. They hit home where it hurt most: at the deep-rooted honour of a true 'Stuka man'. But, at the same time, they left no disciplinary black mark on his record.

At given intervals every unit's punishment register had to be presented to higher authority for inspection. I presented mine: empty pages! Amazed query from on high: How come empty pages? Answer from me: Our unit's discipline is in excellent order. And so it was. Our superiors had ample opportunity to assure themselves of that fact – they inspected us often enough. I'd be the first to admit that my men were no angels, of course. But I never needed to wield the big stick.

It was about this time that Leutnant Stoll-Berberich joined us. He was posted to our Gruppe from StG 2 after having been the only pilot in his Staffel to return uninjured from Dinort's disastrous cross-Channel foray of 16 August. An outstanding personality, he gave no indication of being in the least affected by what must have been a traumatic experience. On every one of his missions with us he was to display the courage and daring, combined with a confidence in his own abilities, that was the hallmark of a good Stuka pilot. (Egon Stoll-Berberich, born 17 June 1913 in Gera/Thüringia, would continue to fly with the Gruppe until the war's end. In 1943 the then Hauptmann Stoll-Berberich was appointed Staffelkapitän of 7./StG 1. On 29 February 1944, the day of his 1,000th combat mission, he was awarded the Knight's Cross.)

Operation 'Seelöwe' [Sealion], the planned invasion of England, was by now rapidly approaching. Preparations by all branches of the Wehrmacht were in full swing and our command, VIII. Fliegerkorps, was standing ready on the Channel coast.

On 24 August my Gruppe was temporarily attached to Oberstleutnant Dinort's Stukageschwader 2. Part of our time was spent at readiness, just in case enemy convoys started venturing into the Channel again. But we were also allowed plenty of time off for training – practice dive-bombing and machine-gun firing against ground targets – in order to give our newer and younger crews the opportunity to get used to supporting the Army in the field: the sort of operations that we could soon expect to be flying over southern England.

There was a nice surprise waiting for me on 27 August. The officers had secretly arranged for a military band to come and serenade me on my birthday. I was speechless! It was my twenty-seventh birthday. I was not especially noted for my shyness, but as I listened to the music being played in my honour I found myself at first overcome with embarrassment. It was quickly dispelled by the genuine joy on the faces of all those present. They were clearly delighted that their 'little surprise' had worked. And it made me realize that their gift was far from little. It could hardly have been bigger: it was an expression of their comradely trust and confidence in me. I felt moved beyond words. It made the loneliness of command, the inevitable burden of every unit CO, that much easier to bear. I decided there and then that it was a fine tradition. And naturally there was a party to follow (an equally fine tradition!).

On 28 August there was to be a dive-bombing exercise against a sea target moored off the coast at Deauville, HQ of VIII. Fliegerkorps. All of StG 2's Gruppen were involved. As a trial counter-measure against enemy fighter attack, something that had to be reckoned with during any operation against England, part of the brief for the exercise called for the pilots of each Gruppe to dive closely one behind the other in order to keep the formations as tight and compact as possible.

A thick haze hid the horizon to seaward. I therefore led my Gruppe towards the target by flying parallel to the coastline. This would give the younger, more inexperienced of my crews something to orientate on. We attacked the dummy target close together as ordered. As I was recovering from my dive and starting to climb away, I saw to my horror two of my Ju 87s plunge almost vertically into the sea! What had happened? I realized almost immediately that the two machines must have collided during the dive. One of the gunners had managed to bail out at the last moment. The two pilots, Oberleutnant Wolfgang Kathe and Leutnant Josef Mühlthaler, and the other gunner, Obergefreiter Georg Zeuler, had all been killed. And this on a training exercise! Again I asked myself, how could we prevent such accidents from happening?

The best solution was obviously practice, practice and yet more practice. But there were strict limits as to just how much flying practice we could put in now. Most of the time we were being held at readiness. We were thus forced to fall back on an altogether more basic procedure in an effort to help our youngsters. On those days when flying was scrubbed, every pilot spent half-an-hour sitting in the cockpit of his aircraft going through a typical mission in his mind – 'flying' it in theory, so to speak. Admittedly, it didn't bring much material benefit, but it got the pilot used to his 'office'; the place where he belonged, the focus of all his thoughts and actions when in combat.

I put in my own half-hours too, of course, and I must say that I found them extremely useful: thirty minutes, completely undisturbed, my thoughts concentrated solely on what I could do to make the next operation safer and more successful, how best I could meet all the possible situations that might suddenly confront me.

29 August 1940 was another day of celebration. I had the pleasure of presenting a number of well-earned decorations to members of my Gruppe. The whole unit

was drawn up on parade under the fruit trees on one side of the field. The recipients' names were read out and they took several paces forward. Men with whom I had flown more than sixty times against the enemy, men who had carried out their missions courageously and successfully, despite the many dangers and often in the face of almost insuperable difficulties. Now I had the privilege of awarding each of them the Iron Cross, First Class, in recognition of their selfless devotion to duty.

That same afternoon we had a high-ranking visitor. Generaloberst Milch, the Quartermaster-General of the Luftwaffe, arrived in his Fieseler Storch for a brief round of talks. They were mainly to do with technical matters and the question of supplies. What did we think of the Ju 87, for example? It was the slowest combat aircraft flying on operations, that's what. Without fighter protection of our own, we stood little real chance against enemy fighters. We would naturally have preferred a machine that handled like a fighter, for then we could have looked after ourselves if we came under attack. But given adequate fighter cover, we were not too badly off with the Ju 87. It was robust and manoeuvrable, yet simple enough in construction for our mechanics to maintain high serviceability rates.

But why were so few Ju 87s being built? We could hardly ever get replacement machines quickly enough to make good our losses in short order. And was there any truth in the rumours we had heard about Ju 87 production being discontinued altogether? No decision had yet been taken on that, but those in the know had high hopes for the twin-engined, single-seat Henschel Hs 129, which had been conceived from the outset as a ground-attack aircraft, was currently undergoing trials, and was expected to replace the Ju 87 in front-line service.

And what did we think of the new automatic recovery system that was now being installed in production Ju 87s? Not a lot, was the short answer to that. It was useless on operations, as it couldn't be manually overridden. We didn't want it, didn't need it, and had it disconnected on all our new machines the moment they were delivered. Once the enemy's Flak gunners cottoned on to the fact that every one of us was recovering and climbing away at exactly the same height and at exactly the same angle they would have had an absolute field day. During this most vulnerable phase of our attack we needed full tactical freedom of movement, which is why we preferred to fly by hand. This enabled us to twist and turn in all directions and thus gave us a much better chance of being able to dodge whatever Flak was being thrown at us.

After a few words with several other officers of the Gruppe, the Generaloberst had to take his leave of us. A flying visit in every sense.

For some time now we had enjoyed the benefit of having had two Flughafen-betriebskompanien [airfield servicing companies], at our disposal: one permanent and one temporary. Attached to flying units, it was the job of such companies to look after the formers' needs at whatever airfield or landing ground they were currently occupying. But on 6 August our temporary supporting company, 5.FBK/StG 2, had been returned to its parent Geschwader. In its place we were now instructed to establish a second permanent airfield servicing company of our own. This we designated 2.FBK/186 (to keep it in line with our first company, which was still known under its original naval designation as 1.FBK/186). The new company began operating on 5 September. During any future transfers, one company would thus be able to move to the new airfield as early as possible prior to our arrival in order to get it ready for us, leaving the second to follow on after it had completed whatever clearing-up work remained to be done on the field we had just vacated.

The missions of 16 and 18 August against enemy airfields and radar stations along England's southern coastline had inflicted prohibitive losses on some of our Stukagruppen. As a consequence, no further Stuka operations had been flown since the latter date. No worthwhile shipping targets had showed their faces in the Channel, and the major industrial targets in Britain were beyond the range of our Ju 87s. In contrast to our inactivity, the bomber and fighter units were flying operations almost non-stop.

We, in the meantime, had reverted to training. Our losses were replaced by new personnel. Individual crews from each of the three Staffeln, plus some members of ground staff, were given short periods of home leave. But the Gruppe continued to be held at operational readiness for Operation Seelöwe, the cross-Channel invasion, for which the Army and Navy were still busily making preparations.

It was during this period of comparative quiet that I began to occupy myself by compiling a list of the Gruppe's pilots, the number of missions each had flown, and the names of those who had been transferred to other units. The basic details are reproduced here in Appendices 1 and 2. I hope they will prove of some interest to the reader by showing the relatively limited number of flying personnel who made up the complement of an operational Stukagruppe – not forgetting, of course, the ground crews, our two airfield servicing companies and our signals platoon.

On 15 September 1940 III./StG 1's temporary attachment to Stukageschwader 2 and VIII. Fliegerkorps came to an end. We were transferred from Falaise in Normandy to St-Pol-sur-Ternoise, some 40km south of St. Omer in the Pas-de-Calais, where we were reunited with our parent Geschwader. There were smiles and handshakes all round when I reported back to our old Kommodore, Oberst-leutnant Hagen. The chain of command was now as follows:

Luftflottenkommando 2:	Generalfeldmarschall Kesselring
II. Fliegerkorps:	General Loerzer
Jagdfliegerführer 2 (Jafü 2):	General Osterkamp
Sturzkampfgeschwader 1:	Oberstleutnant Hagen
III./StG 1 comprising:	7.–9. Staffeln
	1. and 2. FBK/186
	Luftnachrichtenzug III./1

We had already reconnoitred St-Pol and an advance party had been sent ahead to prepare the field for our arrival. As it was an established forward landing ground, a station staff was already *in situ*. Personnel were quartered in private billets in the small township of St-Pol-sur-Ternoise. Scattered around the edges of the field itself there were only a few tents and wooden huts, which were used as ops and readiness rooms and the like, and for the storage of equipment.

While we were settling in and making ourselves comfortable Oberleutnant der Reserve Schellhase revealed his hitherto hidden talents as an 'organizer'. In civil life one of the editors of a large Munich newspaper, Schellhase had been posted to our Gruppenstab as a 'special-duties' officer [O.z.b.V.]. One evening he reported to me that in the local railway station he had discovered an empty goods train, complete with locomotive, that had apparently escaped the notice of 'Dorpmüller' – by whom he meant Dr.-Ing. E.H.J. Dorpmüller, the Reich's Minister of Transport and head of the German State Railways.

He had also managed to locate the train's regular French crew at their homes in St-Pol. Apparently, if we didn't broadcast the fact, they were perfectly willing to drive the train for us should we ever need it. But what good was that? They couldn't simply get up steam and go – they wouldn't know what other traffic was on the tracks. All taken care of, Schellhase assured me. They would check ahead from station to station to see if the route was clear. You could never tell when such a thing might come in handy. All I had to do was turn a blind eye and keep it in mind. That I could manage. And, wouldn't you know it, 'our' train actually did come in very handy on one occasion.

As a precaution against low-level attacks by enemy aircraft, we had received orders to camouflage our machines and disperse them about the perimeter of the field in brick-built blast pens. A very sensible and intelligent move. The only thing that stopped us from complying with these instructions was our total lack of brick-built blast pens! Their construction would be the responsibility of station permanent staff, who were more than happy to have the work carried out, but were unable to do so as they didn't have the necessary materials. Their attempts to obtain the supplies that would be needed were as persistent as they were unsuccessful.

Oberleutnant Schellhase decided it was time that he stepped into the ring. Without informing anyone, he rounded up the French crew and set off in 'our' train for a large depot run by the Organisation Todt – the Reich's labour force – which was stacked high with construction materials of every kind. That same evening the train, fully loaded with building materials, pulled quietly into the siding close to our field. Schellhase came to me to report its arrival. Astonished, I asked him where on earth he had got all the stuff from. What he told me made quite a story.

Apparently, he had called on the services of the French footplate crew to raise steam and clear the journey times and routes with the stations along the way. Accompanied by a sizeable working party and armed with a large briefcase (full of assorted bottles of spirits), Schellhase rolled up to the heavily guarded Organisation Todt depot. The train was waved straight through the main entrance without any questions being asked. After giving the working party instructions on what materials were needed, Schellhase marched off in search of the official in charge. He kept this worthy engaged in conversation, helped along by the contents of his briefcase, while the wagons were loaded. After a while, however, the depot chief began to smell a rat.

Schellhase was forced to come clean. But his explaining that we had been ordered to build dispersal pens for our aircraft didn't interest the Organisation Todt in the slightest. Pointing out that the material could hardly be put to any better or more important use didn't cut any ice either. The head of the depot demanded that the train be unloaded immediately, otherwise he would prevent its departure by force of arms.

It was at this point in his account that Oberleutnant Schellhase had the grace to look a trifle sheepish. The exchange had become somewhat heated by this time, he told me, and when the Organisation Todt official had threatened the use of arms, he admitted that he may have exaggerated things a little. He had responded by saying that he had a radio on board the train and was in constant contact with our Stukagruppe. If there *were* any firing, our aircraft would be overhead in a matter of minutes. It would be far more sensible if he, the depot head, simply let the train depart and forgot about the whole affair. Under strong protest, he was allowed to leave with the train still loaded and got back to us without further incident.

The building material was unloaded and the empty train then sent off to Dorpmüller's railwaymen, where it really belonged in the first place. As far as we were concerned, it had more than served its purpose. Everyone on the field wired in and the brick blast pens were quickly built. Within a few days our aircraft were safely tucked away in them as ordered. But we were nonetheless relieved when it became evident that the Organisation Todt people were keeping the matter quiet. They were apparently more understanding than Schellhase had given them credit for – who knows, they may even have seen the funny side of it too.

The whole enterprise had been far from proper and correct, of course. Legally speaking, we had well and truly overstepped the mark. Our actions had hardly set a good example, but they must be viewed in the light of the times. They also provide a perfect illustration of a higher command's issuing an order while failing to ensure that it could be carried out. For this is exactly what had happened here. We had been given an order, and felt fully justified in falling back on our own devices to comply with it.

From 2 to 15 October my gunner, Feldwebel Baudisch, and I had a welcome spot of home leave. In order to remain readily available to return to the unit if suddenly called upon, we flew in our own Ju 87, via Münster, to Magdeburg-South. There we anchored our machine as per regulations – the further away from the front, the stricter the enforcement of regulations! – and went through the necessary formalities with flying control. Then the leave proper could begin. My wife had come to the airfield to pick me up. Our joy at seeing each other again need hardly be described. We drove to my parents-in-law's place at Bad Salzelmen where my wife was now living with our son, Rainer. With their customary loving kindness, my in-laws had once again pulled out all the stops to make my period of leave as enjoyable as possible for the pair of us. Now nearly eighteen months old, our son was no longer a baby. He had grown into a delightful little fellow that a young father could really get to know and bond with.

Those were days and hours of unalloyed pleasure and delight, even though we knew they were short in number. The war and all that it entailed seemed to fade into the dim distant past. Or perhaps it was simply that my recent experiences at the front were making the present that much more real and intense. The progress of the war was discussed, of course. I was asked about our anti-shipping operations in the Channel. My reply was that we 'sewage-workers' (a tongue-in-cheek nickname that we had given ourselves; the German word for channel and sewer being the same) had been having quite a hard time of it of late.

My wife accepted this with her usual air of equanimity. She clearly trusted in my abilities. Full of confidence, her only comment was: 'Well, you've all been taught how to fly. I'm sure you're doing it properly.' Not a hint of concern in her voice, even though she must have known that as a Stuka pilot I could find myself in some very nasty situations. With her womanly instinct she understood how to isolate me from those larger cares by immersing me in the day-to-day worries of running a home and family. Did she realize, I wondered, just how much of a help and comfort I found that?

On 15 October my leave came to an end. We said our farewells in the hope that the war would soon be over. We didn't know what was brewing on the wider political stage. It seemed fairly certain, however, that, after Britain's rejection of Hitler's peace offer back in July, an armed invasion of southern England was inevitable. But then what? Those at home were still fervently hoping for peace.

Towards evening Baudisch and I landed back at St-Pol. The Gruppe hadn't flown any operations during our absence. I was told the latest news: Operation Seelöwe had been postponed until the spring of 1941! But would an invasion still be possible by then? Time was on the enemy's side. He would be certain to use it to strengthen his coastal defences. We, on the other hand, would have little more to offer than the improvised preparations that had already been put in place. For the Gruppe it meant, first and foremost, settling in for the winter at St-Pol.

We had to come up with something to keep the men occupied during their off-duty hours. Oberleutnant Schellhase, our 'organizer', was already on the job. As the film shows put on by the mobile welfare entertainments people were extremely few and far between, he was busy setting up a permanent cinema for us. In a dump of captured enemy material he had already unearthed some projection equipment, which, he assured me, needed only a few replacement parts to get it working again. He had 'borrowed' a couple of knowledgeable French prisoners-of-war from the Kommandant of a nearby POW camp who could see to this and who would then remain with us as projectionists.

The only thing was, it would mean a trip to Paris to obtain the necessary spare parts. Schellhase set off for the capital with the two Frenchmen. They arrived at about midday and he gave his two prisoners until the following morning to get the parts they said were needed. On the dot of 08.00 hours the next morning they turned up at the agreed meeting place, complete with the parts and grateful for having been able to spend a few hours with their families. For the remainder of our time at St-Pol the pair were carried on the Gruppe's strength as 'attached surplus to establishment'.

A disused old cinema in St-Pol was quickly put back into shape. Schellhase managed to get hold of so many films that we were able to put on one or two shows a day throughout the long winter months. Local Army personnel also became regular visitors. For their part, the Army units in the area combined forces to establish a sports hall and gymnasium, which proved a popular attraction for our men.

On 28 October I received a telephone call from the Army in Abbeville asking for our help. Apparently a stray British barrage balloon had drifted across the Channel and its trailing anchor cable was destroying all the telephone lines in its path. Could we perhaps come and shoot it down? Of course we could. In fact, I decided that I could do with a little flying, not to say target practice myself. I hadn't been in the air for the past fortnight. I soon spotted the rogue balloon. Heading straight for it, I opened up with my two wing machine guns. My salvo hit the target dead centre – not difficult to do with something that size. But I had ventured so close that I suddenly found the side of the balloon looming up like a giant silver wall right in front of me. Heaving on the stick with all my might, I just managed to avoid it. The balloon had crumpled and was descending to the earth in flames – and I had very nearly gone with it! Maybe I was even rustier than I thought.

The sidelining of the Channel-based Stuka units was, in fact, giving us real cause for concern. While the rest of the Luftwaffe was locked in combat against England, we had been condemned to virtual inactivity. As our fighters lacked the range to escort the Kampfgruppen on their longer missions inland, even our bombers had had to abandon their daylight attacks. The growing strength of Britain's fighter defences was taking too heavy a toll of their numbers. Now they were being forced to operate under cover of darkness, flying one or more missions per night.

This prompted us to consider the idea of mounting attacks by individual Stukas – manned by experienced crews – on bright moonlit nights or during those days when the weather forecasts promised sufficient cloud cover. We realized that such tactics were not likely to produce any hugely spectacular results. But we thought the possibility of an occasional success, not to mention the nuisance value alone, warranted giving it a go. After discussing the matter thoroughly with my Staffelkapitäne, we put in an official request suggesting that a small detachment should be moved up closer to the Channel coast to carry out service trials.

Instead of which, on 29 October, we were ordered to join forces with II./StG 1 for a feint attack (dropping no bombs) on Folkestone. The intention was to lure up the defending British fighters so that our own fighters could get to grips with them. We took off at 17.25 hours and flew the mission according to plan, but the enemy failed to rise to the bait. We duly landed back at St-Pol at 18.30 hours having seen neither hide nor hair of the opposition. Was it the restraint shown by Britain's fighters on this occasion, or was it some other reason that persuaded the powers-that-be to send us off on another Stuka mission three days later – and a proper one this time?

On 1 November the Gruppe received orders to attack an enemy convoy in the outer reaches of the Thames Estuary. We were to be provided with a strong fighter escort of two full Jagdgeschwader, those commanded by Mölders and Galland. We based our plan of attack on the formula we had worked out back in the summer. The separate Ketten would seek out the biggest ships in the convoy as follows: 7. Staffel the southern third, 8. Staffel the middle third and 9. Staffel the northern third of the convoy. We would approach from the north, carry out our attack, and then retire at low level while forming up into a *Sauhaufen*. I would fly at reduced speed, changing course slightly now and again, to allow everyone to close up as quickly as possible.

We lifted off at 14.30 hours. At the prearranged rendezvous point our fighters, under the command of Mölders, took up their escort duties. Protected as never before, we set course for the target area. But today the enemy fighters put in an appearance – on time and in numbers. Dogfights were breaking out all around us, as well as above our heads. Wherever you looked: here a fighter going down in flames or trailing smoke, there a pilot slowly descending by parachute. Once in a while a single Spitfire would manage to penetrate the ring of fighters surrounding us. But within seconds one or more of our Me 109s would be sitting on his tail and he promptly lost all interest in pressing home his attack.

The shipping lane leading down from the northeast into the Thames Estuary was crowded with more convoy traffic than we had ever seen in our lives. Both inbound and outbound, vessels of every shape and size as far as the eye could see. Thanks to our excellent fighter cover, each Kette was able to spread out and look things over before launching its attack. Consequently there was hardly a bomb dropped that failed to hit its intended target. Our new tactics were paying off handsomely. Throttling right back after my recovery, I started to weave away at low level to give those behind me the chance to gather together to form the gaggle.

It was at this point that things began to go slightly awry. One of the younger pilots had recovered well after his dive, but had then lost sight of his Kette leader in the haze that hung low over the water. Assuming him to be already far ahead on his way home, the youngster poured on the gas to chase after him. The result was that he himself shot into the lead, while the rest of the gaggle tried to keep up with him. It took quite a while before he was safely rounded up and we all settled down again. Fortunately, only one fighter had tried to attack us while we were sorting ourselves out and we managed to drive him off.

All of our machines returned safely to base. Each Kette (of three aircraft) had claimed a ship sunk. The new tactics of attacking the enemy vessels from astern had proved a success insofar as no machine had been damaged by the explosions of the bombs from the aircraft ahead of it. A few machines had collected one or two bullet holes, but these were quickly patched up.

At debriefing it proved somewhat difficult to assess the true results of the operation, as we had no reliable way of properly estimating the sizes of the ships we had attacked. The best we could do was to go by the number of cargo hatches the vessel had. Each hatch and cargo boom was reckoned to represent around 1,000 grt. This rule of thumb proved reasonably accurate. The only problem was that, in the heat of battle, the individual crews' observations did not always tally

– although this was hardly surprising when you consider everything a pilot had to watch for and worry about during those few vital split seconds of the actual attack. After evaluating all the crew reports, however, III./StG 1 felt confident in claiming 21,000 grt of enemy shipping for no loss!

This was tremendously encouraging. But our success was due in no small part to the excellent fighter protection we had enjoyed. Without it we would scarcely have been able to fight our way through to the convoy, let alone attack it. The fighter pilots too were pleased with the results of their day's work.

The only thing that was still giving us a headache was that period immediately following the attack – between recovery from the dive and assembling into the gaggle for the flight back to base. How could we prevent the Gruppe from becoming completely disorganized, such as had happened today, while bearing in mind that we also needed to protect the younger, less experienced crews while so doing? As chance would have it, it was an order from High Command, which had just come in, that pointed the way to a solution.

The order in question decreed that, due to the recent high rates of loss among unit leaders – and the increasing difficulties in finding suitable replacements – such leaders were no longer to fly at the head of their formations, but were to take up station in the middle of their units and lead from there. My first reaction to this, of course, was: just how do these people imagine a Stuka unit is led into action? We relied entirely on visual signals, which I could only give from the front.

Otherwise, except in cases of emergency, we observed strict radio silence, as the enemy was constantly monitoring our frequencies. The shortest message relayed over the air could be enough to warn the enemy defences of our presence. This had happened to us on one occasion during the campaign in France when we found ourselves on the same frequency as a French unit. No sooner had one of our pilots pressed his transmitter switch and spoken a few words than we heard an excited Gallic voice in our headphones: 'Alloh-Alloh! Shtookah! Shtookah!' After that it was just a matter of time before we had enemy fighters on our necks. And things were not likely to be any different during our operations over England.

Of one thing I was certain, however. I could only lead my Gruppe properly if I was flying at its head. So what about that last mission? As we withdrew at low level from the target area, things had very nearly fallen apart simply because the pilots couldn't recognize my machine and didn't know which aircraft they were supposed to be following. This made me realize that not only did I have to fly at the front of the formation, but also that I would have to apply some form of distinctive markings to my aircraft – and preferably get my Staffelkapitäne to do the same – so that all crews could see who to formate on when assembling the gaggle.

I talked things over with my Staffelkapitäne and we decided that the backs of the undercarriage legs and wheel spats of our machines would be painted a bright yellow. My Iolanthe would have both legs yellow, theirs only one each. Every pilot behind us would thus be able to pick out our aircraft and formate accordingly. If anyone overtook a yellow-legged machine he would automatically be on a charge. And if our additional markings attracted the attention of enemy fighters – so much the better. We stood far more of a chance against them than our younger crews did. My Staffelkapitäne were fully in agreement with these proposals. They thought they were the most sensible solution and the orders were duly given to paint our machines.

Naturally, I had to submit a report to our Geschwaderkommodore, Oberstleutnant Hagen, setting out the measures we were proposing to take. Or perhaps it might be more accurate to say that 'I broke it to him gently' that we had already carried them out! I knew that he regarded the tactical leadership of a unit as a matter that was best left in the hands of the unit's leader. It came as no surprise, therefore, that he gave tacit approval to our scheme. He must surely have been aware that it was based on operational experience.

On 8 November we were again sent out against convoys in the Thames Estuary. Take-off was at 14.00 hours. And again we had two complete Jagdgeschwader to escort us, this time under the overall command of Galland. Everything went as planned, just as before. The Thames presented a similar picture, dogfights were erupting all around us, but our fighters again shepherded us safely to the target.

Our new tactics paid off handsomely. Each Kette claimed an enemy vessel. And regrouping after the attack went without a hitch. As I was throttled well back, the other aircraft quickly caught up with me. To left and right of me pilots were 'sideslipping' to shed their excess speed and not shoot past those clearly visible yellow legs of mine. The *Sauhaufen* was speedily and smoothly formed. Now and again a Spitfire would try to get at the Ju 87s flying on its outer edges, but the enemy pilots were thwarted by the constantly changing composition of our deliberately fluid formation. They found themselves having to break away before they could get in an effective burst for fear of being shot down themselves.

We took a few bullet holes back to base with us, but all aircraft made it and none of the crews had been wounded. One of my wing fuel tanks had to be replaced. It had been quite severely damaged – probably by ship's Flak – but fortunately the tank's self-sealing rubber casing had prevented the fuel from escaping. This was just as well, for otherwise I would not have got home, as the target area had been at the very limit of our range. With a flying time of 1 hour and 47 minutes, we had had little enough fuel reserve as it was. We certainly could not have afforded to give any of it away.

The results of our bombing were once again carefully assessed on the strength of all the crews' combat reports. Today III./StG 1 had sunk some 24,000 grt of enemy shipping without loss to ourselves. And once again our fighters were happy with their day's performance. They had claimed a considerable number of kills, had delivered us to the target area and then brought us safely back again. Everything had gone exactly according to plan. It raised our spirits more than a little.

Three days later, on 11 November, we were ordered to the Thames Estuary for a third time. The Gruppe's twenty-one aircraft, all that we currently had serviceable, began taking off at 12.11 hours. Once again, our fighter escort could not be faulted. At first all went well. Long before arriving over the target area we could already see an unusually large number of big ships sailing in convoy along the northern side of the estuary.

But the enemy seemed to have put more fighters into the air today. Our escorts quickly became caught up in a constant succession of short but vicious dogfights, which then accompanied us all the way to the target. The Me 109s nonetheless managed to keep the Spitfires off our backs for most of the time, enabling us to mount our attack without too much interference. Aiming mostly for the larger vessels in the convoy, each Kette succeeded in hitting its chosen target.

Regrouping on the yellow legs of the lead machines for the flight back to base was also accomplished without undue difficulty. But it soon became apparent that the British fighters had already cottoned on to our new tactic of retiring in a fairly loose, fluid gaggle. While our own fighters were still fully engaged with the Spitfires that had been snapping at our heels throughout much of our approach run, a second and larger force of enemy fighters had been lying in wait for us. Now, when we were about five nautical miles north of Cape Margate – which was our name at the time for the North Foreland – they suddenly came boring in at low level to attack us! Despite our best efforts, we could not prevent one of our number falling victim to a Spitfire. In fact, when we landed back at 14.03 hours it was discovered that *two* of our machines were missing:

Nobody had seen what had happened to 9. Staffel's Unteroffizier Dr Heinrich Oesterreich from Schönau/Chemnitz and his gunner, Gefreiter Anton Sabinarz from Kamp-Lintfort/Düsseldorf. It was presumed that they had been shot down either during the run-up to the target or while diving on the convoy.

Unteroffizier Gerhard Schütz from Hamburg and his gunner, Obergefreiter Georg Brück from Essen, were the 7. Staffel crew that had fallen foul of the Spitfire off Cape Margate.

Once again we had had to suffer the loss of two relatively inexperienced crews, the very ones that we were trying so hard to support and protect until they had amassed sufficient operational know-how. Unteroffizier Dr Oesterreich had been on his seventh op; Unteroffizier Schütz his fourth. But let's face it, on that day's mission – given the length of time we had been in the air and the opposition we had faced – any one of us, even the most experienced, could have bought it.

It had also been a hard day for our escorting fighters. But if they hadn't done such a good job of protecting us, at least on the way in, our losses would undoubtedly have been a lot higher. As it was, the results arrived at during debriefing provided a certain amount of consolation: for the loss of two of their number, our twenty-one machines had sunk seven merchantmen totalling some 37,000 grt. These figures were included in our post-action report and were quoted in that evening's Wehrmacht communiqué, which announced: 'German Stuka units have sunk . . .'

That was a bit rich, we thought, as we listened to the broadcast – 'German Stuka units!' – those 'units' had in fact been no more than the twenty-one machines of our III./StG 1. Even so, we couldn't help feeling a certain pride in the fact that ours was the only Stukagruppe currently engaged by day against England, although we readily acknowledged the part played by our escorting fighters, without whose protection our missions would have been totally impossible.

The next day I visited the Geschwaderkommodore for our usual afternoon chat over a cup of coffee. Oberstleutnant Hagen had just returned from a meeting at Luftflottenkommando 2. He told me that the AOC Air Fleet had been extremely pleased with our previous day's report. He had sent out a reconnaissance aircraft to photograph the convoy before and after our attack. Examination of the pictures it had brought back had shown that seven vessels, totalling an estimated 37,000grt, were missing in the later photographs – exactly the figures we had claimed in our post-action report. Given the difficulty already mentioned of accurately judging a vessel's tonnage from the air – counting hatches and multiplying by a thousand! – it was a sheer fluke that our rule-of-thumb estimation and the official photographic interpretation of the evidence had tallied so precisely. But this didn't stop me from saying to the Kommodore: 'I hope you informed the AOC that we always take great pains to ensure that our reports are accurate.'

It was around now that the Jagdgeschwader commanded by Mölders was withdrawn from the front and returned to the homeland for rest and refit. At the same time an order went out to all those fighter units remaining on the Channel coast restricting the northernmost limit of their area of operations to Cape Margate. This meant that our highly successful attacks on enemy shipping using the far side of the Thames Estuary would no longer be possible. And, in fact, these were to come to an inglorious end on 14 November thanks entirely to a flawed operational order issued by Jafü 2 – Air Fleet 2's fighter commander – to whom we were directly subordinated.

It all began at about 11.00 hours on that date when I received a phone call from Jafü 2's ops officer ordering III./StG 1 to attack an enemy convoy reported to be heading northeast past Dover. Because of the range restriction imposed on our assigned fighter escort, however, we were not to proceed beyond Cape Margate. This then gave rise to an exchange that went roughly as follows:

'When and where was the enemy sighted, how many ships, what speed?'

'Formation of ships sighted off Dover at approximately 09.00 hours, bearing east at medium speed.'

'That means the convoy will already have passed Cape Margate before we can get to the target area. In which case request permission to pursue convoy and attack even if beyond Cape Margate.'

'Margate boundary not to be crossed under any circumstances!'

'Alternative target if the reported convoy is not found within the sea area specified?'

'Then attack other ships in sea area Dover–Margate.'

'No ships have sailed through that area by day for a long time.'

'If no ships sighted, alternative target Dover radio station.'

'If we fly as far as Margate and then detour back to Dover we'll have the entire British fighter force on our backs. Which Dover radio station is to be alternative target? We have target information sheets on three radio stations at Dover.'

'The one with the "mirror"!' (By mirror he meant radar array.)

'Which one is that?'

'We're not sure. Will try to find out and let you know prior to take-off. Otherwise, attack the largest radio station at Dover. Out!'

And that, I thought to myself on the quiet, has to be just about the sloppiest operational order we've ever been given. Such a thing would never have happened under VIII. Fliegerkorps. How on earth was I going to get my Gruppe through such a ridiculous mission as this? We would be parading about like a lot of aerial Aunt Sallies simply begging to be shot down by the enemy's air defences.

It was essential that I displayed my usual air of calm composure when briefing my Staffelkapitäne. But after ending by giving details of the alternative target, I did allow myself one additional comment. If we sighted any vessel at all south of Margate – even if it was just a rowing boat – I would sink it with the three machines of my Stabskette, and all other aircraft were then to return to base immediately with their bombs. Dover radio station was only to be attacked if no ship at all was found.

We took off at 14.22 hours with nineteen aircraft. At the prearranged rendez-vous point we met up with our escorting fighters. They accompanied us northwards until the entire sea area as far as Margate was clearly visible. As I had feared, there was not a single ship to be seen. We turned back and headed south, carefully searching the inshore waters as we went. Nothing! Not even my hoped-for rowing boat. Just the remains of an old wreck showing above the surface. We were familiar with this from earlier operations. The temptation to dump a few more bombs on it was great. But that was out of the question. There was a phrase for that kind of behaviour: cowardice in the face of the enemy. No, the Third Stuka One didn't turn tail. Nothing else for it then – alter course westwards and head for Dover.

There was a solid cloud base at 3,500 metres. We made our approach beneath it; perfect targets for the Dover Flak, which had a reputation for being both plentiful and accurate. Our escorting fighters were clearly aware of this too. They had retired out into mid-Channel well beyond the reach of Dover's gunners. This didn't bode at all well. They obviously wanted to watch the fireworks from a safe distance. We were getting closer to Dover now and were already well within range of the harbour's heavy Flak batteries. But still they held their fire!

I gave a warning to my gunner Baudisch: 'Keep your eyes open! That Flak's too quiet. It must mean there are fighters about!' And there they were. Squadron after squadron of Spitfires came sliding out of the cloud base directly ahead of us. As they approached us head-on we opened up on them with our wing machine guns. But they soared effortlessly past above our heads and began to curve in leisurely towards us for a stern attack. If we were going to bomb the radio station it had to be now or never.

Although we were not yet quite over the target, I gave the signal to start the dive. We went down at an angle of no more than 70 degrees, but the enemy fighters were already amongst us. How those much faster Spitfires managed to stay with us while diving and not overshoot was a complete mystery to me. Our attack, which I had been forced to launch in a hurry, had now degenerated into a complete shambles. Only a handful of my pilots managed actually to aim their bombs at the target – with very poor results – while the rest scattered theirs across the surrounding countryside as they twisted and turned in their attempts to shake off the attacking enemy fighters.

One Ju 87 could be seen going down in flames. The crew had bailed out and were floating earthwards under their parachutes. The Spitfires had the advantage over us, not only in speed, but now also in numbers as well. Each of us was having to fend off two or three enemy fighters simultaneously. At one point I had no fewer than five Spitfires milling around me. Was it my yellow legs that had attracted them? No time to worry about that now. The only consolation was that the odds couldn't get very much greater. The enemy pilots were already getting in each other's way every time they tried to attack me. If any more joined in they would be in real danger of colliding.

We had to have eyes in the back of our heads if we wanted to stay in one piece. I was pulling out all the stops: steep banks, low-speed turns – some even with my dive brakes momentarily extended – sudden climbs, violent skidding sideslips, dummy dives – everything and anything that I could think of to make it more difficult for the faster Spitfires to get in a good deflection shot. But despite all our efforts we couldn't avoid taking numerous hits. It must have been more than ten minutes – or did it just *seem* that long? – before our fighters appeared on the scene and began to wade in. Some relief at last! They'd left us to our own devices long enough this time. But without their intervention, belated as it was, our chances would have been almost nil. Now we were at least able to extricate ourselves from the massive dogfight that was developing and set course for home.

With our feathers well and truly plucked, we landed back at St-Pol at 15.31 hours. Two of our aircraft had been shot down over the British Isles. Three others had made it back across the Channel badly damaged and had forced-landed in France. Nearly every other machine was riddled with bullet holes. Only Oberleutnant Schairer, the Kapitän of 7. Staffel, had returned to base without taking a single hit. Although he had had two or three Spitfires snapping at his heels the whole time, he had somehow managed to avoid every burst fired at him. It was thought that the Gruppe had probably shot down two of its tormentors, but in all that confusion accurate observation had been well nigh impossible and their destruction was by no means certain. Our bombing results were zero. This made our losses, both from 9. Staffel, all the harder to bear:

> Oberleutnant der Reserve Otto Blumers from Heppenheim-an-der-Bergstrasse had been brought down in flames over Dover. He bailed out and was taken prisoner. His gunner, Gefreiter Willy Koch from Lippstadt/Westphalia, was unfortunately killed.
>
> Obergefreiter Herbert Dietmayer from Wartberg/Styria and his gunner, Obergefreiter Johann Schmidt from Dudweiler/Saar, were not seen again after the attack on Dover.

I submitted a full report on the débâcle to our Geschwaderkommodore and requested that he take the matter up with Jafü 2, stressing the fact that this was no way to conduct an operation. The following day Oberstleutnant Hagen and I travelled to Jafü 2 HQ determined to press home the point. General Osterkamp's welcome was friendly and his disarming confession – 'I readily admit, yesterday was an operational error on my part' – completely took the wind out of my sails.

He went on to explain that he had been at his forward command post up on the cliffs and was watching through the scissors telescope as the action above Dover unfolded. If he had been leading the Stuka unit, he said, he would have aborted the mission the moment the Spitfire squadrons appeared. That did it! I found myself letting fly after all, telling the general in no uncertain terms what I had been bottling up inside me since the previous day. If memory serves, my outburst went something like this:

> And just how do you imagine you would have managed that, Herr General? The Ju 87 is the slowest aircraft engaged in the present campaign. The enemy fighters have got nearly twice the speed we have. We couldn't just 'pack up and clear off', even if we had wanted to. And with our meagre armament we're dead ducks against a strong enemy force like yesterday's if our own fighters don't stay on top of things. We have been trained to attack our given targets no matter what the circumstances. But we have to go in fast, using the element of surprise whenever possible, and fly tactically to keep the enemy defences guessing.
>
> What we *can't* afford to do [I went on heatedly] is to stage a flypast along the English coast until every last enemy fighter has taken to the air – at least, not if our own supposed fighter escort doesn't stick close.

General Osterkamp had been listening to my tirade in understanding silence. As an experienced old fighter pilot and formation leader himself, he was no doubt fully aware of the therapeutic benefit of allowing an irate subordinate to 'let off steam' once in a while. He took due notice of my comments, and then very adroitly steered the discussion on to less contentious matters.

The last Stuka attack to be mounted against England by day had thus been a total failure. A failure in our eyes, moreover, that was due entirely to the shortcomings in the orders that had been issued to us prior to the mission. After 14 November we received no further operational orders from Jafü 2 – as they had insufficient fighters to provide us with an adequate escort, we were told. We took this latter with a large pinch of salt. To our minds, there were still enough fighters on hand to make the risks involved in cross-Channel missions worthwhile. Those fighters simply had to be employed in the correct tactical manner.

So what was to happen now? Were we supposed to sit on our backsides and let British shipping sail unhindered in and out of the Thames Estuary in broad daylight while the enemy's defences grew ever stronger? Had our leaders thrown in the sponge because the heavy losses being suffered during operations against England couldn't be made good quickly enough?

A few days later I was sitting with the Kommodore over our customary cup of afternoon coffee. He indicated an aerial reconnaissance photograph that he had brought back with him from a recent visit to Air Fleet HQ. Nicely framed, it was now hanging on the wall of his office. 'Take a good look at that,' Oberstleutnant Hagen said. I did so. It was an aerial shot of what appeared to be a large power station. 'What's the story behind this, then?' I asked. 'Air Fleet gave it to me. It's a "Knight's Cross target".' I thought I wasn't hearing right. 'You've got to be joking,' I said. '"Knight's Cross target"? Since when have there been "Knight's Cross targets"?'

Hagen explained: 'Well, you see, this picture shows the most important of London's major power stations. It's on the eastern edge of the city situated on the south bank of the Thames. Repeated attacks by high-level bombers have failed to knock it out. If it could be destroyed, much of London's electricity would be cut off and the city's armaments industry largely paralyzed. We're supposed to report on whether a Stuka attack would be at all feasible and, if so, what would be required to ensure a reasonable chance of success. What do you think?'

'To start with, I'm not all that keen on the phrase 'Knight's Cross target', Herr Oberstleutnant. It's never been part of any operational order in the past, thank God. But before saying any more, might I perhaps first be permitted to have a look at the maps and target information folders?'

The relevant documentation was placed at my disposal. The maps showed that, as our aircraft were not equipped to carry auxiliary fuel tanks, the target would be at the very limit of our Ju 87s' range. It could, however, just be reached if we flew a direct course there and back, and if the weather conditions were favourable. But any delays or time-loss – evasive action, an air engagement or the like – would reduce our chances of making it back across the Channel to almost nil.

I calculated that three or four direct hits from 500kg HE bombs should suffice to put the power station out of commission, at least for a while. If the attacking force was made up of nine experienced crews with proven bombing records, success, in my opinion, could almost be guaranteed – provided, that is, that the formation wasn't cut to pieces by enemy fighters before reaching the target. This didn't seem very likely, as we would no doubt be provided with a strong fighter escort and would be able to select a day of our own choosing, when we considered the weather for the operation to be just right. In short, it was a target that a Stuka unit flying a 'maximum effort' – or, to quote the exact term used in the official service manual *Air Operations*: 'at optimum operational capacity' – could expect to attack with every chance of success. After much careful consideration, I therefore reported it as such to the Kommodore:

III./StG 1 can attack the power station with good prospects of success. In view of the unusual nature of the operational orders governing this mission, however, the above statement should be made dependent upon the following conditions:

1: None of the crews taking part is to receive any special award or decoration. Reason: The operational morale of the crews remains unbroken; phrases such as 'Knight's Cross target' can only have a detrimental effect. If the destruction of this target is of such paramount importance, Air Fleet must issue their orders accordingly and these will then be carried out by the crews in the knowledge that they are fulfilling the military duties expected of them.

Furthermore:

2: Operation to be flown by nine volunteer crews – I am convinced that all crews will volunteer for the mission – to be selected by the Gruppen-kommandeur: Those most experienced and with good bombing records.

3: Operation to be led by the Gruppenkommandeur.

4: Orders from Air Fleet are to state clearly that this is to be a 'Maximum effort' operation. Reason: In the event of aircraft and crews failing to return, no subsequent accusations of irresponsibility or reckless leader-ship can be levelled at our Gruppe.

5: Fighter cover, within limits of available strengths and operational ranges, to be as requested by III./StG 1.

The Kommodore had been listening attentively. When I had finished he said: 'Regarding Point 3, Air Fleet has already issued instructions that the operation is not to be led by the Gruppenkommandeur. This is to avoid further losses among formation leaders, who are becoming increasingly hard to replace.'

That really was the last straw! And I pulled no punches in telling the Kommodore so:

Leadership of a unit in the air, and especially on a difficult operation such as this, *must* be in the hands of the person with the most experience. And in 'Third Stuka One' that person is the Gruppenkommandeur. I say this out of no sense of self-importance. I base my statement purely on the fact that I have personally led every mission the Gruppe has flown to date. And if this operation is considered too dangerous to risk losing me, I certainly will not ask one of my pilots to take my place!

I had built up quite a head of steam by this time, and ended by requesting that the Kommodore make my feelings on the matter crystal clear to Air Fleet. Oberstleutnant Hagen again showed complete understanding of my latest outburst. He forwarded my report on the feasibility of the operation, together with his own comments on the conditions I had laid down, to Air Fleet HQ . . .

. . . and we never heard another word about it! Why not? Cold feet, perhaps? Suddenly not so important any more? Did they have something else up their sleeve for us? As usual, we weren't told.

Bad weather and night operations

In the meantime our suggestion of conducting trials with single aircraft at night and under bad weather conditions had been given the go-ahead. We therefore transferred a small Sonderkommando up to Ostende-Steene on the Belgian coast. This 'special detachment', drawn from both II. and III./StG 1, consisted of several experienced crews and their supporting ground personnel, all of whom had volunteered to carry out the trials. Among them were Oberleutnants Schairer and Skambraks, the Kapitäne of my 7. and 8. Staffeln, who were to play a particularly active part in the detachment's activities.

At first the trials were restricted to individual aircraft being sent out to attack shipping in the Thames Estuary under the cover of suitably bad weather conditions. Our definition of 'suitably bad' was a combination of ten-tenths cloud – into which we could always disappear if any enemy fighters put in an appearance – with sufficient height and visibility below the cloud base to allow us to make a dive, or shallow attack on any vessel sighted. At this time of year, however, such a combination rarely occurred. And, to complicate things further, the unreliability of our weather forecasts could lead to some nasty surprises.

I found this out for myself on 18 November 1940. According to the forecasters the whole operational area would be covered by solid cloud with a base at around 500 metres or more; in other words, perfect conditions for the type of mission we had in mind.

I took off with Baudisch in the back seat at 15.06 hours. We flew just below the cloud base – ready to duck into cover at the first sign of danger – rounded Cape Margate and headed west into the Thames Estuary. Far ahead of us the sky was growing suspiciously lighter, but we pressed on. On the horizon a large warship hove into view, probably a Flak cruiser that the British were using to protect their eastbound convoys. Then, suddenly, the clouds parted. Above our heads the sky was a dome of bright shining blue! Just a layer of thin haze stretching up from about 1,000 to 1,500 metres that would offer no protection against enemy fighters whatsoever.

What to do now? Abort the mission so close to such a juicy target? Only some four nautical miles now separated us from the warship. I dropped to low level and continued my approach. That should take me below the enemy's radar cover. Perhaps they hadn't scrambled any fighters yet? The ship's long-range heavy Flak opened up at me. It was uncomfortably accurate. The cabin reverberated to the sound of the bursting shells. If the explosions were that loud, they were not far off scoring a direct hit. We were still about three nautical miles away from our target. But we'd never make it through this display of fireworks!

I turned away to the northeast and climbed out of harm's way into the layer of mist at 1,500 metres. I hoped this would make it harder for the ship's range-finders to keep visual track of us. I worked my way around and approached the cruiser again, this time from out of the sun. The Flak did not re-open fire on me until just before I was ready to attack. But I weaved through the bursts to get even closer to the target. I wanted to make my dive as steep as possible, knowing from experience that Flak is not so accurate when firing vertically upwards.

I went into the dive from a position slightly ahead of the ship, aiming for its bow. I let go my bombs at 400 metres and curved away to the west during my recovery. Staying low over the surface of the estuary, I headed towards the English coast. This was the last direction the ship's Flak would be expecting me to take – or so I hoped. Baudisch reported a tall fountain of water where my bombs had exploded some five metres off the ship's bow. 'Shit!' (Most indelicate, but understandable under the circumstances.)

Five metres away wouldn't even scratch a vessel of this size. All for nothing!

The Flak hadn't started firing again yet. They were still busy bringing their guns to bear aft. I was almost out of range before they managed to send a few parting shots after me. Giving the cruiser a respectfully wide berth, I completed a long curve to the south before pointing my nose eastwards for home. It wasn't long until I was back under the protective cover of the cloud base. Altogether, I had been stooging around near the mouth of the Thames Estuary in brilliant sunshine, all on my own, for the best part of twenty minutes. Fortunately for us the British fighters had let our solitary Ju 87 – an almost certain kill – slip through their fingers. Even so, it was depressing enough. I had also failed to hit a very worthwhile target. But these things happened. You just had to accept them.

Other crews enjoyed more success during individual missions of this kind. Over the coming weeks direct hits were scored on a number of enemy vessels.

At the beginning of January 1941 we also despatched a small Sonder-kommando to Berck-sur-Mer, south of Boulogne, to carry out night-attack trials. This detachment also comprised volunteer ground staff and crews from II. and III./StG 1. They faced different problems, however. The most serious of these was the glare of searchlights over the target, which completely blinded the pilot while he was diving. Our makeshift attempts to black out the machines' cockpits were almost wholly ineffective. Once caught in the beam of a searchlight, pilots committed to a dive at night found it practically impossible to escape.

The weather requirements for a night mission were also different. Good visibility and preferably a moonlit sky were the two things needed to enable the crews to navigate visually and locate their targets. But such conditions were equally rare over the Channel at this time of year – and they too, when they did occur, could throw up some unpleasant surprises.

One night Oberleutnant Skambraks attacked a target on the south coast of England. On his way back across the Channel the weather suddenly deteriorated: unbroken cloud low over the water, pitch-black night and almost no visibility beneath it. Unable to find our field, Skambraks flew around over northern France searching for somewhere suitable to land, but without success. Down to his last reserves of fuel, he decided to make an emergency landing. It would be a risky business. In darkness and in poor visibility, judging the suitability of the terrain below for an emergency landing is well nigh impossible. But he was determined to bring his aircraft down in one piece if he could.

Alongside a patch of woodland he spotted what appeared to be a large expanse of open ground. He made his approach but, just as he about to touch down, he suddenly saw the dim outlines of an electricity pylon looming up in front of him. He quickly pushed the stick forward, flattened out and felt his wheels touch the ground. The machine slowed and rolled to a stop – undamaged! Skambraks had flown under a high-tension cable and landed on a flat stretch of meadow in almost total darkness – unbelievable! The next morning his aircraft was refuelled. He took off, carefully avoiding the row of pylons that marched across the field, and landed back at base not long afterwards – happy as a lark, as always, and treating the whole thing as a joke. That lad had no nerves at all!

The results of our trials had shown that individual Ju 87s, flown by experienced crews, could operate by night and in bad weather with a reasonable chance of success. Against the right sort of targets, and under the right conditions, the crews were able to combine their flying skills, their tactical know-how and their determination, to notch up some notable personal successes.

But in February 1941 we also suffered two losses.

On 5 February the 7. Staffel crew of pilot Leutnant Ernst Schimmelpfennig from Ascherbude/Netzekreis and gunner Obergefreiter Hans Kaden from Dresden failed to return from a cross-Channel mission. Their aircraft was seen by another crew shortly after it had attacked a ship off Ramsgate, but it was later reported from England that they had both been killed in action.

On 13 February 9. Staffel's Feldwebel Fritz Lewandowski from Kulkwitz near Leipzig and his gunner, Unteroffizier Bernhard Renners from Oberhausen-

Osterfeld/Düsseldorf, were posted missing after a daylight bad-weather mission against shipping in the Thames Estuary.

The question that now had to be asked was whether the success of these operations could justify such losses, plus the overall cost in time and effort spent constantly at readiness waiting for suitable weather conditions. We were spared the trouble of having to find an answer to this when, in mid-February 1941, we received orders transferring us to Sicily. Our two special trials detachments were immediately disbanded and returned to their parent Gruppen.

Chapter 10
Malta and the Mediterranean

Over Christmas and the New Year of 1940–41 the Gruppe had been stood down. By careful juggling of the duty rosters everybody had managed to get a few days' home leave. I was thus able to spend Christmas with my family at my in-laws. Those joyous, precious hours had sped by as if on wings. All too soon duty had called and it was back to III./StG 1 at St-Pol.

There, much of our time had been occupied in mulling over plans for future operations against England. But at least we had also been able to make use of nearly every minute of suitable weather to despatch individual aircraft across the Channel. We also ensured that the Gruppe's fighting strength and operational readiness were kept on the top line by a rigorous regime of training. This was especially important in preparing those crews newly posted to the unit for their forthcoming baptism of fire. In addition to the set periods of instruction, we got some of our older and more experienced crews to sit down and chat to the youngsters, describing missions they had flown and explaining the various tricks that could be used to get out of a tight corner.

On some of those long winter evenings, when we felt fairly certain that the following day's flying would be scrubbed on account of the weather, the fire was lit in our tiny 'officer's mess' and we would make ourselves comfortable. The mess was actually one of the rooms in our command post that had just enough space to accommodate all the officers of our Gruppe, plus the doctors from the nearby field hospital. For, whenever we settled down in front of the fire with a glass of mulled wine in our hands, we knew it would not be very long before our good neighbours from the field hospital, head doctor Professor Schmidt from Stuttgart and his team of surgeons, came calling.

They seemed to have developed an extraordinary sixth sense that told them when we would be holding one of our cosy evening sessions. But we always welcomed their presence and soon became firm friends. Their contributions to our fireside chats never failed to be both beneficial and enlightening. Because they had experienced much more of life than we had, they saw certain things from a different perspective. With their greater knowledge of external affairs, their outlook was broader and their views perhaps clearer than ours. What they said often made us pause and reflect on the events of the past eight months. For since the closing stages of the fighting in France – while we had been sitting for the most part inactive on the Channel coast – an awful lot had been happening in the outside world:

10 June 1940: Capitulation of the last of Norway's armed forces.

10 June 1940: Italy declares war on France and Britain.

12 June 1940: Soviet ultimatum to Lithuania, subsequent occupation of Lithuania by Soviet troops.

16 June 1940: Troops of the Soviet Union occupy Estonia and Latvia.

19 June 1940: Italian offensive on the French Alpine front.

23 June 1940: Italian offensive brought to a halt.

24 June 1940: Signing of Italian–French armistice in Rome.

28 June 1940: After Soviet ultimatum to Romanian government of 26 June, units of the Red Army occupy Romanian territories of Bessarabia and Northern Bucovina.

3 July 1940: British naval forces attack French fleet at Mers-el-Kebir (near Oran/Algeria). Other French warships interned in Alexandria (Egypt) and in British ports.

4 July 1940: The French Vichy government of Pétain breaks off diplomatic relations with Great Britain.

11 July 1940: Marshal Pétain appointed head of state of Vichy France.

19 July 1940: Hitler's Reichstag offer of peace to Great Britain.

20 July 1940: Lithuania, Estonia and Latvia become Republics of the Soviet Union.

20 July 1940: (A fact unknown to us at the time: Hitler orders the preparation of operational plans for the invasion of the Soviet Union.)

23 July 1940: Romania cedes South Dobrogea [Dobruja] to Bulgaria.

27 July 1940: Romania cedes Northern Bucovina and Bessarabia to the Soviet Union.

4 August 1940: Italian troops advance out of Abyssinia to begin occupation of British Somaliland.

7 August 1940: Start of Italian offensive against British Somaliland.

20 August 1940: Italian troops capture Berbera, the capital of British Somaliland.

27 August 1940: Hitler orders the total blockade of Great Britain.

30 August 1940: German–Italian arbitration in Vienna on realignment of Hungarian–Romanian border. Romania cedes two-thirds of Transylvania to Hungary.

6 September 1940: King Carol of Romania abdicates in favour of his son Mihai (19) after appointing General Antonescu as head of state.

13 September: Italian forces under Graziani advance out of Cyrenaica [Libya] into Egypt, reaching Sidi Barrani.

23–25 September 1940: Attack on the port of Dakar (West Africa) by Free French troops (2,400 men), supported by British naval forces, repulsed by French garrison.

27 September 1940: Signing in Berlin of Axis Tripartite Pact between Germany, Italy and Japan.

8 October 1940: German 'training troops' move into Romania.

12 October 1940: German military mission established in Romania.

23 October 1940: Hitler's meeting with General Franco at Hendaye, intended to bring Spain into the war, ends in failure.

24 October 1940: Hitler meets with Marshal Pétain at Montoire to discuss German–French military alliance. Pétain declines.

28 October 1940: Italian forces in Albania launch offensive against Greece with invasion of Greek province of Epirus.

29 October 1940: British troops land on Crete, and from 3 November on Greek mainland. By end of November 1940 three RAF squadrons based on Crete.

5 November 1940: Franklin Delano Roosevelt elected President of USA for third term.

11–13 November 1940: Successful raid by British torpedo aircraft on Italian fleet in Taranto harbour.

12 November 1940: Visit to Berlin by Soviet Foreign Minister Molotov. No agreement regarding spheres of interest.

21 November 1940: Greek counter-offensive captures Koritza in Albania.

23 November 1940: Romania and Slovakia join Tripartite Pact.

7 December 1940: General Franco again refuses to enter war on side of Germany.

9 December 1940: Launch of British counter-offensive under Wavell in Egypt. Crushing defeat of Italians at Sidi Barrani. Italy's Libyan army destroyed (38,000 prisoners of war).

10 December 1940: Hitler orders transfer of a Luftwaffe Fliegerkorps to Sicily.

13 December 1940: Hitler issues War Directive No. 20 for Operation Marita, the planned attack on Greece intended to relieve pressure on the Italians in the Balkans. *(Unknown to us at the time.)*

17 December 1940: The British capture Sollum on the Egypt–Libya border.

18 December 1940: Hitler issues War Directive No. 21 for Operation

'Barbarossa' in readiness for the attack on the Soviet Union. Preparations
to be completed by 15 May 1941. *(Also unknown to us at the time.)*

19 December 1940: Italian government requests despatch of a German
armoured division and war materiel to Tripolitania [Libya].

28 December 1940: Italy asks for German support in Albania. In the second
half of 1940 German U-boats sink approximately 1,500,000 grt of enemy
merchant shipping.

5 January 1941: British troops capture Bardia in Cyrenaica. 45,000 Italian
prisoners.

6 January 1941: German air units in action against convoys in
Mediterranean for first time.

19 January 1941: Launch of British offensive against Italy's East African
colony of Eritrea.

19 January 1941: Meeting between Hitler and Mussolini at the Berghof.
Germany commits to full participation in the war in the Mediterranean.

25 January 1941: British forces capture Tobruk in Cyrenaica. Italian
garrison surrenders; 25,000 enter captivity.

6 February 1941: British troops capture Benghazi, the capital of Cyrenaica.

8 February 1941: First convoy of German Afrika-Korps leaves Naples for
Tripoli.

12 February 1941: First German troops land in Tripoli.

13 February 1941: General Rommel arrives in North Africa.

Of all the events listed above we, of course, were only aware at the time of those
that had either been announced in the Wehrmacht communiqués or made known
to the general public via the various media. Naturally, the plans of the higher and
supreme commands were a totally closed book to us. The demands of secrecy
were taken very seriously. Nobody was told any more than they needed to know
in order to carry out their own specific duties. And at Stukagruppe level that didn't
amount to very much. Some of the events of which we were then ignorant – such
as, for example, Hitler's preliminary planning of 20 July 1940 for the invasion of
the Soviet Union – have been included in the above chronology as they were to
have a direct bearing on our future operations.

After learning of the signing of the Tripartite Pact between Germany, Italy and
Japan in Berlin on 27 September 1940 we did begin to wonder what effect this
was likely to have on the escalation of the war in the Mediterranean. The Italians
had enjoyed some initial successes in that area but then, by the turn of the year,
had come the unwelcome news of their reversals in Albania and Cyrenaica. This
gave rise to concerns that German forces would be drawn more deeply into the
conflict in the Mediterranean theatre than our leaders had at first intended.

Nor were these concerns unfounded, as was brought home to us in mid-February 1941 when Stukageschwader 1 (Oberstleutnant Hagen), which currently comprised II./StG 1 (Hauptmann 'Toni' Keil) and our III./StG 1, was given orders to transfer to Sicily forthwith. The move was to be made with the utmost urgency – 'by yesterday' if possible!

Our Gruppe's specific orders called for us to stage, via Metz-Frescaty in eastern France, to Munich-Riem, where we would receive further instructions and the necessary paperwork from our Rome liaison HQ for the onward flight down through Italy. Our key ground personnel would also go by air; a Staffel of Ju 52 transports being made available to us for the purpose. The remaining ground staff and our heavy equipment would travel by rail. Notification immediate. Loading height restrictions were to be strictly observed, as the journey would take them through a number of Alpine tunnels.

Spurred on to make all haste, we set about our preparations. Even the orders we were getting, normally so impeccably drafted, showed signs of improvisation, which could only be explained away by the need to hurry. Organizing the land party's vehicles went smoothly enough at first. We'd had plenty of practice during previous moves. But then we hit a snag. Once loaded upon railway wagons, our captured British trucks – which were used, among other things, as a mobile command post and to transport our heavy equipment – would be too high to get through those Alpine tunnels. I therefore ordered the transport officer to remove their wheels and leave them sitting on their axles. His reply: 'Already thought of that and measured them. They'd still be 12 centimetres too high. We'll have to leave them behind.'

Out of the question! Their interiors had too much headroom anyway. We could quite easily chop a good 15 centimetres off the top of the bodywork and then weld the roofs back on. That way we could get them through the tunnels. It was the obvious solution. The mechanics set to work with their blowtorches and within a few hours our vehicle fleet had, quite literally, been cut down to size, and then put back together again so neatly that it was impossible to spot the difference.

On the morning of 19 February 1941 we took off from St-Pol, accompanied by the Ju 52s carrying our essential ground personnel, for the first leg of the transfer flight, via Metz, to Munich-Riem. We landed there at 14.00 hours and were given the details of the remaining stages. Our intermediate stops down through Italy were to be Forli, Foggia, Vibo Valentia (southern Italy) and thence to Trapani in Sicily. The distances involved in some of these stages were close to the maximum range of our Stukas. For the initial leg we were therefore notified of an alternative emergency landing ground at Treviso, north of Venice, which was to be used if we couldn't make it to Forli.

Despite all the urgency and calls for haste, we got no further than Munich on this first day. The met people had forecast 'QBI' – their code for bad weather – with fog and low cloud closing in over the Alps. All thoughts of continuing our flight had to be abandoned for the time being. The Staffel of transport Ju 52s ferrying our ground staff also had to sit it out at Munich. The crews were not fully qualified for blind flying and their Kapitän had previously issued orders that they were only to cross the Alps in conditions of good ground visibility and were, under no circumstances, to attempt to fly through cloud on instruments. For the next two days we fretted and fumed at Munich, waiting for the weather over the Alps to improve, and ready the whole time to take off at short notice. But conditions in southern Bavaria remained so bad that even the storks were walking!

On the afternoon of the second day I telephoned my wife, who happened to be in Berlin. When I told her that we were held up at Munich, she made a spur of the moment decision to travel down on the overnight express to see me. What a disappointment it must have been for her that our meeting was so brief. For the following morning the weather over the Alps was said to be improving and we immediately began preparing to resume our flight south. So it really was a case of 'Hello and goodbye'. But at least we had had another few precious moments together.

It was about midday on 22 February when Innsbruck finally reported that the cloud base in the Inn Valley had lifted to 200 metres, and that in the Brenner Pass it was already more than 100 metres. Further improvement was expected, but it was likely to be of only short duration. Due to the continued urgency of our transfer, time of take-off was promptly fixed for 13.00 hours. I briefed my Staffel-kapitäne on the coming leg of the flight across the Alps. The Gruppe would fly in open line-astern formation with each aircraft staying in sight of the machine ahead of it. We would remain just below the cloud base and keep to the right when flying through the mountain valleys. Should the cloud descend to less than 100 metres from the ground, this would enable us to perform a 180-degree left-hand turn and make our way back to Munich. The Ju 52 transports would follow the same procedure.

Once over the Brenner Pass, each Staffelkapitän was to check his fuel reserves and decide whether he could safely reach Forli, or would have to divert to Treviso.

We took off on schedule and managed to maintain a height of at least 150 metres as we threaded our way through the Alpine valleys. Visibility was only fair to middling, but sufficient to allow us to reverse course if we had to without fear of a mid-air collision. Even so, things were tense enough. We wondered the whole time whether we were going to make it or would have to turn back.

But at last we were through the Brenner. Not long afterwards the cloud began to break up and Italy welcomed us with bright blue skies. One of my Staffeln opted to head for Treviso. With our tanks almost empty, my Gruppenstab and the other two Staffeln landed safely at Forli.

It would have been an enormous help if at least one of us had been able to speak Italian. There wasn't an interpreter to be found. Communication with our temporary hosts was consequently both laborious and time-consuming. Nevertheless we soon established that the field wasn't equipped to handle an overnight stay by a formation as large as ours. The Geschwaderkommodore therefore decided that all those aircraft that could be readied in time to carry on to Foggia before the onset of darkness should do so. Forli possessed no high-speed refuelling facilities. Using hand pumps to fill our tanks also proved a slow business. Nor did the station staff boast a qualified met officer who might have been able to give us a detailed breakdown of the weather we could expect to encounter along the next leg down to Foggia. As it was, all the field's weather clerk could provide was a general area forecast.

Despite the language barrier, we managed to learn that during our coming flight down Italy's east coast the weather would remain calm and we would meet only light winds. Also, if we wanted to make Foggia before nightfall, we would have to take off by 17.45 hours at the latest. There were no charts of the approaches to Foggia airfield. Our only navigational aid was a small-scale map of southern Italy, on which the town of Foggia was marked by a black dot!

When the machines of my Gruppenstab and the two Staffeln that I still had with me were finally refuelled, the Kommodore gave us the go-ahead to carry on to Foggia. We took off from Forli at exactly 17.42 hours. As we flew down along the Italian coast, it didn't take us long to realize that we were battling against much stronger headwinds than had been forecast. An already fresh southerly was blowing straight into our faces and increasing all the time. Our progress was getting slower by the minute. This meant that we would not be able to reach Foggia before sunset, which, in this part of the world, was the equivalent of saying before darkness fell. So it appeared that we would soon be making our first formation landing by night – and at a base totally unknown to us! But we had no other option. I hoped that the airfield at Foggia was at least equipped with reasonable flarepath lighting.

Once the sun had disappeared below the horizon, dusk didn't last long and very soon we were enveloped in pitch-black night. Flying in close formation and with our navigation lights switched on, we continued on course for Foggia, navigating by dead reckoning alone as the blacked-out countryside slid past unseen below us. Then a flashing beacon ahead! That had to be Foggia airfield. Soon we could make out the perimeter lighting and runway landing lights. I knew that some of my younger pilots had never landed a Ju 87 at night before. I therefore led them into the approach exactly as I would by day, a routine they were all familiar with: stay in formation until we were over the field, open up into line-astern as we made a wide left-hand turn, line up with the runway, level off, and touch down directly behind the man ahead.

I landed first, rolled the length of the field, turned off to the left of the runway and sat there in my machine to watch the others come in. They touched down like a well-drilled team, one 'egg-landing' after the other. You couldn't tell the new boys from the veterans. They'd all made it look ridiculously easy. Nevertheless, I could feel the weight lifting from my shoulders after the last one was safely down. Much relieved, I followed him across the field towards a cavernous hangar. I was waved in and taxied inside. Engine off – all switches off – everything in order.

The Italian station commander was there to welcome us. He was brimming over with enthusiasm and obvious delight. The words were pouring from his lips like a torrent in full spate. From the interpreter at his side I was able to gather the gist of what he was saying: never had he witnessed such disciplined formation keeping in the air, nor had he seen such magnificent flying skills as we had just demonstrated in our night landing – he would contact his superiors at once and tell them all about it. Again with the help of the interpreter, I was able to dissuade him from doing any such thing. We were simply glad that all had ended well after unexpectedly finding ourselves in a potentially dangerous situation not of our own making.

The next morning, 23 February, we set off on the next leg of our journey, to Vibo-Valentia on the toe of Italy. Here we came up against new problems. The Italians had received no orders about refuelling our machines. Without an interpreter it took quite some time and effort, not to mention numerous long-distance telephone calls, before they could be persuaded to fill the tanks of our Ju 87s. Then they started urging us to take off again immediately, even though weather conditions over the sea area separating us from our final destination, Trapani on the northwestern tip of Sicily, were very bad and Sicily itself was reporting heavy cloud. Our suggestion that we be allowed to remain at Vibo-Valentia while awaiting an improvement in the weather was flatly rejected by the Italians.

The forecast for the sea area around Sicily gave a cloud base of at least 100 metres. That would just be enough for us to make a low-level overwater flight.

Our only concern was the mountains shown on the map not far from Trapani. There the cloud would be at its thickest. Although our maps of Trapani were extremely poor, they did appear to indicate that – even with the cloud base down to a minimum – if we approached the airfield from the sea, flew in across the harbour and continued to follow the harbour road inland, we would be able to get in without encountering anything too large and solid on the way.

After I briefed the crews as best I could, we took off at 16.20 hours for the final lap of our long transfer flight. Keeping a wary distance from Sicily's northern coast, where the mountains were hiding their heads in thick cloud, we flew west in a loose gaggle low over the water. Rounding the northwestern tip of the island, we turned in towards Trapani. At my signal the formation fell into line-astern ready for the landing. With reasonable visibility extending some one to two kilometres, we swept in across the harbour at an altitude of 50 metres, followed the harbour road as planned, and there ahead to starboard was the airfield.

A wide turn to the right, approach, touchdown. By 18.10 hours we were all safely on the ground. But the weather was atrocious! Low scudding cloud obscured all signs of the mountains shown on our maps. We reported our arrival to Area HQ: Gruppenstab and two Staffeln of III./StG 1, transfer from France completed. Next, with the help of the ground crews of Hauptmann Hozzel's I./StG 1, who were already in residence at Trapani (they had been one of the first Luftwaffe units to be sent to the Mediterranean theatre), we brought our aircraft up to full operational readiness. Only then were we finally able to retire to our assigned quarters. It had been a long day.

We were greeted next morning by brilliant sunshine. When we stepped outside the barracks our eyes widened in disbelief. A high mountain rose sheer almost alongside the field! Good job we hadn't bumped into that imposing lump of rock yesterday. We hadn't expected it to be quite so close. Once again, lady luck had smiled on us. But not everyone had been as fortunate. When 8. Staffel arrived later in the day after their detour to Treviso, they had bad news to impart. Leutnant Helmut Wentorf (born Bremen, 23 February 1919) had suffered engine failure and had been forced to attempt an emergency landing in southern Italy. His machine somersaulted and Wentorf's neck had been broken. (Leutnant Wentorf was buried in Foggia cemetery.)

Another of the Staffel's Ju 87s had also been forced down by engine failure. But its pilot had pulled off a quite remarkable feat. When his engine quit he was over mountainous country. The only level ground anywhere in the vicinity was in the tiny terraced fields clinging to the mountainsides that were then so common in much of hilly rural Italy. Hardly ideal for an emergency landing, you would have thought. But with his propeller windmilling slowly to a stop, the pilot had no other option. He touched down on one of the pocket handkerchief-sized fields and managed to bring his machine to a halt before running over the edge. A healthy combination of luck and skill – not to mention a good helping of steady nerves – had enabled him to achieve the apparently impossible. Both aircraft and crew were all in one piece, but the machine had to be dismantled before it could be removed from its mountain eyrie. It could never have taken off again from such a minute plot of soil. After a lot of work the faulty engine was repaired, the airframe put back together again, and the aircraft returned to operations.

But the worst news of all came from the transport Staffel. Just minutes after lifting off from Munich-Riem two of its Ju 52s had tried to climb through cloud, only to hit the mountains and crash near the town of Rottach at the southern end of the Tegernsee. Together with the Junkers' crews, six members of our Gruppenstab had lost their lives in this tragic incident:

> Oberarzt Dr Hörner (born Würzburg, 27 December 1905), chief medical officer,
>
> Oberfeldwebel Robert Bergmann (born Klein Paschleben/Anhalt, 28 July 1914), NCO i/c Aircraft Servicing Flight,
>
> Unteroffizier Hans Lichtenberg (born Bremen, 13 February 1917), flight mechanic,
>
> Unteroffizier Willi Kräuter (born Neumünster, 30 December 1913), clerk/writer,
>
> Prüfmeister a.Kr. Franz-Ferdinand Jahn (born Lübeck, 18 August 1900), Gruppen-Inspekteur [a.Kr. = 'auf Kriegsdauer'; equivalent to 'hostilities only' or H.O.],
>
> Friedrich Winkler (born Magdeburg, 27 June 1909), Junkers engine fitter (attached).

In addition, seven others had sustained injuries, some of them serious:

> Prüfmeister a.Kr. Bruno Plötz (born Stralsund, 19 February 1899), Gruppen-Inspekteur (H.O.),
>
> Feldwebel Alfred Radloff (born Nehmten/Plön, 30 March 1915), armourer, Gruppenstab: head wound,
>
> Unteroffizier Anton Jene (born Alzey, 26 January 1914), WOp/gunner, 7./StG 1: lower leg fracture,
>
> Unteroffizier Hubert Sassa (born Görlitz, 31 July 1919), WOp/gunner, 7./StG 1: fractured spine and pelvis,
>
> Unteroffizier Walter Meissner (born Danzig, 30 January 1920), WOp/gunner, 7./StG 1: fractured jaw and upper arm,

Gefreiter Erich Schachtschnabel (born Dessau, 14 April 1910), Gruppenstab:
   arm and head injuries,
Feldwebel Karl Bost (born Beeskow, 15 October 1914), Gruppenstab: forearm
   fracture.

Six of the seven injured were rushed straight to Tegernsee Hospital. Feldwebel
Bost was taken to Würzburg Hospital.

And, but for the vigilance and quick thinking of the electrician on duty at
Innsbruck's main power station, our casualties could very well have been much
worse. He had spotted one of the transport Staffel's Ju 52s flying low over the
rooftops of Innsbruck and heading in the direction of the Brenner Pass, where the
cloud base had not risen above 200 metres. As a precautionary measure he had
switched off the power to the high-tension cables running through the pass. His
action probably saved the lives of the crew and passengers aboard the Ju 52. The
aircraft actually *did* brush the wires. But as they were carrying no power, the
machine survived the incident and the pilot was able to turn back and make an
emergency landing.

Even so, the cost of the transfer had been shocking enough. After the bulk of
the crews and key ground personnel had arrived in Trapani and we had been
declared operational, I began to ask myself whether the move had really been so
very urgent.

As far as we were able to gather, the hurried transfer to Sicily of our Gruppe
(together with the Geschwaderstab and II./StG 1) had had something to do with
a planned German–Italian operation to capture the British island fortress of Malta.
The vital importance of this enemy stronghold sitting in the middle of the
Mediterranean was obvious. In order to ensure a safe and regular flow of supplies
to the Axis troops fighting in North Africa, Malta had to be seized. And yet the
operation was never carried out.

When we asked why not, we were never given an official explanation. But
according to the grapevine, the Italians had been unwilling to make available the
troops requested for their part in the undertaking; apparently it was only a matter
of a battalion (or regiment?) of parachutists, or something of that nature.

Be that as it may, the task for the Luftwaffe units based on Sicily had in the
meantime been more or less decided upon: direct and indirect support of the
German supply lines to North Africa. Within this general framework, the specific
job of the Stuka units at Trapani (namely StG 1 with its II. and III. Gruppen, plus
I./StG 1 until the latter's transfer to Africa) was to prevent the British Gibraltar
fleet from interfering with these sea routes.

Upon our arrival in Sicily, StG 1 had been placed under the command of
X. Fliegerkorps. And on 25 February the Korps' AOC, General der Flieger Geisler,

came to Trapani to carry out a visit of inspection. The old seadogs of our Gruppe who had known and respected the then Generalleutnant Geisler when he had been the F.d.Luft (See) [C-in-C Naval Aviation] were more than a little disappointed at his speech of welcome to the assembled troops.

Not a word about the importance and meaning of the operations that lay ahead of us in this new and unfamiliar theatre of war. Not a word about the entirely new kind of missions that we, as an otherwise experienced Gruppe, would now be facing. Just a few platitudes and words of warning about the dangers of southern wines, and a reminder to be on our best behaviour while on Italian soil. That didn't tell us very much at all. We had expected more from our commanding general. Our thoughts, not unnaturally, were focussed on what sort of opposition we were likely to meet in this part of the world. The next day we found out the answer to that for ourselves.

Early on the morning of 26 February 1941 we received orders to fly down to Comiso airfield in the southeast of the island. Because of the distances involved, this was to be the jumping-off point for all our operations against Malta. At Comiso we were given details of our target: the British airfield at Luqa. The enemy bombers and torpedo aircraft that were attacking the German–Italian convoys and transports ferrying troops and supplies to North Africa were based at Luqa and our primary objective was to destroy these aircraft on the ground.

Aerial reconnaissance photos showed that they were dispersed widely apart in individual blast pens. And it was clear from the pictures that these pens were constructed of massive stone blocks. They were so strong that a near miss would have no effect at all. The only way that we could be certain of destroying the enemy machines was by planting our bombs within the walls of the pens and by gunfire.

We planned our raid accordingly. Each pilot was assigned one of the pens identified on the photos. After making a pinpoint attack on his particular target – releasing his bombs at about 450 metres – he would recover, but remain at low level as he crossed the field. This would enable him to use his guns on any aircraft parked on the far side as he swept past. We would then retire southwards, still at low level, and form our customary *Sauhaufen* well out to sea to the south of Malta. I hoped this would be the last place the British would think of looking for us. Our return flight would then take us in a wide sweep around Malta's west coast back to Comiso on Sicily.

The Gruppe took off at 13.15 hours and approached Malta in close formation at an altitude of 3,500 metres. Our fighter escort consisted of Hauptmann Müncheberg's Staffel of Me 109s, plus a number of Italian Macchi fighters. Before reaching the belt of Flak around La Valetta, the Maltese capital, we went into line-astern battle formation. We weaved our way through the bursts of heavy Flak being thrown up at us. Soon we were nearing Luqa and it was time for each of us to pick out his particular target.

Mine was a British aircraft in a pen on the eastern edge of the field. Tip over into a 70–80 degree dive. I got the target centered in my sights and kept it there. At 450 metres I let go my bombs. Easing out of the dive, I headed for another enemy machine parked on the opposite side of the field. Luqa's light and medium Flak was by this time letting fly with all barrels and from all directions. I was right over the middle of the field – barely 200 metres high and still at a nose-down angle of some 30 degrees – when I opened up with my two wing machine guns.

Suddenly – a tremendous jolt, an ear-splitting crash, and my right wing burst open. A direct Flak hit! My Iolanthe immediately fell away steeply to starboard. I automatically punched the stick hard left and yanked it back into my stomach. But it wasn't enough. The centre of my right wing had been blown completely apart. The control surfaces on that side were useless. The wind resistance from my shattered wing was so strong that I could barely hold her, even with full left flap and aileron. I had already retracted my dive brakes. Now I spun the trimming wheel to get her fully tail-heavy.

The Iolanthe responded, but only slowly. The swing to the right had almost ceased, but although I had everything shoved hard left she was still crabbing slightly nose-down towards an open hangar on the far side of the field. I poured on the power and pressed in the tit to give me emergency boost. This finally brought the nose up slightly. Now the battered Ju 87 was tearing across the field at a height of no more than three or four metres and heading straight for the yawning door of the hangar. Inside were three aircraft, which, until the raid started, had presumably been undergoing repair.

If I go, those three will be going with me, I thought, as I sat there helpless, clutching the stick hard into my left side. All I could do was wait to see what happened. The machine's nose had now lifted itself a fraction above the horizontal. Slowly, very slowly, the Ju 87 began to gain a little height. Too slowly? I could already make out every detail of the hangar's interior, right into the farthest corners. But we were still climbing!

Whoosh! Almost as if she herself were putting her all into one final, agonizing leap, my wounded Iolanthe just scraped across the top of the hangar roof.

'Boy, that was close!' I said to my gunner Fritzchen Baudisch. The relief must have been apparent in my voice. But we weren't out of the woods yet. In front of us rose a hill topped by a line of telegraph poles. Not a very large hill as hills go, true, but an almost insuperable obstacle given the sorry state my poor old crate was in. Could we possibly be lucky a second time? We could! We just managed to clear the brow of the hill between two of the telegraph poles without our wheels touching the ground. Telephone wires *kaputt* – aircraft still flying.

Ahead of us the terrain dipped away before opening out into a broad valley that led down to the south coast of the island. That was very convenient for us. Our lame bird wouldn't have taken kindly to many more twists and turns. Very carefully I nudged the rudder pedal with my foot, bringing her round on to course without sacrificing any height or speed. At last we were over open water. The rest of the Gruppe was already making for home far ahead of us, of course. Our mangled wing was slowing us down so much that we hadn't a hope in hell of catching up with them.

We would be more than happy just to stay out of the drink while we crept around Malta back to base. Incredibly, the fuel tanks didn't seem to have been hit. The gauge was showing normal – enough to get us to Comiso. As far as it went, everything appeared to be in order. We were still flying, I said to myself – maybe slowly and awkwardly, and all alone with not another aircraft in sight – but still flying, that was the main thing. It was at that moment that I heard Fritz Baudisch's voice from the rear cockpit: 'Hurricane approaching from astern!'

'Well, shoot it down then, Fritzchen,' I answered as calmly as I could. 'We dare not risk any evasive action, we've just got to keep going.' Fritzchen loosed off a short burst at the Hurricane, more to calm our own nerves than in any hope of doing harm to our eight-gunned opponent, who was now closing in fast on our tail. The enemy opened fire, peppering our wings and fuselage before sweeping past us and making a wide turn to port to get back behind us for another pass. I heard Fritzchen grimly mutter: 'Stoppage!' But with practised fingers he deftly inserted a new firing pin into his machine-gun.

In the meantime the Hurricane was attacking us again. The enemy pilot was a pretty good marksman. His victim, a defenceless, barely manoeuvrable Ju 87, must have seemed like easy meat. Once again, I was conscious of a series of metallic popping noises as a fresh crop of tiny holes sprouted in both wings. Quite a large crop, in fact. Our opponent curved away in front of us once more, clearly intending to make a third pass. But we were still flying! It couldn't go on like this for very much longer. The Hurricane was just setting us up for a fresh attack when, from out of nowhere, another Ju 87 came barrelling in to join the party.

It was Leutnant Theo Nordmann, another straggler from our Gruppe. His bombs had failed to release during his first dive on Luqa and so – against all common sense – he had decided to climb back up and carry out a solo attack long after the rest of us had all hared off home. Now here he was coming to our rescue

– a daring type, this Nordmann! He could see from the state of my machine that I could do little more than try to hold her reasonably straight and level. So, as he didn't have the time to jockey into position to have a go at the Hurricane, he elected instead to fly right across the fighter's nose, forcing it to break away. It was thus Nordmann's machine that collected the enemy's burst this time. Bullets ripped into its flank. The oxygen cylinder exploded, tearing a large hole in the fuselage. But his aircraft was still in the air, and fortunately neither he nor his gunner had been hit.

A few hundred metres behind us the Hurricane was lining up for a new attack on my poor old Iolanthe. The pilot must have been thinking to himself: this can't be happening – how come this Stuka's still flying when the squadrons on the Channel front last summer were reportedly knocking them down in droves? By now he was absolutely determined to send us into the drink. He launched his attack from well astern, reducing his speed as he closed in so that he could get off a really long burst to finish us off once and for all. For the fourth time, our fate hung in the balance.

It was at this moment that Fritzchen Baudisch in the rear cockpit came to life again. Despite all his efforts, his machine-gun was still refusing to fire. But now, galvanized by what he could see going on behind us – and totally out of character for him – he suddenly started yelling a running commentary over the R/T:

> Me 109! – A long way astern – but curving in to get behind the Hurricane – Still miles away – Diving at a hell of a speed! – The Hurricane's almost within firing range. – Me 109's on his tail – Still too far away though. – Hope to God he makes it – The 109's opened fire. – Going full pelt – and at extreme range – But he's got him! – Still firing. – The Hurricane's been hit. – He's on fire – He's going in. – He's shot him down!

The R/T fell silent. I realized I had been holding my breath. Slowly, I let it out. The Hurricane had gone into the sea behind us at a steep angle. Had he been allowed a couple of seconds more, it would have been us now disappearing beneath the waves.

'Escaped by the skin of our teeth again, Fritzchen,' I said to Baudisch. 'You sounded quite excited for a few moments back then, almost as if you were in the thick of the action yourself! Anyway, that 109 deserves a very big thank-you. I must admit, I was starting to find things getting a bit too hot for my liking!' 'Mine too,' my gunner grunted. He was back to his old self again.

Although everything was now quiet all around us, we couldn't count our chickens yet. We still had a long way to go over open water before we reached Sicily. Would our fuel hold out? Had our tanks been hit? The fuel gauges said not.

They were indicating the correct amount of fuel remaining based on the time we had already been in the air. But how was that possible? Both wings had been completely sieved by machine-gun bullets. There was also a huge gaping hole in the right wing close to the starboard outer tank where the metal had been ripped to shreds. And yet the gauges were showing normal? The tanks can't have been punctured. It was nothing short of a miracle!

We had climbed back up to 300 metres and I found that I could keep her at that altitude. The engine was running sweetly enough. We should make it back to Sicily. I tentatively tested the controls of my gallant Iolanthe. But the moment I reduced the revs even a fraction, she immediately tipped over onto her right wing. I could only hold her horizontal at full power and with the stick hard left. Leutnant Nordmann was flying beside me. Sicily came in sight; Comiso. There was only a slight breeze, but fortunately Comiso was quite a large field. It ought to be big enough even for an uncontrolled high-speed landing.

Heading into what little wind there was, I made my approach at low level and with the throttle wide open. I quickly gave Fritzchen the usual string of instructions reserved for any crash-landing that was likely to end up in a somersault: 'Open cabin roof! – Tighten harness! – Remove goggles! – Tuck in knees! – Arms in front of your ugly mug! – *Start praying!*'

Over the edge of the field I chopped the throttle and switched off the ignition. Level out – now wait for the bang! The machine brushed the ground at high speed, jumped back into the air, tipped over onto its right leg – just as I had feared – but then bounced back onto the left leg and proceeded to career across the field, first on one wheel and then the other, before slowly beginning to lose speed. After covering a good two-thirds of its length I cautiously tried the brakes, gently at first, but then harder. The Ju 87 finally came to a stop only about twenty metres from the far end of the field. Despite all the Flak and fighter fire we had taken, the fuel tanks and the tyres had remained unscathed and we'd made it!

We climbed out and inspected the damage. As a memento, I took a couple of souvenir snapshots of my Iolanthe in her present sorry state before she was taken off to have a new pair of wings fitted. It was far beyond the limited capabilities of our field workshops to repair the old ones. In addition to the huge jagged hole that the Flak shell had torn in the wing, our mechanics counted no fewer than 184 bullet holes in the machine. It was almost too much. The aircraft looked like a colander. But the sight of it would have boosted the confidence of any fledgling Stuka pilot. It showed that, if the tanks and radiator weren't hit, the Ju 87 could withstand an incredible amount of punishment.

Leutnant Nordmann had also brought his badly crippled machine down safely. He and his gunner walked around it assessing the damage. The pair were 'more than a little proud' – and quite rightly so – of having got their Kommandeur and his 'A-Anton' out of a very sticky, not to say almost hopeless situation.

Unfortunately, Oberfähnrich Roman Heil (born Würzburg, 28 December 1920) hadn't been so lucky. After being attacked by fighters over Malta, he had been forced to ditch some five kilometres to the west of the smaller neighbouring island of Gozo. After his machine went down, he was reportedly seen swimming in the water with his gunner, Gefreiter Heinrich Stamm (born Wallenbrück/ Herford, 29 September 1918). The pair were later picked up by the enemy's air-sea rescue services and taken into captivity. (Heil was promoted to the rank of Oberleutnant on 1 February 1943 while a prisoner-of-war in Canada.)

The Wehrmacht communiqué of 27 February 1941 reported the day's attack in the following terms: 'Strong bomber and dive-bomber forces of the German Fliegerkorps based in Sicily under the command of General der Flieger Geisler, escorted by German and Italian fighters, have carried out a successful bombing raid against Luqa airfield on the island of Malta. Ten enemy bombers were destroyed on the ground and a number badly damaged. Two aircraft hangars, barrack blocks and a fuel dump went up in flames . . . '

The entry in my flying logbook was more succinct:

26.2.1941 – J9+AH – Ju 87B-1 – Mahlke – Baudisch – Aircraft, Malta Luqa – Take-off Comiso 13.15 – Landing: Comiso 14.45 – Flak hit, wing. Fired on by fighter.

For the next few days our III./StG 1 remained at Trapani awaiting some sign of life from the British Gibraltar fleet. The moment the fleet was reported to be in the Straits of Gibraltar and heading east into the Mediterranean, we would be ordered to immediate readiness. But the British failed to oblige. They had clearly learned from the lessons meted out to them by German Stuka units back on 10 and 11 January:

On 10 January 1941 the first two Stukagruppen to be transferred to Trapani – I./StG 1 (under Hauptmann Hozzel) and II./StG 2 (under Hauptmann Enneccerus) – had attacked a British carrier force in the Mediterranean, scoring six direct hits on the aircraft carrier *Illustrious*. The following day, 11 January, they had sunk the 10,000-ton heavy cruiser *Southampton*. The *Illustrious* suffered further damage from Stuka attack while undergoing repair in Malta's La Valetta harbour and was out of action for more than a year. Other ships, including the Australian cruiser *Perth*, had also been damaged by Stuka dive-bombing.

The British fleet apparently now had such respect for Germany's Stukas that it was careful to keep its vessels well out of range of Trapani's Ju 87s during the hours of daylight. As far as possible, the Malta supply convoys also took advantage of bad weather conditions in order to escape the attentions of our Stukas while en route to La Valetta harbour. The British Gibraltar fleet's forays were confined in the main to protecting the brief high-speed dashes into the western Mediterranean by the aircraft carriers that were ferrying fighter reinforcements to Malta to replace those machines being lost in the defence of the island. The fighters would be flown off from the carriers' decks as soon as Malta was within their range, whereupon the fleet would immediately reverse course and head back to the safety of Gibraltar.

Meanwhile, Malta's bomber and torpedo aircraft were continuing to inflict heavy losses on our ships transporting supplies to North Africa. It was therefore decided that we should attack these enemy aircraft on the island bases. At the same time we were also to be employed against any enemy supply ships arriving in Malta's La Valetta harbour; our orders being to sink them at their berths, preferably before they had discharged their cargos. Neither would be a particularly easy task. Nor was there a guarantee of any lasting effects, even if we did succeed in hitting our assigned targets. Say, for example, we managed to knock out most of Malta's bombers during one of our daylight raids. A radio message back to England was all that would be required for the British High Command to despatch replacement bombers to Malta that same night. And the following day the attacks on our supply convoys would be resumed as normal.

On 4 March, despite poor weather conditions, we were moved down to Comiso again in preparation for a combined attack on Malta by the units of X. Fliegerkorps. A further deterioration in the weather, however, caused the postponement of the operation until the following day. We finally took off from Comiso on the afternoon of 5 March. Our target was Hal Far airfield. Our objective was to destroy the enemy's aircraft on the ground. A Ju 88 unit was also scheduled to bomb the field ten minutes after our attack had gone in. Tactically, the operation was a repeat of our recent mission against Luqa, although on this occasion we were to fly a wide arc out to sea before approaching the target from the east.

We commenced our attack at the time ordered. But while in the dive I realized that the first bombs from the leading wave of Ju 88s were accompanying us down towards Hal Far! Fortunately none of our machines was hit. Nor was our attack in any way disrupted, for all our pilots were concentrating fully on their own targets and few even noticed the missiles falling through the air outside their cockpit windows! The steep dive and low point of release gave us some good bombing results. Our competitive instincts easily persuaded us that we had done far more damage than our comrades in the Ju 88s. To quote the Wehrmacht communiqué again, the announcement of 6 March 1941 read, in part: 'In the Mediterranean theatre German bomber and dive-bomber units, escorted by German fighters, carried out a highly successful attack on the airfield of Hal Far on Malta. They destroyed hangars and barracks, as well as many enemy aircraft on the ground. Our fighters shot down three British aircraft in dogfights over the target area . . .'

Subsequent reconnaissance showed that our Gruppe had indeed been responsible for much of the damage inflicted on Hal Far. But, even so, the raid had been somehow unsatisfactory. The results did not seem to justify the enormous effort involved in mounting such an operation, especially as we had again lost one of our crews. 7. Staffel's Unteroffizier Wilhelm Singer (born Nuremberg, 29 September 1918) and his gunner, Obergefreiter Paul Stapf (born Mindelheim/ Swabia, 6 September 1916), had been shot into the sea by a Hurricane some three kilometres south of Hal Far.

During the night of 22/23 March 1941 a British convoy, escorted by cruisers, had arrived safe and unmolested in La Valetta harbour in Malta. We were given the news early the next morning and immediately despatched down to Comiso. There we were issued with instructions to attack the ships at La Valetta, being ordered to concentrate particularly on a cruiser and two large merchantmen that were berthed in the inner harbour. Time of attack: 15.45 hours. Escort to be provided by a mixed force of German (Me 109) and Italian (Macchi) fighters.

We knew that the British would have a warm welcome waiting for us. La Valetta was already protected by a heavy belt of Flak, and to this would now be added the fire from the ships tied up in the harbour. We would be most at danger from the enemy's light and medium Flak. This could be kept trained on us during the latter part of the dive – those few vital seconds when we had to fly in a straight line in order to hold the target in our sights. The range would grow ever shorter until, finally, we would be practically flying down the barrels of the ships' guns.

Once our bombs had been released we were of course free to manoeuvre. But at low level and at short range, any Flak that was fired at us from dead ahead – even tracer, the only kind we could actually *see* – arrived with such speed that it was almost impossible to avoid. The ships we had been briefed to attack lay almost in the centre of this massed ring of Flak defences. We would make a very juicy target. That we could do nothing about. The only chance we had was to reduce the duration of the attack itself to an absolute minimum. The mission was therefore worked out down to the last detail beforehand in discussions with the crews and with the pilots of our escorts. The fighters would remain with us until the moment we started to dive. During our attack they would move into position low over the sea to the north of Malta and be ready to escort us back to base.

We headed for Malta in close formation, at an altitude of 3,800 metres and in perfect Mediterranean holiday weather: brilliant sunshine, clear blue skies, a gentle breeze and calm seas. We continued on southwards past La Valetta, keeping well away from its hornets' nest of Flak. The first British fighters were already in the air to meet us, but when they tried to attack us they were pounced upon by our escorting fighters. With the enemy thus otherwise engaged, we were free to turn in towards our target unopposed. Approaching from the south, out of the sun, we took up line-astern combat formation. This gave every pilot optimum freedom of tactical movement prior to the actual dive.

A dense flickering of bright flashes on the ground far below indicated that the heavy Flak had opened fire. We promptly executed several sharp turns to right and left in automatic response. A few seconds later the first Flak bursts smudged the sky ahead of us. Others followed in rapid succession until quite a thick curtain of small dirty grey clouds had formed in our path. The enemy were apparently putting up a box barrage, and it was at our exact altitude.

As I led the Gruppe towards the target I kept up a constant weaving. As far as possible, I aimed for those spots in the sky where a fresh grey cloud had just blossomed, for a second Flak shell hardly ever exploded in precisely the same position as the one before it. We could now make out the ships in the harbour very clearly. I gave the signal to start the attack and pushed the stick hard over and across, tipping the machine into a 70–80 degree dive.

The heavy Flak had by now sent up two further barrages: one at medium level and one closer to the ground. They posed no problem. By the time we plunged through those dark, evil-looking clouds of smoke their lead content would have long since dissipated. But then the medium and light Flak suddenly opened up at us with a ferocity and intensity that we had never before experienced. Tangled skeins of tracer came flying towards us from every direction. Like tiny glowing red mice, some flashed past so closely that you felt you could almost reach out and grab them.

But we simply had to ignore the fiery web that was enveloping us. We were nearing the end of the dive and, as the wind was slight, each of us had his target fixed firmly in his sights. For my Stabskette and one of the Staffeln that target was the cruiser; for the other two Staffeln it was the pair of merchantmen. We were down to 500 metres: let go bombs, pull up sharply and corkscrew quickly away in a series of steep twists and turns. Now our only concern was to get back home safe and sound. It wasn't far to the coast, but with the Flak still hammering away at us from all points of the compass our willing Ju 87s – even with their very useful 240km/h – seemed to be no more than crawling along.

The volume of Flak over the target area meant that we had hardly had time to observe the results of our attack. We had, however, been able to see at least one direct hit on each of the vessels, plus a great many very near misses. After passing over the last of the Flak emplacements on the coast we descended to sea level. The extra speed gained in the shallow dive got us out of range of the island's defences that much the quicker, and once over open water we rapidly formed into our now familiar 'gaggle' for the flight back to Sicily.

Our fighter escort had been waiting for us as planned. Now it was their job to keep the British Spitfires and Hurricanes off our backs. Soon we were surrounded by numerous individual dogfights, some being waged as little as five to ten metres above the water. This was where the Italian members of our escort came into their own. Displaying the most incredible mastery of their machines and revelling in their flying virtuosity, they took their Macchis so low down over the slight swell that their propellers were throwing the water up high in their wakes. Skimming only a metre or two above the surface of the sea, they attacked the British fighters from below, claiming a number of successes. I myself saw seven enemy fighters brought down one after the other by the Macchis in this way. Then, abruptly, it was all over as quickly as it had begun. The sky was empty and peace reigned all around us. We were about halfway between Malta and Sicily.

But then a machine of 8. Staffel started to gain height, dragging a long tail of black smoke behind it. I passed leadership of the main group over to my deputy, Oberleutnant Lion, and climbed up after the damaged Ju 87 to see what was wrong. The aircraft was that being crewed by Oberfähnrich Erich Kaubitzsch (born Döbeln near Chemnitz, 22 May 1920) and his gunner, Gefreiter Hans Krumland (born Zetel/Wilhelmshaven, 15 January 1920). Its engine was running in fits and starts – stopping – coming back into life – stopping again – working for a few minutes – before finally giving up the ghost altogether.

Kaubitzsch was fiddling with the fuel injection pump, trying all the tricks he could think of to get his engine going again. But it was no use. The propeller had windmilled to an almost dead stop. The pair therefore decided to bail out. They came down safely enough in the calm water, but unfortunately without their rubber dinghy. Baudisch got our dinghy pack out ready to throw down to them. There was no mechanism in the aircraft to release it automatically. He'd simply have to slide open his canopy and heave it over the side upon my word of command. Quite an awkward business!

I throttled right back, went down low and headed towards the two figures swimming in the water. Just before reaching them I gave Baudisch the order to throw the dinghy out. But we had a stroke of bad luck. The dinghy pack got caught up on our tailplane! I jinked the aircraft about furiously trying to free it, but by the time I had succeeded in doing so we were so far away that it was clearly impossible for the pair to reach it.

Still, they *were* both wearing life-jackets and seemed in good spirits. After a final wave, we therefore set course due north for Sicily. Baudisch was timing our flight on his stopwatch. On his map he then marked the exact spot where we hit the south coast of Sicily. As soon as we landed at Comiso, he immediately climbed into the back seat of the lead aircraft of the first Kette to finish refuelling. While I drove to a telephone to alert the air-sea rescue services, Baudisch was already guiding the three Ju 87s back out to sea along a reciprocal course to where our missing crew had gone into the water.

They found them without any difficulty and began circling the spot. Some ten minutes later an air-sea rescue flying boat from Catania arrived on the scene. It touched down and hauled our two men on board. No more than forty minutes after taking to their parachutes and coming down in the sea – its waters today at near summer temperatures – the pair had been picked up. It had been their first mission!

But although still in his life-jacket and showing no outward signs of injury, gunner Hans Krumland was dead when recovered from the water. He had succumbed to a massive heart attack. His pilot, Oberfähnrich Kaubitzsch, had suffered a nasty flesh wound in his thigh from a 20mm Flak shell ricochet. Despite the calm conditions, it was this that had prevented him from trying to swim to the dinghy we had dropped. He was admitted to Catania Hospital. Two weeks later he was discharged fully fit and able to resume operational duties with us.

Three other crews had failed to return from the attack on La Valetta:

> Pilot Oberleutnant Walter Preiss (born Hartau/Salzbrunn, 3 February 1914) and his gunner, Unteroffizier Paul Horstmann (born Werne/Bochum, 15 July 1916), of the Gruppenstab.
> Leutnant Leopold Jarosch (born Vienna, 8 November 1916) and gunner Grefreiter Josef Jarnuczak (born Gelsenkirchen, 26 February 1917) of 7. Staffel.
> Oberleutnant Hans Ries (born Mannheim, 2 March 1908) and gunner Unteroffizier Walter Philipp (born Mischline/Gross Strelitz) of 9. Staffel.

Stabsfeldwebel Ries never learned of his promotion to Oberleutnant, news of which only came through after the operation had been flown. His gunner,

Walter Philipp, had been rescued from the sea off Malta by the British, but died later that same day. He was buried in the island's St Andrew's Cemetery two days later.

One of the three missing aircraft had exploded in mid-air during the final approach to the target just before we went into the dive. The exact cause was unknown, but its bomb-load may well have been detonated by a Flak hit. The other two had been brought down, either by Flak or fighters, after completing the attack. Again, two of the crews had been made up of relatively green youngsters. But in Oberleutnant Hans Ries 9. Staffel had lost one of its longest-serving and most experienced pilots. As a Stabsfeldwebel he had been in it right from the start, flying his first missions during the campaign against Poland, and later over both France and England.

Given the scale of our losses, the outcome of the raid could hardly be termed a success. Confirming our own hurried observations, post-mission reconnaissance photos showed that we had scored a number of hits on our principal targets. Several bombs that had exploded on the quayside close to the ships must also have caused a bit of damage. The cruiser had certainly taken some direct hits, but was able to put to sea again the next day under her own steam. As we had no armour-piercing bombs capable of penetrating the deck of a modern warship, it was hardly likely that we had inflicted anything more than minor damage to the vessel's superstructure.

As for the two large merchantmen, it was not clear whether their damage was repairable, or whether they were resting on the bottom ready for the scrap heap. Nor did we know, of course, how much of their precious cargo had been destroyed. All in all, the operation had not been one of our better efforts. But we had carried it out as ordered in the face of some very fierce opposition. It had certainly been hard, and not one that any of us was likely to forget in a hurry.

In the middle of March the crews were given a surprise party in the form of a jolly little beer festival. 'Toni' Keil, the Kommandeur of II. Gruppe had indented via the Geschwader for a supply of beer. His Gruppe had been recruited almost exclusively from southern Germany and Bavaria, where beer was regarded as part of the staple diet. In which case, he argued – tongue firmly in cheek – it ought to be included as part of his unit's normal rations. His plea must have found a sympathetic fellow-Bavarian ear somewhere along the line. For among the supplies unloaded from one of the next Ju 52s to fly in from Munich were, to everyone's astonishment, several barrels of best German beer!

The rest of us weren't forgotten. One evening after we had been stood down from readiness, we were all invited out on to the runway to join the party. With a few drinks under his belt, Feldwebel Ebertz – the same Feldwebel Ebertz who had questioned my navigating abilities after we had attacked Esternay railway station in France the previous summer – felt emboldened enough to get something else off his chest that had clearly been bothering him for some little while. He button-holed me and asked if he could speak freely. Permission granted! That was all the encouragement he needed:

'You're very stubborn and determined, Herr Hauptmann, we all know that. But what I don't understand is why you are always so determined to lead us into those areas where the heavy Flak is particularly thick?'

'There's a very simple explanation for that, Ebertz. Hasn't anyone ever told you that when an infantryman is under artillery fire he always tries to take cover in the hole made by the last shell? He knows that the next shell is most unlikely to land in precisely the same spot. It's one of the first things an old soldier learns.'

'Yes, Herr Hauptmann, I've heard about that.'

'Right. Well, it's exactly the same with Flak. Can you remember ever seeing a Flak shell explode in the middle of the cloud of smoke left by the one just before it? Because I can't. And especially not if the Flak is putting up a box barrage, as it usually does over Malta where the sky is always full of little grey clouds. You'd think it would be impossible to fly through them. But it isn't – because they're nothing but smoke! You can fly through them without worrying; nothing's going to happen to you. If you can see the smoke left behind by an exploding shell, you can be sure the shrapnel from it is long gone. But steer well clear of that patch of open sky right next to it. A shell could explode there at any moment and then the air would be full of flying lead!'

Ebertz had been growing more and more thoughtful as he listened to my words. But now a look of almost comical relief crossed his face: 'I see, so we've been doing it right all along!'

Over the next few days we spent the occasional brief period at readiness awaiting orders for an anti-shipping operation of some kind or another. But the only time we were actually sent out was on 26 March when we went looking for an enemy submarine reported in the sea area off Trapani. False alarm! No sign of a submarine or any other vessel far and wide. British naval forces were apparently still unwilling to venture within range of our Stukas. We were very surprised at this. With so much brewing in the Balkans and North Africa, we were expecting daily to hear of a foray by the British Gibraltar fleet into the central or eastern Mediterranean. For it was in these regions that events were now unfolding in rapid and bewildering succession:

1 March 1941: Bulgaria joins the Tripartite Pact (Germany–Italy–Japan).

2 March 1941: Troops of the German 12. Armee cross the border from

Romania into Bulgaria. Great Britain breaks off diplomatic relations with
Bulgaria.

1 March 1941: The first British troops land at Salonika in northern Greece.
From 4 March further British units transferred from North Africa to Greece.
During the period 7–17 March the New Zealand Division lands at Piraeus,
the harbour of Athens.

9 March 1941: Mussolini launches an offensive on the Albanian front. It stalls
after two days.

25 March 1941: Yugoslavia signs the Tripartite Pact in Vienna. Two days later,
on 27 March, Yugoslav General Simonovitch overthrows the government in
Belgrade. The young King Peter accedes to the throne. Yugoslavia revokes
its membership of the Tripartite Pact. On the same day, 27 March, Hitler
issues his War Directive No. 25: '*Blitzkrieg* campaign against Yugoslavia in
conjunction with the attack on Greece.'

24 March 1941: Elements of the Afrika-Korps under General Rommel take El
Agheila. On 30 March Rommel launches a daring counter-offensive by
German–Italian forces in North Africa. On 2 April Agedabia is captured. By
7 April Benghazi, Msus, Derna and Mechili are back in Axis hands. An
attempt to take Tobruk by storm is abandoned on 10 April.

6 April 1941: In the Balkans the combined German–Italian–Hungarian
offensives against Yugoslavia and Greece begins. On 7 April German troops
capture the Yugoslav town of Skoplje. In Greece on 9 April, after heavy and
costly fighting, German ground troops break through the formidable
'Metaxas Line' defences, which had withstood all previous Stuka attacks. On
9 April the Greek army in Macedonia capitulate. Salonika captured.

Meanwhile, we had remained at readiness at Trapani on Sicily. Our task
there, to prevent the enemy's Gibraltar fleet from intervening in the eastern
Mediterranean, had proved unnecessary. The fleet had kept well out of the way.

On 9 April the Geschwaderkommodore, Oberstleutnant Hagen, informed me
that the German Afrika-Korps had urgently requested immediate Stuka reinforcements. But the Gruppe that was scheduled to be sent to North Africa, 'Toni' Keil's
II./StG 1, had not yet completed its tropicalization programme. It would be at
least another two weeks before the engines of all its aircraft had been fitted with
sand filters and other such essential items.

To bridge the gap we, III./StG 1, were therefore to be transferred – with
immediate effect and without any form of tropical equipment whatsoever – to
North Africa. Our key ground staff would accompany us by air transport. But as
a number of our Ju 87s didn't have the necessary modification kits that would
allow them to be fitted with auxiliary underwing fuel tanks, they would not be able

Above: Junkers Ju 87s of I.(St)/186(T) in close formation.

Right and below right: Practising combat formations: Gruppe open arrowhead...

... Staffel echeloned to starboard in Ketten...

... and Staffel line-astern in Ketten.

Above, all: Hennweiler, May 1940: whiling away the hours as men and machines await their first operational mission in the West.

Gruppenkommandeur Major Hagen (*left*) and his TO (technical officer) Oberleutnant Gassmann.

Oberleutnant Heinze.

Leutnant Skambraks.

Oberleutnant Herbst (*right*) and Unteroffizier Kollmitt who, along with their crew chief, were killed while coming in to land at Falaise on 30 June 1940.

III./StG 1 on parade in the orchard for the Iron Cross, First Class, awards ceremony; Falaise, 29 August 1940.

The Quartermaster-General of the Luftwaffe, Generaloberst Milch, arrives by Fieseler Storch to visit III./StG 1.

Generaloberst Milch (*centre, back to camera*) chats to the portly Hauptmann der Reserve Schellhase. An editor of the *Völkischer Beobachter* – the official organ of the Nazi Party – in civilian life, Schellhase was the Gruppe's arch 'organizer'!

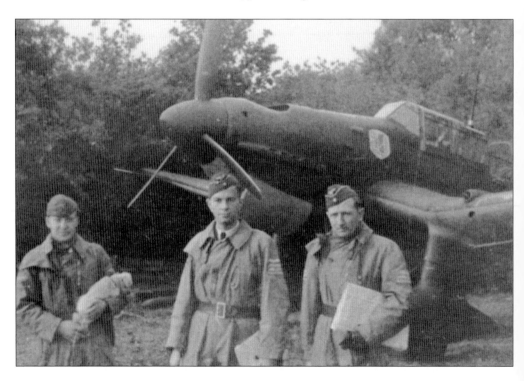

Hauptmann Mahlke (*centre*) with his gunner Unteroffizier Fritzchen ('Little Fritz') Baudisch (*left*) and Oberleutnant Lion (*right*).

7. Staffel's 'J9+AH' taxies out to take off.

Stuka commanders await briefing for 'Adlertag'; Branville, 13 August 1940.
(Author in leather greatcoat facing camera.)

Leaving Falaise for the last time.

Generalfeldmarschall Kesselring, the GOC of Luftflotte 2,
addresses the crews of III./StG 1 at St-Pol.

to make it across the Mediterranean. These machines would instead be collected together into Oberleutnant Heinze's 9. Staffel and placed temporarily under the direct control of the Geschwaderstab. They would stay behind in Sicily and continue to carry out operations from there.

Chapter 11
Operations in North Africa

At 13.35 hours on 10 April 1941 the aircraft of the Gruppenstab, together with those of 7. and 8. Staffeln – their auxiliary tanks topped up to the brim – began taking off from Trapani for the long haul across the Mediterranean to Tripoli. We landed there without incident exactly three hours later.

The two Ju 52s carrying our key ground personnel had already arrived. Inspekteur Schilling, our head admin official, had even tracked down a clothing store where we were able to kit ourselves out with the most important items of tropical clothing: tropical helmets, lightweight khaki shirts, jackets and trousers – not all matching, not necessarily all fitting, but at least suitable for the climate.

Dressed in our new finery we didn't present a very military appearance on the ground. But our Ju 87s would more than make up for that in the air. That was where it mattered. We spent the night in temporary quarters on the airfield and so didn't get to see much of Tripoli itself. We took off at 09.34 hours the next morning for our new base at Derna. We touched down there four hours and 46 minutes later, the longest formation flight – measured in both time and distance – that we had ever made in our Ju 87s. Derna landing ground was perched on the escarpment immediately to the south of the coastal town of the same name, which had been captured by German troops on 7 April. It was one of the many small towns strung along the Libyan coastal highway, now the Afrika-Korps' main supply route.

Derna landing ground: nothing but sand and stones as far as the eye could see. Here nothing grew – no trees to provide welcome shade, no bushes, not even weeds. A single tumbledown building stood at the edge of the field. We were waved in towards it. Apparently this marked our Staffel dispersal areas and the Gruppe's command post. The latter was quickly set up in the lee of one of the ruined walls: an empty bomb crate was stood up on end to serve as a desk and the Gruppe's single field telephone – just connected – was dumped on top of it. Job done! There couldn't have been a finer example of the motto we lived by: 'Where you find the Gruppenkommandeur, that's where you'll find the command post.' It also helped no end in reducing unnecessary paperwork to an absolute minimum.

Situated on the other side of a small road, on the edge of a much larger landing ground, was the operational HQ of Generalmajor Fröhlich – the Fliegerführer Afrika [Air Commander Africa] – under whose command we now came. The large landing ground housed the aircraft of II./StG 2, led by Hauptmann Enneccerus, the Stukagruppe that had been supporting Rommel's troops since the opening of his campaign in North Africa.

I went to see General Fröhlich to report III./StG 1 arrived in Derna with two Staffeln and ready for operations. He welcomed me warmly and sketched in a broad outline of the present situation. He explained to me what our future tasks were likely to be, promising me that there would be no lack of them. Roughly, this is how things stood.

The Afrika-Korps had just captured the town of Bardia on Libya's eastern border and was now pushing onwards into Egypt. But behind the German spearheads the harbour fortress of Tobruk was still being stubbornly defended by British and Australian troops. Yesterday's attempt to take Tobruk by storm had failed. But the capture of Tobruk was vital, not only to prevent the enemy from launching an attack in our rear, but also to shorten our overstretched lines of supply along the one main coastal road in the area.

The Luftwaffe's primary role was therefore to stop any supplies from reaching Tobruk by sea while, at the same time, wearing down the defenders' resistance by constant air bombardment. This, it was hoped, would either force the garrison to surrender, or at least weaken its strength sufficiently to allow its capture by the limited ground forces at our disposal.

General Fröhlich had also summoned Enneccerus, the Kommandeur of II./StG 2, who was to put me in the picture regarding Stuka operations in North Africa. 'Ennec' immediately pointed out to the general that our III./StG 1, with its naval background, would be ideally suited for the anti-shipping role in any forthcoming operations against Tobruk. I certainly had no objection to this, although sadly there were very few of the original old naval hands still serving in our ranks. I could well understand Ennec's distaste for over-water missions. Flying over the open sea in a single-engined aircraft was no rest cure at the best of times. But to do it in Africa, where you could almost hear that one engine choking on the sand it had swallowed, was a real test of nerves – and that's not even to mention the possibility of bumping into enemy fighters while doing so! It was hardly surprising that crews more accustomed to operating over land found it a lot tougher than old seadogs like myself.

I was also happy to accept another of Enneccerus's suggestions. As we were currently only two Staffeln strong, he said, why didn't the Fliegerführer attach the Italian Ju 87 squadron – the so-called 'Pichiatellis', which had been loosely operating with his Gruppe up until now – to III./StG 1 in place of our absent 9. Staffel. The general agreed and issued the necessary orders. He would arrange for interpreters to help overcome the language barrier.

Enneccerus also had some practical tips and advice for us; how to cope, for example, with the sandstorms and scorpions that were both prevalent in these regions. Having taken our boots off, he warned, never put them back on again without first thoroughly checking for scorpions. A warm boot was a favourite hiding place for these venomous little creatures. Armed with this knowledge and a lot more besides, I returned to the Gruppe to brief my unit leaders on the local rules of conduct so that they could, in turn, pass them on to their men.

Welcome as we were as reinforcements in Africa, there was very little in the way of technical or other assistance that could be offered to us. As our deployment was intended merely as a short-term stopgap measure, we had been able to bring with us only the barest minimum of key personnel and essential equipment. There was an awful lot that we had been forced to leave behind, which meant we now had to resort to a great deal of improvisation. Fortunately, our men had had plenty of practice in the art of making do. Our complete lack of transport, however, was a different matter entirely. But we had been in this situation before and knew exactly what needed to be done to solve the problem: we would have to 'organize' for ourselves whatever vehicles were necessary to keep us operational. A small party was therefore sent off into the desert.

Four men – led by Oberleutnant Skambraks, who wasn't going to miss this opportunity – were given enough water and supplies to last them three days. They departed in a borrowed truck. Their destination was a spot in the desert some 200km to the south: Mechili. This was where, four days earlier, on 7 April, Rommel's troops had surrounded and captured a large enemy force. And it was here that our men were to search for any abandoned transport that could be made to run again.

Four days after they had set out the party returned, each of its members at the wheel of a vehicle. The borrowed truck they had driven down to Mechili was now leading four others, ex-enemy vehicles that they had assembled out of the various wrecks they had found littering the Mechili battlefield. That took care of our transport requirements for the next few weeks in Africa. But Skambraks and his little group had two more surprises for us, both very welcome: a large quantity of delicious Australian tinned fruit, and a number of extremely practical folding campaign beds. Needless to say, the fruit didn't last very long. But the beds, which packed away into flat holdalls that could be easily stowed in our machines, were carried with us on all our future moves.

By now we had commenced operations. On the morning of 12 April reconnaissance had reported a ship heading for Tobruk. We were given orders to attack it, and told not to waste any time as a sandstorm was expected. The air was already full of a fine red dust that was making conditions hazy and greatly impairing visibility. By 11.15 hours the Gruppe was in the air.

Our target was somewhere in the sea area to the northeast of Tobruk. We set out in that direction, but as we gained altitude we soon realized that we were rapidly losing all downward visibility. On our seaward side the horizon had already disappeared. We were continually having to sacrifice height in order to stay in sight of the sea beneath us. We were so far out by now that the coastline was just a dim shadow off to our right. Finally, the vague outline of a ship to port ahead. Our target! We would have to head further out to sea before turning in to attack. The weather was not helping: no horizon ahead of us, the land no longer visible behind us.

Ordering the Gruppe into line astern, I curved in towards the vessel. We were flying so low that there was just enough height for a shallow-angle attack. The ship, a merchantman of little more than 3,000 grt, was already sending some well-aimed light Flak up at us. Conditions were still against us. Sharply silhouetted against the all-pervading haze, we must have made perfect targets. Attack! The ship was blanketed by the explosions of our bombs. A tall pillar of steam indicated that her boilers had been hit.

For some unexplained reason Leutnant Buchholz of 7. Staffel failed to recover properly after the attack. His Ju 87 lurched and smashed into the sea a few hundred metres beyond the target. Buchholz and his gunner didn't stand a chance. Did the damaged ship manage to reach Tobruk? We never did find out. The rapidly deteriorating visibility forced us to head back to Derna as quickly as possible. All the signs were that the threatened sandstorm was closer to us than had been expected. And the one thing above all others that had been drummed into us when we arrived in Africa was: 'Never, *ever* fly in a sandstorm. You won't get out of it alive!'

After a flight lasting two hours we eventually landed back at Derna in the most appalling conditions. Three aircraft and crews were missing, although at the time we barely registered this dreadful news, for everybody on the field was fighting hard against the powerful forces of nature. The storm must have been nearing its peak, the wind was howling, and the air was so full of sand and fine dust that it was hard to see anything, hard even to breathe. There was a mad scramble to anchor the aircraft down securely, to get the tarpaulin covers over them and to pack all our small portable items of equipment away into heavy bomb crates.

Then we were all driven down to our billets in Derna. Only a small duty squad of technical personnel remained behind in the large stormproof tent that now served as our command post up on the airfield. Even with everyone working flat out, we had only just got everything done in the nick of time. If anything, the storm was gaining in ferocity and the wind was now so strong that it was almost impossible to keep on one's feet out in the open. Sand was being driven into the smallest cracks and crevices. Sand – sand – everywhere sand – fine grains of sand like reddish-brown flour. On the skin, in the hair, in the eyes, nose and mouth – everywhere sand. Yet between the teeth it felt like grit. And it went on like this for hour after hour. The storm howled and shrieked. The infernal sand brought all activity to a standstill. We could do nothing but get under cover and wait it out.

Sitting in our quarters we tried to work out what had happened to our three missing crews. But there wasn't an awful lot to be learned. 7. Staffel's Leutnant Buchholz and his gunner, Gefreiter David Kerschbaumsteiner, had both been killed almost immediately after attacking the ship. Of that there wasn't the slightest doubt. One crew even claimed to have seen Buchholz's machine fly into a wire fired into the air from the vessel, but this could not be confirmed. Due to the poor visibility, nobody had seen what had happened to the other two crews that failed to return: Feldwebel Holzinger and Gefreiter Anwand, also of 7. Staffel, and Unteroffiziere Wegscheider and Hertz of 8. Staffel. We could only hope that they had managed to land somewhere and were still alive.

The storm continued to rage throughout the night and into the following day. We were being shown in no uncertain terms what a fully-fledged desert sandstorm was really like and exactly what it could do. It kept us pinned to the ground, demonstrating to us in all its savagery just how powerless we were against the primeval forces of nature. Without cover we would never have survived. But during the afternoon of 13 April the wind slowly began to abate. And by evening the sun had broken through. Almost as quickly as it had arrived, the sandstorm was gone. We breathed out!

The ground crews were now faced with a task that was completely new and unfamiliar to them. Using either their hands or empty ration tins, they began scooping incredible quantities of sand out of the innermost recesses of our machines. They had to make sure that all movable parts still actually moved, that all air intakes were free of sand and that the aircraft were fully operational again. It was already too late in the day to fly any missions even if they were, so we decided to take advantage of the calm after the storm – in its truest sense – and have a stroll round the town of Derna in the evening sunshine.

An Easter outing, in fact. With everything that had been happening, we had almost forgotten that today was Easter Sunday. In the company of Oberleutnant Skambraks and our medical officer, Dr Bock, I set out to get at least some impression of the country and the people in this part of North Africa. Behind the high stone walls of some gardens we could see palms, bushes and cacti; occasionally even the odd flower or two. The white-painted buildings in the local styles, with their domed cupolas or flat roofs and squat towers, were particularly attractive and picturesque. They had narrow entry doors, mostly arched, but very few windows; those we saw being mainly small and circular. They were no doubt far better suited to the region's climate than those buildings of European style, which looked nondescript and totally out of place by comparison.

The inhabitants seemed to be going about their normal everyday business. It was such a peaceful scene that you could almost forget that there was a war on. On the streets we saw only children at play and small groups of men. We studied each other with scarcely veiled curiosity. Some of the men smiled in a friendly enough manner, but unfortunately the language barrier prevented any common understanding. Instead, contact was established by means of combined group photos. Some even agreed to having close-up portraits taken. Their splendid features would have been worth painting in oils. True, we saw a lot of poverty. But we also saw calm contentment, and faces that radiated pride and dignity. I got the feeling that these people, leading their uncomplicated lives under the African sun, understood more of the joy of living than many an ambitious and overworked central European. The squeaking and rattling of a column of passing tanks interrupted my reverie and reminded us that a war was being fought not far away.

We were billeted in a hotel-like building that was clean but very sparsely furnished. Our favourite spot was the roof terrace. This was where the officers and officials of the Gruppe took their meals together when the weather was fine. This was also where we gathered to spend our few off-duty hours.

By this time our command post had also acquired some additional creature comforts. As well as the original bomb crate for a desk, the field telephone, and the tent added later, we now had a couple of comfortably upholstered chairs – actually they were the seats taken out of a wrecked car – plus a portable wireless that brought us all the news from home.

We had even found ourselves a car for the more urgent runs that had to be made between our quarters in town and the Gruppe's command post and the HQ of Fliegerführer Afrika up on the escarpment. It was an ancient Adler Trumpf-Junior that was just about ready for the scrap heap. It had a cracked cylinder and would rattle along, emitting the most alarming noises, until all the water that had been poured in at the top had run out of the bottom. In fact, it used far more water than petrol and so could only be used for short journeys, as its radius of action was totally dependent on the amount of water we could take with us each time. Despite its handicaps, the old Adler had an impressive turn of speed – we regularly coaxed it up to 80km/h and more.

One of the mechanics among the small party that had remained in the command post tent up on the airfield during the sandstorm actually *did* discover a scorpion nestling in his boot before he put it back on. It was a good thing we had been warned always to check! From then on none of us removed his boots while on the field, however hot and uncomfortable they became in the 40-degree heat. It was almost laughable: here was a bunch of Stuka flyers who would hurl themselves into a curtain of Flak without batting an eyelid, yet were terrified of such a tiny creature! But it was understandable. It would have been sheer foolhardiness to ignore the danger posed by this miniature assassin.

On 14 April we took off at 06.00 hours to attack fortified positions on the edge of Tobruk town. We started a large conflagration that remained visible for a long time, suggesting that we had perhaps hit a fuel dump. A second mission later that same afternoon was directed against a ship making for Tobruk harbour. My adjutant, Leutnant Martinz, was hit in the radiator during the attack on the vessel. We shepherded him back to the coast and watched as he made a smooth forced-landing in the desert a few kilometres to the west of Tobruk. We had every reason to hope that he would soon be back with us.

Shortly after landing back at Derna we received a surprise visit from the AOC X. Fliegerkorps, General der Flieger Geisler. He was accompanied by General-major Fröhlich, the Fliegerführer Afrika. Under the overall command of Luftflotte 2 (Feldmarschall Kesselring), these two officers were our immediate superiors in Africa. General Geisler again addressed a few words to the aircrews, who had been hastily assembled upon our visitors' arrival. Occasions such as this, however brief, raised the spirits of everyone involved.

But the situation as a whole was less rosy. Despite repeated and very costly attacks, today's attempt to take Tobruk had also ended in failure. After capturing Bardia, Capuzzo and Sollum, the Afrika-Korps' advance had ground to a halt. It had nonetheless been a bold and daring venture by General Rommel, whose forces had consisted of only one German division, the 5th Light, and the Italians.

That evening we received some particularly galling news. Due to some communications foul-up or other, the current situation maps that we had been given were wrong! Although the positions of our forward ground troops in the Sollum area were marked correctly, the enemy's outer defensive ring around Tobruk was shown as being a lot smaller and much closer to the town and harbour than it really was. Only now did we discover that the fortifications around the outer perimeter of the town – some of them a good 16km from the harbour – were, in fact, still firmly held by the enemy and the scene of much bitter fighting. In other words, the enemy's bridgehead around Tobruk was far larger than we had been led to believe.

This had cost us three experienced and courageous crews. For all three aircraft that had failed to return from our first missions in Africa had force-landed in this very area. What must they have felt? Picture the scene for yourself: Nursing your crippled machine back across the sea to the safety of dry land – land that was (supposedly) in friendly hands. There you manage to pull off a successful emergency landing in difficult terrain. From a flying point of view, everything has ended happily. With a sense of relief you climb out of your aircraft and suddenly find yourself surrounded – not by welcoming faces – but by armed enemy soldiers. A very nasty shock!

This slip by an unknown staff officer, however minor it may have seemed, had as good as sentenced three Stuka crews to captivity. But we took comfort from the fact that all had indeed survived their forced landings. Later still we learned that they had been taken to POW camps in Australia.

I found it particularly hard to accept the fact that Leutnant Martinz would not be coming back – that no more would he fly as Number 3 in my Stabskette; that on the ground no longer would he always be at my side as Gruppen-Adjutant. A lively and exuberant young Austrian, Martinz had proven himself a Stuka pilot of sterling worth, someone you could rely on however fraught the situation. On the ground he was the perfect adjutant, tempering his military duties and responsibilities with just the right amount of his native charm and wit. Everyone liked having him around. You felt that he was always prepared to do that little bit more than had been asked of him. He would have found his unnecessary capture especially hard to take. But none of the crews could possibly reproach themselves for having opted to make their forced-landings where they did. Until today none of us had been aware that it was enemy territory.

We remained at readiness throughout 15 and 16 April, but were not called upon to fly any operations. On 17 April we put in an early afternoon attack on Fort Solario, one of Tobruk's many inner defence fortifications.

Then came the morning of 18 April, and with it an operational order from the Fliegerführer Afrika: 'The army at Sollum reports the presence off the coast of an enemy battleship that has been bombarding its positions with heavy calibre gunfire for several days now. III./StG 1 is to locate and sink the battleship. Take-off 09.45 hours. Fighter escort one Rotte [pair] of Me 110s.' There was a rush to attach the auxiliary fuel tanks to their underwing racks and hoist a 500kg bomb into the ventral yoke beneath the fuselage of each machine. Punctually at 09.45 hours the first of III./StG 1's twelve aircraft took to the air.

Heading out to sea, we turned eastwards and began to climb steadily, remaining just in sight of the coast to our right. The two Me 110s took up station, but as we were passing Tobruk they spotted an enemy reconnaissance machine flying in the opposite direction and immediately chased off after it! So much for our fighter protection – just off Tobruk, as well, where the RAF always seemed to have a few fighters on hand. But fortunately we were too far out to be discovered and so continued on our way undisturbed until we reached the Bay of Sollum.

A gathering sea mist was beginning to affect visibility. We flew down into the bay and carried out a thorough search until we were absolutely certain that there were no ships present. The reported battleship must have retired from the area. We set course ENE and headed back further out over the open sea. Our fuel was getting low. We wouldn't be able to spend a lot of time looking for the vessel. We peered into the mist, straining our eyes to see as far as possible. And finally, there off to starboard way ahead of us, we caught a glimpse of a darker shadow. We turned towards it.

It was a ship! It looked like an old-fashioned flatiron on the surface of the water, the typical broad-beamed planform of a large warship. The bone in its teeth showed that it was travelling at high speed. It was making for Sollum Bay and had to be our target. Our four Ketten slid into line-astern battle formation and increased speed ready to attack. As we dived, more details of the vessel became apparent. Strange: on the wide expanse of both fore and after decks there was a circular set of rails. Were they perhaps part of the gun turret mechanism? No time to think about that now. Aim for the bows. Only a very slight wind. Angle of sight one degree. Height 800 metres – 500 metres – bomb release height 300 metres – press the button – bomb gone! Recover and make a left-hand turn – watch for results: a direct hit on the foredeck!

Feldwebel Baudisch confirms: all three of the Stabskette's bombs have hit the foredeck. The second Kette hits full amidships. The vessel's bows are already below the waterline. The third Kette plants its bombs on the afterdeck now rising high out of the water. Within a matter of seconds the huge ship has disappeared ghost-like beneath the slight Mediterranean swell. Our fourth and last Kette, already committed to its dive, could no longer see any trace of the vessel – only a patch of disturbed water. They brought their bombs back to base.

As we set course for home, our thoughts were still with the ship we had just sunk and those unfortunate sailors who had been aboard her. The vessel had gone under so quickly that few would have had the chance to save themselves. Such were the fortunes of war. But we weren't home and dry yet either.

We kept our distance as we crept back past Tobruk, conscious of our lack of escort and all the more grateful to the enemy's fighters for leaving us alone. Even without enemy interference, flying for hours over open water in a single-engined aircraft and attacking a well-defended target, a warship, had been nerve-wracking enough. It had given us too much time to dwell on the fact that our engines were already way past their 100-hour overhaul mark. Instead of being cosseted in a cosy workshop, they had been left standing out in the desert sands of Africa – without filters or any other kind of protection – for so long that you could almost hear them chewing on the sand that they had been forced to swallow. It never ceased to amaze us how much ill treatment our gallant Iolanthes would take without a murmur of complaint. After a flight lasting 2 hours and 35 minutes we landed back at Derna.

But what kind of ship had we sent to the bottom? I tried to get the answer to this question during debriefing. The crews were all agreed on one thing: it had been no modern battleship, that was for sure! Those circular rails on its fore and after decks were more reminiscent of the racer-rings used for the wheeled mountings of older-type ships' turrets. But these could still have fired the heavy shells that had been giving the army around Sollum such a hard time. The vessel obviously hadn't been fitted with an armoured deck; otherwise our bombs wouldn't have caused such devastating damage, sending it down before our very eyes. We came to the conclusion that it could very well have been an elderly shallow-draught coastal monitor, and so that's what we put in our combat report to the Fliegerführer Afrika: '. . . 11.05 hours in sea area NE of Sollum warship or armed merchantman of approx. 8,000 tons, probably an old coastal monitor, attacked and sunk. No losses.'

Afrika-Korps confirmed that the bombardment of Sollum from the sea had stopped. And a few days later we heard from the intelligence services that we had indeed sunk a monitor – mission accomplished.

The following day, 19 April, we were sent out to attack another group of enemy vessels reported to be approaching the coast. This time, however, despite a two-and-a-half hour search of the area indicated, we found nothing and had to return to Derna empty-handed.

On 21 April we took off at 17.15 hours to bomb shipping in Tobruk harbour. Early the next morning we returned to Tobruk; our target being Fort Medauar on the southwestern perimeter of the town's defences. On 23 April we carried out two more attacks on ships in the harbour. We hit a fair-sized ship berthed alongside the 'L' mole and a number of smaller vessels. It was always difficult to assess the effect our bombing had on ships in port. As already mentioned, the results were usually less conclusive than when we attacked ships at sea. For the most part, those in harbour did not have steam up and were not under way. They therefore tended to look very much the same after our attacks as they had done before we bombed them – unless, of course, we happened by chance to hit one loaded with munitions or explosives! But the British clearly found these raids of ours a nuisance, if nothing else. Their Flak always had a warm welcome waiting for us.

A third mission on that 23 April was an evening attack on enemy positions around the Bay of Zeitun to the east of Tobruk.

On the morning of 25 April we sank a large freighter, whose tonnage we estimated to be about 8,000 grt, in the sea area off Tobruk. In the afternoon we went out after a smaller merchantman sighted in the same area. But this vessel seemed to bear a charmed life. Although we fairly plastered it with bombs, the ship's skilful manoeuvring saved it from major harm and meant that we could only claim it as slightly damaged. As we were all running low on fuel, we were unable to leave anyone behind to shadow it and so had to assume that it succeeded in reaching its port of destination.

For the best part of the next week we then concentrated mainly on ground targets around Tobruk, flying as many as three missions on some days. 27 April: Flak emplacements south of the harbour. 28 April: Morning, shipping in the harbour; afternoon, strongpoints – and in between the two, at midday, a ship off Tobruk. 30 April: Defence works close to the harbour. 1 May: Artillery positions NE of Hill 209; then Fort Pilastrino, part of the inner defence perimeter.

During most of these missions against ground targets in and around Tobruk, the Gruppe was accompanied by our Italian Ju 87 comrades of the Pichiatelli squadron.

The Italian Macchi fighters that often escorted us also richly deserve a mention. But it has to be said that our first combined mission with the Pichiatellis was, by our standards, something of a fiasco. Because it had been ordered in a hurry, and due to the language difficulties, we had been able to do little more than simply arrange for the Italians to attach themselves to us as a third Staffel, follow us to the target – an artillery emplacement – and do exactly as we did: bomb release at 500 metres, recovery to the west, and re-form while climbing westwards back to base.

We carried out the attack as ordered. After recovering, I climbed slowly away towards the west, doing my usual weaving act to allow the rearmost aircraft to catch up with me as quickly as possible. We were soon back in formation – but where were the Pichiatellis? They had been tucked in close behind us as we were preparing to dive, but now they had simply disappeared! Finally, against the glare of the setting sun, I spotted a cluster of tiny black dots high up in the evening sky far to the west of us – our missing Pichiatellis. But they couldn't possibly be up there if they had dived with us and bombed from 500 metres as instructed. They had probably let go their bombs at something more like 2,000 metres and then turned round and promptly hoofed it – that wouldn't do at all!

Before our next combined operation, which was to be against enemy troop positions immediately to the south of the town of Tobruk, I therefore enlisted the help of the interpreter to try to explain our tactics to the Staffelkapitän of the Pichiatellis in more detail. I made it clear to him that, when recovering after the dive, I always had to look out for the safety of the last aircraft in the formation. If any pilots got ahead of me and were then attacked by enemy fighters, I would be unable to go to their aid without endangering the entire unit – and this I was not prepared to do. So it would be safest for his squadron to remain firmly in position, even during the dive down to the height of bomb release ordered, and especially afterwards during the recovery phase.

In order to make sure that he had grasped what I had been saying, I spelled out my orders for the forthcoming mission as clearly and concisely as I could: Dive sequence – Stabskette, 7. Staffel, Pichiatelli, 8. Staffel – bomb release 300 metres – recovery northwards at low level across the town of Tobruk – regroup, still at low level, out to sea – once out of Flak range alter course westward.

This time everything went like clockwork. All of us, the Pichiatellis included, gave the target a thorough working over. And when we flew out across the town of Tobruk, the Italians weren't just at rooftop level – they were at street level! As they raced along the roads leading northwards to the sea, they were lost to sight now and again below the roofs of the buildings. It was a demonstration of pure flying skill, enough to gladden the seat of any old pilot's pants. The Pichiatellis were clearly enjoying themselves enormously. At this height the Flak couldn't touch them. In no time at all we were out over the sea and back in formation with the Pichiatellis in their right position. And when we neared Derna they slipped into place in our usual approach and landing pattern as if it were the most natural thing in the world. Full marks, the Pichiatellis.

During debriefing at the command post of the Fliegerführer Afrika, I wanted to congratulate the Pichiatelli Kapitän on his squadron's excellent performance, saying that it had been exactly what we were expecting from them. But he didn't give me the chance. He came rushing up to us, waving both arms about excitedly and shouting in delight. The interpreter could hardly keep pace with his enthusiastic outpourings: 'That was absolutely fantastic! This time we could see our target clearly and we hit it slap bang in the middle. Now at last we know exactly what to do. Up until now nobody has ever bothered to tell us or show us how. Thank you! Thank you!' . . . 'You're welcome, I'm sure.'

After this mission the Pichiatelli squadron flew in formation with us as if they had been part and parcel of the Gruppe from the very beginning. Their enthusiasm rubbed off on the pilots of our escorting Macchis too. In the target area, what we really wanted from a good fighter escort was for two aircraft to remain above us as top cover, two to be waiting for us down at recovery height, and two to accompany us during the dive itself.

The Macchi pilots interpreted this quite literally. Our wish became their command. On the next mission the two Macchis flying level with us took up their positions: one about 100 metres to the right of me, the other the same distance to the left of me. I gave the signal to start the attack, extended my dive brakes and tipped forward into an 80-degree dive – and the two Macchis came with me! How they managed to do that – their machines had no dive brakes, of course – was an absolute mystery to me. Quite simply, those boys could fly. The light Flak couldn't decide which one of us to shoot at first. The enemy gunners were put completely off their stroke. Their shooting hadn't been as poor as this for a very long time.

The two Macchi pilots were clearly having fun. After retiring out of range of Tobruk's Flak defences, I signalled for the Gruppe to close up into arrowhead formation. My two escorting fighters immediately tucked themselves in tightly to right and left of me. Easing off their throttles, they slid smoothly into the slots normally occupied by my two wingmen, forcing the latter, in their turn, to formate on the two intruding Macchis. And so that's how we flew back to Derna, with the Gruppe being led by an extended, mixed Stabskette of five machines: three Ju 87s and two Macchis. We understood each other much better in the air than on the ground. In the air it could all be done without words.

Around midday on 2 May we again attacked a ship in Tobruk harbour. We estimated it to have been about 3,000 grt. If we didn't sink it, we at least inflicted some pretty severe damage. After touching down back at Derna at 14.05 hours we received a message from the Fliegerführer Afrika: 'Gruppe stood down for remainder of day to carry out essential maintenance.' For the first time since arriving in Africa we were finally being allowed a breathing space to undertake all the servicing work that was crying out to be done on our machines. The ground crews soon had the engine cowlings off and began by shovelling out all the fine desert sand that had found its way back into every tiny nook and cranny. There was sand everywhere! It was a miracle our engines were still running. It was almost as if they were actually benefiting from the constant sandblasting they were getting!

In the meantime the aircrews had piled into one of our captured trucks and driven down to the beach for a dip in the Mediterranean. But then, at around 16.45 hours, the field telephone in our command post rang. On the line – something we had never had before – was Generalmajor Fröhlich in person: 'Mahlke,' he began, 'I know I have just stood you down. But could you and your Gruppe go up again today – and as soon as possible?' 'Not for an hour at least, Herr General. The mechanics have started stripping down the engines and the crews will have to be fished out of the Mediterranean. What's it all about, Herr General?'

'Rommel has just been on to me. Apparently the British are making a push out of Tobruk. They're being supported by tanks and have broken through the Italians on the western perimeter. There's an urgent request for an immediate Stuka attack. Top priority!' 'We'll be taking off at 17.50 hours, Herr General, with everything we can get into the air. I'd like some fighter cover.' 'I'll see to it. Thank you, Mahlke. Out.'

'Alarm! Prepare all machines for an immediate mission. Load for land targets. Send a truck down to the beach – Collect all crews and take them straight to Staffel dispersals – Staffelkapitäne to Gruppe command post – Take-off 17.50 hours. *Move!*'

The truck was already on its way to the beach. With a speed and precision born of long practice, the mechanics went to work and soon had the machines fully operational again, the cowlings back on, bombed up, refuelled and re-armed. One after the other the crew chiefs reported their aircraft ready for take-off. The two Staffelkapitäne came tearing up in our old car, announcing that the truck bringing the crews would be along any minute. The men had scrambled aboard still in their swimming gear and were changing into their uniforms on the journey back to the field.

The ops officer called from Fliegerführer Afrika to give us the latest situation report. I passed this on to my Staffelkapitäne together with the plan of attack: Take-off at 17.50 hours to attack enemy troops, and particularly enemy tanks, exploiting the break-out west of Tobruk. Attack in waves, but bomb individually – follow up with ground-strafing for as long as ammunition lasts. Prepare for take-off. The Staffelkapitäne quickly relayed these instructions to their crews who had just arrived. Everyone rushed to their machines – fasten harnesses – close canopies – ignition on – taxi out to take-off line. On the dot of 17.50 hours the first aircraft lifted off. As always here in Africa, they left a thick cloud of sand and dust hanging in the air behind them, from which the remaining machines emerged one by one in rapid succession.

We arrived over the target area. From the air the situation didn't look as threatening as had been made out to us. On our side of the Tobruk perimeter all we could see were several small groups of soldiers, in roughly squad or platoon strength, slowly withdrawing. They didn't appear to be doing any fighting, but were simply marching westwards in relatively good order. We began to bomb the area of the reported breach, attacking in waves and aiming at anything that moved: trucks, a few armoured cars – but also artillery and Flak emplacements, all of which were banging away at a furious rate. Of tanks we saw no sign. Or was that a tank that had just been hit by one of our bombs? To be honest, from up here it looked more like a field kitchen! Dumps of ammunition were exploding. With all the dust and clouds of smoke covering the battlefield it was difficult to see anything at all at times. But even with their bombs gone, our Stukas continued to dive into the maelstrom, searching for targets and firing at whatever they could find.

After completing yet another strafing run our aircraft was suddenly hit by a burst of machine-gun fire from the ground. As chance would have it, the rounds just missed the gunner's seat armour and caught Feldwebel Baudisch in the thigh. I heard him give a soft groan over the R/T: 'I've been hit. Several bullets in the top of my left thigh. Losing a lot of blood.' 'Can you put a tourniquet on it?' I asked, as I immediately hauled the aircraft round and headed west, away from the battlefield. 'No, the wounds are too high up.' 'Can you hold on then until we get to the nearest fighter field at Gazala? About ten or fifteen minutes?' 'Hope so,' he answered weakly.

In the rear-view mirror I could see the face of my loyal 'Fritzchen' Baudisch. It was drained of all colour. He looked in a really bad way. But in the aircraft I couldn't get to him; couldn't help him. Minutes counted now, perhaps even seconds. The nearest and quickest place to get medical aid was the Army's casualty clearing station. I knew this was the large tent marked with the Red Cross, which was situated on the supply road skirting the Tobruk perimeter at the point where it branched off the main coastal highway. I turned towards it.

The 'supply road' was nothing more than a broad swath of desert that had been worn flat by the wheels of the countless trucks driving along it. At the moment, luckily, it was free of all traffic. I touched down on it and taxied quickly across to the casualty clearing station, leaving a cloud of dust in my wake. I pulled up right in front of the tent. Some medics came running out. 'Be careful!' I yelled to them, 'The engine's still running – watch out for the propeller! Go round to the rear cockpit from the tail.' They carefully lifted my badly wounded gunner from his seat and carried him straight to the operating table only metres away inside the tent. He was in good hands now.

Meanwhile, I had been looking around me. The ground on all sides was a mass of small sandy hummocks and stunted clumps of grass. Between the grass the sand had formed into deep drifts, interspersed with large areas of loose shingle. I would never be able to lift off again from here. Only the 'road' immediately behind me was free of obstacles and suitable for a take-off. But I couldn't taxi back out to it, or even turn in a tight circle from where I was now standing, without running the risk of tipping my machine onto its nose. I beckoned to a nearby group of soldiers and asked them to heave the tail of my Ju 87 round so that I was pointing back in the direction I had come from. That did the trick. I taxied carefully back out on to the road, which was being kept clear for me, pushed the throttle forward, lifted off smoothly and set course for Derna.

The sun was going down. Then it was night. There wasn't a dusk in these parts.

In Derna no one would be expecting me to arrive now. As I approached the field, I should have fired off a recognition flare. But I couldn't. That had always been Fritzchen's job – which is why the flare pistol and cartridges were stowed in the rear cockpit. I ought to have remembered to bring them up front with me before taking off from the clearing station. But I hadn't, and now it was too late – I couldn't reach them.

This meant I would have to reckon with a welcome from our own Flak gunners as I came in 'unannounced', and their shooting was a lot better than I would have liked in my present situation. I therefore tried to sneak in at low level and my wheels had actually touched the ground before the field's light Flak defences opened up at me. Fortunately, the cloud of dust I was kicking up persuaded the gunners that I was coming in to land, not to strafe, and they immediately ceased fire again.

As I taxied in to dispersal, the ground crews came rushing up to me, their concern written large on their faces. The rear cockpit was empty! Where was Baudisch? I calmed their fears with a brief explanation about what had happened, saying that I was sure all would be well with him. (A few days later Feldwebel Baudisch was brought back to Derna and placed in the care of the medical air evacuation Staffel. He was subsequently flown to Trapani where he received further treatment – and where, after our own return to Sicily, we were also able to keep an eye on him.)

When I reported to the Fliegerführer Afrika command post I found everyone there in the best of spirits. General Rommel had just rung through to say: 'Situation at Tobruk resolved by Stuka intervention. Many thanks.' Only then did it occur to me. That's right! As I left the area with the badly wounded Baudisch, I now remembered seeing what I presumed to be the same small groups of soldiers that I had noticed marching westwards on my arrival, only this time moving back eastwards – although, as far as I could tell, they still didn't appear to be engaged in any fighting.

On the afternoon of 4 May Fliegerführer Afrika's operations officer had another mission for us. We were ordered to attack a large merchantman of some 10,000grt that reconnaissance had reported about to be entering Tobruk harbour. I very much doubted that the British would risk sending such a large vessel into Tobruk at this time. 'That's got to be a hospital ship,' I said, 'What did it look like?' The ops officer obviously questioned the reconnaissance pilot before answering: 'No Red Cross markings seen. Vessel white with a green stripe around the hull.' 'Those are the colours of a hospital ship. There's got to be a red cross painted on it somewhere. Suggest sending the fighters at Gazala up for a second look, it wouldn't take them long.'

The ops officer ordered the Gazala readiness section to scramble. After about ten minutes the fighters radioed back: 'Vessel displays hospital ship markings. Fired at us with light and medium Flak as we approached.' But a hospital ship wasn't supposed to do that. And so the order to attack it was confirmed.

The ship had in the meantime entered Tobruk harbour and was already tied up at the quay when we arrived high overhead. I had ordered the attack to be made in a steep dive, with bomb release set at 500 metres. A veritable wall of Flak came up to meet us; not just from the Tobruk defences, but from the target vessel as well. Even by Tobruk's standards, it was an impressive display – and we were in the middle of it! Swarms of red fireflies were flashing past my cockpit windows. They were growing ever thicker and getting ever closer. There's going to be one hell of a bang any second now, I thought. This is not looking at all good.

The needle of my altimeter was just unwinding past the 1,000-metre mark when a sudden change in wind direction forced me to turn and correct my angle of dive in order to keep the target in my sights. In this much Flak I'm never going to make it down another 500 metres, I said to myself, but before it gets me I can at least let go a few live ones. (The fuzes in our bombs armed them a second or two after they had dropped away from the aircraft.) I therefore pressed the bomb release button prematurely – at a height of about 700 metres – but continued to dive, expecting to hear that big bang and meet my end at any moment. But nothing happened! I recovered at low level and then raced out to sea before slowing down to set about the usual routine of getting the Gruppe back into formation. So it hadn't been the end after all! There must have been quite a sizeable hole in that wall of Flak. And, incredibly, we had all dived straight through it without getting as much as a scratch.

But our target had also had more than its fair share of luck as well. It had taken only one hit – from one of my small 50kg underwing bombs that had struck its upper deck and torn a gash in its side. All the other aircraft that had followed me down had been so badly thrown off by the change in wind direction that they were still turning and trying to compensate for it when they reached the 500-metre point of release. Consequently, every one of their bombs had missed, exploding off to one side of the vessel. The ship developed a list, but was nonetheless able to leave Tobruk harbour under its own steam later that same night. By the following morning it was beyond the range of our Ju 87s.

In place of the wounded Baudisch, the Gruppe's technical officer, Oberleutnant Hartmann, had accompanied me on this mission. Starting back in the days of the Polish campaign, Hartmann had amassed an awful lot of back-seat experience. But even he admitted that he had never before seen so much red tracer flying past so close. He was as amazed as I was that we had come out of it with our hides intact. (Perhaps it wasn't just a case of nerves on my part after all?)

On 7 May the Pichiatelli joined us for two attacks on Tobruk's water distillation plant. With a cloud base down to just 300–500 metres, the first mission had to be flown at low level and achieved only marginal results. After the weather had improved and the cloud had lifted, a second attack from a higher altitude scored several direct hits and explosions were seen among the installations.

When we landed back at Derna after the latter raid there was a surprise waiting for me. As I clambered out of the cockpit, the members of the Gruppenstab and representatives from all three Staffeln greeted me with an enormous bunch of flowers! (Where on earth had they managed to find flowers, I remember thinking to myself.) Oberwerkmeister Nigbur, the Gruppe's master mechanic, was also there with a large placard bearing the inscription:

'Heartiest congratulations on your 100th mission!'

So it had been my 'hundredth'! The fact that the ground personnel kept such an accurate record of the aircrews' missions proved just how close were the ties that bound us together. Whenever we took off on an operation they were up there with us in their thoughts, worrying about us until we were all safely back down again. The moment we appeared over the horizon they stopped what they were doing to count the returning aircraft. Only when all were accounted for did normal work resume. A sign of true comradeship. A celebratory drink – Thank you, every single one of you!

My hundredth also happened to be the last mission the Gruppe was to fly in North Africa. Our return flight to Trapani, via Wadi Tamet, was scheduled for 8 May 1941. And with our temporary desert deployment at an end, it was on this date that we said farewell to North Africa.

Chapter 12
Trapani/Sicily

After the briefest of stops for refuelling at Wadi Tamet, we landed back at Trapani at 13.45 hours on 8 May 1941. We had been forced to leave two Ju 87s and their crews behind at Derna because of engine trouble. They were to follow on later under the command of 7. Staffel's technical officer, Leutnant Nordmann, once their problems had been sorted out. The engine of one of the aircraft was not firing properly on two cylinders. The necessary replacement parts were not available in North Africa, which meant that it could not be fixed. But despite the ailing engine, Theo Nordmann nonetheless decided to risk the flight back across the Mediterranean anyway. A born optimist, our Theo!

He took off in the company of two Ju 52 transport aircraft, but in the middle of the Mediterranean, somewhere near the island of Pantelleria, his engine finally quit. It had simply had enough. Nordmann was forced to ditch. The crew of one of the Ju 52s dropped him a dinghy. But they had misjudged the strength of the wind and it fell quite a distance away from the pair in the water below. Hampered by his life-jacket, Nordmann couldn't swim fast enough to reach it. Realizing it was his only chance, he discarded the jacket and struck out for the fast disappearing dinghy. If only the wind weren't so strong!

Nordmann was swimming for his life. With his last ounce of strength he managed to catch up with the dinghy and haul himself into it. Not only that, he was somehow able to paddle it back and pick up his exhausted gunner. But then they could do no more. Their hands were so cold and stiff that they couldn't even prise open the watertight tin containing emergency provisions and – more importantly – a signal pistol and flares. This latter was to have dramatic consequences.

The two Ju 52s landed at Trapani as dusk was falling. They were immediately despatched back out to the area where Nordmann's machine had gone in with orders to maintain contact. But in the darkness they were unable to find the dinghy. Down below, Nordmann could hear the Ju 52s flying backwards and forwards close above his head, but he had no way of attracting their attention. He still couldn't get at the flare pistol. The metal container it was in had been too tightly and securely closed.

The following morning we requested permission to send one of our Staffeln out on a grid search. But permission was denied. The entire Gruppe was to remain at immediate readiness at Trapani. Apparently we were awaiting orders to attack the British Gibraltar fleet, which had reportedly chosen now – of all times – to venture out into the western Mediterranean. The Geschwader *did* send three of its reconnaissance Me 110s to search for our missing crew. By a cruel twist of fate, only one returned. In the prevailing low cloud and poor visibility the other two had crashed into the mountains of Pantelleria. The efforts of the air-sea rescue services, both local and from Pantelleria naval station, also proved unsuccessful in finding Nordmann and his gunner.

The uncertainty surrounding the British Gibraltar fleet's intentions kept us pinned to the ground at Trapani throughout the next two days. It was very hard to sit there doing nothing, trying to come to terms with the fact that hope for our two missing comrades was fading with every passing minute.

On the third day I was summoned to the telephone. A long-distance call from Tripoli. Who on earth could be phoning me from North Africa? 'Leutnant Nordmann here,' a cheerful voice announced. 'Great God above – Nordmann? Is that you? Well, hurrah and many happy returns! How in heaven's name did you end up in Tripoli? We couldn't come out to look for you, we've been held at immediate readiness for the past couple of days.'

'We were rescued by an Italian floatplane. A civilian Ala Littoria machine that was on its way to Tripoli with a full load of passengers. The pilot spotted our dinghy and came down to pick us up, even though there was a heavy swell running – the sea must have been a good three or four. But that lad could definitely handle his aircraft! He managed to take off again, despite the conditions and his machine being overloaded, and took us along with him to Tripoli. There's an aircraft that happens to be leaving here tomorrow bound for Trapani. We're getting a lift back on that.' Everyone was overjoyed when I passed on the news.

An 'enforced mission'

Prior to the Nordmann incident – on the very next day after our arrival back from Africa, in fact – we had been transferred post-haste down to Comiso. The weather could not have been worse, but we were told to prepare for an immediate attack on a large convoy of British ships that had been reported making for Malta. We had no aircraft out shadowing the enemy, and so the exact position of the vessels was not known. The operation was therefore to be carried out in the form of an armed reconnaissance: first find the ships and then attack them. And in these conditions!

On the way down from Trapani to Comiso we had already had to contend with a cloud base of 100 metres and visibility of little more than two kilometres. Out to sea large areas of layered cloud had been reported. In this sort of weather we stood very little chance of even finding the ships (which is probably why the British had risked sending them past us to Malta in daylight in the first place). But High Command regarded the destruction of the convoy before it reached its destination to be of such vital importance that it ordered us to mount the attack with 'optimum operational capacity' – in other words, another 'maximum effort' job. We were being forced to go ahead with it come what may.

And so we took off at 13.15 hours and set course for the target area. Our battle with the weather began almost immediately. With only a medium-strength wind we were able at first to fly above the lowest of the many layers of cloud and maintain a height of about 100 metres. Over our heads, at 300 metres, the cloud was solid. We couldn't climb any higher, for if we got caught in the cloud above us we would never be able to find the ships. Meanwhile the cloud below us, scattered at first, had become thicker and thicker until it too was now a solid unbroken mass. We would have to make our way down through it if we wanted to regain surface visibility.

I ordered the aircraft into closed Gruppe line-astern formation – each machine right behind the other in one long unbroken line with no gaps between the individual Staffeln. Experience had taught us that this was the easiest formation to fly in extremely bad visibility. I could hold the Gruppe together with little danger of mid-air collisions. We continued slowly to lose height through the cloud. At 50 metres we could just make out the white crests of the amorphous slate-grey waves below us. Beneath the cloud, visibility was now down to one kilometre and worsening. The wind had strengthened and storm-like gusts were shaking the aircraft, making instrument flying ever more difficult. Visibility now a bare 500 metres! If we had known the exact position of the enemy convoy, we might have been able to do something about it. But to search for ships in a sea area of any size under these conditions was simply asking too much. In this kind of witches' brew we'd need a hell of a lot more luck than we'd had so far today.

In fact, I'd settle for just keeping the Gruppe in the air and in reasonable safety. Battling against this weather, we'd just about reached the limits of what could be asked of a formation of Ju 87s. I only hoped I hadn't already overstepped those limits. I decided that I would have to abort the mission despite all its urgency. If we succeeded in getting everybody back to base in one piece today, we'd have done all that was humanly possible under the circumstances. After just forty-five interminable minutes in the air, we bowed to the forces of nature again and landed back at Comiso still carrying our bombs. I was hugely relieved when all were safely down on the ground. We topped up our tanks and waited for an improvement in the weather. Perhaps we would have better fortune later on.

Just to make sure that we had covered all eventualities Oberleutnant Heinze, the Kapitän of 9. Staffel, took off again with his wingman on a target and weather reconnaissance flight. After some time had passed the wingman returned alone. He brought with him the tragic news that after attacking an enemy submarine about five kilometres to the northeast of Malta's La Valetta harbour, Oberleutnant Heinze had himself been attacked by three Hurricanes. He had last been seen disappearing into cloud with the three British fighters on his tail. The visibility in the area was so atrocious that the wingman had lost sight of both Heinze and the surfaced submarine. Heinze and his gunner, Unteroffizier Kummerhofe, were posted missing.

The weather in the whole sea area between Sicily and Malta was showing no signs of improvement. In the evening we were therefore ordered by X. Flieger-korps to return to Trapani. The loss of Oberleutnant Heinze had hit the Gruppe hard. He had been with us since the very beginning and was one of the unit's most experienced pilots. He had flown twenty missions during the Polish campaign. Then, after the loss of Hauptmann Blattner at the start of the *Blitzkrieg* in the West, he had taken over command of our old third Staffel, 3.(St)/186(T), shortly before its redesignation as 9./StG 1.

During our recent temporary deployment to North Africa it had been Ober-leutnant Heinze's 9. Staffel that had remained in Sicily. From there they had continued to experiment with night attacks by individual machines similar to those we had mounted while based on the Channel coast. Now, however, the target was not England, but Malta. Heinze had been describing the Staffel's activities to me only the evening before:

Night operations by single Ju 87s against Malta
    Most days we were simply being held at readiness in case we were required to go out against enemy shipping. But as nothing was happening on this front I suggested that, whenever the weather was suitable, we be allowed to continue with the same sort of experimental attacks by night that we had been making against England. I was given the go-ahead. Our primary target was to be the torpedo workshops at La Valetta. This was where the torpedoes used in the air attacks on our North African supply convoys were stored and tested. Situated right by the harbour, the workshops would be easy to spot on bright moonlit nights.
    The problems we faced were similar to those encountered over southern England, if not worse. The extent of the defences concentrated around La

Valetta meant that our aircraft were usually picked up by the searchlight batteries very early on in their approach. And once coned by that many lights, a pilot would be so blinded by the glare that there was every danger of his completely losing control of his machine. He wouldn't even be able to read his turn-and-bank indicator in the reflected glare. We tried all sorts of ways to black out our cockpits, but none of them was any good. If the pilot *did* manage to escape from the beams, he would normally try to set up another attack. But the constant glare from all the searchlights waving about played havoc with our bombing accuracy. Despite that, however, the distinctive layout of the harbour area – even individual ships identified as suitable alternative targets – were usually clear enough to allow us to achieve some results.

Navigation also presented a bigger problem for the crews than it had done over England. We were no longer just hopping across the Channel. Here we were faced with a much longer over-water approach flight, at night, in an aircraft that was not exactly equipped for blind flying. The abilities and flying skills of the crews were tested to the limit, as the horizon was often invisible, with the sea, low-lying mist and night sky all merging into one. To provide some sort of navigational aid on the way down from Trapani, a beacon was set up at Comiso. And with the individual aircraft attacking at intervals of about ten to fifteen minutes, the almost constant searchlight activity in the target area was also a handy guide that could be seen from quite a considerable way away.

Heinze had also arranged for the Staffel's attacks to be synchronized with other bomber and reconnaissance activity over the island. The flares dropped during these high-altitude operations proved a great help in illuminating the target area at night for our dive-bombers. But this hadn't prevented 9. Staffel from suffering several losses. On 19 April two crews had failed to return from early morning missions against Valetta harbour, both timed for around 05.00 hours: Leutnant Steeg with gunner Gefreiter Gündert, and Leutnant Teutloff with Obergefreiter Klein. And on 4 May Unteroffiziere Becker and Wiersgowski had been reported missing after attacking La Valetta's harbour installations at 03.00 hours.

Despite the loss of three of its crews, the results of the Staffel's nocturnal raids on La Valetta were nonetheless considered successful enough, according to Heinze, for him to be given orders to continue with them. Apparently, the justification for this decision was not just the harassment factor, but also the indirect contribution it was believed they were making towards the safety of the African convoys. But then, early in May, night operations against Malta were suddenly called off. This reversal of policy – or so it was rumoured – came about after intervention by the Pope.

All this Heinze had told me only yesterday. And now we had to go on without him. He had made the ultimate sacrifice. Oberleutnant Karl Lion from Saarlouis was immediately appointed Kapitän of 9. Staffel. He too had been a successful member of Hauptmann Blattner's 3.(St)/186(T) – under its original designation of 4./186 – during the Polish campaign. Then, in the general reshuffle after the fall of France, when I had been appointed to the command of III. Gruppe, it had been Oberleutnant Lion I had selected to take with me as my Gruppe Ia, or operations officer.

Since that time Lion had flown on every one of the Gruppe's operations as one of the two wingmen in the Stabskette alongside me. A master of his craft both in the air and on the ground, he was another of our most experienced and successful pilots. A modest man by nature, he was also one of the most reliable, and the best comrade anyone could wish for. In his capable hands the men of 9. Staffel would be well looked after.

By now the campaign in the Balkans was all but over. A lot had happened while we had been in Africa:

11 April 1941: Hungary aligns itself with the Axis powers. That same day Hungarian troops march into Yugoslavia.

12 April 1941: German troops enter Belgrade.

17 April 1941: The Yugoslav Army surrenders (344,000 prisoners).

20 April 1941: Greek Epirus Army capitulates.

27 April 1941: German troops enter Athens.

30 April 1941: All of mainland Greece in German hands (223,000 Greek prisoners, plus 22,000 British troops captured on the Peloponnese after the evacuation of 50,732 men in the period 24–30 April).

The rapid success of these operations had been due in no small measure to the Luftwaffe, whose order of battle in the Balkans had included eight bomber Gruppen, seven Stuka Gruppen, eight fighter Gruppen, two Zerstörer Gruppen, one ground-attack Gruppe and three long-range reconnaissance Staffeln. We had not been part of this force and even now, after our return from North Africa, we were still being held at Trapani doing practically nothing. In the greater scheme of things, however, perhaps our presence alone was having the desired effect, for no British warships had ventured anywhere near us during the hours of daylight. Only once had enemy vessels been reported in our area. That had been the convoy of 9 May, when the weather had been so bad that it had ruled out any possibility of our mounting an attack.

Although we had been ordered to remain at readiness for the next few days, the Gruppe's ground staff now received instructions to pack all their equipment and prepare for transport by rail to Cottbus in Germany. This was to allow them to be ready and waiting for us when we flew back home at some point in the very near future for a brief period of rest and refitting.

To maintain our technical readiness in the interim, each aircraft's chief mechanic was to remain behind with us at Trapani. They were all given a quick course of instruction qualifying them as aircraft mechanic/gunners, which meant that they would now be eligible to fly on operations with us. We also kept back a small party of technical specialists. When the time came for us to fly back to Germany, each of these latter would have to squeeze into the rear cockpit alongside the crew chief-cum-gunner. Meanwhile, our regular wireless-operator/gunners had been ordered to accompany the ground party making the journey to Cottbus by rail.

These rather unusual measures led us to suspect that there was something in the offing. Certain items of recent political news from the outside world had also been giving us pause for thought. On 10 April the Soviet Union had declared a state of martial law. In Moscow three days later a five-year non-aggression treaty had been signed between the Soviet Union and Japan. And on 6 May Josef Stalin, already the Secretary of the Communist Party of the Soviet Union, had also been appointed President of the Council of People's Commissars.

But none of these items prepared us for the shock we got on 10 May 1941 when it was announced that Rudolf Hess, deputy leader of the Nazi Party and second only to Hitler in the hierarchy, had flown to Scotland and parachuted from his aircraft not far from Glasgow. His successor, Martin Bormann, took office two days later on 12 May.

Rudolf Hess in Britain! Even the least politically astute among our ranks could appreciate that this was an event of outstanding importance. Speculation was rife and theories abounded. Opinions ranged from total disbelief to the certainty that this marked a major political turning-point. Many saw it as a prelude to negotiations and secretly nursed the hope that it would bring an early end to the war. How quickly such hopes blossomed, only to wither away again for lack of sustenance. We got the impression that our propaganda was playing down the significance of the event and trying to deny its importance. We soon realized that Great Britain was making no effort to capitalize on it either. Everyone's hopes were dashed. The war went on.

20 May 1941 saw the launch of Operation 'Merkur' [Mercury], Germany's airborne invasion of Crete. The initial landings met fierce opposition from British and Greek troops. This was probably one of the main reasons why our Gruppe

was suddenly and unexpectedly called upon to add its support to the invading forces. On 21 May we received orders to transfer to Athens-Tatoi at midday the following day, 22 May 1941, with an intermediate stop for refuelling at Grottaglie on the heel of Italy en route.

Chapter 13
Operation 'Merkur' – Crete

With our ground personnel somewhere on their way north by rail to Cottbus in Germany, we took off from Trapani at 12.10 hours on 22 May 1941 for Athens-Tatoi. After a refuelling stop at Grottaglie in Italy, we touched down in Greece at 18.00 hours. Upon our arrival we were back under the direct control of Stab StG 1 (Oberstleutnant Hagen) as part of General von Richthofen's VIII. Fliegerkorps. And didn't we notice the difference! Hardly had we climbed from our aircraft before new orders were being issued to us, clearly and concisely, together with all the necessary maps and reconnaissance photos we would require for our coming missions in this new and unfamiliar theatre of war.

The next morning we were to move down to Argos-South on the Peloponnese and commence operations immediately. Fuel and bombs sufficient for our needs would be there waiting for us. The only thing that couldn't be provided was additional ground staff. This meant that not only would our crew chiefs have to fly every mission with us as rear-seat gunners, but that when we returned to base afterwards – instead of a well-deserved break – they would also be required to service the aircraft, including refuelling and re-arming, in order to get them ready for the next operation. It was a lot to ask, but the men were all in good heart.

At 04.55 hours on 23 May we left Athens-Tatoi for our new base at Argos-South, where we landed at 05.25 hours. Argos, we discovered, was just a large expanse of brown sandy soil with a few sparse patches of thin grass dotted here and there about its surface. An awful lot of sand and dust, in fact, but fortunately not as bad as in Africa. The men immediately set to work bombing-up and refuelling the machines. We weren't kept waiting long before the first orders arrived from VIII. Fliegerkorps. The Luftwaffe was systematically trying to sink all enemy shipping in the sea areas around Crete – those vessels bringing fresh reinforcements to the island, as well as those evacuating troops. Our specific instructions: attack and sink any ships found at anchor in Suda Bay on Crete's northern coast.

We took off at 12.05 hours in rapid succession, despite the enormous quantities of dust stirred up by the leading Ketten, and headed south for the target area. In close formation we flew at some 3,000 metres in glorious sunshine down across the Peloponnese and then out over the Sea of Crete. Not a sign of the enemy anywhere, just brilliant sunshine, blue skies and a blue sea – the perfect ingredients for a summer holiday. But despite the idyllic backdrop, our nerves were growing tauter and our senses becoming ever keener the closer we got to the target. This was our first mission in an area that was new to us. We knew from experience that this meant keeping our wits about us. We had to be extra careful, ready for any eventuality – especially for anything different from what we had been used to in the past. Every operation flown in totally new and strange surroundings was an adventure into the unknown. It demanded the utmost vigilance and lightning-fast reactions to ensure not just success, but survival.

Crete gradually came into view. And there was Suda Bay. We could see a lot of little ships, but very few larger ones. In the face of some moderate Flak we split up into separate Ketten before attacking. The wind was slight and constant, the bombing results correspondingly good, and the mission accomplished without any undue fuss. We regrouped and headed for home, touching down back at Argos-South after 2 hours and 55 minutes in the air. This was to set the pattern for the majority of our coming operations.

The crew chiefs, who a moment before had been our back-seat gunners, got to work at once refuelling and re-arming the machines. Orders for the next mission were already in: same again – go and sink the ships in Suda Bay. Two hours after landing we were back in the air. This time we found a slightly bigger vessel of about 5,000 grt, which went down after taking a couple of direct hits. We also hit several of the smaller ships. We sustained no damage during our attacks and all returned safely to Argos-South where we landed at 19.35 hours.

We were dog tired by this time. But the aircraft again had to be serviced and got ready for the first mission early the next morning. Only when this was done could we grab a bite to eat and get some much-needed sleep. We had already been given our orders for the following day, 24 May:

> Take-off at first light for armed reconnaissance of the sea areas en route to, and around the island of Crete. Destroy all enemy ships sighted, particularly troop transports sailing to or from Crete. You are free to attack *all* vessels within areas specified, as no friendly shipping in vicinity. If no ships found, alternative target enemy troop positions at Canea.

By 05.05 hours on the morning of 24 May we were already aloft. The weather conditions and visibility were perfect. From our altitude of 3,000 metres we could scan a vast area of sea. But that didn't help us much today. It was as if the surface of the water had been swept clean. Despite all our searching, not a single ship came into view. The whole way to Crete there was not a ship to be seen. In the entire sea area around the island, not a ship to be seen. After nearly three and a half hours spent staring fruitlessly at the sun-dappled water, I was finally forced to opt for the alternative target, which we bombed to considerable effect at 08.45 hours. With the last drop of fuel remaining in our tanks we landed back at Argos-South eighty minutes later. Exactly five hours' flying time! Our longest ever operational flight, but unfortunately also one of the least rewarding. The crews rapidly refuelled and bombed-up the machines ready for the next mission on the list.

Two hours later and we were off again. Our target this time was a bridge to the west of Canea on Crete, which we successfully bombed at 13.35 hours. Returning to Argos-South at 15.00 hours, we duly reported that the mission had been carried out as ordered and that nothing untoward had occurred. That wasn't strictly true, however. Something *had* occurred. But it was the Gruppe's business and nobody else's. When we were about halfway to Crete two aircraft had suddenly dropped out of formation and set off back in the direction of home. We were a long way out to sea, nothing but water all around us and not a speck of land anywhere in sight. I had my own thoughts about what was going on. Either this pair really did have engine trouble – in which case they were unlikely to make it back to Argos-South and there would be little chance of our finding them and fishing them out of the drink – or (as I hoped) they had simply turned back for some other, completely minor reason and would be there waiting for us when we landed after the mission.

I had every sympathy with a pilot who preferred to play it safe. The strain on our engines of late had been enormous. Not only were they long overdue for their scheduled overhauls, they had also been operating for very nearly a month in the sand and dust of North Africa without filters or any other kind of special protection. Now we were trusting them to carry us for hours on end over the open sea far from the sight of any land. I must admit that I found myself glancing at my own instruments a lot more frequently than usual – especially the oil pressure gauge. We were all quite used to the fact that the needles of our oil pressure gauges always vibrated badly. On some aircraft they jumped about from high to low and back again for no apparent reason whatsoever. But now the sight of my needle's erratic movements was scaring the life out of me, even though I knew full well that it was the instrument's normal behaviour and not a portent of some imminent engine malfunction.

And so, as we neared base after completing the mission, I was anxious to see whether our two missing aircraft would be there waiting for us. And they were. After I had taxied in the two pilots lost no time in reporting to me, eager to explain the reason for their early return. There had been something wrong with their oil pressure – the needles of their gauges had been waving about all over the place!

'You scoundrels!' I said – or words to that effect – 'you simply turned round and went home! You ought to know by now that those needles are always moving about. It's just that it has never bothered you in the past when we were flying over land. But once you're over water it suddenly worries you! Your two machines will not be touched or checked in any way. They will remain exactly as they are. They'll simply be refuelled, and for the next mission you are to exchange aircraft with your section leaders.' This had the desired effect. After returning from the next mission the section leaders confirmed that the two machines were perfectly in order. Naturally, nobody wanted to be accused of letting the side down again like this in future. And from then on all such signs of nerves disappeared – or were kept well under control. The lesson had been learned. And among ourselves the whole incident was quickly forgotten.

We flew three operations in all on 25 May. The first two, at 07.00 hours and 13.50 hours, were directed against enemy troops in the Alikianou area to the south-west of Canea and achieved good results. But the problem of assigning specific targets when we were carrying out missions in close support of our own troops was proving insoluble. Our lengthy over-water approach flights meant that by the time we reached Crete the situation, and the positions on the ground, could have changed dramatically. Unfortunately, VIII. Fliegerkorps' attempts to overcome this difficulty by sending details of the target to the attacking force by radio shortly before its arrival over the target area didn't work with our Gruppe. It was now that we began to regret not having our regular wireless-operator/gunners with us. Without them, long-range W/T traffic was not possible. Our temporary rear-seaters couldn't read Morse. And the radio equipment in our machines couldn't be relied upon to pick up R/T messages relayed over longer distances, as it only operated on certain frequencies that had to be tuned in and set prior to take-off.

Our targets, therefore, also had to be set before we took off from Argos-South. This meant a gap of something like two hours until the time of our attack. Despite this, the outstanding efficiency of VIII. Fliegerkorps' operations staff ensured that we never lacked for targets. And for the third and last of our three missions on 25 May the target was shipping off the port of Heraklion, which we attacked to good effect at 17.55 hours. During the course of this long day we had spent a total of eight-and-a-half hours in the air. And that wasn't all: in between each mission the crews had also had to refuel and re-arm their own aircraft. It was asking a lot of any man. But everyone had turned to with a will that was, quite honestly, little short of inspiring.

Since our transfer to Greece Feldwebel Popisch had been flying with me as my gunner. Popisch was the Gruppenstab's Flugzeugoberfeldwebel, or senior NCO in charge of servicing, and, as such, was responsible for the smooth running of all technical matters necessary to maintain our aircraft at maximum operational readiness. These duties had kept him on his feet day and night since our arrival at Argos-South and he had hardly been able to snatch a wink of sleep. For the final mission of 25 May, and for the next few after that, I therefore took Gefreiter Twenhöfel along as my gunner instead. Feldwebel Popisch was none too happy about this. But he could appreciate the fact that the essential work he was carrying out on the ground to keep our machines operational had to take precedence. He also saw the sense in my prescribing him a good dose of shut-eye. We didn't know how long we would be expected to go on like this, and so it seemed only sensible to husband what little resources we had.

At 10.00 hours on 26 May we attacked an enemy tented encampment south of Skines on Crete. When we got back to Argos we were held at readiness, but in fact flew no more missions for the rest of that day. The crews welcomed the chance to catch up on some much-needed sleep.

27 May saw us fly three further missions over Crete. In the first, directed against shipping in Suda Bay at 09.05 hours, we scored hits on a number of vessels. They were all fairly small, however, the largest of them being little more than 2,000 grt by our reckoning. This first operation was followed by a mission flown in direct support of our airborne forces around Heraklion. After several days of fierce and costly fighting, they had established a firm foothold in the town and were now preparing to push east and south. Our job was to clear the roads to the southeast around Episkopi, which was known to be clear of all friendly forces. This meant we were free to attack any troops we found on the roads or taking cover to either side of them.

We flew at low level up and down the roads around Episkopi, bombing any worthwhile targets we came across and machine-gunning individual vehicles of every description. The large number of olive groves lining the roads provided the enemy with excellent cover. The troops hiding under the trees were extremely difficult to spot, even from our very low altitude. On the other hand, there was very little Flak to speak of. We were thus able to take our time in searching out our targets. When we found something we attacked almost at leisure – individually or in waves – until all enemy movement on the ground had been brought to a halt. Altogether we spent a good thirty minutes over the target area, from 14.50 to 15.20 hours, before finally turning for home. That evening we took off for another anti-shipping mission in the sea area around Crete. Again we found only smaller vessels, among them an unidentified minor warship of just a few hundred tons, which we attacked and sank at 18.30 hours.

After the repeated attacks on enemy ships in Crete's numerous bays and coves, it was now becoming very difficult to tell which of the many apparent wrecks were in fact still afloat and thus worthwhile targets. Following the amazing successes achieved by VIII. Fliegerkorps' other Stuka Gruppen during their operations against the British Mediterranean Fleet at the start of the campaign and prior to our arrival in Greece, it seemed as if the enemy no longer dared send any larger vessels – either major warships or merchantmen – into the sea areas now dominated by our Stukas. In the light of this, VIII. Fliegerkorps was now reckoning with the possibility that the enemy might try to stage another 'Dunkirk' – in other words, use a flotilla of small ships to reinforce his troops on Crete or, in the last eventuality, to evacuate the island. From now on we were therefore ordered to attack even the smallest of seagoing vessels with machine-gun fire. Just how effective such an attack could be we were to find out the following afternoon.

At 04.45 hours on the morning of 28 May we had taken off for an armed reconnaissance of the sea area around Crete. Having found it free of all enemy shipping we finally resorted to bombing our alternative target, enemy ground positions at Retimo, at 07.10 hours. In the afternoon we had then spent a good hour, up until about 15.30 hours, attacking road traffic around the town of Tymbaki on the island's southern coast.

Our return flight took us out across Suda Bay in the north. It was here that I spotted a small, cutter-like vessel riding at anchor and clearly ready for sea. He's just waiting for darkness before making a dash for it, I thought to myself. We'll have to try and put a stop to that if possible. I went down low, got the vessel lined up in my sights and opened fire with my two wing machine-guns, aiming to hit it at the waterline. If I didn't sink it, that would at least keep the crew busy pumping ship. But I was a fraction too high. I curved round to make a second run. This time I went down even lower. So low, in fact, that I would only just be able to clear her mastheads. Or so I thought. For suddenly, right in front of my nose, there was an enormous explosion! It was so close that there was no time to think of taking any evasive action. No time to think? There wasn't even time to react!

It was too late – we were right in the centre of a gigantic fireball! The shock wave hurled our gallant Iolanthe upwards like a storm-tossed leaf. We felt the tremendous jolt beneath our backsides. Ship's planking was flying all around us – above us! – in front of us! – beside us! The air was full of terrifyingly solid lumps of wood and metal. And we were slap-bang in the middle of this tumbling mass of ship's debris. But a moment later and we were through it. Absolutely incredible!

The engine was running smoothly, the rev counter was showing normal. That meant the propeller hadn't been hit. After we had recovered from our initial shock we checked the wings for damage – all in one piece. As soon as we landed we inspected our aircraft . . . and couldn't find a scratch on it. But how on earth was that possible when so much junk – and big junk, at that – had been flying round our ears? If the crews in the other machines hadn't seen for themselves how the cutter exploded right in front of us, and how we flew straight through the resulting fireball, they would never have believed our story. It would have been dismissed as a 'line-shoot' of truly epic proportions.

But our survival today had not been of our own making. To use another elegant old infantry expression: 'The dear Lord had stuck his big fat thumb into things once again.' Either that, or he had drafted in a whole flock of guardian angels to look after us – one angel on its own wouldn't have been enough to do the job. Be that as it may, we thanked our Maker with all our hearts that we were still breathing. After such an experience you really appreciated the gift of life that much more.

On 29 May we coupled another unproductive armed reconnaissance of the waters off Crete with a 'road-cleansing' sweep of the Pirgos area in the northwest of the island. Nothing special to report. But it was nonetheless a special day for me: my wife's birthday. Another gift for which I was, and always would be, truly thankful.

At around midday on 30 May our target was the British signalling station on the tiny island of Gavdhos, to the south of Crete, and any vessels that might be drawn up on the beach there. Another incident-free mission to grace the pages of the logbook. Although we were no longer finding any shipping during our armed reconnaissance flights over the sea areas around Crete by day, reconnaissance had established that over the past few nights the British had been evacuating troops from the island under cover of darkness.

Late that afternoon we were therefore transferred from Greece down to Heraklion on Crete's northern coast. The town's airfield had just been captured by our paratroopers and we were to use it as a jumping-off point for a sweep of the seas to the south of the island at first light the following morning. This, it was hoped, would enable us to catch some of the night's evacuation shipping before it withdrew out of range. Our orders were to prevent any vessels we found from escaping south across the Mediterranean to Egypt. To do this we were to carry our maximum bomb load and forgo the use of auxiliary fuel tanks.

Laden with bombs, we touched down at Heraklion at 19.15 hours that evening. A station commander was already in office. He showed us to our quarters for the night: a barracks block on the edge of the field in an area which, he said, had only just been cleared by the paratroops before darkness fell. My Staffelkapitäne and I followed the commander into the deserted building. By the light of our torches we could see that the walls of the large empty rooms were absolutely alive with bugs – great long marching columns of bugs! That's all we needed now, to be infested with lice only a matter of days before our return to the homeland. Out! We fled, leaving the field – or rather, the walls – to the bugs. As a precaution we had brought our Australian folding beds along with us in the aircraft. It was pleasantly warm, and so we set them up under the wings of our Ju 87s and settled down to spend the night in the open.

Around midnight the airfield was attacked by British bombers, which spread a carpet of incendiaries over the whole area. We raised the alarm, or as much of an alarm as was possible – or necessary – against the backdrop of noise and fireworks created by the raid itself, and ordered our men to take cover at the edge of the field. The ground here was strewn with huge boulders and lumps of rock, which offered at least some degree of protection against the machine-gun fire that was being sprayed down on us from every side. Pressed tightly against the boulders, it was now our turn to be at the receiving end of a ground strafing – and thoroughly unpleasant it was too. With no slit trenches or dugouts anywhere nearby, we just had to lie there and take it as bullets ricocheted off the rocks, whining and whistling around us in all directions.

The British made one strafing run after another. They were directing their fire mainly against our aircraft, which were standing completely unprotected out in the open around the edge of the field not far away from us. Under the starry night sky they were clearly visible, silhouetted against the sea of tiny flames from the countless incendiaries that were still glowing and guttering all over the surface of the landing ground. The raid finally came to a close. The sound of the enemy's engines faded into the distance. We crept from our hiding places and took stock: on the far side of the field a single machine was burning – a Hurricane, which the British had been forced to leave behind when they evacuated Heraklion. Despite a number of minor bullet holes, the Staffeln reported all their aircraft fully serviceable. No losses.

It was still dark when the time came to start preparing for the next morning's mission. 'Up you get!' I called to my gunner, Gefreiter Twenhöfel, who was still sitting huddled up underneath our machine: 'Time to get moving!' 'I can't, Herr Hauptmann,' he answered plaintively. Can't? – What on earth was the matter with him? Twenhöfel had been fast asleep when the raid began. Apparently he only fully woke up when the incendiaries started raining down and machine-gun bullets began kicking up the dust right next to him. Then he ran for dear life – straight across a clump of cactus and through several pools of oil or tar from a bullet-holed drum.

And now here he sat, his legs black and swollen, his feet a mass of deeply embedded cactus thorns that he couldn't pull out, a figure of abject misery. He was in considerable pain and couldn't put any weight on his feet. But he insisted on his comrades helping him into his flying gear and lifting him up into the aircraft. As he pointed out, he wasn't going for a walk – gunners fly their missions sitting on their backsides! (Nonetheless, when we returned to Argos-South he had to be taken off operations to give him a chance to recover, whereupon Feldwebel Popisch immediately reclaimed his position in the back seat as my regular gunner/ acting.)

At 06.05 hours on 31 May we took off from Heraklion at first light as ordered for an armed reconnaissance mission against a flotilla of British warships that had been reported in the sea area to the south of Crete. Although there wasn't a cloud in the sky, visibility was greatly reduced by the early morning mist. But it was sufficient to allow us to search the given area thoroughly and find it completely devoid of shipping. No British flotilla, not a single vessel of any kind to be seen. Without our auxiliary fuel tanks we soon reached the limit of our range and had to turn round and head back to Heraklion.

By now the visibility was beginning to improve somewhat. We were flying at an altitude of 3,500 metres in order to be able to scan as much of the sea area below us as possible. Then, in the thinning mist off to starboard far ahead of us, we caught sight of a large ship. It was on a southerly heading and travelling at high speed, judging by the bow wave it was pushing in front of it. The vessel was obviously in a great hurry. That was our target. We could now see that it was a large passenger liner – something that no self-respecting Stuka pilot could possibly miss. We prepared to attack.

As we neared the target, it struck me as odd that we were getting no Flak from the ship. Couldn't they identify us yet because of the sea mist? They'd soon find out. Line-astern attack formation – dive! The needle of the altimeter unwound past the 2,000-metre mark. Now more details of the vessel could be made out. But it wasn't until I was down to about 1,500 metres that I realized it appeared to be wearing hospital ship markings. The thought flashed through my mind: troop transport or hospital ship? Then there was no longer any doubt about it. The vessel was clearly finished in all the internationally recognized markings of a hospital ship – even if its paintwork was streaked with rust and very faded.

I was already pulling out of my own dive as I yelled a warning over the R/T to all the other aircraft: 'Abort – hospital ship! Do not attack! Abandon dive – do not release bombs!' The discipline in the unit was excellent. Not a bomb fell.

We encountered no other vessels of any kind and so landed back at Heraklion empty-handed. The reconnaissance aircraft that had been covering the same area and beyond, much further down into the Mediterranean, also reported the entire sea area to be free of enemy shipping. The British fleet was no longer in evidence anywhere near Crete. That same evening we were transferred back to Argos.

The 'hospital ship incident' continued to be the main topic of conversation among the crews for quite some time afterwards: 'I tell you, that captain must have needed a double brandy when he saw us all screaming down on him in one bloody great long line!' . . . 'He could count himself lucky that we even noticed his filthy dirty paintwork!' . . . 'That hospital ship business was just a lousy trick. He was evacuating British footsloggers from Crete, I'd stake my life on it. He was sailing as a troop transport pure and simple!' . . . 'He certainly was in one hell of a hurry!' . . . 'No, that was never a hospital ship, not in a thousand years!'

After our earlier experiences at Tobruk, I too was fairly certain in my own mind that the hospital ship had been engaged in evacuating troops from Crete. It was probably crowded with men below decks, but of course that couldn't be seen from above. So what else should I have done, other than let the vessel continue on its way? According to the international laws of sea warfare any ship so marked was strictly taboo. That was something we had been taught during our days in the Navy. And quite rightly too.

The captain of the vessel had also very cleverly kept his nerve and refrained from opening fire on us. If he hadn't, it was highly unlikely that he and his ship would have survived. He knew his maritime law, and he could thank his lucky stars – and the German Navy – that the same code of conduct had been drummed into us during our officer training. I for one was glad that no bombs had been dropped. Even today – even though I found out after the war that this particular hospital ship had indeed been evacuating troops from Crete – I still feel the same. The British naval high command was none too fussy about the protection offered by the sign of the Red Cross. In contrast, our actions had been perfectly correct. They may even go some little way in balancing the often distorted picture given of the German fighting soldier. I myself am more than happy to be labelled: 'Stupid, but honourable.'

After our return to Argos-South we flew only one more mission over the Mediterranean. This was on 2 June when we were ordered to provide cover for a convoy of ships heading southeast out of Piraeus. It was the first to take reinforcements and supplies to Crete by sea. After the initial bloody and extremely costly battles fought by our paratroops to gain a foothold on the island, Operation 'Merkur' – the airborne invasion of Crete – had finally been brought to a successful conclusion.

And now, for the first time since the beginning of the war, the Gruppe was being recalled to the homeland for a short period of rest and refitting. On 3 June we left Argos and set course northwestward. After a refuelling stop at Foggia, we landed at Treviso in northern Italy at 15.04 hours. We were to remain here overnight, which gave us just enough time for a brief visit to nearby Venice. The Geschwaderkommodore, Oberstleutnant Hagen, had arranged to borrow a car and was more than happy to take us along. Two whole hours in Venice! The number of lasting impressions that we took away with us after so short a time was truly astonishing – we even managed the obligatory feeding of the pigeons in St Mark's Square. But it would have required much more time really to appreciate all the magnificent sights and wonders that this enchanting city had to offer. Another time perhaps – after the war.

The following day we resumed our journey home, via Kitzingen, to Cottbus, where we finally touched down at 18.35 hours on 4 June 1941. We had been given just fourteen days to get our aircraft back up to full operational readiness. With everyone lending a hand, we soon had the engines out of our machines and loaded aboard transport ready to be taken away for a complete – and long overdue – overhaul. Then we set to and tackled all the outstanding paperwork. Once this had been put into some sort of order, the whole Gruppe was free to enjoy a week's leave. Only a small party stayed behind in Cottbus to attend to the necessary maintenance work, take delivery of stores and supplies, and look after any replacement personnel who turned up during our absence. The supply and support services once again demonstrated their customary efficiency and skill. By 16 June – two days ahead of schedule – III./StG 1 was already back up to full establishment in both men and machines.

Most of the gaps torn in our ranks by the recent fighting were perforce filled by mainly young and inexperienced crews. But the spirit of the old members of the Gruppe was quickly assimilated by the new. They too were determined to prove their worth to the best of their abilities. Our only concern with these replacement crews was their limited amount of time in the air. To help them get used to the aircraft they would be flying in combat, we gave them every opportunity to carry out practice flights . . . and look, there's one coming back from just such a flight now. He's approaching to land – but he's much too high! – Give her more power, lad, more power! – Go round again – Pour on the power! But, of course, he couldn't hear us – unfortunately. He levelled out and performed a perfect three-point landing . . . while still 20 metres up in the air!

Then he let the poor old crate come down like an express lift. No aircraft could stand up to that sort of punishment. Not even the faithful and otherwise forgiving Iolanthe. It was a total wreck! Almost brand new – and now nothing but scrap! Luckily, the pilot was able to scramble out of the wreckage completely uninjured. Even luckier, for him, was the fact that we were able to put in a lot more practice with him before taking him with us on his first combat mission. To our relief, it soon became apparent that such extreme errors of judgement tended not to be repeated. The newcomers were eager to learn. Most found their feet very quickly and it was encouraging to see how rapidly they established themselves as valued members of the Gruppe.

We were now waiting with a mixture of expectation and suspense for what the coming days might bring. We had no idea what plans were being hatched behind the closed doors of the world's political leaders. The excitement surrounding the news of Rudolf Hess's flight to Britain back on 6 May seemed to have fizzled out. The event had since been effectively hushed up. Whatever results may have been hoped for had obviously failed to materialize. But on Germany's eastern borders something was clearly brewing.

There were rumours of Soviet forces massing along the frontier, perhaps with the intention of attacking us from the rear. Of rumours there were more than enough – of hard facts very few. The only thing that we knew for sure was that we would be told in due course all that we needed to know to carry out the task awaiting us. That and no more. We didn't know for example that two days earlier, on 14 June, Hitler had called his army group and army commanders together to inform them of the reasons for, and purpose behind, his forthcoming campaign against the Soviet Union. Our own orders for this 16 June read simply: 'Prepare for transfer at short notice.'

Early on the morning of 17 June 1941 we received the transfer order itself:

> III./StG 1 to transfer to Dubovo-South. Flying elements to take off during afternoon, singly and at intervals of approximately five minutes. Flight to be made at low level so that landing and dispersal of machines cannot be observed from across adjacent border. Absolute secrecy to be maintained. Kommandeur III./StG 1 to report on arrival to ops officer VIII. Fliegerkorps, Major von Heinemann, at Korps' HQ located Arys-Rostken for further instructions. Upon arrival at Dubovo-South the Gruppe will operate as part of StG 1 under the direct command of VIII. Fliegerkorps.

This immediately brought the Gruppe to life. The necessary orders were quickly issued. We had been through this procedure so often in the past that most of it was now done almost automatically.

Chapter 14

The Russian Campaign

The command post of the AOC VIII. Fliegerkorps was a bustling hive of activity when I reported there punctually at 13.00 hours, as ordered, for a briefing from Major i.G. [of the General Staff] von Heinemann, the Korps' Ia. In short, concise sentences he quickly put me in the picture regarding VIII. Fliegerkorps' current situation and future role in the campaign against Russia. All the while, messengers were hurrying in and out and a bank of field telephones was in constant noisy use. It was a scene of orderly chaos. Heinemann dealt calmly and efficiently with the questions that were coming at him from all sides. His answers were brief and to the point, leaving no room for any later misunderstandings or misinterpretation. The perfect model of a staff officer, he was dispensing instructions and inform-ation with assurance and clarity in equal measure.

Despite the constant interruptions, I was soon in possession of all the facts or, at least, all the facts that I needed to know today, and not a single thing more. The confident and controlled manner in which Heinemann handled his enormous workload was impressive. It was a virtuoso performance that commanded respect.

All the maps and aerial photographs required for our first missions against the Soviets had already been put together for us. After I had been issued with these, I was again reminded of the need for absolute secrecy and then dismissed to return to my Gruppe at Dubovo-South. If everything else went off as smoothly and efficiently as VIII. Fliegerkorps' preparatory staff work, then nothing could go wrong. Or could it? At least we now knew exactly where we stood: we were actually going to invade Russia! But in the quiet hours of that evening, when there was time to consider the enormity of the undertaking, doubts began to creep in.

An attack on Russia – wasn't it Adolf Hitler who had written in his *Mein Kampf* that Germany must never again let herself be drawn into a war on two fronts? Had he forgotten those words? Hadn't every military operation against Russia in the past foundered – brought to a halt sooner or later by the sheer vastness of her territories? Would it be any different today – with our modern weapons and faster means of transport – than it had been in the time of Napoleon? Questions such as these couldn't simply be ignored. But only the future held the answers. For us the present offered only one certainty: the certainty that our leaders would be demanding the very highest level of operational commitment and achievement from all forces engaged in the fight against Russia.

And just what *were* those forces in terms of Luftwaffe dive-bombers? I knew, of course, that our Gruppe would be operating as part of VIII. Fliegerkorps. In addition to its bomber, fighter and reconnaissance units, this Korps – one of two under the overall command of Luftflotte 2 – controlled four Stuka Gruppen in all: II. and III./StG 1, plus I. and III./StG 2. The Korps also included a Me 109-equipped ground-assault Gruppe, II.(Schl)/LG 2, plus a single ground-assault Staffel, 10.(Schl)/LG 2, which was still flying Henschel Hs 123 biplanes.

Among the units comprising II. Fliegerkorps – the second of Luftflotte 2's two component Korps – were the three Gruppen of Stukageschwader 77. Finally, in the far north, one of Luftflotte 5's commands – the Fliegerführer Kirkenes – deployed a single Stuka Gruppe, IV.(St)/LG 1, on the Norwegian–Finnish border. Altogether, the number of Stukagruppen deployed for the coming attack on Russia thus totalled exactly eight.

On the eve of the invasion, details of the so-called 'Commissar Law' were made known to the troops. This 'law' formed part of the set of orders laid down by Adolf Hitler on 6 June 1941 relating to the conduct of the war in the east and was headed 'Guidelines for the liquidation of Soviet political commissars'.

Of more relevance to us, the first operational orders for the campaign against Russia were now issued. While the bulk of the Luftwaffe's forces would be launching their offensive in the tried and tested *Blitzkrieg* fashion of first destroying the enemy's air power by targeting it in the air and on the ground, our opening attacks were to be directed against the command structure of the Soviet ground forces. The targets assigned to our crews were three enemy army staff headquarters situated in the town of Kalvarja on the East Prussian–Lithuanian border.

While the ground crews were out on the field in the blackness, working by the light of shaded torches to get the aircraft ready, the pilots pored over the maps and aerial photographs, each imprinting his own particular target firmly in his mind. We were scheduled to cross the border and carry out our attacks at first light simultaneously with the initial advance of the ground troops.

Exhaust flames began to flicker and splutter in the dispersal points around the edge of the field. The noise of engines shattered the stillness of the night. Red, green and white navigation lights emerged slowly from the camouflaged dispersals and seemed to be wandering about almost haphazardly in the pitch darkness as the pilots taxied out and formed up into their respective Ketten. At exactly 02.30 hours on 22 June 1941 the three machines of my Stabskette lifted from the ground as one. We had left a thick cloud of dust in our wake, which must have reduced visibility for those behind us to almost nil. Despite this, their lights could be seen emerging from the cloud at short, regular intervals as each Kette took off hard on the heels of the last. Like trios of tiny glow-worms they scurried across the unseen woods and fields below as they quickly closed up on us.

'Staffeln all present and correct in close formation,' reported Leutnant Michl, who was flying as my gunner on this mission. We reached the rendezvous point where we were to join forces with II. Gruppe. Our orders called for us to fly together as far as the border. There we were to separate, with II. Gruppe attacking their targets in the same area immediately prior to us. In the first pale glimmerings of dawn the outlines of villages, roads and railways could just be made out – or at least guessed at – through the mist blanketing the ground beneath our wings. But of our other Gruppe there was no sign. We circled the rendezvous point until our watches told us that they must already have set course for the target area. Then we turned east ourselves to follow in their tracks.

We crossed the frontier. It was a peculiar sensation: another new and unknown theatre of war, another new and unknown enemy. Once again we would have to get used to a new opponent, his methods of fighting and the strength of his defences. There shouldn't be any particularly nasty surprises in store if the information we had been given was correct and fully up to date. But we were always on the alert for surprises of any sort when flying a combat mission. We had to have our wits about us in order to be able to react at any moment. But at first everything remained quiet. The Soviets still seemed to be fast asleep. They were about to get quite a wake-up call!

Ahead of us the first of II./StG 1's bombs began exploding on their targets. Pillars of flame shot up from the ground, multiplying and merging into one great inferno of fire and smoke. Then it was our turn. A few untidy puffs of dirty grey cloud dotted the sky here and there. The enemy Flak gunners had at last woken up. At first their fire was so uncoordinated and unsure that it didn't look at all dangerous. Certainly nothing to worry old Stuka hands like ourselves.

The pilots had by now identified their individual targets. We dived almost vertically, each Kette close behind the other. The bombs went screaming down and did their work in a matter of seconds. The ruins of the staff headquarters disappeared beneath a pall of dust, billowing smoke and leaping flames. We re-formed and returned to base in tight formation, landing back at Dubovo at 03.48 hours. As always, the crews were immediately surrounded by the ground staff: 'Well, how did it go?' – 'What happened?' – 'How was it?' 'Nothing to it! They were all still tucked up in bed. We managed to wake them up though!'

Maybe there had been nothing to it for us veterans. But for some it had been a major event: *their first operational mission!* It was perhaps just as well that nothing untoward had happened, for now the object of all that training had been achieved.

The ultimate test – the first successful operation – was finally under their belt. All the talk in the classroom of the opposition they would be facing had suddenly become reality. Now they had to get used to the highly unpleasant feeling that the enemy was actually shooting at them, was trying to bring them down – and might even succeed in doing so. This acceptance of ever-present danger would ultimately bring with it a sense of calmness and self-confidence. With experience they would learn to differentiate between what was important and what could safely be ignored.

But experience would also teach them that there are certain situations where what was needed was a large slice of luck. Call it what you will: fate – providence – a guardian angel – divine intervention – or just plain luck; there was not one old Stuka pilot who couldn't quote you numerous examples where a generous helping of luck alone had helped him out of a very tight corner. Look around you at these experienced old hands and you'll begin to understand what the ancient Romans were getting at when they said: '*Fortes fortuna adjuvat*' – 'Fortune favours the brave'.

And so it was time to congratulate our younger and newer comrades. They had cleared that first all-important hurdle to future successful operations. The warm handshakes from their Staffelkapitäne and the other crews said it all. They had been through it themselves, and understood all too well exactly how the first-timers were feeling.

But there was no time to dwell on such matters now. The enemy had to be hit and hit hard by the full weight of German arms right from the very start of the campaign. The barracks that was serving as the Geschwaderstab's ops room was alive with activity. Telephones were constantly ringing. Reports and orders were being passed back and forth. There was a continual coming and going. The Geschwaderkommodore, Oberstleutnant Hagen, as ever the quiet eye in the centre of the storm that was raging all about him, calmly acknowledged my report of the Gruppe's first mission before handing me the orders for the second, already issued by VIII. Fliegerkorps: 'Attack the River Niemen crossings at Grodno!'

The orders came accompanied by a sheaf of maps and aerial photos of the town of Grodno. The Kommodore spelled out the operation in detail: 'The Niemen crossing points are to be blocked. But only the approach roads – the bridges themselves are not to be damaged. They will be needed for our own troops' advance. Take-off: 05.45 hours. When will you arrive over target?' 'At about 06.20 hours, Herr Oberstleutnant.' 'Good, that will do. Everything clear?' 'Jawohl! Beg to report Third Stuka One ready for mission as ordered!'

I quickly rang my adjutant from the Geschwader ops room to give him some advance warning of the coming mission. This would allow the crews a little more time to prepare. A large part of the success of any operation depended on the thoroughness of the preparations. Then I jumped into the Gruppe's new car and raced back along the badly potholed country lanes to our landing ground. This car was our prized possession and was normally looked after and driven with great care. Only on trips such as this, to and from an urgent briefing, was it thrashed to the limit.

At the Gruppe command post the pilots were already bent over what maps and aerial photographs they had been able to find of the immediate target area. Now I assigned each Staffel its specific objectives. Routes, times, formations and the actual sequence and method of attack were all discussed. The Staffelkapitäne drove off across the field, each to his own dispersal area. There the aircraft were ready and waiting. While the crews were being briefed, the mechanics had been giving their machines a final once-over, checking the engines and making sure that everything in the cockpit was securely stowed and fastened down. The last thing a pilot wanted during a steep dive – when all his attention needed to be focussed on the target – was to have some loose item of equipment flying around his ears! The crews climbed aboard their aircraft. They were strapped in, the engines sprang into life, and for the second time on this first morning of the war against Russia our Iolanthes taxied out to the take-off line – time: 05.45 hours.

The mission went off exactly as briefed. The enemy's Flak was a little heavier this time, but still not heavy enough to pose any serious threat to our manoeuvrable Ju 87s. Our bombs blew deep craters in the approach roads to the bridges that we had been ordered to block. Several houses collapsed, spilling their debris into the streets and creating additional barriers. The bridges would still be usable, but only after a fair bit of clearance work had been done. Satisfied with the outcome, we returned to base at 06.45 hours and reported to Geschwader HQ: 'Mission accomplished as ordered. Bridges at Grodno undamaged but effectively blocked. All aircraft returned safely.'

To my surprise the Kommodore rang back almost at once: 'You've done even more than you thought. The GOC has expressed his appreciation and sends his congratulations. Signals intelligence picked up a plain language radio message from Grodno calling for help: "Army staff wiped out!"' 'We saw no signs of that, Herr Oberstleutnant, but if the enemy staff was headquartered in those buildings that are now scattered across the road, then it could well be true!'

Blow followed upon blow. While the ground staff were busy checking, refuelling and re-arming the aircraft, the crews took advantage of the brief pauses between ops to grab forty winks. They needed to be as fresh as possible for each new mission. The nights were now short and every minute of daylight – from dawn until the onset of darkness – was used to the full. It was late when the Gruppe finally landed back after the last mission of a long and arduous day; a day that had proven totally successful and had cost us not a single casualty. The exit roads out of Olita (10.40 hours), the bridges at Vizna (15.10 hours) and Vilna (20.15 hours) had all been blocked and made impassable to enemy supply and troop movements. Above all, the new crews had been given the chance to prove themselves and get the feel of Gruppe operations. They had experienced the enemy's defences and taken them in their stride. They had performed like true Stuka flyers and they had all returned safely.

We had flown five missions in all on this opening day of the war in the east. First take-off: 02.30 hours. Final landing: 21.08 hours. The next op had already been ordered for the following morning; take-off at 03.30 hours. It promised to be a short night. But before turning in the crews had to give a full account of the day's events to our ground personnel, each and every one of whom had played his part in contributing to the Gruppe's success.

On the second day of operations against the Soviet Union, 23 June 1941, our first two targets were the railway networks around Lida and to the south of Vilna. Our bombs tore up the railway embankments in numerous places. Several goods trains, including one carrying either self-propelled guns or light tanks, were trapped on short lengths of track and partially destroyed. We also used our machine-guns to 'de-steam' a number of locomotives. It was quite a sight to see our bullets puncturing a loco's boiler and watching the steam jet out in all directions like a mechanical porcupine ruffling up its quills in self-defence! Our engineers would be none too pleased at having to repair the track in so many places. And I'm sure the railway officials would rather have taken over locomotives that were in full running order. But our top priority at the moment was to block the enemy's supply routes and obstruct his lines of retreat.

The next job was to block the exit roads out of Lida. As there were so many of them, plus a number of possible detours, it required two missions effectively to seal them all off. When we approached Lida for the second time, the town centre was a mass of flames. We had hit a fuel dump during our first attack and a strong wind had now spread the fire across the whole town. The Soviets seemed to be making no attempt to fight the fires – or if they were, their efforts were having no effect whatsoever. Dense clouds of smoke rose high into the air and the smell of burning penetrated into our cockpits. Our bombs rained down a second time, closing those exit roads still passable, until every single escape route was blocked and the roads had been turned into cratered stretches of rubble.

During the day's low-level missions our machines had received one or two scratches from the increasingly wild ground fire. Luckily none of the crews was hit and the slight material damage to the aircraft was quickly made good. All machines were fully serviceable again in time for the next mission.

So far we had only seen the occasional Soviet fighter. The stubby Ratas with their large radial engines swiftly made themselves scarce whenever they caught sight of us. Now we found out the reason for this lack of aerial opposition: on 22 June, the first day of the campaign in the east, the Luftwaffe had claimed a staggering 1,811 Soviet aircraft – 322 brought down by fighters or Flak, the remaining 1,489 destroyed on the ground! The figures were scarcely conceivable. Never before in the annals of air warfare had so many aircraft been destroyed in the course of a single day – nor were they ever likely to be again. This feat of arms by the Luftwaffe stands alone.

It was scarcely conceivable – yet true. And we were among those now reaping the benefit. Discounting the one or two single Soviet fighters glimpsed from afar – none of which had shown the slightest inclination to come any closer and get involved with us – these first missions of ours had been flown without any contact with the enemy in the air whatsoever.

24 June brought a change of emphasis in our operations. As the Soviet air force had to all intents and purposes been knocked out, we were to be sent even deeper into the enemy's hinterland to try to prevent all movement in his rear areas. Early that morning we attacked and blocked the exits from Molodeczno, a town straddling the main Vilna–Minsk railway. Long convoys of heavy supply trucks were threading their way all unsuspectingly through the narrow streets. Many of our bombs burst among the vehicles heading out of town on the western exit roads. The railway crossing received a direct hit just as the head of one of the convoys was starting to cross. A number of vehicles were destroyed or set on fire. A train standing nearby was badly damaged. All exit roads were sealed off. In Baranovichi, our next target, we also brought all through traffic to a temporary halt.

But then something happened that wasn't at all according to plan.

Shot down in flames behind Soviet lines!

24 June 1941: For the third time today, at 14.14 hours, we took off from Dubovo to attack the enemy. Our mission was to disrupt Soviet supply lines by destroying the northern exit routes out of Minsk. Once this had been accomplished, our secondary task was to attack any enemy convoys found on the roads to the northwest of the town.

Broken cloud shone brilliantly white beneath our wings. Below that the Russian landscape was a picture of peace and tranquility basking in the summer sun. But our eyes were diligently scanning the skies around us. If there *were* any Soviet fighters about, we wanted to spot them in plenty of time to be able to defend ourselves. This mission was taking us much deeper into enemy territory than any we had flown in the past two days: a good 200km beyond our own armoured spearheads. In the distance far ahead of us we could see a vast expanse of smoke and flames: Minsk! Other units had been there before us and had already done their work. The gaps in the clouds had been steadily closing all the while. Now we found ourselves in attack formation above a sea of solid cloud that was effectively hiding Minsk from our view. Suddenly, from behind, came a warning yell: 'Achtung! Enemy fighters!'

I see them! But they're too far away to reach us before we start to dive. And that's the best way of eluding them – get down into the clouds. With a shout of 'Let's go!' I tipped onto one wing and led the Gruppe into a steep dive towards our target. For a few seconds wisps of white cloud flashed past outside the cockpit windows. And then we were through. In front of us – below us – lay the town of Minsk. Alter the angle slightly to line up on that large road junction – Take her down a little closer – Press the bomb release button – Pull out.

'Direct hit!' came the voice of Feldwebel Wüstner, who had taken over as my gunner just the day before. I looked around for the other aircraft and for any enemy Flak or fighters. Everything appeared to be perfectly in order. The Gruppe was all present and correct. No enemy fighters either attacking or even pursuing us. One final brief glance back at the target: large mushrooms of smoke above the road junction where our bombs had exploded.

We went into our usual recovery routine and wound our way out of range of the ring of Flak batteries encircling the town. Then it was time to head northwest for a low-level sweep of the roads in that area. In the very first village we came to we found a long convoy of heavy trucks standing motionless. In the middle of the column was a quadruple Flak gun mounted on a truck chassis. It was already spitting fire from all four barrels – that was my target! I had to silence that gun before it hit any of our aircraft. Roaring down the road at low level directly towards him, we must have been presenting him with an ideal, almost stationary non-deflection target.

I let fly at him with my two MG 17 wing machine-guns. My aim was good. But the Russian was still firing too – straight back at me and with twice as many barrels. He wasn't using tracer bullets, so I couldn't see where his fire was going. It was only by the muzzle flames from his four barrels, which were constantly flickering like a gas ring, that I could tell there was an awful lot of lead in the air. And as his aim was also good, it was presumably all heading in my direction.

Suddenly, a deafening bang! – The engine had collected a packet, a very nasty packet! – Cordite smoke from a high-explosive shell filled the cockpit. – This didn't look good. – Hope nothing vital has been hit. – Uh, oh! Uh, oh! – A thick stream of oil had started to gush out of the tank in front of me. Within a matter of seconds rivulets of hot oil from the punctured tank and pipes had covered everything in a black viscous film – the cabin windows, the instrument panel, my face. Keep calm! Slide the cockpit canopy back. Turn west and start to climb, at least for as long as everything keeps running.

It was still a good 120km back to our own lines. We'd never make it. We radioed for another aircraft to come to our assistance. Somewhere in this part of Russia there must surely be a level stretch of ground large enough for two aircraft to land on – and for one aircraft with four occupants to take off from again?

Wüstner repeated our radio call for help: 'One aircraft to formate on Anton!' A Ju 87 closed up alongside us. It was piloted by a young Fähnrich who had been posted to our Gruppe only days before. I could no longer read either of my compasses, and my maps were smothered in oil and totally illegible. It was only with great difficulty that I was able to keep my eyes open and see anything at all. I therefore signalled to the Fähnrich to take over the lead and set course westwards. But he misunderstood my hand signals. I could almost hear him thinking: What on earth does the Old Man want now? Finally, he must have decided that I was motioning him to carry out another attack on the convoy, for he banked down and away back towards the village.

We were completely on our own again. Our engine coughed a couple of times – and came to a dead stop. The oil that was sloshing around on the cockpit floor had somehow caught fire. It was burning with an even blue flame and giving off a cloud of bluish-black smoke. Bail out? Not a wise move. The road below us was packed with columns of marching Russian troops. To the right of the road the ground was swampy. If we jumped out here we'd be rounded up the moment we hit the ground, and then it would be a bullet in the back of the neck. That was definitely out! So just sit tight and look for a suitable spot for an emergency landing – somewhere where we wouldn't be observed, as far away as possible from the road and those enemy troops, and preferably near a wood where we could find cover. A tall order. And if our aircraft exploded before we found what we were looking for? That was a risk we would have to take. It was our only chance.

Without power we were already losing height. But we might just make that small meadow on the edge of the wood, which we could now see. It really was an awfully small meadow, and there was a deep ditch, or sunken path of some kind, running along the front of it – but we would have to give it a go, there was no other option. With our dead engine our angle of descent was far too steep. At this rate I reckoned we would smash straight into that damned ditch. All that was needed to clear it was a quick burst of power. The only problem was, I didn't *have* any power! So there was going to be one hell of a bang any moment now. Or was there?

Just before the ditch I deliberately slammed the machine down onto the ground. I knew from past experience that the Stuka's oleo legs could withstand a tremendous lot of punishment. And, sure enough, the aircraft had come down so hard that it bounced into the air again, cleared the ditch and came back down in the tiny field on the far side of it. The trees at the other end of the field were already hurtling towards us, but no more than ten metres from the edge of the wood we went into a high-speed ground loop and shuddered to a stop. One of the tyres had been punctured, either by enemy Flak or from that first hard touchdown, and this had given us just that added bit of braking power that we'd needed.

With a few quick movements Wüstner had removed his MG 15 machine gun from its mounting. We jumped out of the aircraft and dived for cover in the wood, burrowing under some low-hanging fir branches. From our hideout we could still just see our Iolanthe.

The wood was also uncomfortably small and surrounded on all sides by open fields. Farm labourers were working in one or two of them. Fortunately, our aircraft had come down behind a low hillock and was hidden from their view when we made our short dash for the shelter of the trees. By the time the first of the farm workers had got to the top of the small rise and could see our machine, the Iolanthe was well alight and burning fiercely. None of them dared approach any nearer for a closer look. The ammunition in the wings was also alight and going off in all directions. Then the fuel tanks exploded. The farm hands must have thought that nobody could have got out of that inferno alive.

In the meantime we had been looking all around us and weighing up the situation. The terrain was totally unsuitable for movement by day. We'd have to stay hidden in what little shelter this thin stand of firs provided until darkness fell. We had crept into the best bit of cover we could find. Like animals at bay we watched for the first signs of the enemy and tried to interpret every slight noise that reached our ears. The sound of an approaching truck was unmistakable. It drew to a halt. A group of Soviet soldiers climbed down from it and started walking towards our aircraft. They disappeared from our sight as we backed deeper into the thicket. 'If they decide to comb this wood we're going to be in real trouble,' I whispered to Wüstner.

There was a noise of someone or something gradually moving towards our hiding place. It was coming closer – a metallic clatter not unlike the rattling of mess tins. We held our breath and peered out, trying to identify the source of the mysterious noise. It was getting nearer – it stopped – then came closer still – it would be on top of us any moment now. We sensed movement. And from around the edge of the trees right next to us there appeared . . . a cow! A herd of grazing cows had been slowly making its way towards our small wood.

It was all we could do not to laugh out loud in sheer relief. But we mustn't relax our guard for a second. Those Soviet soldiers from the truck were still somewhere very close to hand. Then we saw them making their way back to their vehicle. They clambered aboard and drove away. All clear! They too must have come to the conclusion that we had been burned in the wreckage of our machine. Our trusty Iolanthe had served us well right up to the very end, when she was nothing more than a small heap of glowing embers and ashes. Now at last we could settle down and make ourselves comfortable in our hideaway among the firs. Wüstner dug into his pocket and produced a crumpled cigarette packet. Six whole cigarettes! They were all the provisions we had and he very generously offered to share them out among the crew – three each.

Everything else, including our maps unfortunately, had gone up in flames along with the aircraft. Incredibly, we were both all in one piece, not a bone broken. And at the moment that was the most important thing. To lift our spirits we each lit up a cigarette and then held a grand council of war.

Neither of us had the slightest doubt that we would make it back. The only question was, how? Duty was calling, so how do we get back to our own lines as quickly as possible? We knew that our spearheads had just completed the encirclement of a large body of Soviet troops near Lida, so they must be at least 80 to 100km away still. We would be bound to meet our advancing tanks at some point within that distance. But we couldn't be sure exactly where or when. There was little likelihood of our finding any transport hereabouts, and so our only option was to start walking westwards and simply keep going until we bumped into them.

'One thing's for sure,' Wüstner kept repeating, 'I'm not going to end up breaking rocks in some godforsaken stone quarry in the Urals. My uncle told me too much about that after his experiences in the First World War.' I was in full agreement and assured him that I had no intention of letting myself fall into Soviet hands either. Our first priority therefore was to get out of this neighbourhood unseen. We didn't dare move until dusk, however, and so we allowed ourselves a few hours' rest in our thicket hidey-hole to make up for all the sleep we'd missed over the past few nights.

As darkness began to fall we crept back out towards our aircraft hoping perhaps to find at least a map still intact. But all we saw was a glowing pile of ashes and the silhouette of a Soviet sentry. Bidding a silent farewell to the remains of our faithful old bird, we set off westwards. At first we crawled through a field of growing corn until we were sure that the sentry guarding our machine would no longer be able to see us. We soon realized that we couldn't cover the whole 80–100km on our hands and knees. So we got to our feet and started walking quite openly straight across the fields like a pair of farm workers. The stars in the night sky were as good as any signpost to guide us on our way. In fact, it was a perfect summer's evening, and would have been just right for a pleasant stroll – if we didn't have to be constantly on our guard not to bump into any Russians. On top of that, the heat of the day had given us a raging thirst. And our last bite to eat had been so long ago that it was hard to recall.

'It'd be nice to find a fat juicy chicken around here somewhere,' Wüstner said. He had quite a reputation in the Gruppe as a cook who specialized in such delicacies, and he too was clearly feeling the pangs of hunger. But chickens seemed to be a scarce commodity in these parts. We walked through a sleeping village on the lookout for something to eat, but found nothing. We couldn't even find the village well. Finally, we came across a thin trickle of water – it hardly merited being called a stream – that ran sluggishly through a boggy field. It looked pretty foul and was probably the outflow from a nearby farmyard. 'We'll just wet our lips,' we said to each other, before throwing ourselves full length and gulping down the delicious muddy nectar. As we did so, the words of warning from the Gruppe MO kept ringing in our ears: 'Don't touch the local water because of the danger of cholera!'

Feeling refreshed we continued our march westwards. Only gradually did it occur to us that we might perhaps have drunk too much of the slimy yellowish brew. But we justified our actions by telling each other that it didn't matter whether we died from thirst or from cholera – the end result was the same. Whatever the outcome, the water had given us fresh strength and we started to make better time. Later we came across a natural spring of bubbling, crystal clear water. We drank our fill. We drank so much, in fact, that we deceived our empty stomachs into thinking they were full and were even able to forget our hunger for a short while. On we plodded, through forests, valleys and fields.

The sky began to lighten. We crawled into some thick bushes on the edge of a wood where we could enjoy a short nap, and which would provide us with ample cover for the rest of the day. Not far ahead of us lay a small village. There was no sign of movement. Maybe it would give us an opportunity to 'liberate' a chicken or some fresh milk come the evening. But the morning was so cold that we were frozen almost solid after only an hour. We therefore decided to get moving again to warm ourselves up. The cornfield bordering the wood was glistening from a heavy dew. This provided sufficient refreshment until we found another spring, where we drank and had an early morning wash.

By the time the sun had fully risen we were making our way through a large forest. The day grew steadily hotter. A sunny glade tempted us into having a brief rest, before the urge to continue our homeward march brought us to our feet again. We walked for hours through that forest. By about midday we finally emerged on the far side, where the country opened out into a broad vista of fields and meadows. In the far distance we could see a number of cows dotted about, a welcome sight for hungry and thirsty warriors whose knees were beginning to give out. Unfortunately, there was a man or woman watching over every single animal. They must have had some unpleasant experiences with cattle thieves hereabouts in the past.

Not wishing to reveal our presence, we kept to the edge of the forest until we came to an isolated farmhouse backing on to the trees. We approached it cautiously. We decided to knock on the door. If things looked like getting nasty, we could always dash back into the cover of the forest again. If only we knew whether we were on Russian soil, or on territory that had previously been Polish. We might get a friendlier reception from the Poles, now that they had spent nearly two years under Soviet subjugation.

While we were deliberating, we saw two young farm lads coming towards us. Direct action was called for. We beckoned them over and asked: 'Russki or Polski?' 'Polski,' they replied. The four of us then launched into an animated discussion that was conducted entirely in sign language. If anybody had been watching us they would surely have fallen about laughing. The two Polish youngsters first pointed at our pistols saying: 'Nix boom-boom!' We replied by pointing to our open mouths: 'Nix boom-boom if we munch-munch.' This puzzled them just as much as our speaking in German. But after quite a bit more pointing and arm waving, they finally grasped what we were trying to get across and led us to the farmhouse. This was their family home and they quickly explained our needs to their father. He politely invited us into the house.

In the poor but spotlessly clean farm parlour we were given a warm and friendly welcome. A glass of vodka was offered to us, and then the good people produced all that they had in the way of food: sour milk, butter and bread. Delicious! While we were enjoying our meal the farmer managed to explain to us, by means of sign language alone, that the Russians had taken almost everything they possessed: their boots – the whole family was bare-footed – their smoked hams, all their other winter provisions, and even one of their *panje* carts; the small two-wheeled carts that seemed to be the standard mode of transport throughout this region. It was reassuring to find that he had nothing good to say of the Russians.

After some initial difficulties, we were also able to discover exactly where we were. The farm was situated seven kilometres north of Woloszyn. They told us that Lida, the town where we could be certain of meeting up with our own troops, was very far away. How far? It must be more than 100km, they thought.

So we still had quite a considerable distance to go! Any chance of borrowing one of the remaining *panje* carts? The farmer rejected that out of hand. He wanted to help us but, in his opinion, he'd never get all the way to Lida in one of his carts. And the language barrier meant that it was out of the question for us to try it on our own. We therefore decided that the best thing to do would be to sit it out where we were and let the German Army come to us. We got the distinct impression that we would be safe enough here with these Poles. We indicated to the farmer that we expected German tanks to be here in two days at the most, and asked that he and his sons keep an eye open for any military activity in the area, either the approach of Russian troops or the arrival of our own tanks.

We then retired to the barn to catch up on some more much-needed sleep. At intervals we would also climb up into the roof to scan the surrounding countryside. But we saw nothing suspicious. In the evening we went back into the farmhouse. The same meal as we had been given at lunchtime was again placed before us: bread, butter and sour milk. Sheer delight. The old man sidled up to us, hand held in front of his mouth, and whispered: 'Tanks – German tanks – Woloszyn!'

What? They've got this far already? Our spearheads must have continued their advance eastwards, leaving the troops following on behind to mop up the Soviet forces encircled around Lida. The temptation to set out for Woloszyn straight away was almost unbearable. But night had now fallen and caution was called for. Perhaps the Poles simply wanted to get rid of us. In the darkness it would be all too easy to walk straight into a Soviet ambush.

It made much more sense to stay here for the night. We asked the farmer if he would take us to Woloszyn in his cart at first light. He said he would get his eldest son to do it. The rest of the night remained quiet. At dawn a sturdy little pony was harnessed to the *panje* cart. Soon we were bumping along the rock-strewn, potholed and overgrown track that led to Woloszyn. 'God almighty, I've not been bounced around as much as this since I was on my mother's knee!' . . . 'It's just as well we don't have to go all the way to Lida like this!' . . . 'Now I understand what that farmer meant when he said his cart would never make it all the way to Lida. He was right.'

Wait! – What's that? – Off to our right several tanks were hidden along the edge of a small wood. Their camouflage and the dim early morning light made it impossible to tell if they were ours or the enemy's. All we could see was that they were watching us through their binoculars. We had already jumped down from our rattletrap of a cart and were making our way across the field towards them. No hesitation now. We'd just have to trust to luck. We didn't even know the day's password, by which we could have clearly identified ourselves to them as German servicemen. In lieu of this we simply shouted at the tops of our voices: 'Hallo there! Are you German?' No answer.

We were wearing our pistol belts under our flying overalls, in the hope that this would make us appear less military from a distance. But our right hands were in our overall pockets clutching our pistols – for all the good that would do: two pistols against a troop of tanks. But we had no choice. We were now approaching much more slowly and cautiously. When we were almost at the edge of the wood we stopped and tried calling again: . . . 'Hallo! German? We're a German Stuka crew – shot down!' 'Right you are!' replied a calm voice as several tank men emerged from the shelter of the trees. We covered the last few metres at a run. The stress and strain of the last couple of days – and the tension of these final few minutes – were instantly forgotten in the sheer relief of meeting up with our comrades.

The commander of the small armoured troop, a typical combat Unteroffizier, saluted and introduced himself to us. 'It's marvellous that you've got this far already,' I told him. 'We arrived yesterday evening,' he explained. 'We're the leading unit, a recce troop, sent out here as flank protection for the night. We were just about to break camp. We've been given orders to push on!' 'Before you go, could you possibly spare us a couple of cigarettes?' 'Of course.' Whole packets of cigarettes were pressed into our hands. 'Take them. We'll get ourselves some more later on,' the tank men assured us.

Then the Unteroffizier pulled out his map and showed us the route we should take. The country between here and Woloszyn had been cleared of the enemy. We nodded. 'All the best then, comrades – and good luck!'

Somebody produced a camera and took a quick group photo to record the chance encounter. Then we were off. We ran back across the field to the farmer's son who had been patiently waiting. We climbed up on the back of the cart and sat there as carefree as a couple of little children on a day's outing, legs swinging, hardly conscious of the jolts and bumps as we continued on our way to Woloszyn.

Next to the fountain in the town square stood a German soldier in full combat gear. We jumped down from the cart and went over to him: 'We're German airmen, shot down over Russia. Take us to your commanding officer, please.' 'He's over there,' he answered somewhat sourly. As we walked along the street to the building indicated, he followed close on our heels, pistol in hand. Just as we were about to go through the door he shouted in a loud voice: 'Herr Leutnant, here are two Russian flyers.' 'No, my lad, that's not what we said. Two German Stuka flyers *shot down* by the Russians during a low-level sweep near Minsk,' we explained laughingly as we unzipped our flying overalls to reveal our German uniforms.

The Leutnant was in charge of a supply convoy that was heading for the front. He was apologetic, but he simply couldn't spare a vehicle to take us back to Dubovo. Luckily, a despatch rider was going back part of the way along the road that formed the main axis of advance in this region and he gladly gave us a lift on his motorcycle combination. Then it was a case of continuing on by stages, hitching a lift on whatever vehicle was returning to the rear. Eventually we came to a landing ground occupied by a tactical reconnaissance Staffel, whose Kapitän got one of his pilots to fly us back to Dubovo-South.

Rather grubby and bedraggled, we landed back at our base just before dusk on the evening of 27 June. As we had arrived in a machine of another unit, we weren't recognized at first. Nobody took much notice of us at all. But as we made our way across the field towards our Gruppe command post, we began to get one or two quizzical, disbelieving looks. Our 'Benjamin' – the youngest member in any unit was always the 'Benjamin' – came walking towards us carrying two large buckets of water. When he caught sight of us his mouth dropped open and his eyes nearly popped out of his head. Quickly putting his buckets down, he dashed off towards our HQ building as fast as his legs could carry him to give the word.

The news spread like wildfire: 'The Old Man's just got back with Feldwebel Wüstner – they're both OK!' I had to smile to myself. I was all of twenty-seven, and to them I was 'The Old Man'. Wüstner and I had no doubt aged considerably over the past couple of days – but even so. In no time at all we were surrounded by our comrades, all wanting to shake us by the hand and wish us 'Happy Birthday' on our lucky escape and safe return. The joy in the eyes of these men, who had been with us through thick and through thin, was in itself a joy to behold. A truly humbling experience. The other pilots quickly conjured up a bottle of champagne from somewhere or other. Toasts were drunk as we gave our first brief account of what had been happening to us. Then my car pulled up alongside our little group and I was whisked away.

Five minutes later I was standing in front of our Kommodore in the Geschwader command post and reporting: 'Hauptmann Mahlke and crewman Feldwebel Wüstner returned from mission of 24 June. Both uninjured. Aircraft destroyed in enemy territory.'

The Kommodore, Oberstleutnant Hagen, an officer and commander revered by us all, had risen to his feet and was coming towards me. Quite unashamedly, he took me squarely in his arms like a son, saying: 'God in heaven, Mahlke – to think that you've actually managed to make it back! And so quickly. I can scarcely believe it.' I could tell from his face that he was fighting to hold back what I hoped were tears of joy. He was quite a man, our Stuka Kommodore – a true comrade in every sense. 'We've had the devil's own luck again, Herr Oberstleutnant,' I said. And over an excellent cognac I proceeded to describe everything that we had been through since our crash landing.

Then came the first bit of official paperwork following our sudden reappearance: our names were removed from the 'Missing in action' list! 'Have you written to my family already, Herr Oberstleutnant?' I asked anxiously. 'To be perfectly honest, I hadn't been able to bring myself to do it yet.' 'Thank God for that.'

Another crew had also failed to return from the mission of 24 June. But 9. Staffel's Leutnant Friedrich Bornemann and Gefreiter Franz Jordas hadn't been as lucky as us. They had been attacked by enemy fighters near Kazyn, some 25km northwest of Minsk, and had gone down in flames from a height of only 200 metres. Neither had managed to escape from the burning machine before it hit the ground and exploded. 9. Staffel had also suffered another loss earlier today, 27 June, when Leutnant Adalbert Schilling and Gefreiter Hermann Gutschalk had been killed in action during an attack on Volkovysk.

The German advance continues

In our absence the Gruppe had been just as busy as it was during the first forty-eight hours of the campaign against the Soviet Union when, as part of VIII. Fliegerkorps, we had supported 9. Armee and Panzergruppe 3 in their breaching of the enemy's frontier fortifications to the east and southeast of Suwalki. In the few days since, the front had shifted a long way further east. The Army's fast armoured spearheads had driven deep into enemy territory. The so-called 'cauldron' battles – the encirclement of large bodies of Soviet troops – around Grodno–Bialystok and Minsk had been raging since 25 June. The shattered enemy units were trying desperately to form a new line of defence. But whenever they attempted to make a stand they were promptly attacked by superior German forces and forced to flee for their lives again.

The Luftwaffe's task now was to cut off the Soviets' lines of retreat and prevent their escaping from the armoured pincers that were inexorably closing in around them. Once encirclement was complete, our ground forces would be able to turn their entire weight against the cauldron, battering it into submission and ultimate surrender.

Since 25 June our attacks had therefore been aimed at stopping the hordes of Soviet units streaming eastwards. Complete stretches of railway track were torn up by our bombs. Bridges were destroyed. Numerous temporary crossing points that had been thrown across waterways by the Soviets in their frantic attempts to escape the advancing German tanks were knocked down almost as quickly as they were erected. At many places along the riverbanks large untidy collections of abandoned vehicles of every kind showed where Soviet units had tried, and obviously failed, to find a place shallow enough to ford. Our bombs rained down on the thousands of enemy troops trapped by these bottlenecks, sowing death and destruction and adding yet more confusion to the already panic-stricken masses. Although the altitude at which we operated spared us most of the grisly details, the scenes of carnage were terrible to behold.

By midday on 28 June Wüstner and I were back in the air again in a new machine. At about 13.00 hours the Gruppe destroyed the bridges at Yerenichi. In the evening at around 20.20 hours we sent the Baksztu bridges crashing into the River Beresina. Our armoured spearheads had by this time advanced so deep into enemy territory that we were anxiously awaiting the order to transfer forward ourselves. This would greatly reduce the distance to the target areas, which were presently costing us a lot of time and effort that could be put to far better use.

The transfer order finally arrived late on 28 June. But it was not what we expected. We were to move forward to Baranovichi, southwest of Minsk. Fair enough – but upon arrival there we would be placed under the command of II. Fliegerkorps; to be more precise, under that Korps' Nahkampfführer 2 [Close-support Commander 2] General Fiebig. Our advance ground party, with all our most essential personnel and items of equipment, had already left Dubovo five days previously on the orders of VIII. Fliegerkorps. Unfortunately, however, they were not making for Baranovichi, but another destination entirely. So we wouldn't be seeing them again for quite some time.

This was a considerable blow. But problems such as this were there to be solved. It was simply a matter of reorganizing in detail and getting every single one of us still present to increase his workload. Whenever situations like this arose it never ceased to amaze me just how much could be achieved by a handful of dedicated and experienced men.

Before calling it a day, I discussed all the measures that would have to be taken to complete our somewhat unexpected move with our company chief, Hauptmann der Reserve Holzmann. The three Staffelkapitäne were also present to receive my orders. But, as usual, it was Holzmann who would have all the worry and hassle of getting our motley collection of remaining vehicles to the new base by road. And I prayed that, as usual, he would pull off another of his miracles and get them there in record time.

By the early morning of 29 June everything was ready. The shadows of the transport aircraft we had been promised flitted low over the field. Despite the thick morning mist, they landed safely and without any fuss. 'Not bad, those boys turning up right on time in spite of this lousy weather,' I heard one or two of our men comment approvingly. The few items of equipment that we still had with us were quickly loaded on board the Junkers. The commander of the transport unit had already been given his instructions as to the route he was to take. As soon as the fog lifted, we took off for our first big hop forward into occupied Russian territory.

The airfield at Baranovichi was visible from quite a distance away. It was identifiable by the numerous wrecked and burned-out Soviet aircraft scattered across its surface. Like all the other airfields in the border areas, it was impressive testimony to the Luftwaffe's massed assault on Soviet air force bases during the opening days of the campaign – in particular, those initial devastating attacks of 22 June.

As we circled the field, we soon spotted the empty corner that had been assigned to us as our dispersal area. Piles of bombs and fuel drums had already been stacked there in readiness for our arrival. We taxied in and immediately set to work getting ourselves organized. The base signals section brought us a field telephone, which they connected up and left on the grass beside our machines – the first physical evidence of our command post-to-be. Then the transport Junkers bringing in our ground staff and equipment touched down. While the mechanics got straight on with the job of preparing our Ju 87s for operations, everybody else lent a hand putting up our tents alongside the edge of the field close to the dispersal points.

In the midst of all this feverish activity we suddenly got word that the transport machine carrying most of our admin staff, together with the cooks, their kitchen equipment and all our provisions for the next few days, had been shot down in flames by Soviet ground fire. We had little hope that any of our men had survived or, if they had, that they would be able to make their way forward to us on foot. Search aircraft had been sent out. They returned without sighting anything. But our worst fears were soon confirmed. News came through that the Ju 52 had crashed close to the Slonim–Baranovichi forest road, some four kilometres to the south of Yeziernica. It had probably been brought down by the lorry-mounted quadruple Flak gun that was found abandoned 200 metres from the crash site.

Five members of our Gruppenstab had lost their lives: head of the admin office Regierungsinspekteur Schaak from Dragupönen, our cook Unteroffizier Benz, Junkers mechanic Markwitz, armourer Obergefreiter Elsner and Gefreiter Pütz of our general-duties staff. What a terrible blow. Only a few short hours earlier they had all been excited at the prospect of being in the first transport accompanying us forward into enemy territory. Now all we could do was pay them our last respects from afar.

This tragedy forced us to concentrate on our needs, both immediate and for the near future. Our provisions were quickly replaced. The airfield's base staff and the nearby Army units, who were always more than willing to help 'their' Stukas whenever they could, gave us more than enough to tide us over.

When I reported the Gruppe's arrival to the Nahkampfführer 2, he painted a broad outline of the situation in our new sector and explained what he had lined up for us. We were to operate in direct support of our armoured units, in particular the Panzergruppe Guderian. Our task would be to clear the way immediately ahead of Guderian's leading tanks and deal with any serious resistance they might come up against. We would have our hands more than full, I was promised.

The moment our machines had been armed and refuelled, the Staffeln began taking off one by one on their separate missions. The orders started to pour in. These were close-support operations in the truest sense. No sooner had one Staffel returned to base than it was bombed up, re-armed, refuelled and sent out again. Bridges were demolished, Soviet tanks were attacked – either on the move or when hidden hull-down in ambush – marching troops were strafed and their columns dispersed.

These shuttle missions, flown almost without a break, had one major drawback as far as my small Gruppenstab, or HQ staff, was concerned. We were constantly tied to the telephone and so snowed under with all the paperwork necessary to keep our three Staffeln in the air, that we hardly flew any operations ourselves. The Kommodore did his level best to console me: 'That's one of the crosses a Kommandeur has to bear,' he commiserated, 'not being able to accompany his units every time they take off on a combat mission.' But as soon as we had settled into our new routine, we made sure that we were up there with one or other of our Staffeln whenever time allowed. Thus it was that I found myself back in the air on 30 June, with Gefreiter Foisner as my gunner, attacking the newly repaired bridge at Yerenichi, which we successfully destroyed for a second time at 16.20 hours.

In the early hours of 1 July we were roused from our slumbers by the telephone. The wake-up call from the Nahkampfführer's ops officer was brief and to the point: 'The armoured train is back. Go and get it!' 'Right!'

The Army – perhaps I should say a small unit of shock troops – had stormed the railway bridge across the River Beresina at Svislocz and established a bridge-head on the far side, which they were defending tenaciously against large numbers of Soviet troops. Yesterday evening, however, the enemy had brought up an armoured train. One of our Staffeln had driven it off, but had not succeeded in destroying it. Now it had returned and was back in action against the small group of German troops clinging grimly to their bridgehead. We took off immediately, not wanting to let it slip through our fingers again. We found it standing in the same spot as it had been when attacked the evening before. Its 'lucky escape' then still rankled with the Staffel involved.

As we approached we could see the locomotive getting up steam. This time we were going to make sure. Our first bombs went down exactly where intended: on the tracks in front of, and behind the armoured train. Now it was nailed fast and couldn't move more than a few metres backwards or forwards. It presented a much

easier target for the following aircraft. The shock waves from the bombs deton-
ating close alongside the wagons at the front and back of the train toppled them
from the rails and onto their sides. But a couple of bombs exploded among the
trees quite some distance from the tracks. The two pilots were mystified. Their
approach and dives had been perfect, and they had laid their eggs practically on
top of the armoured wagon in the middle of the train.

The puzzle was solved when they got back to base. Their Staffelkapitän and
some of the other crews had been watching their attacks. They had indeed hit the
domed gun turret of the middle wagon – but their bombs had simply bounced off
the sloping armour and flown in a wide arc before exploding harmlessly in the
woods bordering the railway line. Tough luck! But another valuable lesson had
been learned for the future: when attacking an armoured train, go in low and 'lob'
the bombs into its flanks. Never mind, this was one armoured train that had now
been put well and truly out of action.

On foot behind Soviet lines for the second time

To the north of us our armoured spearheads had also crossed the Beresina at
Borisov, where they had managed to establish a somewhat larger bridgehead. The
Soviets had reacted furiously and were throwing everything they had into the
battle to push the Germans back across the river. Our troops were equally
determined to retain their foothold on the eastern bank of the Beresina and were
defending the bridgehead stubbornly against overwhelming enemy odds.

The fighting was bitter. Strong enemy armoured forces were approaching down
the Moscow highway and were nearing Borisov. Our task was to help relieve the
pressure on our comrades in the bridgehead for as long as possible by mounting
non-stop attacks in Staffel strength against the oncoming Soviet armour. A job
after our own heart! Whenever our troops on the ground were in a jam, it was
always a pleasure to help them out.

This time the Staffeln took off at slightly longer intervals. Soon they were over
Borisov. The Soviet Flak was paying close attention to us. Their shooting wasn't
bad – but it wasn't all that good either. We could afford to ignore it. Our interest
was focussed entirely on the area surrounding the bridgehead on the eastern bank
of the Beresina. Our target was enemy armour. And there it was! Hordes of Soviet
tanks and trucks all bearing down on the thinly held bridgehead. More tanks could
be seen massing in the many small woods and thickets on either side of the main
road. A wealth of very juicy and worthwhile targets.

'Preparing to dive.' I said. Feldwebel Wüstner, who was in the back seat again
today, calmly replied: 'All clear behind.' The usual final adjustments as I pointed
the nose downwards. Our chosen victim, a medium tank, slid slowly into the

centre of my sights. I let go the first bomb – recovered – watched for the result – missed! Ten metres away from the target – oh, sh . . . ame! That won't do at all. Have another go. While the following aircraft were still dropping their first bombs, we had climbed high enough to make a second attempt. The same target – and this time a direct hit! The Soviet tank slewed sideways and began to brew up. He was done for! On to the next. But this one was destroyed by somebody else's bomb before I could even line my sights up on it. Quick change of target: our second bomb detonated close alongside another tank, which first spewed a brief ball of flame before then commencing to burn fiercely.

The tanks advancing along the road had posed the most immediate threat. Once these had been either destroyed or immobilized, we unloaded the rest of our bombs on the machines half-hidden in the woods nearby. Then it was the turn of the trucks. We each made several strafing runs until the road was littered with their burning wreckage. With our bombs gone and our fuel and ammunition running low, it was time to turn west and head for home to refuel and re-arm. We flew at low level, machine-gunning everything we came across on the way: troop positions, gun emplacements and vehicles. We crossed back over the Beresina north of Borisov. Soon we would be approaching our own lines, so extra care was called for. We didn't want to let fly at our own troops by mistake!

As we flew at treetop height over an area of forest, we spotted a Soviet artillery emplacement among the trees. The enemy gunners dashed for cover as we roared past above their heads. I climbed a fraction and then banked round in a shallow dive to strafe the gun positions before resuming our course westwards.

Bang! An ear-splitting crack. A bright tongue of flame lanced out of the engine cowling. We'd been hit. Thoughts raced through my mind: Altitude? – Ten metres above the forest – Windscreen already covered in oil – Open cockpit canopy – Ahead of us to starboard, a cutting through the trees that seemed to widen out into a clearing – Make for it!

I tramped hard on the rudder pedals, lining the aircraft up with the cutting and levelling her out for an emergency landing. 'Tighten harness! – Open canopy! – Prepare for emergency landing! – Get ready in case we somersault!' I shouted over the R/T to Wüstner. The engine had stopped. It was already well ablaze and burning like a blowtorch. The flames were licking into the cockpit. The intense heat was becoming unbearable – high time to get out of here.

I tried to slam her down as hard as possible. If I could wipe the undercarriage legs off there would be less chance of the machine cartwheeling. She hit the ground hard in an area dotted with thick, almost metre-high tree stumps – and the undercarriage stayed put! But if we managed to miss the tree that I could just make out ahead of us, we should have a clear run out into the clearing.

The cockpit windows were by now completely covered in oil. It was impossible to see out. We were hurtling along through the cutting in the woods at breakneck speed. The heat of the flames forced me out of my seat. I undid my harness, heaved myself upwards and stood on my seat, my hands gripping the edge of the canopy frame. I balanced there like a demented surfboarder as my Iolanthe continued to career madly between the tree stumps. There was absolutely nothing more I could do – just hang on for now, and prepare to launch into a forward roll off my seat the moment I felt her start to somersault.

The tree that had stood in our way had been snapped off by our right wing as we tore past it. Luckily, the impact had also straightened us out and we were now heading down the centre of the cutting towards the clearing ahead. Our speed finally began to slacken. At this rate my idea of a forward roll might even work – providing I didn't land on my back on top of one of the tree stumps. Our brave bird was still keeping her tail resolutely on the ground. We had emerged into the clearing by now and the machine had almost come to a stop. Her nose began to tip forward slightly – the moment of truth! No! She sank slowly back on to her tail and stood there. Stood there, as smoke poured out of her and she began to burn.

I quickly jumped down from my perch and peered into the rear cockpit. Wüstner seemed to be hunting for something. 'Get out! I yelled up at him. 'Out, man! Out! Get a move on! She's going to go up at any moment!' 'Hang on, just got to find my rations bag,' he answered calmly. He obviously remembered the last time we were in this situation and wasn't going to go hungry again. Having found what he was looking for, he too now clambered out clutching his rations bag and water canteen in one hand.

All this while the Staffelkapitän and the other crews had been circling above us, watching (and photographing) our emergency landing. We waved up to them to indicate that we were OK. But then the squealing and rattling of tank tracks sent us hurrying into the cover of the nearby trees. Soviet light tanks! We pushed deeper into the wood before stopping to catch our breath. Behind us we could hear the sound of our comrades machine-gunning the enemy tanks. They were keeping them occupied so that we could make good our escape. Well done, lads, much appreciated! They must have stayed above us for a good fifteen minutes before they had to break off and head home to refuel. There hadn't been a hope of any of them attempting to land and pick us up. There was nothing but forest far and wide, and the only clearing in the vicinity – the one we had come down on – was uneven and pitted with shell holes.

Not to worry, we could make it back on foot just as well. This time we were not too far away from our own troops. The quickest way to get to them would be to strike southwestwards. We started off at the double in this direction and kept running until we could no longer hear the tanks behind us. Then we stopped for a rest in some thick undergrowth and had a cigarette: 'Saints alive! I didn't think we'd be that lucky a second time!' 'That was some landing you pulled off among all those tree stumps,' Wüstner remarked. 'It was nothing to do with me. The old crate very kindly did that all by herself. From the moment our wheels touched the ground I was standing on my seat. It was getting much too hot around my feet and, besides, it was the only way I could see where we were going.' 'That explains it. I was wondering how the Herr Hauptmann had managed to get out so quickly.' 'A lucky escape for both of us. I think that calls for another "birthday" cigarette.'

We might have survived the worst, but we couldn't afford to relax our guard just yet. There were Soviet soldiers in the woods all around us. We had some way to go, and would have to be on the alert the whole time. In the background artillery fire of every calibre was pounding away in all directions. One or two shells even landed quite close to where we were hiding. That was all we needed. We began to get a pretty good idea of what our comrades on the ground had to put up with every day. Our cigarettes were almost finished. It was high time to get moving again.

The undergrowth gave way to open forest floor. Clutching our pistols in the pockets of our flying overalls, we cautiously made our way through the trees, still heading southwest, but watching for danger on all sides. 'Pssst!' Wüstner warned. Soviet soldiers ahead of us. We crouched behind a thin screen of ferns. There were only two of them. They were slouching along, apparently intent on nothing more than making their way to the rear and safety. 'Let's grab them!' Wüstner whispered in my ear. 'It'd be quite something to turn up back at base with a couple of prisoners in tow!' 'Have you forgotten what you said last time about breaking rocks in the Urals?' I hissed back. 'We'd be far better leaving them alone. They'd only be a millstone around our necks. We don't know what's going to happen next. If we run into a larger bunch, our two pistols aren't going to be of much use. And we'd very likely end up hammering rocks after all.'

Wüstner admitted that I was right. He confirmed his aversion to the Urals and their stone quarries, and saw the sense in our letting the two hapless Russians go. They wouldn't get far anyway. Our troops would be sure to pick them up fairly quickly. Once the pair were out of sight we continued on our way. There were numerous trenches and fieldworks in the area we were passing through. We took extra care whenever we came across any. But there were no signs of life. They had all been abandoned. Darkness was falling by this time and it had begun to rain. We were again without a compass, and with no stars to guide us it was becoming increasingly difficult to keep to the right direction. Then the heavens opened and the rain really started to come down – we were soaked to the skin in seconds. 'Everything else, and now this filthy weather.' But moaning wouldn't help. The most sensible thing to do would be to find some sort of shelter and wait for first light.

We huddled under a large tree, but it was no use. The raindrops found their way down through the leaves and were, if anything, even heavier by the time they reached the ground. We gave this up and crawled under some smaller saplings instead. We still got wet through, but at least we didn't spend the night walking around in circles. Then, to add to our misery, swarms of gnats and midges descended upon us. 'Damn and blast!' I could hear Wüstner swearing softly to himself. 'It's cold – it's wet – and now these bloody things. It could only happen in Russia.'

The artillery was still hammering away all around us. If we could only tell which of the guns were ours, it would give us a clue in which direction to go. But we lacked the trained ear of the infantryman. A battery suddenly opened up close to hand. We began worming our way through the undergrowth towards it. The firing stopped as abruptly as it had begun. We waited for it to start again. When the next salvo sounded, however, it seemed to be coming from much further away. The battery had changed its position. They were probably Soviet guns covering the enemy's retreat.

We finally recognized a familiar sound among the general background rumble of duelling artillery: the sharp, flat crack of 88mm Flak guns being used in the ground-support role. Now we had a definite point to make for. We set out towards the 88s, our stride lengthening as we followed forest paths, forded a stream, breasted through plantations of young trees and wound our way through dense woods. A faint noise stopped us in our tracks. We listened intently. It was the whine of a self-starter. 'Those must be our tanks up ahead – we've made it!'

Shortly afterwards – it was about 04.00 hours on the morning of 2 July 1941 – and we were peering out at a road lined with the countless vehicles of one of our long supply columns. We stepped out of the bushes and approached a sentry thickly bundled up against the early morning chill. 'Hands up!' he shouted, releasing the safety catch on his rifle the moment he caught sight of us. 'More than happy to oblige now! You can save your bullets, comrade. We're a Stuka crew, shot down near Borisov, trying to make our way home.'

We were as happy as a pair of mud larks. Soon we were surrounded by a circle of other thickly swaddled figures who stared at us sleepily but wide-eyed. 'Well, have you got the coffee on already?' I enquired breezily. 'It's just heating up.' 'Heating up? Sorry, can't wait for that. Is there a staff HQ anywhere nearby?'

Comiso, 26 February 1941: Hauptmann Mahlke (*left*) in conversation with Oberleutnant Schairer, the Kapitän of 7. Staffel, after the Gruppe's attack on Luqa.

The starboard wing of Mahlke's Ju 87 showing the damage caused by the Flak hit during the attack on Malta's Luqa airfield on 26 February 1941. Photo taken immediately after return to Comiso, Sicily.

Trapani, Sicily: Major Hozzel (*left*), the Kommandeur of I./StG 1, discusses a coming operation with Hauptmann Mahlke in III./StG 1's mobile command post, an almost brand new British Army truck captured near Dunkirk. This was one of the vehicles whose roof had to be lowered so that it could be transported by rail through the Alpine tunnels.

III./StG 1's command tent up on the plateau above Derna is furnished with 'all the comforts of home'.

On the roof terrace of the Gruppe's quarters in Derna. From left: Mahlke,
'Theo' Nordmann, Skambraks (Kapitän 8. Staffel) and Schairer (Kapitän 7. Staffel).

The GOC X. Fliegerkorps, General der Flieger Geisler – accompanied by the Fliegerführer Afrika,
Generalmajor Fröhlich (in lighter leather greatcoat) – visits III./StG 1 at Derna and addresses the assembled
aircrews. (Mahlke in background between Geisler and Fröhlich.)

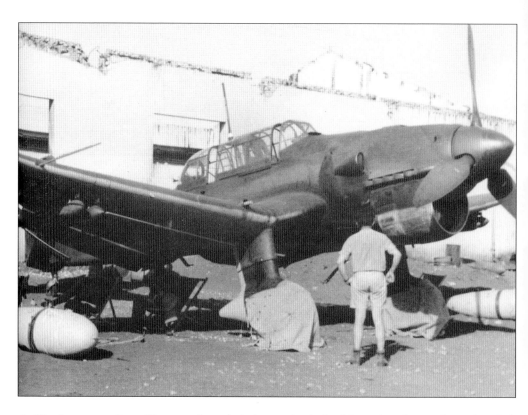

Ju 87 and crew at readiness. The crew relax in deck chairs in the shade of the starboard wing. The auxiliary fuel tanks, already topped up, lie on the ground ready to replace the two 50kg underwing bombs if a long-range mission is ordered. Note the tarpaulins protecting the tyres from the heat of the African sun, and the yellow-painted rear sections of the mainwheel leg and spat.

Five ground crew struggle to lift a fully loaded fuel tank on to its mountings.

Underwing tanks in place, Ju 87s kick up sand during a typical desert take-off, April 1941.

Bombing Tobruk's Fort Medauar, 22 April 1941.
Take-off from Derna, 09.40 hours; land back at
Derna, 11.06 hours.

Oberstleutnant Hagen pictured in Venice during the
brief stopover at Treviso, northern Italy, while en
route from the Mediterranean back to Germany.

Two Russian tanks that drove one on top of the other into a Stuka bomb crater in their efforts to escape a dive-bombing attack. Both tanks were abandoned almost undamaged by their crews.

On 1 July 1941 Hauptmann Mahlke's machine was hit by ground fire and he had to make a second forced landing in enemy territory. Having emerged from the cutting through the woods seen in the background, the Stuka sits in the open with smoke pouring from its engine. This photograph was taken from another of the Gruppe's aircraft that was circling the crash site keeping Russian tanks occupied until Mahlke and his gunner could find cover.

A portrait of Hauptmann Mahlke taken some time after the award of the Knight's Cross on 16 July 1941. The traces of the burns to his face, suffered when he bailed out of his blazing Stuka on 8 July 1941, are still clearly visible.

Already showing signs of wear and tear, one of III./StG 1's new Ju 87Ds taxies from its snow-covered dispersal early in 1942.

A Ju 87D is bombed up in Russia some time during the summer of 1942. Note the yellow-painted wheel spat as first introduced by Mahlke during the Battle of Britain two years earlier.

By the war's end III./SG 1 was a ground-attack unit equipped with Focke-Wulf Fw 190s.

'There's an armoured division HQ – about a hundred metres down the road and then into the woods on the right.'

We followed these directions, found the armoured HQ quite easily, and woke the divisional orderly officer from his short and no doubt well-deserved night's sleep. He soon got things organized. First, a quick breakfast and some very welcome coffee, and then a truck to take us to Minsk. The driver attached himself to a convoy that was heading to the rear. 'The woods around here are crawling with Soviet stragglers,' he explained. 'It's better to travel in company – slowly but safely.' We didn't mind at all. A few extra minutes now didn't matter in the least. In fact, we spent most of the journey catching up on our own sleep so that we would arrive refreshed and ready for action.

Despite travelling in convoy, we made reasonably good time and it was not long before we were approaching the outskirts of Minsk. The town's main airfield was occupied by a tactical reconnaissance Staffel who agreed to help us on our next leg. While they were getting their Fieseler Storch runabout ready, we had a quick shave and brush-up to make ourselves look presentable again. 'Where is it exactly that you want to go?' asked the Staffelkapitän who was filling out the flight plan. 'Back to Baranovichi. But perhaps we could have a quick look at the other airfield near here first? Our Gruppe may have moved forward already.' 'Sounds like a good idea to me.'

As the Storch headed for the neighbouring field, I could already see some of our Ju 87s parked around its perimeter. Excellent! This would save us wasting a lot of time. We touched down and taxied over towards the Stukas. The men working on them were craning their necks trying to see who was in the Storch. They knew from past experience that the arrival of one these little machines usually meant a visit from some brass-hat or other. But then one of them recognized me and I saw the word quickly being spread around the dispersal area.

As soon as the Storch came to a stop it was ringed by a sea of smiling faces all wanting to congratulate us on our safe return. The Staffelkapitän pushed his way through the throng to make his report: 'One Staffel transferred forward from Baranovichi to Minsk-South as ordered. The other two Staffeln carrying out a combat mission en route. They should be arriving any minute now.' 'Good, thank you. I'm afraid we were forced to make the transfer by a more roundabout route. So tell me, what's happening here?' 'We've only just arrived ourselves and haven't been given any fresh orders yet.' 'We've come at just the right time then. Let's get cracking. Have the aircraft refuelled and bombed up in readiness. Then get yourselves settled in while we wait for further orders.'

The Gruppe command post was quickly set up and the telephone connected. It wasn't long before our first operational orders came through. The single Staffel took off on its first mission from Minsk-South. The other two touched down shortly afterwards and their Kapitäne reported to me. How had we managed to turn up here, they then wanted to know. I promised to tell them all about it that evening. At the moment there was work to be done. Later we described our second brief hike behind enemy lines. Apart from that decidedly unorthodox emergency landing, there hadn't been very much to it. We passed it off with a joke: 'Wüstner and I have decided that in the next war we're going to volunteer for the infantry – that way we'll know from the start that we'll be walking everywhere!'

But in reality there was little to joke about. Today, 2 July 1941, had seen the loss of an 8. Staffel crew in the same area along the River Beresina. Leutnant Kurt Hoffmann and Gefreiter Hermann Becker were shot down into the woods some ten kilometres to the east of Borisov while attacking Soviet ground troops.

And 3 July was to deal us another bitter blow. The Gruppenstab's Oberleutnant Jochen Berkhoff and Gefreiter Johann Foisner failed to return from a mission to the northwest of Beresino. They too were strafing enemy ground troops when they were brought down close to the forest road between the towns of Beresino and Schoramz.

Chapter 15
Ground-Support Operations

There were still many small groups of Soviet soldiers, cut off from the main body of the retreating Red Army, hiding in the woods surrounding Minsk-South. They had carried out several unsuccessful attacks on the field over the last few nights. As a precaution we therefore decided to increase our normal number of sentries when darkness fell. Before that, however, we sent out some foraging parties of our own to scour the area by daylight for abandoned vehicles and any other items of equipment that the Soviets might have left behind, and which we could make use of until our ground columns turned up.

It wasn't long before the first of our men returned. They had discovered a deserted Soviet camp nearby and had brought back with them some very welcome tents. At least we would have shelter for the night. Then Leutnant Heimlich, who had set out riding pillion behind an armed motorcyclist to search for vehicles, came back and reported proudly: 'Two officers and fifty enemy soldiers captured. One truck, one fuel bowser and one equipment trailer found. Prisoners delivered to station guardroom. Vehicles towed away for minor repairs – they'll be in full working order by the morning.'

'That's quite a haul,' I said. 'How did you manage to get hold of the prisoners?' 'They suddenly appeared out of the cornfields while we were inspecting the vehicles. They were stragglers. They didn't seem to have the faintest idea what they were supposed to do next.'

Not long after this our own two ground columns finally arrived – one from the north and the other from the south. Their appearance was greeted with both excitement and relief. Now things could get back to some sort of normality. Our company chief, Hauptmann der Reserve Holzmann, who had been in command of the main column, was a typical boisterous Bavarian and not one to hide his true feelings. When we saw him coming across to make his report, we already knew what his first words would be. They were always the same after every transfer. But this time he started shouting while still some distance away from us – just so we wouldn't be in any doubt.

'Never in my entire life have I known a transfer like it!' he yelled in his broad, almost incomprehensible Bavarian dialect before launching into his report and a blow-by-blow description of the ground party's journey. 'The roads! You've no idea of the state the roads were in! The ruts were so deep one of the trucks ended up on its side. Almost every trailer came adrift. We were continually having to halt so that the workshops could make new couplings before we could get going again. Stop, start – it was never ending. Then we leaguered for the night in some forest or other – sentries posted, of course. I was making my rounds when one of the infantry types on guard duty suddenly popped out from behind a tree to tell me that the woods were still full of Soviets! We'd stumbled into the front line! Naturally, we stayed put where we were – quiet as mice. Not a sound the whole night long. Then in the morning we had to wait until the roads were cleared. For hours we sat there – hours! I tell you, you can't imagine what we've been through . . .'

He still had a lot more to tell us about the troubles he had had in getting through. But we explained that it would have to wait until the evening. The Staffeln had been given orders to carry out a series of continuous rolling attacks, which would keep us all fully occupied throughout the day.

Our other ground column – the original advance party, which we had almost given up for lost – had undergone similar trials and tribulations during its ten-day odyssey on the road since departing Dubovo-South. But it had made some lucky finds too, and turned up bearing tubs of butter, cartons of tea and a lot of other treasures that had been 'saved' from going to waste in an abandoned Soviet supply convoy. The difficulties that had to be overcome during these transfers, however, can only really be understood and appreciated by those who themselves took part in the great advance of the summer of 1941 and are familiar with the conditions in Russia during that period.

In the meantime our spearheads had reached the River Dnieper at Rogachev. We helped soften up the crossing points and then supported our ground troops during the actual assault on the river by keeping up constant attacks on the enemy's defensive positions on the far bank. I flew on two such missions with Oberleutnant Hartmann, the Gruppe's new TO, or technical officer, in the rear seat. Hartmann had wanted desperately to get in on the action, and so now joined Unteroffizier Hilberger and Leutnant Michl as the third of my trio of 'acting gunners' who flew with me more or less in rotation as their other duties permitted.

Generaloberst Guderian's armoured units were now advancing eastwards from Borisov along the Minsk–Moscow highway towards Smolensk. We were ordered to make another move forward in order to keep in close touch with them. Our destination was a small landing ground still under construction near the village of Dokudovo, close to the main highway. The first aircraft to land there were a small group of Ju 52s carrying a company of infantry whose job was to secure the area for us. The giant 'cauldron' battle around Minsk was not yet over, and the only territory to the east of the town that was in our hands was the narrow strip along the highway carrying supplies to our armoured spearheads.

We transferred up to Dokudovo on the evening of 5 July after first flying a mission against enemy artillery and tanks to the east of Bobruisk on the way. We touched down on our new field at 19.05 hours, not very long after the infantry had landed. And, just to show it *could* be done, our entire ground organization also arrived later that same evening!

The supply services performed magnificently, keeping us well stocked with munitions and fuel. The number of missions that we were being ordered to fly meant that we were soon consuming considerable quantities of both these commodities. But whenever supplies started to run low and we were beginning to wonder whether we would have enough for the next mission, several Ju 52s would come swooping in to land, delivering fresh loads and relieving us of our worries.

When we first touched down at Dokudovo and I had reported the Gruppe's arrival to Nahkampfführer 2's ops officer, he wasn't joking when he welcomed us to the 'most forward airfield on the Eastern Front'! It must be admitted that we felt a certain pride when we were told this. But we were far more pleased by the fact that, with the front only a few kilometres away, it would save us an awful lot of time getting to and from our target areas. On top of this, troops serving close to the front line were often better supplied than those further back who were not within the immediate combat zone.

This wasn't simply a matter of priorities. The nearer the front you were, the greater the opportunities for a little 'self-help'. Take our IVa, or stores inspector, for example. This much-harassed official was responsible for the Gruppe's physical well being. The Soviet collective farms hereabouts still had sufficient produce available to contribute to our daily ration requirements. And it was much easier and quicker for the IVa to get his provisions from the local farmers rather than from the official supply depots and rations stores many kilometres distant. He became a sort of wholesale buyer for the area and greatly enjoyed making the rounds of the collective farms, most of whose Soviet overseers and commissars had taken to their heels prior to our arrival.

We were careful not to touch any of the pitifully few personal possessions or foodstuffs that the Soviet authorities had allowed the farm workers to keep simply in order to be able to survive. They were grateful for this and their initial fear of the foreign invaders soon turned to trust. Occasionally they would even come to the field to present us with some of their produce as a gift. But it was not always possible for every German unit advancing through the area to treat the small farmers with quite the same consideration, as the following incident illustrates.

A farmer came to our Geschwaderkommodore one day with a tale of woe. A group of soldiers had milked his cow – his only cow, whose milk provided the sole source of nourishment for his wife and four children. Now he was afraid that the animal itself would be stolen some day soon. To prevent this, he pleaded for an 'official certificate' to the effect that he was permitted to keep his one cow and its milk for the use of his family. The Kommodore had a kind heart. He gave him a certificate as requested, signed with a flourish, and bearing the official stamp of Stukageschwader 1.

The next day the farmer reappeared waving his piece of paper and lamenting loudly. Below the Oberstleutnant's signature and the rubber stamp, another hand had written: 'The cow is dead! We were out of grub: Gefreiter . . . (name and unit).' After a moment's hesitation, the Kommodore joined in the guffaws of laughter. After all, what else was the unknown corporal supposed to have done? His unit had presumably outstripped its supplies and he had no doubt been ordered to find something for the men to eat! The bewildered farmer was not forgotten, however. He was given a replacement cow from another collective that had one to spare.

In the meantime, we were flying one operation after the other. The Soviets were constantly throwing in more and more fresh units in their efforts to stop the advance of our ground forces. Endless convoys of tanks, artillery pieces and trucks were streaming westwards along the main highway from the direction of Moscow–Smolensk. Many of them were destroyed by our bombs and machine guns before they could reach the front and be deployed against our troops.

Now that our ground personnel were once again back with us and at full establishment, the Gruppenstab could also play a larger part in operations. On 6 July, with Oberleutnant Hartmann as my gunner, I flew two missions against enemy tanks: one to the southwest of Senno, the other close to Kochanovo. The following day we had to abort one mission because the oil tank filler cap of our machine had not been properly secured and excessive loss of oil forced us to return to base early. But we put in three other ops on this 7 July. The first saw us again attacking enemy tanks near Kochanovo. Then we bombed artillery columns on the march in the Belavichi area, before engaging yet more tanks around Tolochin.

We destroyed a number of tanks by direct hits, but also immobilized or put out of action many more with near misses. During the later stages of the war near misses would come to count for very little, for by then the enemy could quickly recover and usually repair most of his armoured vehicles abandoned on the battlefield. But during these opening weeks of the campaign, when the German Army was advancing rapidly, any immobilized tank was effectively a total loss to the retreating enemy, even if the vehicle's crew did manage to escape.

An example of this was captured on film by the then Oberleutnant Kaiser, commander of an 88mm Flak battery, who photographed a pair of Soviet tanks abandoned in a crater left by a Stuka's bomb. The tanks had not been hit or damaged in any way, but in their attempts to escape the falling bombs both had driven blindly into the same crater, one on top of the other. The Flak battery used one of its heavy tractors to pull the two tanks out of the crater and found that both were still in perfectly good running order.

If the number of enemy air raids on our field was anything to go by, our operations must have been hurting the Soviets badly. They seemed intent on knocking us out on the ground. The enemy bombers usually came over at night, but also sometimes tried to sneak in at dawn or dusk. Our vigilant Flak crews sent quite a few down in flames into the surrounding swamps, and forced many more to break off their attacks before dropping their bombs. Those that *did* manage to get through caused very little material damage. Our Gruppe suffered no losses whatsoever among either personnel or aircraft.

It may have been this lack of success by night that prompted the Soviets to risk a daylight raid on one occasion. But it cost them dear and was never repeated. Although our base was very close to the front, our fighters scrambled in time to intercept the formation of nine enemy bombers just short of the field. A brief, dramatic air battle took place in full view of all those of us watching from the ground. It was a truly amazing spectacle. In a matter of minutes – no, seconds – every single one of the nine Soviet machines was shot down. Nine columns of smoke were still climbing lazily into the air around the field as the Me 109s, which shared the base with us, came back in to land. They were given a rapturous welcome by those who had witnessed the whole thing.

This short interlude gave a terrific boost to our own ground personnel, who were otherwise working non-stop repairing the damage – some of it serious – that our machines were now suffering during their low-level shuttle missions against the enemy's ground forces. For unlike many of our previous opponents, Russian troops tended to stand firm when under air attack. Rather than dive for cover, most would blaze away at us with whatever weapons they had to hand. And as infantry weapons did not use tracer bullets, we were often unaware of the volume of enemy fire that was being directed at us. It was only when we returned to base and saw the enormous number of bullet holes in our machines that we realized just how much lead we had been flying through.

But we didn't all return to base. It was inevitable that this amount of fire would result in casualties and we sadly suffered several losses during this period. At about 11.00 hours on 7 July Leutnant Horst Suckrow of 9. Staffel was brought down by ground fire during an attack on Malo Gorodno, east of Velyavichi. Suckrow was killed, but his gunner managed to bail out and make his way back to our lines. At about the same time another 9. Staffel machine also fell victim to ground fire while attacking enemy troops near Gubailovichi, east of Belavichi. Here too the pilot, Leutnant Hans Rudorf, lost his life while his gunner survived; Gefreiter Erich Braune being admitted to hospital with a broken ankle. And on 8 July yet a third 9. Staffel crew was shot down, this time by Soviet fighters while bombing enemy tanks near Latigalskiye. Pilot Feldwebel Karl Dietz and gunner Gefreiter Bodo Leonhardt both parachuted from their burning machine. Feldwebel Dietz was found by our troops and taken into hospital suffering burns and bullet wounds in his backside. Gefreiter Leonhardt joined the list of those missing in action.

These were grievous losses, just as grievous as all the previous losses we had suffered. And yet here in Russia there was something subtly different about them – they were somehow not quite so distressing. It certainly wasn't due to the fact that the tempo of operations left us hardly any time to grieve. No, it was something else – something that we had not noticed, or had not been conscious of before. Here on the Eastern Front, whenever we carried out our low-level attacks immediately in front of our comrades on the ground – dropping our bombs singly on the gun emplacements and machine-gun nests that were holding up their advance, and then strafing the enemy's trenches until our ammunition was exhausted – we could actually *see* the results. We saw our troops getting to their feet and dashing forwards, often waving up at us as they did so, to storm the Soviet lines that we had been attacking only moments earlier.

That was it! Here we had finally come to understand what our close-support missions really meant to our comrades on the ground. Without our help, how much more blood would those troops have had to shed in order to achieve their objectives? We were needed here like we had never been needed before. This knowledge made us all the more determined to give of our best. It also made it that little bit easier to accept our inevitable losses.

My last mission with 'Third Stuka One'

The telephone in the Gruppe command post was ringing again. It had been doing so throughout the whole morning of this 8 July 1941, mostly minor matters. 'Nahkampfführer's Ia on the phone for the Herr Hauptmann!' the operator called across the room. 'This will be an operational order! Stand by . . .' I took the phone.

'The 17. Panzerdivision has been surrounded by strong enemy armoured forces. According to latest reports the Soviets are bringing up even more heavy units. The Gruppe is to mount shuttle missions against enemy tanks and artillery in the area southwest of Senno to relieve pressure on 17. Panzerdivision.' 'Jawohl! Understood!'

The Staffelkapitäne were already reporting to the command post. The purpose of the mission was explained to them and the details quickly sketched out: time and place of rendezvous with fighter escort, our own times and order of take-off. 'Right, synchronize watches: 10.21 hours – counting – Now! Let's make a good job of it and give the tank boys a bit of room to breathe!'

The Staffeln lifted off, one shortly after the other. It wasn't far to the target area. We were there in twenty minutes. Now it was a case of getting our bearings. It was not easy to fix our exact position above this unfamiliar patchwork of country lanes and small villages. Aha! There's the road we'd been told to look out for – or was it just a broad track winding through an area of marshy ground? Whatever it was, it was jammed full of Soviet tanks, nose to tail in one long column, and all heading towards a village that we could now see was occupied by our troops.

Our troops? More accurately: two tanks, four self-propelled guns and just a handful of men, part of the spearhead of the 17. Panzerdivision that had set up a defensive position in this village. The leading Soviet tanks were already very close to the first houses. Our lads down there were soon going to be in serious trouble.

We lost no time in diving to the attack. Our first bombs, released singly, went down along the road on and among the column of enemy tanks. One or two exploded violently. Smoke poured from several others as they began to brew up. But now what's happening? Were our eyes deceiving us? Obviously an order had been given. For suddenly every tank on the road turned simultaneously to either right or left! They were frantically trying to disperse in order to present less of a target for our bombs. But in their desperation to get off the road they drove at full speed into the swamps flanking it on either side! One after the other they started to sink into the morass – some seemed to nosedive straight down, other settled more slowly on an even keel, giving their crews just enough time to escape through the turret hatches.

In the back seat Hartmann was yelling almost incoherently. His excitement was infectious and I found myself joining in. The enemy tanks were disappearing into the swamp so quickly that we found it hard to count them – there must have been twenty at least! Those twenty wouldn't be doing our comrades any more harm. But there were plenty more closing in on the village from other directions. From up here the olive-brown Soviet tanks looked like so many nasty little insects as they crawled across the open fields, twisting and turning wildly to throw us off our aim, or crept under trees and bushes trying to hide from us.

We distributed our remaining bombs among these new targets. But there were still so many of them left that we flew back to base at top speed to re-arm and return for a second attack. Our tank men needed all the help we could give them. When we landed at Dokudovo a quick glance around the dispersal areas showed that all our aircraft had made it back safely; no crews missing. The mission had been a total success.

The mechanics and armourers immediately swarmed over the machines, bombing up and re-arming them ready to take off again. Each and every man was – as always – determined to do his job as rapidly and efficiently as possible. They were all highly skilled and absolute masters of their particular trades. No onlooker could possibly appreciate the vital importance of the work they were doing. It wouldn't have appeared all that spectacular to the casual observer. But these men were at their posts night and day, dedicated to keeping us flying, and conscious of the fact that the slightest negligence or lapse of concentration on their part could spell the difference between life and death for their comrades in the air.

Each took enormous pride in *his* machine's being the best: always in top condition and ready for action, the engine as smooth as silk, its guns never jamming, its bomb-release systems in perfect working order. And if an aircraft should return from an op with combat damage, they lost no time in carrying out whatever repairs were necessary to make it serviceable again. Were they perhaps even a little proud if 'their' machine came back bearing the scars of battle? Not at all – quite the opposite, in fact. They would much prefer to see it return, mission successfully accomplished, undamaged and all in one piece. Not because that meant less work for them, you understand, but simply because of the odd sense of affection they felt towards what was, after all, just an inanimate piece of machinery – rather like the driver who lavishes care and attention on his car and can't bear to see it scratched or dented in any way.

While in the command post I had put through a call to the Ia of Nahkampf-führer 2 to give him a preliminary report on the success of our mission: 'We really caught them on the hop.' I told him, 'We accounted for quite a few enemy tanks knocked out or disabled, and then chased at least twenty more into the swamps . . .' 'My spies have already been in touch with me,' the Ia interrupted, 'not with all the details of course, but I've got a couple of radio messages from the encircled Panzerdivision here in front of me. According to one of them, the observers on the ground estimate that your Gruppe has just wiped out an entire Soviet armoured brigade – sixty tanks either totally destroyed, put out of action or forced off the road into those swamps. The second message is addressed to your unit and simply says: "Bravo the Stukas!"'

'That's music to an old Stuka pilot's ears. The men will be as pleased as Punch when I pass it on to them. But unfortunately there are an awful lot of enemy tanks still active in the target area. We ought to put in another attack straight away – unless, of course, you have a more urgent job waiting for us?' 'No, carry out another mission against the same target.' 'Jawohl! I'll report further when we get back. We'll take off as soon as possible. Out.'

The Staffelkapitäne had reappeared in the command post. This time things took slightly longer. Before briefing them on the next mission we had to assess the results of the last. Every crew had witnessed so much during our attack on the enemy tanks that it was not at all easy to include everything that had happened and boil it down into a concise combat report. But eventually the job was done. 'The mission was a resounding success!' I said in summing up. 'Well done, all of you. You can inform your crews of a message from 17. Panzerdivision: "Bravo the Stukas!" The second mission will be a repeat of the first. Same targets. But we'll take off at slightly longer intervals so that it won't be too crowded over the target area.'

While the aircraft were being refuelled and re-armed, the crews had taken the opportunity to have a bite of lunch. The Staffeln then took off at the times and in the sequence agreed upon during the briefing. The ground fighting was still raging furiously when we arrived over the target area. The enemy was throwing in all his reserves. We had a lot on our hands. But by the time we had finished the Soviets had lost many more of their tanks and assault guns.

When we returned to base for the second time there was another message from 17. Panzerdivision waiting for us: 'Stuka assistance invaluable.' Like the earlier message, it was hard to describe the joy we felt at receiving these few short words. It meant a lot to us that our comrades on the ground – despite being engaged for hours in a bitter and bloody battle – had somehow found the time to send a brief message of thanks and appreciation. We had seen the results of our bombing for ourselves and knew that we had inflicted further considerable losses on the enemy. But there was an added satisfaction in having it confirmed in this way and knowing that we had been instrumental in helping the men of the 17. out of a very tight corner. We had carried out the orders we had been given – exactly as was expected of us.

We were then sent out for a third time to mop up any remaining Soviet forces still in the same area. The situation had by now been stabilized, however. Things had eased considerably and our main priority would be to prevent the enemy from bringing up any further reinforcements. Our three Staffeln had already departed on this third mission by the time I started to taxi out with my two wingmen.

But we were held at the take-off point. I was wanted on the telephone. It was the Nahkampfführer's ops officer again with a last-minute addition to our orders: 'A message has just come in. A Flak battery has been cut off by enemy tanks near the village of Latigalskiye. It is rapidly running out of ammunition. Immediate help is urgently requested. Get all aircraft not yet airborne over there as soon as you can.'

'The three machines of my Stabskette are the only ones still on the ground here. We can take off for Latigalskiye in ten minutes. Request you keep a couple of fighters in the target area as cover until we arrive.' 'Fighters will remain over the target area. Out.'

We were hurriedly preparing for this new mission when who should turn up but the head doctor of the field hospital at St-Pol in France, with whom we had spent many a pleasant evening chatting in front of the fire during the previous winter. He and his chief surgeon had set up shop nearby and had come over to visit us. We were delighted to see them both. Unfortunately, we had to make it brief, as we had to go and help that Flak battery out of trouble. Our visitors fully understood. They were quite prepared to wait until we got back. It should take us about an hour, I told them. And then we were off.

For the third time today we found ourselves circling above the same patch of enemy territory. We pinpointed the spot given in our operational orders and started looking for the Flak battery and the enemy tanks. But we could see no sign of either. We widened our search area. They can't have just vanished! I went down a little lower and called over the R/T to my gunner Hartmann: 'Keep your eyes well peeled. Watch the sky while I try to find the Flak battery.' 'Understood,' he replied, before adding, 'three Me 109s off to starboard.' 'Good!' I answered, 'They'll keep us out of trouble. Now, where the hell is that Flak battery?'

I took her down even lower. From this height we ought to be able to see *something*, however well camouflaged it might be. But still no sign of the battery, or any evidence of the position it had been occupying. At last I did spot four Soviet tanks. They didn't seem to be threatening any Flak battery. In fact, they didn't appear to be in action at all. But they were the only enemy tanks to be seen. So, just to be on the safe side, we decided to attack these tanks first and then return to the search for the battery in our old target area. We selected a heavy tank that was nosing its way along a country lane. Our bomb fell short, but we had probably damaged the tank. At any rate, it was no longer moving. I had just begun to climb again, when suddenly. . .

'Heavy machine-gun fire from the wood behind us!' reported Oberleutnant Hartmann. I automatically started to weave from side to side, the manoeuvre that we normally employed to put ground gunners off their aim. But then I thought to myself: Hold on a minute! Our own troops have just sent up recognition flares from the edge of that wood behind us. There can't be any Soviets left in it! I looked over my shoulder to see for myself what was going on. Sweet Jesus! Now we were for it!

An enemy fighter was sitting right on our tail. At that very moment he loosed off a long burst that ripped into our left wing. Even as he zoomed past us, climbing away to port, a second fighter was already boring in – and then a third. They were so close that they couldn't miss. We collected a full salvo from each. The left wing fuel tank had immediately burst into flames – and now the right tank was ablaze as well.

The enemy fighters had really caught us napping this time. But how was that possible? The answer was tragically simple. Our attackers had been MiGs – the first we had ever seen. With their pointed noses and streamlined shapes they looked very similar to our Me 109s. Up until now the only Soviet fighters we had encountered had been the stubby little Ratas with their blunt radial engines. And so we had mistaken the MiGs for the German fighters we had been told would be in the area. It was our own fault – and now we were paying for it.

'Out!' I yelled to Oberleutnant Hartmann as soon as I had coaxed our burning bird up just high enough to allow us to take to our parachutes. The machine was a goner, anyway. An emergency landing was out of the question as flames were by this time roaring out of both inboard wing fuel tanks and streaming back along the fuselage on either side of the cockpit. The wings could come off at any moment. All we could do now was to try to save ourselves. I had slid my canopy back. I daren't use the automatic release to jettison it altogether in case it interfered with Hartmann's escape from the rear cockpit.

I finally saw him climb out of his seat and hurl himself through the flames alongside to get clear. At last! Now it was high time that I followed suit. The fierce tongues of flame were already licking at my hands and face. I jumped – felt myself get caught up on something – and then fell free. But I was still surrounded by the unbearable heat of the flames from the burning fuel. I knew I mustn't open my parachute yet. If I did so while falling through the air still engulfed in the blazing comet's tail from my doomed aircraft, the parachute silk would catch fire and that would be the end. So I forced myself to wait until I was out of the flames.

At last I sensed the air around me getting cooler. I tugged at the D-ring of my 'chute and felt it give slightly. Did I still have enough height for the canopy to open? We'd been at a bare 700 metres when I jumped, and I'd already been falling for quite a while now. I was still falling, and nothing was happening. Still nothing! And what could I do about it? Absolutely nothing!

I had automatically closed my eyes tightly against the heat and the flames. Now, with great difficulty, I opened my swollen eyelids and peered downwards. I wasn't more than 100 metres from the ground! A few more seconds, and . . . ? In those few seconds something flashed through my mind's eye – Wertheim, 6 December 1939: an aircraft had crashed in a ploughed field, and I could still see the two medics using forceps to gather up bits of the crew. Any moment now, I found myself thinking – and you won't even have a medic to pick up the pieces.

Whoa! A muffled crack above my head. The harness yanked me upwards. The parachute had opened! At last – and about time too. Thud! The lines had hardly had time to unfurl from the blossoming 'chute before I found myself sitting on my backside on mother earth A quick look around reassured me that there were no enemy troops in the immediate vicinity. But where was Hartmann – Oberleutnant Hartmann – my gunner? I couldn't see his parachute in the sky above me.

I thumped the release disc of my parachute harness and shrugged myself free of the straps. I tried to prop myself up and get to my feet, but my left arm was hanging limply by my side. My face and hands felt as if they were on fire. Otherwise I seemed to be in reasonably good order. I tried shouting for Hartmann, but got no answer. Nor could I see any signs of him. I began to get an uneasy feeling, but I didn't have the strength to go looking for him. I had to get away from here, had to find somewhere to hide. If any Soviet soldiers *did* turn up, the first place they'd start searching was where the parachute had come down. And in my present state, I was in no condition to put up any kind of fight.

Not far away stood one or two farmhouses and a barn. I slowly made my way towards them. An old couple appeared in the doorway of one of the houses. I approached them, hoping that they would be able to help me bandage my wounds. But they waved me away, pointing instead to the barn. I turned in the direction indicated and carefully opened the small door into the barn. It was half empty. Like a wounded animal I clambered painfully across piles of junk and rusty farm implements to the hay piled on the far side. I climbed up it to give myself a vantage point. There were plenty of small gaps in the dilapidated thatched roof. I peered out but there was nothing to be seen. I really ought to have made a larger hole to get a better view, but the weeping burns on my hands and face stopped me from doing so. I didn't want to risk getting any dirt in them – who knew when I would be able to have them properly bandaged.

The sun beating on the thatched roof was making the interior of the barn very hot and stuffy. I felt myself becoming drowsy. Initially I had noticed hardly any pain at all, but now reaction was setting in and I was in agony. I desperately wanted to sleep! But I knew I mustn't – that could be fatal. Instead, I stretched out on the hay to conserve what strength I had left in case there were any more nasty surprises in store for me. Just don't go to sleep, I kept repeating to myself, as I lay there listening intently to every little noise.

Engines! The sound of motorcycle engines in the distance. The noise gradually grew louder until I could recognize the unmistakable sound of German BMW motorcycles. Our motorcycle troops were out looking for us. From the uneven but growing noise of the engines, the sudden bursts of power, I could tell that the motorcyclists were bumping their way across the newly ploughed fields in my direction. When they got close to the barn, the engines were switched off and everything was suddenly quiet. It was time to reveal my presence.

I jumped down from my nest in the hay – and fell flat on my face. I had forgotten all about my useless left arm. Picking myself up, I edged slowly out of the door. And there they stood: two armed motorcyclists in full combat gear. Talk about a welcome sight! I called across to them, although with my mouth now completely swollen from my burns, it came out as more of a croak. They hurried over and I felt myself being helped by strong but gentle hands. Thanks, comrades!

They sat me in the sidecar of their motorcycle combination and we drove, or rather bounced back across the ploughed fields to their company HQ. My God! That short journey was a nightmare! I was no longer in any state to be rattled and shaken about like that. But we were heading back towards friends. The sense of joy and feeling of safety this gave me almost made me forget the pain of my injuries. The motorcyclists told me that it was their company commander who had sent them out to look for us. They had caught a glimpse of a parachute opening, but it had been so close to the ground that they hadn't had time to see any more before it disappeared behind a hill. When we arrived at the headquarters, the company CO himself applied the first emergency dressings to my wounds. He also promised me that his men would continue the search for Hartmann. Where on earth was he, my gallant comrade? Had he made it down safely as well?

I was next taken by car to the divisional field dressing station. As if in a dream, I was only dimly aware of all that was going on around me. The car came to a halt. Experienced hands lifted me carefully on to a stretcher and I was carried into a cattle shed. Or rather, what had previously *been* a cattle shed, but now – painted white and spotlessly clean throughout – was serving as the 17. Panzerdivision's field dressing station. I was informed that I was in the village that the division's spearheads had been so stubbornly defending since early this morning – the very same village, which had been the target of the enemy tanks we had destroyed earlier in the day.

A doctor was bending over me. 'Straight into the operating theatre,' I heard him order softly. Then somebody was holding an ether mask in front of my face: 'Start counting.' I started counting – could almost taste the strong odour given off by the ether – counted some more – breathed in some more ether – counted – breathed in some more eth . . . and I was gone. Out like a light.

When I came round my first question was: 'Where is Oberleutnant Hartmann, my gunner?' 'He didn't make it,' I was told, 'He jumped out before you but for some reason wasn't able to open his parachute in time.' At that I broke down and cried. I had done all I could. I'd managed to keep our burning aircraft in the air just long enough for him to bail out. I'd slid my hood back rather than jettison the entire canopy, in case it prevented him from escaping from the rear cockpit. And yet I still hadn't been able to save him. I hadn't been able to bring my friend and comrade home. As a pilot that failure hit me particularly hard.

I myself was now just about at the end of my strength. Despite this, I felt secure and absolutely safe, even though I could tell from the noise of battle all around us that fierce fighting was still going on not far away. In the dressing station the doctors and medics carried on with their work calmly and methodically as if all was peace and quiet beyond the shed's wooden walls. They had removed the bullet from my left shoulder, splinted the fracture in my upper left arm and had bandaged the second and third degree burns on my face and hands after smothering them in layers of boracic ointment a good half-a-centimetre thick. All in all, things didn't appear too bad. I was being well looked after and in no great pain.

I asked if I could send a radio message and dictated what I wanted to say to one of the medical orderlies: 'Message to Nahkampfführer 2 via Panzergruppe Guderian: Kommandeur Third Stuka One shot down in flames. Gunner Ober- leutnant Hartmann killed. Hauptmann Mahlke wounded, rescued by own forces. Expect to return to unit in about three days.'

This latter was greeted by a general burst of laughter. 'What's so funny?' I demanded, 'I don't see there's anything to laugh about.' Without saying a word, another orderly held a hand mirror up to my face. Even I had to admit that my three-day estimate was more than a little optimistic. In fact, it looked like I was in for a long haul. My head was nothing but a huge white, round ball of gauze, beautifully crafted, its smooth surface punctured by four tiny holes for eyes, nose and mouth!

That same night several of us were placed in an ambulance, which followed the fighting troops forwards for a short way until we emerged on to the main highway. This then took us back to the field hospital at Borisov, where the doctor in charge was my old friend and acquaintance from Stuttgart, Professor Schmidt. The hospital was housed in a large brick schoolhouse. When we arrived there our stretchers were carried up the stone steps to the main entrance of the building by a group of elderly men, bearded but strongly built, who were apparently Russian prisoners of war. They took great care with us, and showed such solicitude that I couldn't help thinking how right and natural it seemed for friend and foe to be so compassionate towards each other once the fighting was over and they were allowed to be just 'normal human beings' again.

As my burned flesh slowly began to heal, it produced an absolutely revolting, evil-smelling fluid. I could smell my own stink, day and night, with every breath I took. The stench really brought me low and I felt as foul as I smelled. One day I was standing in a queue in one of the hospital corridors waiting for treatment, when I saw an orderly who looked vaguely familiar. 'Do you know Hauptmann Mahlke, the Stuka pilot?' I asked him. When he nodded, I continued: 'Well, I'm Mahlke. I'd appreciate the opportunity to say a quick hello to your head doctor if he has a moment to spare.' 'I'll tell him immediately,' the medic replied.

It wasn't long before Professor Schmidt appeared. 'What have they been doing to you?' he enquired, as he handed me a lit cigarette that he had thoughtfully inserted into a cut-down cardboard cigar holder: 'I knew that as a long-time smoker you'd appreciate nothing more than a cigarette. It's not good for you, of course, but it can't do much more harm at the moment either.' And how right he was! A cigarette had never tasted so good. He also said he'd keep an eye on my progress – at least until he and his staff were ordered to move forward again. He didn't think they'd be permitted to take me with them, he added.

He too must have known that my recovery was going to be a lengthy process. I found myself with a lot of time on my hands. Time to reflect on what had happened on that final, fateful mission. Until that moment we had only ever seen the enemy's Rata fighters. When we encountered his MiGs for the first time we didn't recognize them as the enemy, but mistook them for our own Messerschmitts. It wasn't until they were right on top of us, and their opening bursts had set our fuel tanks on fire, that Hartmann had reported: 'Heavy machine-gun fire from the wood behind us.' And by then, of course, it was too late. We were already burning. We had let ourselves be shot down without a fight. But that's how quickly these things can happen when your attention is focussed on the ground and you're searching for comrades who urgently need your help.

It was during this time too that I received a letter of appreciation, dated 15 July1941, from the Air Officer Commanding, Luftflotte 2, Generalfeldmarschall Kesselring.

While reading through it I thought back on the many difficult and dangerous missions that the Gruppe had flown in the past. In the media these had often been portrayed to the public as tremendous successes. But in our own close little circle of comrades we had privately joked that: 'The thanks of a grateful Fatherland will be following along later.' Now, as I held the letter from my commanding general in my bandaged hands, I was struck by a sudden thought – the thanks of a grateful Fatherland had finally caught up with me.

Afterword

Helmut Mahlke was right. The thanks of a grateful Fatherland *had* finally caught up with him. On 16 July 1941, just eight days after he had bailed out of his burning aircraft to the north of Burbin, Hauptmann Helmut Mahlke was awarded the Knight's Cross. He was the first serving member of III./StG 1 to receive this prestigious decoration.

But his hopes of returning to his unit in 'about three days' were wildly optimistic, as he himself had very soon realized. In fact, the combat mission flown on 8 July 1941 – his 159th of the war – was to be his last. After recovering from his wounds he did not return to operations, but spent the remainder of the war in a succession of staff appointments, mainly on the Eastern Front. However, although Helmut Mahlke's own operational career may have been over, 'his' Gruppe – III./StG 1 – would remain in action until the very end.

Throughout the late summer and early autumn of 1941, III./StG 1 – still under the command of II. Fliegerkorps – continued to support the armoured spearheads of Army Group Centre as they advanced on Moscow. After covering the crossings of the River Beresina, the Gruppe had next participated in the breaching of the River Dvina line and the capture of the towns of Polotzk and Vitebsk to the north of the main Minsk–Moscow highway.

With its northern flank thus secured, Army Group Centre then turned its attention to the taking of Smolensk, an important rail and transport junction just to the south of the highway. III./StG 1 played an important role in the ensuing 'cauldron' battle of Smolensk. During the battle's final phase, on 2 August 1941, 8./StG 1 lost its Staffelkapitän when the irrepressible Oberleutnant Günter Skambraks failed to return from an attack on Soviet Flak emplacements.

The battle of Smolensk ended on 5 August with the defeat and capture of large parts of three Soviet armies. For the next two weeks the Gruppe remained south of the highway, supporting the ground forces in the battles of Roslavl, Rogachev and Gomel. Having already moved forward from Dokudovo to Schatalovka [Shatalovo], a large airfield some 55km SSE of Smolensk, III./StG 1 was then transferred the same distance again down to newly captured Roslavl as part of the Luftwaffe build-up for the forthcoming attack on Kiev, the great industrial city on the River Dnieper and capital of the Ukraine.

The 'cauldron' battle of Kiev would rage for more than five weeks, from 21 August to 27 September 1941. At its close almost the entire Soviet Southwest Front had been destroyed and nearly two-thirds of a million Russian prisoners taken. While engaged against Kiev the Gruppe was awarded its next two Knight's Crosses. The first of them went to a long-serving Staffelkapitän, Oberleutnant Hartmut Schairer of 7./StG 1, who was decorated on 30 August 1941. The second recipient was 8. Staffel's Leutnant Theodor Nordmann, who was similarly decorated on 17 September 1941.

('Theo' Nordmann, who had come to Helmut Mahlke's aid after the disastrous attack on Malta's Luqa airfield back on 26 February 1941, and had later been fished out of the Mediterranean by a civilian Italian floatplane, would himself be promoted to the rank of Oberleutnant in October 1941 and appointed Staffelkapitän of 8./StG 1 shortly thereafter.)

It was also during the battle of Kiev that III./StG 1 welcomed a new Kommandeur. Since Helmut Mahlke's wounding, the Gruppe had been led in an acting capacity by Oberleutnant Peter Gassmann. But on 19 September 1941, when it finally became clear that Mahlke would not be returning to operations – or, at least, not for a very long time – Oberleutnant (later Hauptmann) Peter Gassmann officially took over as Gruppenkommandeur of III./StG 1 in his stead. Gassmann had been one of the original members of 3.(St)/186(T) and had seen service with this Staffel in Poland. At the end of the campaign in France, however, when the then Gruppenkommandeur of III./StG 1, Major Walter Hagen, had been appointed Geschwaderkommodore of StG 1, it was Gassmann whom he had selected to take with him as his new Geschwader-TO [technical officer]. Hauptmann Gassmann had been serving with the Geschwaderstab ever since.

After the capture of Kiev, III./StG 1 returned north and next participated in the 'twin' battles of Vyazma and Bryansk. They then supported the advance on the towns of Orel and Tula, the latter less than 200km from Moscow. Now back under the command of VIII. Fliegerkorps, the Gruppe operated briefly out of Schatalovka, before transferring forward to Orel shortly after that town's occupation by German forces on 3 October.

The main German offensive against Moscow was launched on 4 October and III./StG 1 remained in action to the south and southwest of the Soviet capital for the next two months as the Russian weather closed in and conditions steadily deteriorated. The Gruppe's last move forward in 1941 took it to Yuchnov, another town to the southwest of, and just under 200km from Moscow. The ground forces were even closer to the enemy capital. On 5 December 1941 advance elements of Army Group Centre were reported to be only eight kilometres from the city's edge.

But the German offensive had finally ground to a halt, beaten by the sub-zero temperatures – down to minus 40 or more at times – and snowdrifts many metres deep. Luftwaffe units found it almost impossible to operate in such conditions. And on 6 December 1941 III./StG 1 was withdrawn from the front and returned to Schweinfurt in Germany to rest and re-equip.

During the two months spent at Schweinfurt the Gruppe exchanged its ageing Ju 87Bs for the new Ju 87D variant. Aerodynamically refined and capable of carrying a heavier bomb load, the Ju 87D also featured twin machine guns in the rear cockpit. This went at least some way towards addressing the problem of the Stuka's notoriously weak rearward-firing defensive armament, one of the matters that had so concerned Helmut Mahlke.

In February 1942 the Gruppe was ready to return to the Russian Front. But the war in the east in 1942 was to be very different from that which III./StG 1 had experienced in 1941. Hitler had changed his strategy completely. Moscow was no longer the primary objective. The main emphasis of operations was now to be focussed in the south: towards Stalingrad and the oilfields of the Caucasus.

In the north, the German Army would spend much of 1942 grimly defending the territory it had gained the previous year. And it was to the northern sector that III./StG 1 was heading.

Staging via Neukuhren on the Baltic coast, the Gruppe moved up to Gostkino and Gorodez, south of Leningrad, where it came under the command of I. Flieger-korps. III./StG 1's Ju 87Ds were immediately thrown into the thick of the action – not clearing a path for advancing German spearheads as their predecessors had done during the first heady weeks of the campaign in the east, but supporting beleaguered German troops trying desperately to contain a series of Soviet counter-offensives.

Together with I./StG 2, also newly arrived back in Russia after re-equipping with Ju 87Ds, III./StG 1 was instrumental in bringing to a halt one such major counter-offensive by the Red Army that had penetrated deep into the seam between Army Groups North and Centre. The two Gruppen also flew many missions in support of the nearly 100,000 German troops encircled and cut off in the Demyansk 'pocket' by Soviet forces. Both Demyansk, to the southeast of Lake Ilmen, and the much smaller 'pocket' at Cholm some 100km away, had been ordered to hold at all costs until they could be relieved.

It was to the northwest of Cholm on 13 April 1942 that another link to the past was broken when a Stuka took a direct hit from enemy Flak and its crew were forced to bail out into Soviet captivity – for the crew in question consisted of pilot

Oberfeldwebel Hans Ebertz, the ex-butcher from Mühlheim who had questioned Helmut Mahlke's navigational abilities during the campaign in France, and gunner Oberfeldwebel Fritz 'Fritzchen' Baudisch, who had occupied the back seat during so many of Mahlke's missions.

After helping to stabilize the situation along the army group boundaries, III./StG 1 was next involved in operations further to the north. Beginning in April 1942, the Gruppe spent over two months on the Leningrad front. It was a busy period. They dive-bombed targets in and around Leningrad itself; they attacked the Soviet shipping that was trying to run supplies across Lake Ladoga into the besieged city; and they bombed and strafed a large body of enemy troops – the remnants of another failed Red Army counter-offensive – who were trapped to the south of Leningrad at Lyuban. At the height of these operations, on 25 May 1942, Gruppenkommandeur Hauptmann Peter Gassmann was awarded the Knight's Cross.

By June 1942, with the bulk of the Luftwaffe's strength concentrated in the south in support of the main German summer offensive against Stalingrad and the Caucasus, III./StG 1 was one of the few Stuka Gruppen that remained to cover operations on the northern and central sectors. As such, it was employed in what was known as a 'fire brigade' role, being rushed back and forth many hundreds of kilometres from one trouble spot to another. Inevitably, losses began to mount. On 19 July Hauptmann Hartmut Schairer, the long serving Staffelkapitän of 7./StG 1, was killed when his damaged aircraft crashed in flames near Staraya Russa, northwest of Demyansk, after an attack on enemy tanks.

Schairer's regular gunner Oberfeldwebel Heinz Bevernis, who had flown with him since the *Blitzkrieg* in France, also died in the crash. Bevernis would be awarded a posthumous Knight's Cross on 19 September 1942. He was the first wireless-operator/gunner of the entire Stuka arm to be so honoured.

Despite the lengthening casualty lists during the closing months of 1942 – Schairer's successor at the head of 7./StG 1, for example, was killed less than seven weeks after being appointed – one veteran from the days of the original I.(St)/186(T) was still going strong. In August 8./StG 1's 'Theo' Nordmann flew his 600th Stuka mission of the war.

The unremitting tempo of operations during this period had been having a serious effect on the already failing health of Gruppenkommandeur Hauptmann Peter Gassmann. More and more of his duties were being assumed by his deputy, the Staffelkapitän of 9./StG 1, Hauptmann Heinz Fischer (who had first joined the Gruppe at the time of 9. Staffel's night raids on Malta). But when Heinz Fischer and his gunner were killed in a freak accident on 26 October – it was reported that they had unwittingly flown through an artillery barrage and that the tail of their machine had been blown off by a shell – the matter of finding a suitable replacement Kommandeur for the Gruppe became something of a priority.

On 4 December 1942 Hauptmann Gassmann was finally forced to relinquish command. He would spend the next eight months in hospital, first in Russia and then in Berlin. The officer selected to take his place as Gruppenkommandeur of III./StG 1 was Oberleutnant Nordmann. He was to remain in command for just sixteen weeks. But, like Helmut Mahlke before him, he firmly believed in leading from the front. In February 1943 he flew his 700th operational mission, and on 17 March 1943 Nordmann became the first serving member of III./StG 1 to be awarded the Oak Leaves to his Knight's Cross.

(Ten days after receiving the Oak Leaves 'Theo' Nordmann left III./StG 1 to take command of III./KG 101. By the beginning of 1945, promoted in the interim to Major and now wearing the Oak Leaves with Swords, Nordmann was Kommodore of Schlachtgeschwader 3, a ground-attack wing equipped with Focke-Wulf Fw 190s. With very nearly 1,200 combat missions under his belt, Major Theodor Nordmann was killed in a mid-air collision with another Fw 190 over East Prussia on 19 January 1945.)

Nordmann's successor as Kommandeur of III./StG 1 was the first 'outsider' to command the Gruppe. The highly decorated Hauptmann Friedrich Lang (he had been awarded the Oak Leaves five months earlier) had spent his entire operational career to date with Stukageschwader 2, which he had joined back in the summer of 1938. But although he had never served with III./StG 1, Friedrich Lang was no stranger to the Gruppe. Like most military organizations, the Luftwaffe's Stuka arm was a fairly close-knit community and its founder members all knew one another. It was Lang who had so graphically described the Neuhammer tragedy to Helmut Mahlke.

By April 1943, the time of Hauptmann Lang's appointment as Gruppen-kommandeur, III./StG 1 had been transferred down from the northern to the central sector of the front, where it came under the command of 1. Flieger-Division. The battle of Stalingrad had just been fought and lost, and now the Red Army was beginning the advance that – in two short years – would take it all the way to Berlin.

On the central sector the Soviets were pushing hard towards Orel and Kursk. Orel had been the Gruppe's first base upon its move down from Gorodez in the north earlier in the year. And it was from here that III./StG 1 would play its part in the last major German offensive in the east: Operation 'Zitadelle' [Citadel] – the Battle of Kursk.

The Gruppe had already helped to blunt the Soviet drive on Orel. It had flown countless missions against the enemy's armoured units and had destroyed numerous bridges along their lines of advance. It had also participated in a devastating raid on Livny, the town that was the hub of the Red Army's rear-area supply network behind the Orel front.

But 140km to the south the Soviets had succeeded in capturing Kursk and pushing even further westwards. This had created a large salient, or 'bulge' in the German front line. Operation 'Zitadelle' – Hitler's last great gamble in the east – was intended to eliminate this bulge by launching simultaneous attacks on it from both the northern and southern flanks, pinching it off, and destroying those Soviet forces trapped inside it.

On the morning of 5 July 1943, the opening day of 'Zitadelle', III./StG 1 mounted an attack on Kursk railway station, which lay in the very heart of the enemy salient. Although successful, this was the last dive-bombing raid deep behind enemy lines ever to be flown by the Gruppe. Just over a week later 'Zitadelle' was called off. Henceforth, III./StG 1 would be employed almost exclusively in direct support of German ground forces on the battlefield.

In the immediate aftermath of 'Zitadelle' the Gruppe was attached to Gefechts-verband Kupfer. This Stuka battle group – formed around StG 2 and led by that unit's Kommodore, Major Dr.jur. Kupfer – was made up of all the Luftwaffe close-support units on the northern flank of the salient. It was hoped that this concentration of strength would be able to contain the advancing Red Army. And on one occasion the battlegroup actually *did* succeed in bringing a major Soviet armoured offensive to a grinding halt. This was said to be the first time in military history that such an offensive had been smashed by air power alone.

But this was very much the exception. Nothing could now stop the Soviet juggernaut. The whole Wehrmacht was in retreat. For III./StG 1 this first meant vacating Orel and retiring the 120km to Bryansk. From there they continued steadily to fall back westwards, via Karachev, Sechinskaya, Polotzk and Gomel to Bobruisk.

The days of the Ju 87 dive-bomber as an effective weapon of war in the east were coming to an end. On 18 October 1943 the term 'Stuka' all but disappeared from the Luftwaffe's order of battle when a major reorganization of all ground-support forces resulted in every Stuka Gruppe (bar one) being incorporated into a greatly enlarged *Schlacht*, or ground-attack arm. The title Stukageschwader (StG) was done away with and replaced by Schlachtgeschwader (SG). Helmut Mahlke's erstwhile III./StG 1 would now be operating as III./SG 1. (Although it would be several more weeks before the Gruppe began using its new designation – see e.g. Appendix 5.)

It was the intention to equip all the ex-Stuka Gruppen with single-seat Fw 190 ground-attack fighters. Such an ambitious conversion programme could not be carried out overnight, of course, and many units were to soldier on for weeks, if not months, flying their venerable Junkers. In November 1943, for example, III./SG 1 retired briefly to Vilna, where they received the latest version of the Ju 87D. This had been specially modified for low-level ground-support operations. The underwing dive brakes had been removed and the two forward-firing wing machine guns had been replaced by harder-hitting 20mm cannon.

Thus equipped, III./SG 1 was promptly despatched down to the southern sector where, in the weeks that followed, they were kept fully occupied supporting the German armies that were attempting to stop the Soviet advance through the Ukraine: the 4. Panzerarmee to the north of Kiev, and the 1. Panzerarmee and the reconstituted 6. Armee (the original 6. Armee having been destroyed at Stalingrad twelve months earlier) at Krivoi Rog and Nikopol.

But by the end of 1943 III./SG 1 was back at Bobruisk on the central sector under the command of Luftflotte 6. In February 1944 they transferred the 275km up to Polotzk, close to the boundary with the northern sector. The operations they flew from Polotzk in support of German ground forces defending Vitebsk, and from Orscha close to the main supply highway west of Smolensk early in March 1944, were to be the Gruppe's final missions on the Ju 87. By the middle of March 1944 III./SG 1 had returned to Vilna in Poland, this time to begin converting to Fw 190s.

The fast and highly manoeuvrable Focke-Wulf, with its powerful radial engine, fully retractable undercarriage and advanced electrical systems, was a far cry from the ageing Junkers and a number of casualties were suffered during the eight-week conversion course.

While training on the Fw 190 the Gruppe underwent its last change of command. Major Friedrich Lang had flown his 1,000th combat mission on the Ju 87 out of Orscha on 7 March. The following month, after a year in charge, he departed for a training post. His place at the head of III./SG 1 was taken by Hauptmann Karl Schrepfer, a long-time member of II./StG 1. Hauptmann (later Major) Schrepfer would remain in command of the Gruppe for the final twelve months of the war.

(It was also at this time, incidentally – on 31 March 1944 – that the now Major Helmut Mahlke, currently serving as the Ia, or operations officer of Luftflotte 6 headquartered at Priluki in the northern Ukraine, was awarded the German Cross in Gold to add to his Knight's Cross.)

By mid-May 1944 training had been completed and III./SG 1 was declared fully operational again. With its full establishment of forty-seven brand new Fw 190s the Gruppe was based at Radzyn, southeast of Warsaw. But Hauptmann Schrepfer's unit of ground-attack single-seaters bore very little resemblance to

Hauptmann Mahlke's dive-bombing Stuka Gruppe of old. Its operational role was entirely different. The Soviets were massing for their great summer offensive of 1944. This would take the Red Army to the gates of Warsaw and the frontiers of eastern Germany – and III./SG 1 was standing squarely in its path.

The Soviet assault was launched on 19 June 1944. It heralded the final phase of the Gruppe's wartime career: a fighting withdrawal to Berlin in the face of overwhelming enemy air and ground superiority. Within a month III./SG 1 had been reduced to less than half-strength and was operating out of Warsaw-Okecie.

In early September its twenty Focke-Wulfs were rushed up to Insterburg (Chernyakhovsk) to help repulse an enemy thrust into East Prussia. By mid-October the Gruppe was back in Poland. Based at Bielice, it kept up its attacks on advancing Soviet armoured forces for the remainder of the year and into 1945. In November 1944 Oberleutnant Kurt Goldbruch's 8./SG 1 had been briefly taken off operations at Bielice to retrain with Panzerschreck underwing rockets. These specialized anti-tank missiles were capable of knocking out the heaviest Soviet tanks. But it was too little too late. Nothing could stop the victorious Red Army now.

On 16 January 1945 Oberleutnant Otto Hulsch, who had first joined III./StG 1 at the start of the campaign against Russia and had been awarded the Knight's Cross just prior to the Gruppe's conversion to the Fw 190, was leading 7./SG 1 in an attack on enemy tanks near Warsaw when he was shot down by Soviet fighters. Twenty-four hours later the Polish capital fell to the Russians. The next, and ultimate prize was Berlin.

But after retreating to the German border, III./SG 1's Focke-Wulfs were ordered up to the Baltic coast. Their task now was to try to halt the northernmost flank of the enemy pincers closing in on Hitler's capital. But here too they were forced to give ground. From Danzig they retired, via Kolberg (Kolobrzeg), to Garz on the island of Rügen. With the threat to Berlin growing by the day, however, it was not long before they were moved back down closer to the capital – first to Prenzlau, and then to Oranienburg.

The final Soviet assault on Berlin was launched before dawn on 16 April 1945. Later that same day Leutnant Walter Hoffmann of the Panzerschreck-equipped 8./SG 1 – another of the Gruppe's recent Knight's Cross recipients who had first joined III./StG 1 in June 1941 – was brought down by enemy fighters in the Berlin-Oranienburg area.

On 24 April 1945 Stalin announced to the world that the Red Army had entered Berlin. With the end only days away, III./SG 1's remaining machines (which now also included a handful of 'long-nosed' Fw 190Ds) returned north to the Baltic. After a brief stop-over at Wismar, the unit made its final move of the war: to Flensburg-Weiche, hard by the Danish border, to await the arrival of British forces.

The Gruppe's history had thus come full circle. It ended little more than 60km from where it had begun less than six years earlier with the official activation of I.(St)/186(T) at Kiel-Holtenau on 10 September 1939 – and only a kilometre or two further from the village of Heikendorf, on the far side of Kiel Bay, where Generalleutnant Helmut Mahlke (retd.) died on 26 December 1998.

III./StG 1 Pilot Roster
At the Close of the Campaign in France

Name and Rank	*Place and Date of Birth*	*Combat Missions*		
		Poland	*France*	*England*

Gruppenstab

Mahlke, Hptm. Helmut (Gp.Kom.)	Berlin-Lankwitz, 27.8.13	–	60	11
Lion, Oblt. Karl (Ia)	Saarlouis, 5.11.10	19	57	13
Martinz, Lt. Hans (Adjutant)	Hirt/Carinthia, 10.6.14	–	55	9

7. Staffel

Schairer, Oblt. Hartmut (St.Kap.)	Nagold, 16.9.16	–	60	12
Schimmelpfennig, Lt. Ernst	Ascherbude, 11.6.16	–	60	6
Kühdorf, Obfw. Karl	Plauen i.V., 13.2.11	–	36	5
Jenster, Fw. Jakob	Cleves, 14.3.17	–	34	8
Stiebitz, Obfw. Herbert	Neukirch/Laus., 27.9.12	–	–	12
Blysch, Uffz. August	Hindenburg, 7.8.17	–	–	8
Berk, Uffz. Rudi	Grosskamsdorf, 23.12.13	–	–	6
Singer, Uffz. Willi	Nuremberg, 29.9.18	–	–	4
Schütz, Uffz. Gerhard	Hamburg, 8.4.17	–	–	4
Holzinger, Fw. Franz	Stuttgart, 18.8.13	–	–	5
Berkhoff, Oblt. Jochen	Berlin, 2.11.16	(Newly posted)		
Fischer, Oblt. Heinz	Berlin, 22.5.17	(Newly posted)		
Buchholz, Fhr. Heinz	Nordhorn, 30.11.19	(Newly posted)		

8. Staffel

Skambraks, Oblt. Günter (St.Kap.)	Tilsit, 1.12.16	–	54	10
Heimlich, Lt. Adolf	Graz, 27.3.16	–	53	11
Viertel, Obfw. Willi	Breslau, 5.9.11	–	52	20
Märgner, Fw. Kurt	Karlsmarkt, 28.3.18	–	48	13
Dietze, Fw. Rudolf	Heynitz, 10.2.17	–	39	5
Bartsch, Fw. Walter	Breitenhain, 29.4.14	–	3	2

Name and Rank	Place and Date of Birth	Combat Missions		
		Poland	France	England
Reuss, Fw. Otto	Bierlingen, 1.4.17	–	8	4
Wiesnet, Fw. Fritz	Ingolstadt, 26.11.15	–	–	4
Wegscheider, Uffz. Anton	Welden/Landsberg, 14.10.17	–	–	5
von Stein-Lausnitz, Oblt. K.U.	Wongrowitz, 9.6.14	–	–	5
Stiegler, Uffz. Hans	Wilhelmshaven, 4.6.18	–	14	5
Wetter, Fw. Ernst	Gelsenkirchen, 22.4.15	–	–	5
Ebertz, Fw. Hans	Mühlheim, 26.8.14	–	48	3
Wentorf, Fw.		(Newly posted)		
Teutloff, Lt. Dietrich	Rheydt, 17.9.20	(Newly posted)		
Schalanda, Fhr.		(Newly posted)		

9. Staffel

Name and Rank	Place and Date of Birth	Combat Missions		
Heinze, Oblt. Ulrich (St.Kap.)	Halle, 21.12.14	20	61	8
Golleritz, Oblt. Julius	Rechnitz, 15.8.17	–	51	10
Ries, Stbsfw. Hans	Mannheim, 2.3.18	15	48	7
Gerken, Fw. Heinz	Zwickau, 22.11.15	18	55	6
Becker, Uffz. Heinrich	Berleburg, 31.7.14	–	–	10
Oesterreich, Uffz. Heinrich	Schönau/Chemnitz, 21.8.19	–	–	7
Lewandowsky, Uffz. Fritz	Kulkwitz, 15.7.14	–	–	4
Küster, Uffz. Karl	Liekwegen, 14.7.14	–	–	8
Dietmayer, Gefr. Herbert	Wartberg, 24.5.20	–	–	4
Tittel, Fw. Rudolf	Görlitz, 29.9.17	17	–	4
Blumers, Lt.d.R. Otto	Heppenheim, 26.4.10	–	6	3
Preiss, Oblt.		(Newly posted)		
Zühlke, Lt.		(Newly posted)		
Schupp, Lt.		(Newly posted)		
Rudorf, Fhr. Hans	Häger/Bielefeld, 6.3.20	(Newly posted)		
Steeg, Ofhr. Klaus-Jürgen	Essen, 28.10.20	(Newly posted)		

Pilots of I.(St)/186 (T) and III./StG 1 Killed or Missing in Action, 1939–40

Name and Rank	Place and Date of Birth	Combat Missions			Fate
		Pol.	Fr.	Eng.	
Czuprina, Uffz. Wilhelm	Hindenburg, 23.10.15	3	–	–	3.9.39: KiA Hela
Rummel, Oblt. Hans	Suhl/Thur., 10.11.10	10	–	–	14.9.39: KiA Gdingen
Urbons, Uffz. Herbert	Marunen, 6.2.16	12	–	–	6.12.39: KAS Wertheim
Blattner, Hptm. Erich	Konstanz, 19.4.08	18	2	–	11.5.40: KiA France
Heyden, Oblt. Hanfried	Düsseldorf, 28.7.17	16	8	–	14.5.40: KiA France
Hemke, Uffz. Fritz	Bokel, 18.6.14	–	9	–	14.5.40: KiA France
Strehler, Fw. Walter	Greppin, 16.1.16	–	?	–	14.5.40: KiA France
Ellerlage, Ofhr. Hans-Jürgen	Kiel, 17.2.17	–	7	–	14.5.40: KiA France
Troll, Oblt. Dietrich	Rüstringen, 18.5.12	–	12	–	1.6.40: MiA Channel
Stengel, Lt. Walter	Munich, 2.10.18	–	26	–	1.6.40: KiA France
Idel, Fw. Heinz	Altroggen, 6.5.15	19	17	–	5.6.40: KiA France
Dietz, Fw. Richard	Burgsolms, 6.4.14	14	55	–	16.6.40: KiA France
Ullrich, Uffz. Heinz	Schönebeck, 9.4.16	–	44	–	16.6.40: KiA France
Herbst, Oblt. Wolf-Dietrich	Emmagrube, 25.10.15	–	55	–	30.6.40: KAS France
Torngrind, Fw. Herbert	Wojene, 16.4.14	–	46	4	8.8.40: MiA Channel
Walz, Gefr. Ernst	Walddorf, 23.9.20	–	–	1	8.8.40: MiA Channel
Kathe, Oblt. Wolfgang	Halle/Saale, 16.5.13	–	–	–	28.8.40: KAS France
Mühlthaler, Lt. Josef	Munich, 30.9.16	–	3	–	28.8.40: KAS France
Schütz, Uffz. Gerhard	Hamburg, 8.4.17	–	4	–	11.11.40: MiA Thames
Oesterreich, Uffz. Heinrich	Schönau, 21.8.09	–	–	7	11.11.40: MiA Thames
Dietmayer, Ogefr. Herbert	Wartberg, 24.5.20	–	–	?	14.11.40: MiA Dover
Blumers, Oblt.d.R. Otto	Heppenheim, 26.4.10	–	6	?	14.11.40: PoW Dover

(KAS: Killed while on active service. KiA: Killed in Action; MiA: Missing in Action; PoW: Prisoner-of-War)

Appendix 3

Pilots of I.(St)/186(T) and III./StG 1 Posted Away, 1939–40

Name and Rank	Place and Date of Birth	Combat Missions			Destination
		Pol.	Fr.	Eng.	
Serwottka, Uffz. Richard	Zabern, 23.9.18	–	–	–	On activation of I./186 in September 1939 posted away from 1./186 to Stuka-Schule Kitzingen
Stoffel, Uffz. Siegfried	Liegnitz, 7.12.17	–	–	–	„ „
Grosche, Uffz. Wolfgang	Zwickau, 30.5.18	–	–	–	„ „
Heutmann, Uffz. Rudolf	Freistadt, 14.3.16	–	–	–	„ „
Götz, Uffz. Ewald	Münster/W., 17.1.17	–	–	–	„ „
Bremkamp, Uffz.					On activation of I./186 in September 1939 posted away from 2./186 to Stuka-Schule Kitzingen
Tietjen, Uffz.					„ „
Sirrenberg, Uffz.					„ „
Krohn, Uffz.					„ „
König, Uffz.					„ „
Schubert, Fw. Gustav	Königszelt, 11.11.16	17	–	–	18.2.40: Stuka-Schule
Tittel, Uffz. Rudolf	Görlitz, 29.9.17	17	–	–	„ „
Bode, Hptm. Helmut (Gp.K.)	Metz, 15.10.07	–	45	–	11.6.40: III./StG 77
Holtgraefe, Fw. Willi	Bodenfelde, 4.12.14	–	44	–	„ „
Ebertz, Fw. Hans	Mühlheim, 26.8.14	–	48	–	26.6.40: Lippstadt
Hagen, Obstlt. Walter	Kiel, 16.3.1897	?	?	?	2.7.40: StG 1 (Ges.K.)
Gassmann, Oblt. Peter	Bonn, 4.12.10	18	?	?	2.7.40: StG 1 (Ges.TO)
Schmidt, Fw. Richard	Sorau, 1.1.16	–	51	–	3.7.40: St-Sch. Otrokowitz
Ostmann, Oblt. Klaus	Schöppenstedt, 26.9.12	–	–	3	8.8.40: Hospital
Reiter, Uffz.d.R. Roland	Hundsheim, 22.3.14	–	–	1	„ „
Vaupel, Fw. Wilhelm	Essen, 9.8.15	–	46	3	18.8.40: St-Sch. Jesau
Reuss, Fw. Otto	Bierlingen, 1.4.17	–	8	4	18.9.40: St-Sch. Graz
Bartsch, Fw. Walter	Breitenhain, 29.4.14	–	3	2	17.10.40: Lippstadt
Wiesnet, Fw. Fritz	Ingolstadt, 26.11.15	–	–	4	20.10.40: JG 27

Name and Rank	*Place and Date of Birth*	*Combat Missions*			*Destination*
		Pol.	*Fr.*	*Eng.*	
Kühdorf, Obfw. Karl	Plauen i.V., 13.2.11	–	36	5	29.10.40: JG 26
Dietze, Fw. Rudolf	Heynitz, 19.2.17	–	39	5	” ”
Gerken, Fw. Heinz	Zwickau, 22.11.15	18	55	6	4.11.40:JG 54
Blysch, Uffz. August	Hindenburg, 7.8.17	–	–	8	12.12.40: Erg.-Gr.
Märgner, Fw. Kurt	Karlsmarkt, 28.3.18	–	48	13	17.12.40: Erg.St./StG 1

(Some of the above pilots subsequently returned to the Gruppe, e.g. the wounded after recovery in hospital, and those temporarily posted to various Stuka schools and Ergänzungs (replacement) units as instructors.)

Appendix 4

Ground Personnel Killed, Missing or Died on Active Service, 1939–45

Name, rank and date of birth only. For details see Appendix 5

Benz, Uffz. Fritz (5.4.19)
Bergmann, Obfw. Robert (28.7.14)
Bremer, Gefr. Eberhard (16.3.21)
Burger, Ogefr. Xaver (30.8.19)
Degenhardt, Obfw. Josef (28.7.15)
Elsner, Ogefr. Josef (26.7.18)
Ewers, Gefr. Johannes (31.1.07)
Frische, Ogefr. Fritz (17.9.19)
Grüneberg, Uffz. Karl-H. (12.12.19)
Holzmann, Maj. Georg (9.8.1890)
Hörner, OstA. Dr. Otto (27.12.05)
Jahn, Mstr. Franz-Ferdinand (18.8.1900)
Knitzatka, Ogefr. Norbert (26.2.18)
Kräuter, Uffz. Willi (30.12.13)
Kressler, Uffz. Herbert (4.7.17)
Lichtenberg, Uffz. Hans (13.2.17)
Lohberg, Obfw. Helmut (3.2.11)
Markwitz, (Ju.Monteur) Paul (8.8.09)
Mildenberger, Ogefr. Karl (17.7.17)
Neu, Ogefr. Walter

Nigbur, Obfw. Paul (18.12.12)
Opel, Uffz. Josef (18.6.16)
Peuker, Ogefr. Gerhard (8.10.22)
Podak, Ogefr. Gerhard (16.6.17)
Pütz, Gefr. Theodor (20.2.21)
Rastetter, Gefr. Gustav (8.3.21)
Rottmüller, Gefr. Josef (18.5.17)
Schaak, Reg.Insp. Karl (22.11.14)
Schug, Uffz. Erich (16.10.16)
Spermann, Ogefr. Josef (5.10.21)
Stenzel, Gefr. Bruno (10.1.13)
Timm, Flg. Herbert (15.5.22)
Timmel, Flg. Egon (2.6.20)
Wagner, Flg. Erich (28.4.20)
Weidner, Oblt. Joachim (8.3.22)
Wenzel, Ogefr. Alfred (19.2.03)
Wiedemann, Obfw. Johann (20.5.12)
Winkler, (Ju.Monteur) Friedrich (27.6.09)
Wittig, Uffz.d.R. Heinz (31.5.14)

Extracts from I.(St)/186(T), III./StG 1 and III./SG 1 Casualty Reports

(The numeral in front of the date of each entry is the number of the original report.)

Casualty reports Stuka 3./186

1: 3.9.39   Czuprina, Uffz. Wilhelm; pilot 3./186 (Hindenburg, 23.10.15)

2: 3.9.39   Meinhardt, Funkmaat Erich; gunner 3./186
            (Adersleben/Halberstadt, 16.4.14)

Crew failed to return from mission against Hela submarine base.

3: 14.9.39   Rummel, Oblt. Hans; pilot 3./186 (Suhl/Thuringia, 10.11.10)

4: 14.9.39   Blunk, Oberfunkmaat Fritz; gunner 3./186 (Flensburg, 31.10.11)

Crew killed in attack on Gdingen naval base. Wreckage of aircraft found near Oxhöft Spitze battery. Crew buried alongside wreckage. Identification definite. Re-interred Danzig-Silberhammer.

Casualty reports I.(St)/186(T)

1: 11.5.40   Blattner, Hptm. Erich; St.Kpt. 3./186 (Konstanz, 19.4.08)
            Fernholz, Fw. Karl; gunner 3./186 (Gelsenkirchen, 26.9.15)

Crew failed to return from attack on tanks in Montmedy area. Aircraft crashed 1km north of Montmedy.

1: 11.5.40   Ullrich, Uffz. Heinz; pilot 3./186 (Schönebeck/Elbe, 9.4.16)
            Bornemann, Fw. Werner; gunner 3./186 (Greifswald, 8.9.09)

Crew missing. Last seen over German-held territory returning from combat mission, signed Hagen, Major and Gruppenkommandeur.

2: 14.5.40   Heyden, Oblt. Hanfried; pilot 1./186 (Düsseldorf, 28.7.17)
            Cords, Lt.d.R. Helmut; gunner 1./186 (Stettin, 30.4.13)

Crew killed in air combat. Aircraft shot down by fighters, seen to crash between Florenville and Chiny. Grave 13 metres to left of Izel–Chiny road.

2: 14.5.40   Hemken, Uffz. Fritz; pilot 1./186 (Bokel/Oldenburg, 18.6.14)

Kopania, Uffz. Otto; gunner 1./186 (Malschöwen/East Prussia, 25.2.20)

Aircraft failed to return from combat mission. Crew killed. Aircraft crashed after air combat 10km east of Sedan. Presumed location of aircraft in woods to east of Sedan.

2: 14.5.40   Strehler, Fw. Walter; pilot 2./186 (Wolfen/Bitterfeld, 16.1.16)

Hüsch, Gefr. Heinrich; gunner 2./186 (Moers/Lower Rhine, 6.8.19)

Crew killed in air combat in Florenville region. Bodies found and buried by troops of I./Inf.Regt. 230 SE Brevilly, 12km east of Sedan, on 7/8.6.40.

2: 14.5.40   Reuss, Uffz. Otto; pilot 2./186 (Bierlingen/Horb, 1.4.17)

Hecht, Uffz. Ernst; gunner 2./186 (Berlin, 4.2.18)

Initially reported missing in action after air combat in Florenville region. Uffz. Hecht killed in area between towns of Malton and Chemency. Uffz. Reuss returned wounded. Discharged from hospital and returned to Gruppe 29.7.40.

2: 14.5.40   Ellerlage, Ofhr. [Oberfähnrich] Hans-Jürgen; pilot 3./186 (Kiel, 17.2.17)

Froese, Uffz. Alfred; gunner 3./186

(Regau/Preussisch Holland, 22.3.15)

Killed in action. Air combat SE Sedan. Uffz. Froese buried in military cemetery of 71. Inf.Div. 6km south of village of Pin (18km east of Florenville), signed Hagen, Major and Gruppenkommandeur.

3: 22.5.40   Blumers, Lt.d.R. Otto; pilot 3./186 (Heppenheim, 26.4.10)

Wenzel, Uffz. Gerhard; gunner 3./186 (Grünewald/Pomerania, 4.7.15)

Blumers made emergency landing in burning aircraft between Arras and Agnez after air combat. Taken to Aachen hospital with first-degree burns and bullet in back. Wenzel killed in action, body burned in aircraft. Buried 100 metres to right of Warluis–Duisans road. Blumers returned to unit 14.7.40. Admitted to reserve hospital Würzburg 10.8.40 for operation to remove bullet from upper right arm.

3: 22.5.40   Bartsch, Fw. Walter; pilot 2./186 (Breitenheim, 29.4.14)

Philipp. Uffz. Walter; gunner 2./186 (Mischline, 25.12.25)

Crew wounded in action against enemy fighters south of Arras. Crash-landed. Bartsch first-degree burns, bullet graze to head, impact wounds to head and left leg. Philipp impact wounds to head. First treated by mobile medical unit Guise. Philipp released from hospital and returned to unit 11.6.40; Bartsch 29.7.40.

4: 1.6.40   Müller, Uffz. Julius; gunner 2./186 (Gimbweiler, 2.11.17)

Wounded in air combat with enemy fighters. One bullet wound in shoulder, two bullet wounds in leg. Evacuated from Guise to homeland by Ju 52. Released from hospital fit for duty and returned to unit 19.8.40.

4: 1.6.40   Troll, Oblt. Dietrich; pilot 1./186 (Rüstringen/Oldenburg, 18.5.12)

Rampf, Fw. Walter; gunner 1./186 (Freiburg/Breisgau, 24.8.13)

Crew missing in action. Failed to return after air combat 10 nautical miles north of Dunkirk.

4: 1.6.40   Stengel, Lt. Walter; pilot 3./186 (Munich, 2.10.18)

Horstmann, Uffz. Paul; gunner 3./186 (Werne, 15.7.16)

Stengel killed in air combat over Mardyck near Dunkirk. Buried by troops of 5./Inf.Regt. 176 in field grave at Loon-Plage, 4.6.40. Horstmann returned injured with impact wound to upper right eyelid and fractured bone in right hand. Returned fit for duty 3.6.40.

5: 5.6.40   Idel, Fw. Heinz; pilot 3./186 (Altroggen/Rahmende, 6.5.15)

Dziallas, Ogefr. Heinz; gunner 3./186 (Spalitz, 5.2.18)

Crew killed in action. Failed to return from combat mission. Shot down 5km NW of Corbie, probably by 20mm Flak. Engine fire. Aircraft executed a half-roll. Canopy was jettisoned. What next happened to crew unknown. Crash site with two graves 2.5km east of Lamotte-Brebières between Amiens–Corbie railway line and River Somme, signed Hagen, Major and Gruppenkommandeur.

6: 12.6.40   Obermeier, Obfw. Heinz; gunner I./186 (Hamburg, 10.5.14)

Wounded by ground fire at height of 300 metres 5km north of Esternay after dive-bombing attack. Bullet through upper left arm, bullet lodged in upper left arm, bullet graze to lower left arm. Admitted to 6. Field Hospital Soissons. (This mission flown as gunner to Gruppenkommandeur Major Hagen.)

6: 15.6.40   Timmel, Flg. Egon; mechanic 1.FBK/III./StG 1
(Schwepnitz/Kamenz/Saxony, 2.6.20)

Automobile accident. Buried in grounds of Quillmont estate Bucancy, 8km south of Soissons.

6: 16.6.40   Dietz, Fw. Richard; pilot 3./186 (Burgsolms, 6.4.14)

Kortenhaus, Uffz. Hans; gunner 3./186 (Herne, 20.3.17)

Ullrich, Uffz. Heinz; pilot 3./186; (Schönebeck/Elbe, 9.4.16)

Heine, Ogefr. Heinz; gunner 3./186 (Struveshof, 2.10.17)

Both crews killed in action near Beaune railway station SW of Dijon. Aircraft crashed in enemy territory, either from Flak or mid-air collision. Dietz and Kortenhaus buried in individual graves Beaune local cemetery. Ulrich and Heine near Beaune railway station.

6: 30.6.40   Herbst, Oblt. Wolf-Dietrich; pilot 2./186 (Emmagrube, 25.10.15)

Kollmitt, Uffz. Franz; gunner 2./186 (Tollack/East Prussia, 11.4.19)

Schug, Uffz. Erich; crew chief 2./186 (Neuwied/Rhineland, 16.10.16)

Killed in crash on final approach to landing 4km SE Falaise. Buried Falaise local cemetery.

7: 30.6.40   Wieber, Fw. Friedrich; aircraft mechanic 7./StG 1
(Remscheid, 24.12.14)

Admitted to hospital severely injured in motorcycle accident. Released from hospital and returned to unit 4.1.41.

Casualty reports III./StG 1

8: 25.7.40   Meissner, Uffz. Walter; gunner 7./StG 1 (Danzig, 30.1.20)

Wounded 15km SW Portland Bill. Bullet lodged in left thigh. Admitted hospital Potigny. Returned to unit 29.7.40.

8: 25.7.40   Stillinger, Ogefr. Josef; gunner 8./StG 1 (Pfarrkirchen, 2.3.19)

Killed after attack by enemy fighters over Channel 45km north of Cherbourg. Bailed out but drowned. Body not recovered.

9: 8.8.40   Ostmann, Oblt. Klaus; pilot 8./StG 1
                      (Schöppenstedt/Wolfenbüttel, 26.9.12)

Wounded in action 20km south of Isle of Wight. Bullet lodged in right knee, kneecap shattered. Bullet graze to right arm. Admitted hospital Valognes.

9: 8.8.40   Reiter, Uffz. Roland; pilot 9./StG 1 (Hundsheim/Vienna, 22.3.14)
                      Renners, Ogefr. Bernhard; gunner 9./StG 1 (Oberhausen, 30.6.13)

Wounded in air combat SW of Isle of Wight. Both received wounds to shoulder. Admitted Valognes hospital near Cherbourg. Renners returned to unit 1.11.40.

9: 8.8.40   Torngrind, Fw. Herbert; pilot 9./StG 1
                      (Wojene/North Schleswig, 16.4.14)
                      Bauer, Gefr. Heinrich; gunner 9./StG 1 (Adelshein/Buchen, 1.10.17)

Crew missing in action after air combat with enemy fighters during attack on enemy convoy SW of Isle of Wight.

10: 8.8.40   Walz, Gefr. Gottlob; pilot 9./StG 1
                      (Walddorf/Calw, Württemberg, 23.9.20)
                      Schütz, Gefr. Robert; gunner 9./StG 1 (Idstein/Taunus, 4.4.20)

Crew missing in action after air combat with enemy fighters during attack on enemy convoy SW of Isle of Wight.

11: 28.8.40   Kathe, Oblt. Wolfgang; pilot 8./StG 1 (Halle/Saale, 16.5.13)
                      Zeuler, Ogefr. Georg; gunner 8./StG 1
                      (Ramsenthal/Bayreuth, 30.7.14)
                      Mühlthaler, Lt. Josef; pilot [?] 1.FBK/186 (Munich, 30.9.16)

Killed in crash after mid-air collision during dive-bombing practice 1km north of Deauville. Buried Falaise Catholic cemetery.

12: 11.11.40   Schütz, Uffz. Gerhard; pilot 7./StG 1 (Hamburg, 8.4.17)
                      Brück, Ogefr. Georg; gunner 7./StG 1 (Essen, 18.3.19)

Missing after air combat with enemy fighters over Thames Estuary 5 nautical miles north of Margate. Fate unknown.

12: 11.11.40   Oesterreich, Uffz. Dr. Heinrich; pilot 9./StG 1 (Schönau, 21.8.09)

Sabinarz, Ogefr. Anton; gunner 9./StG 1 (Kamp-Lintfort, 21.7.18)

Missing Thames Estuary grid area 1237; probably shot down by British fighters.

13: 14.11.40   Blumers, Oblt.d.R. Otto; pilot 9./StG 1 (Heppenheim/Bergstr., 26.4.10)

Koch, Gefr. Willy; gunner 9./StG 1 (Lippstadt/Westphalia, 15.11.16)

Shot down by enemy fighters during attack on Dover radio station. Koch killed, Blumers captured by British.

13: 14.11.40   Dietmayer, Ogefr. Herbert; pilot 9./StG 1 (Wartberg/Styria, 24.5.20)

Schmidt, Ogefr. Johann; gunner 9./StG 1 (Dudweiler/Saar, 14.11.19)

Missing (after air combat) during attack on Dover radio station. Ogefr. Schmidt declared dead.

14: 6.1.41   Pfeifer, Gefr. Heinz; gunner 7./StG 1 (Könitz/Saalfeld, 15.3.18)

Admitted St-Pol hospital with suspected typhus.

14: 6.1.41   Lion, Oblt. Karl; pilot III./StG 1 (Saarlautern, 5.11.10)

Admitted Kiel-Wik naval hospital with duodenal ulcer.

15: 5.2.41   Schimmelpfennig, Lt. Ernst; pilot 7./StG 1 (Ascherbude, 16.11.16)

Kaden, Ogefr. Hans; gunner 7./StG 1 (Dresden, 5.11.19)

Missing after individual harassment attacks on enemy convoy off Ramsgate. Report from Britain confirmed killed in action.

16: 13.2.41   Lewandowski, Fw. Fritz; pilot 9./StG 1 (Kulkwitz nr. Leipzig, 15.7.14)

Renners, Uffz. Bernhard; gunner 9./StG 1 (Oberhausen-Osterfeld, 30.6.13)

Missing after individual bad weather harassment attack on shipping in Thames Estuary. Failed to return.

17: 22.2.41   Hörner, Oberarzt Dr. Otto; chief medical officer III./StG 1 (Würzburg, 27.12.05)

Bergmann, Ofw. Robert; NCO i/c servicing, III./StG 1 (Klein Paschleben/Anhalt, 28.7.14)

Lichtenberg, Uffz. Hans; flight mechanic III./StG 1 (Bremen, 13.2.17)

Kräuter, Uffz. Willi; clerk/writer III./StG 1 (Neumünster, 30.12.13)

Jahn, Prüfmstr.a.Kr. Franz-Ferdinand; Inspekteur (H.O.) III./StG1 (Lübeck, 18.8.1900)

Winkler, Friedrich; Junkers engine fitter attached III./StG 1 (Magdeburg, 27.6.09)

Above all killed during transfer flight by Ju 52 transport from Munich-Riem to Italy. Aircraft crashed near Rottach on Tegernsee lake. Following all injured in same incident:

Plötz, Prüfmstr.a.Kr. Bruno; Inspekteur (H.O.) III./StG 1
(Stralsund, 19.2.1899). Severe injuries.

Bost, Fw. Karl; general-duties III./StG 1 (Beeskow, 15.10.14).
Forearm fracture.

Radloff, Fw. Alfred; armourer III./StG 1 (Nehmten/Plön, 30.3.15).
Head wound.

Jene, Uffz. Anton; gunner 7./StG 1 (Alzey, 26.1.14). Lower leg fracture.

Sassa, Uffz. Hubert; gunner 7./StG 1 (Görlitz, 31.7.19).
Fractured spine and pelvis.

Meissner, Uffz. Walter; gunner 7./StG 1 (Danzig, 30.1.20).
Fractured jaw and upper arm.

Schachtschnabel, Gefr. Erich; Gruppenstab III./StG 1 (Dessau, 14.4.10).
Head and arm injuries.

18: 22.2.41   Lohberg, Obfw. Helmut; master mechanic 7./StG 1 (Posen, 3.2.11)

Died of circulatory collapse in Luftwaffe hospital Arras.

19: 23.2.41   Wentorf, Lt. Helmut; pilot 8./StG 1 (Bremen, 23.2.19)

Killed in emergency landing. Broken neck. Buried Foggia cemetery Italy.

20: 26.2.41   Heil, Ofhr. Roman; pilot 7./StG 1 (Würzburg, 28.12.20)
            Stamm, Gefr. Heinrich; gunner 7./StG 1
            (Wallenbrück/Herford, 29.9.18)

Ditched in sea 5km west of island of Gozo after air combat in Malta area. Crew seen swimming. Taken into British captivity (Canada). Heil promoted to Oblt. on 1.2.43.

21: 5.3.41   Singer, Uffz. Wilhelm; pilot 7./StG 1 (Nuremberg, 29.9.18)
            Stapf, Ogefr. Paul; gunner 7./StG 1 (Mindelheim/Swabia, 6.9.16)

Crew killed in action. Crashed in sea 3km south of Hal Far/Malta after air combat with Hurricane.

21: 23.3.41   Jarosch, Lt. Leopold; pilot 7./StG 1 (Vienna, 8.11.16)
            Jarnuczak, Gefr. Josef; gunner 7./StG 1 (Gelsenkirchen, 26.2.17)

Missing in action during attack on La Valetta, Malta. Probably shot down by Flak or fighter.

21: 23.3.41   Preiss, Oblt. Walter; pilot III./StG 1 (Hartau/Salzbrunn, 3.2.14)
            Horstmann, Uffz. Paul, gunner III./StG 1 (Werne/Bochum, 15.7.16)

Missing in action during attack on La Valetta, Malta. Probably shot down by Flak or fighter.

21: 23.3.41   Ries, Stfw. Hans; pilot 9./StG 1 (Mannheim, 2.3.08)
            Philipp, Uffz. Walter; gunner 9./StG 1 (Mischline/Gross-Strelitz)

Ries missing in action, as above. Philipp killed. Rescued from sea off Malta by 4 Sqn. RAF, died 23.3.41. Buried St Andrew's Cemetery/Malta 25.3.41.

21: 23.3.41   Kaubitzsch, Ofhr. Erich; pilot 8./StG 1 (Döbeln, 22.5.20)

                    Krumland, Gefr. Hans; gunner 8./StG 1 (Zetel, 15.1.20)

Engine damaged in air combat. Crew bailed out 20km south of Sicily. Kaubitzsch recovered badly wounded (cannon shell wound right thigh) by air-sea rescue service. To hospital Catania. Krumland recovered from sea dead.

22: 11.4.41   Zühlke, Lt. Werner; pilot 9./StG 1 (Zanow/Pomerania, 4.5.20)

                    Feldeisen, Ogefr. Hans; gunner 9./StG 1 (Söllichen/Bitterfeld, 23.4.20)

Crew killed in action by Flak or fighter during attack on Ta Venezia airfield Malta.

23: 12.4.41   Buchholz, Ofhr. Heinz-Wilhelm; pilot 7./StG 1 (Nordhorn, 30.11.19)

                    Kerschbaumsteiner, Gefr. David; gunner 7./StG 1
(Klein-Refling, 13.8.21)

Missing, probably killed, during attack on ship entering Tobruk. Parachute cable fired from vessel [?].

23: 12.4.41   Holzinger, Fw. Franz; pilot 7./StG 1 (Stuttgart, 18.8.13)

                    Anwand, Gefr. Rudolf; gunner 7./StG 1 (Wiese über Breslau, 15.7.20)

In captivity (Australia). Probable emergency landing due to damaged radiator. Landing not observed due to bad visibility.

24: 14.4.41   Martinz, Lt. Hans; adjutant and pilot III./StG 1
(Hirt nr. Klagenfurt, 10.6.14)

                    Pohl, Uffz. Helmut; gunner III./StG 1 (Königsfeld, 5.12.18)

In captivity (Australia). Emergency landing behind enemy lines in Tobruk after dive-bombing attack on enemy merchantman in Bay of Tobruk. Martinz promoted Oblt. 1.10.41.

24: 19.4.41   Steeg, Lt. Klaus; pilot 9./StG 1 (Essen, 28.10.20)

                    Gündert, Gefr. Anton; gunner 9./StG 1 (Würzburg, 26.8.14)

                    Teutloff, Lt. Dietrich; pilot 9./StG 1 (Rheydt, 17.9.20)

                    Klein, Ogefr. Friedrich; gunner 9./StG 1 (Graz, 3.3.19)

Both crews missing after attack on La Valetta harbour Malta at approx. 05.00 hours.

25: 2.5.41   Baudisch, Fw. Fritz; gunner III./StG 1 (Breslau, 19.6.18)

Wounded during combat mission west of Tobruk.

25: 4.5.41   Becker, Uffz. Heinrich; pilot 9./StG 1 (Berleburg, 31.7.14)

                    Wiersgowski, Uffz. Karl; gunner 9./StG 1
(Datteln/Westphalia, 28.11.18)

Missing after attack on La Valetta harbour Malta at approx. 03.00 hours. Wiersgowski declared dead.

26: 9.5.41   Heinze, Oblt. Ulrich; St.Kpt. 9./StG 1 (Halle/Saale, 21.12.14)

Kummerhofe, Uffz. Anton; gunner 9./StG 1 (Essen, 18.3.16)

Attacked and chased by three Hurricanes after attack on submarine 5km NE La Valetta. Nothing further observed due to bad visibility. Kummerhofe declared dead.

26: 23.5.41   Rottmüller, Gefr. Josef; aircraft mechanic 8./StG 1 (Munich, 18.5.17)

Crashed near Castellamare/Sicily during transfer flight. Died from burns to body. Buried cemetery Trapani/Sicily.

27: 24.6.41   Bornemann, Lt. Friedrich; pilot 9./StG 1 (Langenstein/Harz, 24.5.21)

Jordas, Gefr. Franz; gunner 9./StG 1
(Döschma/Mährisch-Trübau, 9.3.17)

Killed in action after attack by fighters near Minsk. Crashed on fire from height of 200 metres at Kazyn, approx. 25km NW Minsk.

28: 27.6.41   Schilling, Lt. Adalbert; pilot 9./StG 1 (Marktoberdorf, 24.2.20)

Gutschalk, Gefr. Hermann; gunner 9./StG 1 (Rathenen, 15.5.19)

Killed in action during attack on Volkovysk at approx. 15.00 hours.

29: 30.6.41   Schaak, Karl; Inspekteur III./StG 1 (Dragupönen, 22.11.14)

Benz, Uffz. Fritz; cook III./StG 1 (Karlsruhe, 5.4.19)

Markwitz, Paul; Junkers mechanic attached III./StG 1
(Dortmund, 8.8.09)

Elsner, Ogefr. Josef; armourer III./StG 1 (Oberwöldorf, 26.7.18)

Pütz, Gefr. Theodor; general duties III./StG 1
(Cologne/Bickendorf, 20.2.21)

Killed during transfer flight by Ju 52 east of Slonim close to Slonim–Baranovichi forest road. Probably hit by ground fire. Aircraft crashed in flames 4km north of Yeziernica. Apparently brought down by truck-mounted quadruple Flak gun found abandoned 200 metres from crash site.

30: 2.7.41   Hoffmann, Lt. Kurt; pilot 8./StG 1 (Emmerich, 1.5.18)

Becker, Gefr. Hermann; gunner 8./StG 1 (Platten/Wittlich)

Killed in action during attack east of Borisov on River Beresina. Crashed into woods 10km east of Borisov.

30: 3.7.41   Berkhoff, Oblt. Jochen; pilot III./StG 1 (Berlin, 2.11.16)

Foisner, Gefr. Johann; gunner III./StG 1
(Kefermarkt/Upper Danube, 30.3.18)

Killed in action during attack NW Beresino close to Beresino–Schoramz forest road, signed Mahlke, Hauptmann and Gruppenkommandeur.

31: 7.7.41   Suckrow, Lt. Horst; pilot 9./StG 1 (Insterburg/East Prussia, 1.12.20)

Killed in action during attack on Malo Gorodno east of Velyavichi at 11.00 hours. Aircraft shot down by ground fire.

31: 7.7.41   Rudorf, Lt. Hans; pilot 9./StG 1 (Häger/Hall/Westphalia, 6.3.20)
                          Braune, Gefr. Erich; gunner 9./StG 1 (Berlin 2.1.20)

Hit by ground fire and crashed during attack on enemy troops at Gubailovichi east of Belavichi at approx. 11.00 hours. Lt. Rudorf killed (buried Somry cemetery 6–7km east of Belavichi). Gefr. Braune taken to Reserve Hospital 4 Wiesbaden with broken ankle.

32: 8.7.41   Dietz, Fw. Karl; pilot 9./StG 1 (Ansbach, 24.3.17)
                          Leonhardt, Gefr. Bodo; gunner 9./StG 1 (Finsterwalde, 15.3.20)

Shot down by fighters during attack on tanks at Latigalskiye. Fw. Dietz wounded. Three bullets in buttocks and burns. Admitted to hospital. Gefr. Leonhardt missing.

32: 8.7.41   Hartmann, Oblt. Walter; TO and gunner III./StG 1
                          (Königsaue/Saxony, 5.11.20)

Killed in action against fighters over woods to north of Burbin (during mission as gunner to Gruppen-kommandeur).

33: 8.7.41   Mahlke, Hptm. Helmut; Gruppenkommandeur III./StG 1
                          (Berlin-Lankwitz, 27.8.13)

Wounded in action against fighters over woods to north of Burbin. Second-degree burns to face and hands, bullet wound/fracture left shoulder. Admitted field hospital Borisov.

33: 13.7.41   Brunner, Uffz. Alfons; gunner 7./StG 1 (Karlsruhe-Daxladen, 3.7.13)

Wounded near Gusino. Flak splinter in thigh. Admitted field hospital Borisov. From 18.7.41 reserve hospital Krotochin.

33: 17.7.41   Schorpp, Lt. Wilhelm; pilot 8./StG 1 (Karlsruhe, 17.1.21)
                          Grenz, Fw. Max; crew chief/gunner 8./StG 1 (Küstrin, 21.1.07)

Shot down 3km east of Krischev after attacking columns on the Krischev–Roslavl road. Lt. Schorpp killed. After emergency landing a large tree trunk fell across cockpit trapping pilot. Lt. Schorpp burned to death in aircraft. Fw. Grenz escaped landing unharmed. Evaded capture and returned to unit 25.7.41.

33: 21.7.41   Mötefindet, Lt. Heinz; pilot 9./StG 1 (Eilsdorf/Oschersleben, 10.2.20)
                          Rauschdorf, Ogefr. Kurt; mechanic/gunner 9./StG 1
                          (Einbeck/Hildesheim, 19.2.19)

Missing in action after attack on mobile columns near Gusino at approx. 13.15 hours, signed Gassmann, Oberleutnant and Gruppenkommandeur (acting).

34: 21.7.41   Schmidt, Uffz. Heinrich; armourer 7./StG 1
(Butzbach/Hessen, 30.6.17)

Becker, Ogefr. Otto; armourer 7./StG 1 (Neundorf/Bernburg, (4.1.19)

Serno, Gefr. Jakob; mechanic 7./StG 1
(St Peter am Wallersberg, (4.4.20)

Wounded by enemy fire during flight in Ju 52 transport. Aircraft made emergency landing on fire.

34: 23.7.41   Degenkolb, Ogefr. Werner; gunner 7./StG 1 (Syrau/Plauen, 4.1.18)

Wounded during enemy low-level attack on Schatalovka airfield. Bullet through left knee, bullet lodged in right knee.

34: 28.7.41   Mildenberger, Ogefr. Karl; mechanic 8./StG 1 (Kaiserslautern, 17.7.17)

Both legs shattered by explosion of Russian bomb fuze Schatalovka airfield. Location of grave Schatalovka-East airfield, right-hand side of road opposite water tower.

35: 2.8.41   Skambraks, Oblt. Günter; St.Kpt. 8./StG 1
(Tilsit/East Prussia, 1.12.16)

Hilberger, Uffz. Richard; gunner 8./StG 1 (Frankfurt-am-Main, 27.4.17)

Shot down east of Stodolichze railway station while attacking Flak positions in Voroshilovsk area. Crew bailed out. Missing.

35: 2.8.41   Stahmer, Lt. Franz; pilot 8./StG 1 (Hamburg, 9.5.20)

Fahrner, Gefr. Karl; gunner 8./StG 1
(Gramastetten/Lower Danube, 16.10.19)

(No details given.)

36: 9.8.41   Buchmann, Gefr. Josef; gunner 9./StG 1
(Gross Kreuzendorf/Neisse, 26.1.20)

Wounded during combat mission near Kletnya southeast of Roslavl. Splinter in right foot. Admitted hospital Warsaw.

36: 13.8.41   Nigbur, Obfw. Paul; NCO i/c servicing 8./StG 1
(Herten/Westphalia, 18.12.12)

Grüneberg, Uffz. Karl-Heinz; mechanic 8./StG 1
(Barfeld/Alfeld, 12.12.19)

Wagner, Flg. Erich; mechanic 8./StG 1 (Kitzerow nr. Stettin, 28.4.20)

Killed in enemy bombing raid on Schatalovka-West airfield. Location of graves Schatalovka-East airfield opposite water tower, signed Gassmann, Hauptmann and Gruppenkommandeur (acting).

37: 24.8.41   Reinbold, Uffz. Albert; pilot 7./StG 1 (Baden-Baden, 14.12.16)

Jasulski, Uffz. Bruno; gunner 7./StG 1 (Danzig-Langfuhr, 11.5.19)

Aircraft made emergency landing on fire at approx. 08.25 hours in enemy territory some 3km north of Lojv on River Dnieper. One crewmember seen to bail out beforehand. Both missing in action.

38: 10.9.41   Wilm, Ogefr. Günter; gunner 8./StG 1 (Rahlbude nr. Danzig, 9.5.19)

Wounded in right arm by 20mm cannon shell during attack on railway line south of Rommy.

38: 17.9.41   Küster, Uffz.d.R. Karl; pilot 9./StG 1 (Liegwegen/Stadthagen, 14.7.14)

Wounded in right ankle by machine-gun bullet during attack on enemy tanks north of Scharitza. Forced landing due to oil tank damaged by machine-gun fire.

38: 18.9.41   Rothe, Uffz. Gerhard; gunner 8./StG 1
                   (Neutsch nr. Neusa/Oder, 11.11.19)

Wounded in right thigh by infantry ground fire southeast of Rommy.

39: 13.11.41   Härtel, Lt. Hans-Werner; pilot 8./StG 1 (Niederhirschfeldau, 25.11.19)
                    Lohmaier, Uffz. Josef; gunner 8./StG 1
                    (Wilpertskirchen/Bavaria, 1.10.19)

Crew missing in action near Serpuchov. After recovering from dive aircraft last seen heading in northerly direction (enemy territory).

40: 13.2.42   Ströbitzer, Uffz. Hans; pilot 9./StG 1 (Sternberg/Amstetten, 29.12.18)
                   Lach, Ogefr. Erich; gunner 9./StG 1 (Liebesmühl/East Prussia, 11.1.20)

Hit by Flak at low level during attack on Krechno/Russia. Aircraft crashed and caught fire. Crew killed. Ströbitzer buried Krechno, 33km SW Chudovo.

40: 20.2.42   Schütte, Hptm. Heinrich; Gruppenkommandeur (acting) II./StG 2
                   (Gartatovo/Posen, 13.10.09)
                   Meyer, Fw. Johann-Georg; gunner II./StG 2
                   (Hohe am Berg/Bamberg, 21.1.16)

Missing. Shot down by enemy fighter while assembling 10km NW Sieverskaya. Operationally subordinated to III./StG 1 a short time earlier. Hptm. Schütte in Russian captivity (see signature on propaganda leaflet dropped by enemy).

40: 23.2.42   Goede, Lt. Horst; pilot 7./StG 1 (Stilheide, 5.12.19)
                   Raetz, Hans-Joachim; Sonderführer [uniformed civilian specialist]
                   (Gabersdorf/Silesia, 24.8.15)

Killed in action. Crashed after direct hit from Flak over Maluska. Goede bailed out; died of wounds. Raetz went down with aircraft.

41: 27.2.42   Kaubitzsch, Lt. Erich; pilot 9./StG 1 (Döbeln, 22.5.20)
                   Schmidtke, Uffz. Horst; gunner 9./StG 1 (Königsberg, 18.12.15)

Killed in action. Shot down by Flak over Glybochka after attacking enemy positions. Buried 10.3.42 in Sessye pol Yanka, 10km SSW Lyuban, SE Leningrad, on River Tigoda.

41: 28.2.42   Hamer, Obfw. Wilhelm; NCO i/c servicing 8./StG 1
                   (Kröss nr. Oldenburg/Holstein, 11.7.13)

Wounded. Bullet through upper left arm during enemy air attack on Gostkino airfield.

41: 29.2.42   Schubert, Obfw. Gustav; pilot 9./StG 1 (Königszelt, 11.11.16)

Wounded during combat mission west of Kuzino. Flak splinter through left hand.

42: 25.2.42   Rastetter, Gefr. Gustav; driver 9./StG 1 (Karlsruhe, 8.3.21)

Developed hypothermia during transfer from Neukuhren to Gostkino 22.2.42. Admitted military hospital Pleskau [Pskov]. Died 25.2.42.

42: 28.3.42   Fally, Ogefr. Ludwig; gunner 7./StG 1 (Mödring/Horn, 20.7.21)

Killed in action. Died in aircraft crash 2–3km NW Minasdno Bor after direct Flak hit. Pilot bailed out.

42: 29.3.42   Wiesnet, Obfw. Fritz; pilot 8./StG 1 (Ingolstadt, 26.11.15)

                  Jungmayer, Obfw. Fritz; gunner 8./StG 1
                  (Gieselhöring/Lower Danube, 30.7.14)

Killed. Crashed while attempting emergency landing with damaged engine after attack on enemy fighter base Soltsy. Buried cemetery West Soltsy.

43: 31.3.42   Heinz, Uffz. Hans; pilot 9./StG 1 (Leipzig, 24.1.20)

                  Bothe, Gefr. Leonhard; gunner 9./StG 1
                  (Markersdorf/Sudetenland, 21.4.19)

Shot down by Flak 20km east of Lubin on the Leningrad–Moscow railway line. Pilot killed, buried Molody. Gunner admitted to Field Hospital 21. Put aboard hospital train 'Balbino' for transport to Germany 4.4.42.

43: 1.4.42   Pollak, Uffz. Georg; gunner 8./StG 1
                  (Hindenburg/Upper Silesia, 15.6.20)

Ju 87 damaged by ground fire. Attempted to bail out 1km NE Sussolovo, 7.5km SW Staraya Russa, but parachute caught on tail and crashed to death with aircraft. Buried Sussolovo village.

43: 4.4.42   Podak, Ogefr. Gerhard; aircraft mechanic, 9./StG 1
                  (Königsberg, 16.6.17)

Died of illness Gorodez. Body taken to military hospital Pleskau for burial.

44: 13.4.42   Ebertz, Obfw. Hans; pilot 8./StG 1 (Mühlheim/Ruhr, 26.8.14)

                  Baudisch, Obfw. Fritz; gunner 8./StG 1 (Breslau, 19.6.18)

Missing in action. After direct Flak hit crew bailed out over enemy territory 15km NW Cholm (10km from own lines). Captured by Russians.

45: 23.4.42   Bruhn, Obfw. Erich; pilot 9./StG 1 (Prinzert/Fürstenberg, 12.9.15)

                  Kohl, Uffz. Richard; gunner 9./StG 1
                  (Hockenheim/Mannheim, 11.10.20)

Shot down by fighter in area Kerest [probably Krechno?] on Volkhov sector. Crew bailed out. According to interrogation report of Russian POW Glanzev, Dimitri (Tver, 1905; civilian occupation farmer), member of a medical battalion, 1002. Inf.-Rgt. (305. Div.), Kohl landed in the middle of a

Soviet mortar battalion. He tried to escape in the direction of the German lines, but was caught and surrounded by the men of the mortar battalion. The injured Kohl, who had already suffered wounds to the arm and leg, was then shot at close range by the battalion commissar, the Jew Slavinski. The bullet entered Kohl's temple, destroyed his left eye and exited from the centre of his forehead. The Soviet soldiers protested loudly at their commissar's action. Kohl's wounds were bandaged by a medical orderly and he was then placed in the care of the medical battalion. He recovered quickly and was even able to take short walks in the fresh air supported by Glanzev. According to Glanzev, Kohl refused to divulge any military information, despite often being questioned. Commissar Slavinski took his documents and passed them on to battalion HQ. At the end of May Kohl was transported to the Russian interior. By that time his recovery was such that his life was no longer in danger.

46: 24.4.42   Dietz, Obfw. Karl; pilot 9./StG 1 (Ansbach, 24.3.17)
           Kubies, Uffz. Walter; gunner 9./StG 1 (Gelsenkirchen, 15.3.20)

Shot down during attack on Leningrad naval base. Carried out deadstick emergency landing and returned to unit 24.4.42. During landing Dietz suffered slight injuries to face. Kubies wounded in right hand.

47: 12.5.42   Fischer, Oblt. Heinz; St.Führer 9./StG 1 (Kiel, 22.5.17)
           Hümmer, Uffz. Ernst; gunner 9./StG 1 (Gelsenkirchen, 15.4.19)

Emergency landing after hit in starboard fuel tank during attack on enemy tanks near Lipovik. Crew returned to unit 13.5.42. During landing Oblt. Fischer suffered torn right eyelid, bruise to shinbone, haemorrhage and compression left forearm.

48: 16.5.42   Borries, Lt. Hans-G.; pilot 8./StG 1 (Königsberg, 8.5.20)
           Ortner, Uffz. Rudolf; gunner 8./StG 1 (Götzis/Feldkirch, 28.4.20)

Direct Flak hit 5km NE Smerdinya in Pogostye region. Crew bailed out of burning aircraft. Probably captured by Russians.

49: 22.5.42   Breikschat, Uffz. Alois; pilot 9./StG 1 (Wanzleben, 3.4.19)
           Zickbauer, Uffz. Josef; gunner 9./StG 1 (Hessendorf, 11.12.19)

Shot down by Flak over Krilovchina. Crew slightly wounded. Recovered by German front-line troops, signed Schairer, Hauptmann and Gruppenkommandeur (acting).

50: 22.5.42   Kittl, Uffz. Georg; pilot III./StG 1 (Schliersee/Upper Bavaria, 6.8.15)

Posted to III./StG 1 on 22.5.42. Crashed and killed near Rauen during transfer flight to unit.

50: 22.5.42   Maas, Ogefr. Karl; pilot 8./StG 1 (Homberg, 30.11.21)
           Best, Ogefr. Walter; gunner 8./StG 1
           (Bruchenbrücke/Friedberg, 6.5.18)

Killed in action 10km NW Demyansk. After attacking target aircraft caught fire and dived vertically into a swamp. Bodies not recovered.

50: 28.5.42   Kersting, Uffz. Willi; pilot 8./StG 1 (Bochum, 23.9.19)

Rodenbröker, Uffz.; gunner 8./StG 1 (Paderborn, 17.10.20)

Forced landing during combat mission near Schlüsselburg. Crew slightly wounded.

51: 13.6.42   Wittig, Uffz.d.R. Heinz; ground crew 7./StG 1 (Goldberg, 31.5.14)

Died of acute alcohol poisoning at Gorodez 09.00 hours. At 23.00 hours 12.6.42 blood-alcohol level measured 5.0. On 16.6.42 blood sample taken from body measured 3.85.

51: 14.6.42   Treskatsch, Uffz. Artur; pilot 7./StG 1 (Schlachow/Lauenburg, 14.4.20)

Laufen, Ogefr. Johann; gunner 7./StG 1
(Wefelen/Aachen Land, 11.11.19)

Combat mission. Pilot wounded. Burns to both feet. Admitted hospital Luga. Gunner killed. Buried Veshki military cemetery.

51: 17.6.42   Heinrich, Lt. Karl; pilot 7./StG 1 (Hegendorf/Löwenburg, 15.12.19)

Killed on combat mission. Buried WNW Semitzi, grid area 19192, signed Gassmann, Hauptmann and Gruppenkommandeur.

52: 12.7.42   Burger, Ogefr. Xaver; armourer StabsKp. (Peterstal/Kempten, 30.8.19)

Drowned while bathing in Lake Vrevo near Gorodez. Body not recovered.

53: 19.7.42   Schairer, Hptm. Hartmut; St.Kpt. 7./StG 1 (Nagold, 16.9.16)

Bevernis, Obfw. Heinz; gunner 7./StG 1 (Barth/Pomerania, 11.12.14)

Hit by enemy fire while returning from combat mission and crashed near Staraya Russa. Crew killed. Buried Military Cemetery III Solzy. [Author's note: This was Schairer's 562nd and Bevernis' 462nd combat mission!]

54: 14.8.42   Dietz, Obfw. Karl; pilot 9./StG 1 (Ansbach, 24.3.17)

Kupies, Uffz. Walter; gunner 9./StG 1 (Gelsenkirchen, 15.3.20)

Hit by Flak at height of 500 metres during attack on enemy positions 2km NE Pochinok (48km NW Bolchoff near Orel). Machine dived vertically into ground. Exploded and burned on impact. Crew killed.

55: 18.8.42   Nagl, Uffz. Fritz; pilot 8./StG 1 (Behamberg, 5.2.18)

Altenhölscher, Ogefr. Wilhelm; gunner 8./StG 1 (Gladbeck, 7.12.14)

After recovering from dive at height of 800 metres crashed in no-man's land 500 metres north of Vosti, 60km north of Bolchoff on River Zhysdra. Cause of crash unknown.

55: 23.8.42   Hagn, Uffz. Johann; pilot 8./StG 1 (Vienna, 2.12.18)

Paul, Uffz. Walter; gunner 8./StG 1 (Oppelsdorf 24.1.20)

Crashed during landing approach Orel-Nikulichi. Non-combat mission. Crew killed. Buried military cemetery Orel-West airfield on highway to Orel, signed Rohkrähmer, Hauptmann and Special Duties Officer.

56: 30.8.42   Timm, Flg. Herbert; aircraft mechanic 8./StG 1
(Augustenau/Colmar, 15.5.22)

Bremer, Gefr. Eberhard; aircraft mechanic 8./StG 1
(Burhave/Wittmund, 16.3.21)

Killed Gorodez airfield when taxiing Ju 87 rammed by He 111. Buried in grounds of Vlodarskoye estate on road from Lyublino to Koneserye.

57: 31.8.42   Tillmanns, Lt. Harald; pilot 7./StG 1 (Cologne-Lindenthal, 20.6.21)

Killed in action. Hit by 20mm Flak and crashed in flames near Mga. Buried NE Mga.

57: 4.9.42   Houben, Uffz. Paul; pilot 9./StG 1 (Geilenkirchen, 25.7.21)

Dittberner, Uffz. Albert; gunner 9./StG 1 (Oranienburg, 7.1.22)

Combat mission. Aircraft exploded in mid-air 8km NE Mga. Crashed. Crew killed.

57: 5.9.42   Hanne, Lt. Erich; pilot 7./StG 1
(Clauen über Lehrte/Hildesheim, 19.3.20)

Killed in action. Shot down by infantry fire Mikhailovsky, NE Mga.

58: 10.9.42   Strankmann, Uffz. Herbert; pilot 9./StG 1
(Friedeburg nr. Stade, 29.3.20)

Arnold, Ogefr. Kurt; gunner 9./StG 1 (Gautsch-Markkleeberg, 6.8.20)

Aircraft crashed 500 metres north of Tortolovo, 12km NE Mga, after direct Flak hit. No parachutes seen. Crew killed, signed Gassmann, Hauptmann and Gruppenkommandeur.

59: 14.9.42   Thiele, Uffz. Johannes; pilot 7./StG 1 (Euba/Chemnitz, 29.11.19)

Vielwerth, Ogefr. Hermann; gunner 7./StG 1
(Ingolstadt/Bavaria, 2.10.20)

Crew killed in action. Aircraft shot down over Tortolovo, probably by light Flak, crashed and burst into flames on impact.

60: 21.9.42   Henning, Fw. Wilhelm; pilot 7./StG 1 (Fährendorf, 10.7.18)

Wenzel, Uffz. Martin; gunner 7./StG 1 (Berlin, 4.12.20)

Crew killed in action. Direct Flak hit. Aircraft crashed east of Tortolovo, 10km east of Mga, signed Holmann, Major and Gruppenkommandeur (acting).

61: 26.10.42   Fischer, Hptm. Heinz; St.Kpt. 7./StG 1 (Berlin, 22.5.17)

Zethmeier, Uffz. Fritz; gunner 7./StG 1 (Scheinfeld, 12.8.18)

Crew killed 1km NE Strelitzi. Aircraft probably hit either by Flak or artillery shell, exploded and crashed.

61: 30.10.42   Hennig, Fw. Wilhelm; pilot 9./StG 1 (Bernburg, 25.6.19)

Schattauer, Uffz. Karl; gunner 9./StG 1 (Vienna, 27.9.19)

Probably damaged by Flak 11km north of Mga (grid area 10143). Forced landing on German-held territory. Crew admitted to hospital slightly wounded.

62: 7.11.42   Bremer, Ogefr. Gerhard; pilot 9./StG 1 (Schwerin, 6.11.19)

At start of combat mission from Krasnogvardeisk airfield, machine failed to lift off and crashed into equipment hut on airfield perimeter. Bremer admitted to Field Hospital 502 Krasnogvardeisk with concussion, signed Lang, Hauptmann, (pp) Gruppenkommandeur.

62: 1.12.42   Stroba, Fw. Joachim; pilot 8./StG 1 (Schwientochlowitz, 26.9.20)

During transfer flight from Idriza (100km west of Velikiye Luki) to Gorodez machine ran into bad weather front – snow showers and fog – and crashed 8km east of Koroye-Selo airfield. Pilot killed.

62: 6.12.42   Pommer, Obfw. Wilhelm; pilot 8./StG 1 (Neukrin/Anklam, 8.12.14)
                   Wagner, Fw. Walter; gunner 8./StG 1 (Flensburg, 9.12.13)

Machine ran into area of bad weather (probably iced-up) and crashed during transfer flight from Gorodez to Königsberg-Devau for major overhaul. Crew killed.

62: 6.12.42   Leder, Uffz. Martin; pilot 9./StG 1 (Waldenburg/Altwasser, 20.11.21)
                   Günther, Uffz. Horst; gunner 9./StG 1 (Hartha nr. Döbeln, 11.1.20)

Crew missing in action. Forced landing area Strelitzi, SE Lake Ilmen, after hit by Flak, signed Nordmann, Oberleutnant and Gruppenkommandeur (acting).

63: 10.12.42   Pörksen, Lt. Heinz; pilot 7./StG 1 (Kiel, 27.7.21)
                   Schrewe, Ogefr. Friedrich; gunner 7./StG 1
                   (Anröchte/Westphalia, 3.2.23)

Combat mission against artillery positions 25km east of Schlüsselberg. Damaged by Flak over enemy territory 5km ESE Robochy-Posselok, east of Schlüsselburg. During return flight at height of approx. 1,000 metres aircraft hit in engine by light Flak. Both cockpit canopies immediately jettisoned. Aircraft went into dive shortly thereafter. Shortly before impact one crew member was seen to bail out and land apparently unharmed (in enemy territory). Whether it was pilot or gunner who bailed out could not be established.

64: 11.12.42   Bleckl, Oblt. Karl; St.Führer 7./StG 1 (Vienna, 26.9.19)
                   Büchner, Uffz. Georg; gunner 7./StG 1 (Grosszöbern/Plauen, 25.5.21)

Aircraft hit by Flak 1km west of Novo-Sokolniki during combat mission. Crew bailed out. Pilot returned to unit uninjured. Gunner wounded, fractured thigh, hospitalized.

65: 30.12.42   Martens, Lt. Gerhard; pilot 8./StG 1 (Nordhof/Amrum, 19.8.21)
                   Borghoff, Uffz. Ferdinand: gunner 8./StG 1 (Vorhelm/Westphalia,)

Crew killed in action. Shot down by enemy fighters while attacking armoured train east of Velikiye-Luki and enemy positions in northern part of Velikiye-Luki. Crashed in enemy territory 2km west of Velikiye-Luki.

65: 30.12.42   Steinböhmer, Uffz. Heinz; gunner 8./StG 1
              (Münster/Westphalia, 14.12.18)

Severely wounded in head by enemy fighter fire during attack on armoured train east of Velikiye-Luki. Aircraft returned to base. After landing, Uffz. Steinböhmer admitted to military hospital Idriza, signed H. Meyer, Oberleutnant and Special Duties Officer.

66: 2.2.43   Stenzel, Gefr.Bruno; Stabskp. III./StG 1
             (Wiesenrode/Kreis Rawitsch, 10.1.13)

Committed suicide 19.45 hours with rifle shot to head, signed Steffen, Oberleutnant and Adjutant (acting).

67:   Holzmann, Major d.R. Georg; Stabskompanie chief III./StG 1
      (Nuremberg, 9.8.1890)

Died Luftwaffe Hospital Berlin-Reinickendorf after illness.

68: 23.2.43   Kruse, Uffz. Hugo; pilot 7./StG 1 (Minden/Westphalia, 3.9.20)

             Baumgärtner, Uffz. Werner; gunner 7./StG 1
             (Burghausen/Upper Bavaria, 4.2.22)

Probably damaged by Flak during attack on enemy troop concentrations in Katovichi (Chisdra area). For some unexplained reason, after recovery from dive turned full 180 degrees and flew deeper into enemy territory. Radio calls to pilot remained unanswered. Crash not observed. Probably in forest NE Sagorichi 44/2/B area Chisdra. Crew reported missing. According to unconfirmed statement by Russian prisoner, two German flyers captured by Russians on day of crash. Further enquiries unsuccessful.

69: 2?.2.43   Michel, Uffz. Willi; pilot 9./StG 1 (Scheppach/Kreis Öhringen, 19.9.19)

             Winter, Ogefr. Raimund; gunner 9./StG 1
             (Faimingen/Dillingen, 9.10.22)

Crew killed in action. Shot down by infantry fire during attack on enemy positions at Alexandrovka SE Livny. Aircraft burned on impact.

69: 28.2.43   Spermann, Ogefr. Josef; armourer 9./StG 1
             (Darme/Kreis Lingen, 5.10.21)

Killed Orel. Jumped on to moving truck but unable to keep hold. Slid off and killed by trailer. Buried military cemetery Orel-West.

69: 9.3.43   Geipel, Uffz. Waldemar; pilot 9./StG 1 (Oelsnitz/Zwickau, 8.6.22)

             Biesold, Ogefr. Günther; gunner 9./StG 1 (Sangershausen, 1.4.21)

Combat mission, take-off 13.20 hours. Shot down by Flak while attacking tanks 5km north of Chisdra. Aircraft burned on impact in enemy territory and destroyed. One parachute observed, location Poliki, signed Lang, Hauptmann and Gruppenkommandeur.

70: 20.4.43   Sabinsky, Fw. Rudolf; pilot 9./StG 1 (Berlin-Bohnsdorf, 11.6.19)

Neuhaus, Uffz. Wolfgang; gunner 9./StG 1
(Bad Suderode/Aschersleben, 22.9.19)

During attack on Flak positions at Gorbachevka Station aircraft received direct hit on tail, went into immediate spin and hit ground. Did not catch fire. Report by witness Uffz. Hudler: 'During 20.4 attack on Gorbachevka Station aircraft Sabinsky/Neuhaus hit by heavy Flak 11.20 hours. Tail unit blown completely off. Aircraft landed on back close to Flak battery. No parachutes seen. Uffz. Hudler, Stab III./StG 1'; signed Panse, Leutnant and Adjutant.

71: 22.4.43   Klaflinger, Uffz. Karl; pilot 7./StG 1
(Suban nr. Schorting/Upper Bavaria, 17.7.18)

Fuchs, Uffz. Otto; gunner 7./StG 1 (Brotterode/Thuringia, 5.2.21)

Crew killed. Crashed Baranovichi 21.4.43 during searchlight cooperation exercise. Buried 23.4.43 military cemetery Baranovichi.

73: 1.6.43   Schwarz, Fw. Willi; pilot 7./StG 1 (Deutsch Eylau/West Prussia, 6.1.16)

Pachler, Uffz. Karl; gunner 7./StG 1 (Linz, 22.4.20)

Crashed west of Yamskaya-Sloboda after direct Flak hit. Aircraft seen to burn on impact. Witness reports by Uffz. Karl Fiala and Uffz. Robert Kopsa, both 7./StG 1.

74: 12.6.43   Wenzel, Ogefr. Alfred; driver Stabskp. (Berlin, 19.2.03)

Drowned 16.00 hours while bathing without permission in River Oka. Buried military cemetery Orel.

75: 15.6.43   Detzer, Lt. Alfred; pilot 8./StG 1 (Marienweiher, 9.7.19)

Töpfer, Uffz. Gerhard; crew chief 8./StG 1
(Gersdorf/Chemnitz, 25.9.20)

Shot down by direct Flak hit during mission against tanks assembling near Tevemzy and troop concentrations in Micheikinski. Aircraft burned on impact NE Budiegovichi.

75: 15.6.43   Geyer, Oblt. Johann; pilot 7./StG 1 (Vienna, 3.1.21)

Killed in forced landing 2km east of Klinzy. (Non-combat mission.)

76: 20.6.43   Pelz, Uffz. Edgar; gunner 9./StG 1 (Heinersdorf/Neisse, 31.12.15)

After aircraft had been hit in engine by Flak, Pelz and his pilot bailed out at a height of approx. 150–200 metres over friendly territory 18km north of Bolkhov. For some unexplained reason Uffz. Pelz failed to open parachute. Killed on impact with the ground.

77: 21.6.43   Kubitzer, Obfw. Josef; pilot 8./StG 1 (Klausberg, 14.8.14)

Huning, Uffz. Günther; gunner 8./StG 1 (Essen, 8.7.21)

Combat mission against artillery positions (take-off Orel-East 05.50 hours). Direct Flak hit while diving on target at Czenychino (near Novossil). Aircraft burned on impact. (According to witness statement by gunner Uffz. Ofenböck: Flak hit tail unit.) Crew killed.

78: *21.6.43*   Wiedemann, Obfw. Johann; ground staff 8./StG 1
(Riedlingen, 20.5.12): killed

Bergbauer, Uffz. Heinrich; general duties 8./StG 1 (Dorfbach/Passau, 7.7.17): seriously wounded, right leg splintered, left thumb shot off

Fulde, Ogefr. Werner; driver 8./StG 1 (Oberpilau, 6.8.20): slightly wounded

Löffel, Ogefr. Kurt; driver 8./StG 1 (Gallowitz, 10.4.21): slightly wounded

Donath, Ogefr. Johannes; 8./StG 1 (Grünau/Zittau, 6.1.20): slightly wounded

Körnschild, Ogefr. Heinrich; (Zeitz/Saxony, 22.8.21): slightly wounded

The above casualties were suffered during a Russian air attack on Orel-East (Prokurovka) airfield.

79: *5.7.43*   Knepper, Uffz. Kurt; pilot 8./StG 1 (Neu-Seifersdorf, 19.1.16)
Kiefer, Ogefr. Alfons; gunner 8./StG 1 (Orscholz)

Crashed from low altitude at airfield Orel-North upon return from combat mission. Reasons unknown. Uffz. Knepper killed, buried military cemetery Orel. Ogefr. Kiefer slightly wounded, admitted Field Hospital 615 Orel.

79: *5.7.43*   Heil, Uffz. Heinz; pilot 7./StG 1 (Pforzheim, 19.8.19)
Schramm, Ogefr. Gerhard; gunner 7./StG 1 (Zschopau, 5.3.23)

Combat mission against artillery positions in small wood west of Maloarchangelsk (between Orel and Kursk). Take-off Orel-East 02.45 hours. Dived on target in grid area 63534. Apparently damaged by Flak during dive and flew off eastwards trailing smoke. No further sightings. No response to radio calls. According to Russian propaganda leaflet both crewmembers in Russian captivity. (Crew posted to III./StG 1 on 3.7.43 from I./StG 151 Pancevo near Belgrade, where StG 1's Ergänzungsstaffel was based.) Report compiled 20.7.43, signed Berberich, Hauptmann and Staffelkapitän.

80: *5.7.43*   Rohde, Oblt. Hermann; St.Kpt. 9./StG 1 (Hasewald, 25.5.20)
Hupas, Fw. Adolf; gunner 9./StG 1 (Frauendorf/Oppeln, 21.11.18)

Hit by Flak during attack on troop assembly areas in village of Podoyan and forced to make emergency landing 7km west of Senkova. Aircraft overturned. Crew slightly wounded.

81: *11.7.43*   Seiffert, Uffz. Horst; pilot 8./StG 1 (Langenberg/Thuringia, 17.11.20)
Lachmann, Uffz. Hans; gunner 8./StG 1 (Berlin, 2.10.19)

Both wounded during combat mission. Engine hit by Flak, burning aircraft force-landed 08.45 hours near Pogoryelovzy 35km south of Orel. Pilot, burns to lower right leg and face. Gunner, shell splinter in right shoulder.

82: 12.7.43   Alscher, Uffz. Herbert; pilot 8./StG 1
(Rotenbach/Kreis Waldenburg, 7.5.21)

Henning, Uffz. Friedrich; gunner 8./StG 1 (Berent/Danzig, 15.11.19)

During return from combat mission aircraft collided with another machine, made contact with ground and overturned near Alexandrovka, 22km north of Orel. Crew slightly wounded.

82: 13.7.43   Artner, Uffz. Ernst; pilot 7./StG 1 (Mitteradel/Lower Danube, 8.8.20)

Fiala, Uffz. Karl; gunner 7./StG 1.

During attack north of Zhetucha (Orel region) at 12.55 hours aircraft took direct hit from light Flak and crashed in Russian territory. Burned on impact. Crew killed.

83: 14.7.43   Böttinger, Fw. Heinz; gunner 8./StG 1 (Bochum Langendreer, 10.6.17)

Wounded by light Flak SE Bobrik. Shell splinter in lower left leg.

83: 14.7.43   Buchholtz, Lt. Werner von; pilot III./StG 1 (Rostock, 24.6.20)

Etzelsdorfer, Uffz. Josef; gunner III./StG 1 (Schöndorf, 27.2.22)

Shot down by Russian Flak near Dudorovski during attack on tanks in area Dudorovski–Dudorovo–Medynzevo. Gunner missing after seen bailing out. Pilot severe burns to face.

84: 19.7.43   Kersting, Lt. Willi; pilot 9./StG 1 (Borkum, 23.9.19)

Schattenier, Uffz. Karl; gunner 9./StG 1 (Vienna, 27.9.19)

Aircraft exploded in mid-air during attack on village of Vetrovo, SW Bolchoff. Cause unknown. No parachutes seen. Crew killed.

84: 19.7.43   Lippmann, Lt. Hans-E.; pilot 9./StG 1 (Aussig/Elbe, 28.3.21)

Starboard fuel tank on fire after Flak hit. Bailed out west of Kolmy-Kovo but parachute caught on tail. Severely injured.

84: 19.7.43   Kern, Uffz. Emil; gunner 9./StG 1 (Nussdorf/Pfalz, 9.11.19)

Three Flak hits to aircraft west of Kolmy-Kovo. Slightly wounded.

84: 20.7.43   Hennig, Fw. Wilhelm; pilot 9./StG 1 (Bernburg, 25.6.19)

Direct hit in cockpit from light Flak during dive on target near Bychki. Severely wounded.

[Note: From this point until entry 94 it appears that the units casualty returns were either not submitted or not filed in the proper sequence; they are reproduced here in the order given in the German edition. Dates marked * have been amended from the German original. *Report 86* of 21.7.43 was 21.2.43 in the original; *Report 86* of 26.7.43 was 26.1.43; *Report 89* of 16.8.43 was 16.3.43.]

84: 17.7.43   Tigges, Ogefr. Günther; gunner 7./StG 1 (Celle, 2.11.20)

Severely wounded in right leg during fighter attack NE Glasovo.

85: 17.7.43   Knitzatka, Ogefr. Norbert; driver Stabskp. (Vienna, 26.2.18)

Killed in enemy bombing of Konefka near Orel. Buried Orel military cemetery.

85: 17.7.43   Kritzner, Ogefr. Helmut; crew chief Stabskp. (Gössnitz, 28.3.21)

Severely wounded in enemy bombing of Konefka near Orel.

85: 17.7.43   Schlosser, Ogefr. Rudi; crew chief 9./StG 1 (Zwoda, 17.4.20)

Slightly wounded in enemy bombing of airfield Orel-East.

86: 21.7.43*   Ayerle, Obfw. Karl-L.; pilot 9./StG 1 (Augsburg, 12.7.18)

   Magna, Ogefr. Wilhelm; gunner 9./StG 1
   (Harpenfeld/Osnabrück, 22.2.18)

Forced to make emergency landing SE Orel after attack by enemy fighter. Crew slightly wounded.

86: 26.7.43*   Fiedler, Fw. Hans; pilot 8./StG 1 (Kronach, 16.11.20)

Slightly wounded by shell fragment right arm.

86: 17.7.43   Grabinger, Ogefr. Egon; gunner 9./StG 1 (Amberg, 27.7.20)

Slightly wounded by bomb fragment during attack by Russian aircraft on airfield Orel-East.

86: 14.7.43   Böcker, Uffz. Rolf; pilot 8./StG 1 (Ulm, 16.1.22)

Slightly wounded over Dudorovo (combat mission). Taken to Reserve Hospital I, Löwitz.

86: 20.7.43   Schmid, Fw. Friedrich; pilot 8./StG 1 (Pastetten nr. Munich, 29.9.18)

   Ofenböck, Uffz. Otto; gunner 8./StG 1 (Wiener Neustadt, 27.9.22)

Crew slightly wounded in forced landing near Solotarevo (combat mission).

87: 2.8.43   Rahmel, Lt. Gregor; pilot 8./StG 1 (Cologne-Lindenthal, 18.10.21)

   Lange, Uffz. Heinz; gunner 8./StG 1 (Görlitz, 16.2.20)

Crew slightly wounded in forced landing near Ordzhonikidsgrad (combat mission).

87: 3.8.43   Heimke, Lt. Ernst; pilot 9./StG 1 (Locknitz, 27.5.22)

   Malik, Uffz. Paul, gunner 9./StG 1 (Kihnau, 23.10.22)

Combat mission. Crew slightly wounded by Flak near Gosterul.

87: 15.07 43   Buchholz, Lt. Hans; pilot 7./StG 1 (Emden, 24.11.19)

   Kopsa, Uffz. Robert; gunner 7./StG 1 (Vienna, 9.9.18)

Take-off Orel-East for combat mission against Melekhovo. Attacked SE Yagodnaya by enemy fighters. Emergency landing. Pilot died in hospital, gunner severely wounded.

88: 5.8.43   Kuhnle, FhjFw. Karl; pilot 8./StG 1 (Schwäbisch-Gmünd, 19.6.19)

   Winterle, Uffz. Rolf; gunner 8./StG 1 (Pforzheim, 25.3.10)

Take-off Ivanovka (near Bryansk) 08.40 hours for attack on village of Kutafino (50km SW Orel). Aircraft received direct Flak hit and crashed 4km NW Kutafino. Burned on impact, crew killed.

89:16.8.43*   Kuhn, Uffz. Walter; pilot 9./StG 1 (Zschopau/Dresden, 30.3.19)

                Hunze, Uffz. Karl; gunner 9./StG 1 (Barfelde/Hildesheim, 15.6.21)

Attacked by enemy fighters over enemy territory 10–15km south of Kosselsk. Emergency landing. Nothing further seen. Crew missing.

89: 8.8.43   Schönbein, Ogefr. Willi; crew chief 8./StG 1 (Dresden, 9.5.18)

Shot in foot while cleaning pistol. Accidental wounding.

91: 2.8.43   Fasold, Uffz. Wilhelm; pilot 9./StG 1 (Cologne-Ehrendorf, 22.2.22)

                Mauser, Uffz. Alois; gunner 9./StG 1

Attacked by enemy fighters near village of Vanovka east of Karachev. Pilot slightly wounded, gunner died in hospital 2.8.43.

91: 8.8.43   Beck, Obfw. Max; pilot 8./StG 1 (Karlsruhe, 24.11.12)

                Hlafka, Uffz. Friedrich; gunner 8./StG 1 (Vienna, 1.2.21)

Both slightly wounded by Flak during attack on Flak positions in Studenka area.

92: 15.8.43   Preikschat, Uffz. Alois; pilot 9./StG 1 (Wanzleben/Magdeburg, 3.4.19)

                Zickbauer, Uffz. Josef; gunner 9./StG 1 (Hessendorf, 11.12.19)

Crashed north of Malistovo after direct Flak hit. Aircraft burned on impact. Crew killed.

93: ??.8.43   Frische, Ogefr. Fritz; armourer 7./StG 1 (Barntrup, 17.9.19)

Killed in partisan attack near Bryansk (between Kolzovka and NE Styashnoye). Buried military cemetery Sechinskaya.

94: 13.8.43   Barde, Uffz. Felix; gunner 7./StG 1 (Paulwitz/Schleswig, 10.9.20)

Combat mission. Severely wounded by Flak near Gravelovo.

95: 20.8.43   Lindemann, Fw. Johann; pilot 9./StG 1 (Bögerwald, 13.3.18)

                Grabinger, Ogefr. Egon; gunner 9./StG 1 (Amberg, 27.2.20)

Take-off Sechinskaya 05.00 hours for attack on enemy troops concentrated in woods south of Troyanovski, SE Ssevsk. Hit by Flak approx. 8km SE Ssevsk. Aircraft last seen flying northwards. (According to previous report crew had returned to unit on 6.8.43 after an earlier forced landing behind enemy lines.) Again declared missing in action 20.8.43.

95: 20.8.43   Weintraut, Uffz. Rolf; gunner 9./StG 1 (Hamburg, 8.5.22)

Combat mission east of Ssevsk. Slightly wounded in neck by bullet fragment from heavy machine-gun.

96: 23.8.43   Rohde, Oblt. Hermann; St.Kpt. 9./StG 1 (Pasewalk, 25.5.20)

                Palm, Uffz. Martin; gunner 9./StG 1 (Essen, 1.2.16)

Crashed 1,500 metres west of Klinzy immediately after recovery from dive-bombing attack. Cause unknown. Aircraft burned on impact, crew killed.

97: 29.8.43   Müller, Uffz. Ernst; pilot 8./StG 1 (Eibelshausen/Dillkreis, 30.10.19)
Böttinger, Fw. Heinz, gunner 8./StG 1 (Bochum-Langendreer, 10.6.17)

Aircraft destroyed in mid-air by explosion of own bombs after Flak hit over Ugriza. Crew killed.

98: 30.8.43   Kohl, Uffz. Eduard; gunner 7./StG 1 (Trier, 8.7.23)

Slightly wounded by Flak NE Essmann. Shell fragment in right shinbone. 5cm of bone damaged.

98: 4.9.43   Rahmel, Lt. Gregor; pilot 8./StG 1 (Cologne-Lindenthal, 18.10.21)
Lange, Uffz. Karl-H.; gunner 8./StG 1 (Görlitz, 16.2.20)

Direct Flak hit in engine. Grid area 35-343/1-300,000. Crew bailed out over enemy territory and made way back to own lines. Pilot severely wounded (first- and third-degree burns to head, neck and left arm). Gunner slightly wounded (contusions and skin abrasions).

98: 4.9.43   Riedelbauch, Uffz. Heinrich; pilot 7./StG 1
(Wunsiedel/Nuremberg, 8.12.20)
Huxold, Uffz. Rudolf; gunner 7./StG 1
(Obenkirchen/Hannover, 26.8.22)

Shot down by enemy fighters near Leonovo, 11km SW Yelnya. Crew bailed out over enemy territory. One crew member caught on aircraft's tail unit. Uffz. Riedelbauch made way back wounded to own lines. Admitted to Military Hospital 2/609 on 11.9.43 with burns to face, neck and both hands. Gunner missing, believed killed.

99a: 12.9.43   Jokisch, Uffz. Heinz; pilot 8./StG 1 (Radewell/Merseburg, 18.10.19)
Tomaselli, Uffz. Willi; gunner 8./StG 1
(Volkmarode/Brunswick, 9.3.22)

Aircraft hit by Flak near Olsufyeski. Crew bailed out. Slightly wounded, compression injuries.

99: 15.9.43   Gerbl, Fw. Max; pilot 7./StG 1 (Munich, 31.7.13)
Martin, Fw. Wilfried; pilot 7./StG 1 (Vienna, 18.4.19)
Ebeling, Uffz. Friedrich; gunner 7./StG 1 (Oldenburg, 15.8.21)
Throne, Uffz. Heinz; gunner 7./StG 1 (Hagen, 20.8.21)

All severely wounded during enemy bombing raid on Schatalovka airfield. Fw. Gerbl died of wounds in Orscha hospital 21.9.43.

99: 16.9.43   Wiedemann, Fw. Karl; pilot 7./StG 1 (Munich 4.11.21)

Missing near Tychayevo. Direct Flak hit while attacking group of forty enemy tanks 10km north of Duchovchina. Aircraft on fire. Crew bailed out over Russian territory.

100: 16.9.43   Hopf, Uffz. Herbert; gunner 7./StG 1 (Weida/Thuringia, 7.5.21)

Missing as Fw. Wiedemann above.

100: 18.9.43   Müller, Uffz. Siegfried; pilot 7./StG 1 (Mönchweiler, 14.12.18)

                Voss, Uffz. Hans; gunner 7./StG 1 (Blankensee/Mecklenburg, 1.10.20)

Killed SE Kosolez when aircraft hit ground after recovering from dive.

100: 19.8.43

Note: The 7./StG 1 crew Uffz. Kopp/Uffz. Voss reported missing in action south of Alexandrovka on 19.8.43 have returned to unit uninjured.

101: 21.9.43   Degenhardt, Obfw. Josef; master mechanic 7./StG 1
                (Saarlautern, 28.7.15)

                Opel, Uffz. Josef; crew chief 7./StG 1 (Delmenhorst, 18.6.16)

Killed in Russian air raid on Novosybkov.

                Winter, Ogefr. Hubert; driver 7./StG 1 (Munich-Schönberg, 8.5.21)

Wounded in Russian air raid on Novosybkov.

102: 26.9.43   Schmitt, Lt. Heinz; pilot 9./StG 1 (Hornau/Wiesbaden, 9.8.23)

                Zoller, Uffz. Franz-X.; gunner 9./StG 1 (Augsburg, 4.4.21)

Exploded in mid-air during attack on Alexandrovka. Cause unknown. Crew killed.

103: 30.9.43   Amthor, Lt. Richard; pilot 7./StG 1 (Brückenau/Mainfranken, 14.2.22)

Took off in Fieseler Storch tasked with reconnoitring site for new airfield. Came under fire from partisan-controlled area near Bobruisk. Severely wounded by explosive bullet left thigh. Admitted Reserve Hospital V/239 Bobruisk.

104: 4.10.43   Peuker, Ogefr. Gerhard; driver StbsKp. (Hulderhof nr. Brieg, 8.10.22)

                Walter, Ogefr. Heinrich; driver StbsKp. (Blocksee/Schleswig, 10.7.16)

Soviet air raid on Bobruisk. Ogefr. Peuker killed 20.30 hours. Ogefr. Walter severely wounded by bomb splinter in right eye.

104: 9.10.43   Birke, Uffz. Herbert; pilot 9./StG 1 (Buchwalde nr. Breslau, 10.10.20)

                Gutenthaler, Uffz. Edmund; gunner 9./StG 1
                (Weidlingen nr. Vienna, 29.5.20)

Forced landing Koslovo after aircraft hit by Flak. Pilot died of wounds in hospital 10.43 hours 21.10.43. Gunner slightly wounded.

104: 14.10.43   Hagedorn, Uffz. Günter; pilot 7./StG 1 (Magdeburg, 6.11.21)

                Veit, Ogefr. Johannes; gunner 7./StG 1 (Duisburg, 28.2.21)

Shot down during attack on distillery north of Lenino while diving on Flak emplacement. One crew member, probably gunner, seen to bail out over enemy territory. Crew missing.

104: 19.10.43   Seiffert, Uffz. Horst; pilot 8./StG 1 (Langenberg/Thuringia, 17.11.20)

Slightly wounded in left arm by infantry fire during combat mission near Gluchez.

105: 12.11.43 Leucht, Uffz. Werner; pilot 9./StG 1 (Auerbach, 20.12.20)

Kasparek, Uffz. Rudolf; gunner 9./StG 1 (Teschen/Kattowitz, 10.4.22)

Böhnel, Gefr. Otto; crew chief 9./StG 1 (Wolfstein, 15.10.23)

Non-combat mission. Aircraft crashed 10km west of Zwiahel, cause unknown. Gunner killed, buried military cemetery Zwiahel. Pilot and crew chief slightly wounded.

105: 22.11.43 Kater, Flg. Heinz; pilot 7./StG 1 (Karlsruhe, 14.4.21)

Direct Flak hit 2km west of Alexandrovka, NW Gomel. Aircraft overturned during emergency landing. Pilot killed.

106: 11.12.43 Klemm. Uffz. Rudolf; pilot 7./StG 1 (Vieselbach/Weimar, 27.1.23)

Crashed and killed during check flight with Ju 87D-5. Took off unofficially in QBI [bad weather] conditions, without flight plan, without checking weather and without informing flight control. Buried war cemetery Zagret near Vilna without military honours.

107: 6.3.44 Wiedemann, Uffz. Carl; pilot 7./SG 1 (Munich, 4.11.21)

Aircraft damaged by Flak near Bogorodichko. Slightly wounded (strained vertebrae) during forced landing in friendly territory. Gunner Uffz. Barde uninjured.

108: 10.12.43 Kressler, Uffz. Herbert; crew chief 7./SG 1 (Leipzig, 4.7.17)

Injured spine falling down stairs at the Gaststätte Drei Löwen [Three Lions Inn] Vilna. Died of injuries in Hospital 2/605 Vilna on 15.12.43.

109: 19.12.43 Jentzsch, Uffz. Heinz; gunner 7./SG 1 (Borddorf nr. Leipzig, 3.7.19)

Slightly injured in forced landing at Ignalino during 'circuits and bumps'.

110: 31.12.43 Alfs, Ogefr. Alfred; driver 9./SG 1 (Deichhausen/Wesermarsch, 5.8.20)

Koppitz, Ogefr. Hermann; driver 9./SG 1 (Peisteritz/Breslau, 15.1.21)

Both received slight head wounds from mine explosion.

111: 24.2.44 Krause, Uffz. Karl; pilot 9./SG 1 (Remscheid, 7.9.22)

Schlabitz, Uffz. Heinz; gunner 9./SG 1 (Liegnitz, 20.9.21)

Crashed after direct Flak hit 3km NE Verichev. Aircraft burned on impact. Crew killed. Ju 87D-5.

112: 7.3.44 Westermeier, Ofhr. Karl; pilot 9./SG 1 (Munich, 14.8.23)

Malik, Uffz. Paul; gunner 9./SG 1 (Kuhnau, 23.10.22)

Crashed after direct hit from heavy Flak east of Ostrov-Yeryev (grid area 05424). Aircraft burned on impact. Crew killed.

113: 10.3.44 Dressel, Ogefr. Günther; pilot 7./SG 1 (Berlin, 10.3.23)

Heer, Ogefr. Hans; gunner 7./SG 1 (Gelsenkirchen-Buer, 25.2.22)

Shot down in flames by Flak NE Novoye-Sela (grid area 05423). Crew killed.

114: 2.3.44   Löhe, Uffz. Edmund; pilot 7./SG 1.

According to notification from 2./SG 152, took off in Fw 190 for transfer flight Posen–Rahmel. Probably ran into snowstorm and crashed in Bay of Danzig.

114: 10.3.44   Heimke, Lt. Ernst; pilot 9./SG 1.

Overturned in Fw 190 while landing at Rahmel. Seriously injured (fractured fourth vertebra). Expected to remain in naval hospital Gotenhafen 4–6 weeks.

115: 30.3.44   Beck, Stbsfw. Max; pilot 8./SG 1 (Karlsruhe, 24.11.12)

Bailed out of Fw 190 during 'circuits and bumps' Vilna. Seriously injured.

116: 24.4.44   Lützelberger, Ogefr. Karl; armourer 9./SG 1
                  (Schleusingen/Thuringia, 7.11.23)

While Ogefr. Geissenhörner was checking his service pistol, a round was accidentally discharged and hit Ogefr. Lützelberger in left thigh. Taken to Military Hospital 909 Vilna, signed Lange, Major and Gruppenkommandeur.

117: 5.5.44   Fischer, Oblt. Hans-Joachim; pilot 7./SG 1
                 (Weissenfels/Saale, 9.12.19)

Fw 190 caught fire when landing after 'circuits and bumps' Vilna airfield. Pilot severely injured. Admitted Hospital 606 Vilna.

118: 24.6.44   Bertram, Gefr. Harald; pilot 9./SG 1.

Killed in Fw 190F-8 shot down by enemy fighters NW Gomsa.

118: 30.6.44   Leucht, Fw. Werner; pilot 9./SG 1.

Fw 190G-8 took direct Flak hit in right wing 6km east of Baranovichi. Crashed 6km short of base. Pilot killed. Buried military cemetery Baranovichi.

119: 28.6.44   Schrepfer, Hptm. Karl; GpKdr. III./SG 1 (Augsburg, 10.2.17)

Slightly wounded by Flak splinter in right eye during combat mission west of Bobruisk. Fw 190F-8.

119: 9.7.44   Kopf, Fw. Ernst; pilot 7./SG 1 (Dornbirn/Vorarlberg, 31.3.18)

Took off from Kobryn in Fw 190F-8 to attack enemy armoured spearheads in village of Piotrovichi, east of Slonim. Pilot missing. Fate not observed due to strength of enemy defensive fire.

119: 13.7.44   Wieschalla, Fahnenjunker-Oberfeldwebel Willibald; pilot 8./SG 1
                  (Karlsruhe/Oppel, 7.7.14)

Missing in Fw 190G-8 during attack on enemy forces in area Pruzana–Baresa–Kartuska.

118a: 5.7.44   Schmid, Obfw. Friedrich; pilot 8./SG 1
                  (Pastetten/Kreis Erdingen, 29.9.18)

Took off Kobryn 04.15 hours for combat mission in area east of Nieswiecz. Missing near Lesna, 25km SE Baranovichi. Fw 190G-8.

118a: 8.7.44   Richter, Uffz. Heinrich; pilot 9./SG 1 (Aken/Kreis Calbe-Saale, 8.4.22)

Took off in Fw 190G-8 from Kobryn 08.15 hours. Second attack of day against enemy trucks and vehicle columns to north of Nova Mysz (grid area 54862). Missing in target area. Fate not observed.

118a: 10.7.44   Hartwig, Uffz. Heinz; pilot 9./SG 1 (Friedrichsrode/Thuringia, 14.3.21)

Combat mission in Fw 190. Severely injured bailing out 15km NW Kobryn. Fractured lower leg and damage to knee joint. Admitted local hospital Kobryn.

120: 19.7.44   Klüber, Hptm. Wilhelm; pilot 7./SG 1 (Nuremberg, 28.1.14)

Fw 190F-8 'Yellow A' shot down by direct Flak hit at Hainovka (grid area 33195). Aircraft seen to burn on impact. Pilot killed.

120: 25.7.44   Eisbacher, Lt. Johann; pilot 7./SG 1 (Voitsberg, 2.5.22)

Fw 190 'Yellow C' attacked by enemy fighters south of Siedlce. Fate not observed. Pilot missing.

120: 26.7.44   Wagner, Obfw. Josef; pilot 7./SG 1
                 (Vilsbiburg/Lower Bavaria, 21.12.12)

Fw 190 'Yellow M' shot down by light Flak SE Yanrovo (grid area 2237). Aircraft burned on impact. Pilot killed, signed Schrepfer, Hauptmann, (pp) Gruppenkommandeur.

121: 27.7.44   Mühlhaus, Uffz. Karl; pilot 7./SG 1
                 (Roitham/Kreis Vöcklabruck, 5.12.20)

Fw 190 'White C' missing during combat mission in Siedlce–Kaluscyn area.

121: 28.7.44   Neu, Ogefr. Walter; aircraft mechanic 7./SG 1 (Legitten/Kreis Labiau)

Accidentally killed when Fw 190 he was working on at Warsaw-Okecie was rammed by Me 109 taxiing out to take off.

122: 1.8.44   Prior, Fw. Lothar, pilot 7./SG 1 (Vienna, 1.6.21)

Fw 190F-8 'Yellow F' missing near Magnuschev north of Debbin. Despite lengthy search of area nothing found to establish fate.

123: 2.8.44   Ewel, Fw. Gerhard; pilot 9./SG 1 (Berlin-Charlottenburg, 17.7.18)

Fw 190F-8 'White B' crashed for reasons unknown during transfer flight from Warsaw-Okecie to Bielice. Pilot killed.

123a: 21.8.44   Szielasko, Ofhr. Arthur; pilot 8./SG 1 (Völklingen/Saar, 24.4.23)

Fw 190F-8 'Blue M' hit by Flak and crashed to west of road 3km SE Schirwindet. Aircraft burned on impact. Pilot killed.

124: 7.10.44   Seiffert, Fw. Horst; pilot 8./SG 1 (Bad Gandersheim/Harz, 4.12.24)

Fw 190 'Black 9' airfield Bielice. Aircraft lifted off too soon during emergency scramble, stalled, rolled over on to left wing and crashed from height of 30 metres. Pilot killed.

125: 13.10.44 Müller, Ofhr. Heinz; pilot 7./SG 1 (Vienna, 8.3.22)

Fw 190 'White 8' shot down by medium Flak while diving on target at Nieperef (grid area 13513). Aircraft seen to burn on impact. Pilot killed.

125: 13.10.44 Bauer, Uffz. Eduard; pilot 7./SG 1 (Vienna, 8.3.22)

Fw 190 'Yellow 5'. Shot down by enemy fighters SW Lipniki (grid area 13152) after attacking target at Lipniki. Aircraft seen to burn on impact. Pilot killed.

125: 13.10.44 Lange, Uffz. Joachim; pilot 9./SG 1
  (Tangerhütte/Kreis Stendal, 14.2.23)

Fw 190 'Yellow 7': Presumed shot down by Flak 6km SE Mackheim. Aircraft seen to burn on impact. Pilot killed, signed Schrepfer, Hauptmann.

126: 13.10.44 Faymonville, Ogefr. Paul; pilot 8./SG 1 (Aachen, 4.2.23)

Fw 190 'Blue 8': Combat mission north of Warsaw. Pilot had to bail out of damaged machine (Flak hit) over home base Bielice. Haemorrhage left thigh.

126: 21.10.44 Freischmidt, Uffz. Rudolf; pilot 7./SG 1
  (Hillesheim/Kreis Trier, 21.8.21)

Fw 190 'White 5': Shot down by enemy fighters. Aircraft seen to burn on impact. Wreckage found 500 metres NW Mlodchianovo, 3km south of airfield Nasielsk. Pilot killed.

127: 17.6.44 Faymonville, Ogefr. Paul; pilot 8./SG 1 (Aachen, 4.2.23)

Fw 190 'Blue L'. Non-combat mission. Aircraft somersaulted while landing airfield Pastovichi. Concussion and impact wound to left eye.

127: 25.7.44 Buchholtz, Oblt. Werner von; pilot Stab III./SG 1 (Rostock, 24.6.20)

Fw 190 'Black D': Rammed by another machine during take-off Warsaw-Okecie on combat mission. Concussion.

127: 1.8.44 Panse, Hptm. Werner; pilot 7./SG 1.

Fw 190 'Yellow A': Bailed out of burning machine after attacking target SE Gora-Kolyava (grid area 121591). Severely wounded. Second- and third-degree burns to face and neck.

127: 11.8.44 Herrmann, Obfw. Edgar; pilot 8./SG 1 (Karlsruhe, 26.1.17)

Fw 190 'Blue C': Lightly wounded in action against enemy fighters. Bullet splinters in left side of face and neck.

128: 16.1.45 Hulsch, Oblt. Otto; St.Führer 7./SG 1 (Rochau, 14.9.21)

Knight's Cross winner. Shot down in Fw 190 'White 1' after air combat with ten Il-2s and six La-5s and Yak-9s in grid area 03792. Aircraft seen to burn on impact. Pilot killed.

128: 17.1.45 Schubert, Oblt. Gustav; St.Kapt. 9./SG 1 (Königszelt/Silesia, 11.11.16)

Oak Leaves winner. Fw 190 'Yellow 1': Shot down by Flak 6km SW Kroschin (grid area 83495) after attacking enemy tanks in grid areas 83497 and 83495. Aircraft seen to burn on impact.

128: 17.1.45   Dietz, Uffz. Erich; pilot 8./SG 1 (Bad Cannstadt nr. Stuttgart, 17.12.22)

Fw 190 'Black 10': Crashed on take-off for combat mission from airfield Kornen near Berent (grid area 85964). Cause unknown. Aircraft burned on impact. Buried military cemetery Berent in West Prussia, Grave Row No. 11, signed Schrepfer, Major and Gruppenkommandeur.

129: 19.1.45   Flegel, Hptm.d.R. Rudolf; pilot 7./SG 1 (Frankfurt-on-Oder, 19.7.08)

Fw 190 'White C': Injured spine in emergency landing after combat mission grid area 9352. Admitted reserve hospital Chemnitz. Light injuries.

129: 31.1.45   Heidrich, Lt. Waldemar, pilot 7./SG 1 (Rastatt/Baden, 11.5.24)

Fw 190 'White 11': Injured spine in emergency landing after combat mission grid area 85793. Admitted Berent sanatorium. Light injuries.

130: 20.1.45   Vogel, Uffz. Siegfried, pilot 9./SG 1 (Dresden, 9.12.18)

Missing. Fw 190 'White 5': Emergency landing near Königsdorf during transfer flight from Hohensalza to Bromberg 20.1.45. Vogel was seen by one of the Gruppe's Feldwebeln in Landsberg a.d. Warthe on 22.1.45. He was trying to obtain a travel warrant in order to get back to the unit as quickly as possible. But as he only had a combat flight pass on him, it seems likely that Vogel was picked up by the military police and pressed into service with another unit.

130: 11.2.45   Lyke, Fw. Heinz; pilot 7./SG 1 (Lehrte/Hannover, 8.10.21)

Fw 190 'White 5': Force-landed due to engine damage during combat mission in grid area 85787. Impact wound to head and concussion.

131: 15.2.45   Petzold, Obfw. Lothar; pilot 7./SG 1 (Guhrau/Silesia, 5.9.16)

Fw 190 'White 3': Force-landed during combat mission in grid area 84411. Suffered two impact wounds to head and back sprains.

131: 23.2.45   Krahe, Gefr. Helmut; pilot 8./SG 1 (Urnitz/Cologne, 25.3.24)

Fw 190 'Yellow 5': Failed to return from attack on enemy infantry positions on west bank of River Vistula opposite Graudenz. Fate not observed. Pilot missing.

131: 28.2.45   Herrmann, Obfw. Edgar; pilot 8./SG 1 (Karlsruhe, 26.1.17)

Fw 190 'Yellow 5': Crashed from a height of approx. 400 metres into swampy area between Bast and Güldenhagen, 10km NW Köslin, during transfer flight from Stolp-West to Kolberg. Cause unknown. Pilot killed.

131: 28.2.45   Zastera, Uffz. Helmut; pilot 8./SG 1 (Kriesdorf/Aussig, 3.10.23)

Aircraft set on fire by enemy action during combat mission. Pilot bailed out over enemy territory. Missing.

131: 1.3.45   Wagner, Obfw. Georg; pilot Stab III./SG 1
(Heidelberg-Rohrbach, 12.8.14)

Fw 190A: Shot down by enemy fighters east of Baldenburg, SW Rummelsburg. Aircraft burned on impact.

132: 2.3.45   Stobbe, Fw. Horst; pilot 7./SG 1 (Danzig, 21.10.20)

                Ewers, Gefr. Johannes; crew chief 7./SG 1 (Kiel-Holtenau, 31.1.07)

Fw 190: During evacuation of Kolberg airfield this machine was to be ferried to Workshops Section 26/III at Oranienburg. Pilot took his crew chief (Gefr. Ewers) with him. Aircraft failed to arrive. Details of fate could not be established.

132: ??.3.45   Lyke, Fw. Heinz; pilot 7./SG 1 (Lehrte/Hannover, 8.10.20)

Shot down by enemy fighters. Crashed into River Oder near Postejuck, between Autobahn bridge and Stettin.

132: ??.03.45   Schirm, Uffz. Julius; pilot 8./SG 1 (Stuttgart/Münster, 23.10.21)

Fw 190 'Yellow 8': Shot down by enemy fighters near Schöningen, 15km SSW Stettin. Severe wound to upper right arm.

133: 11.3.45   Centurier, Lt. Wilhelm; pilot 9./SG 1 (Stargard/Pomerania, 30.11.23)

Fw 190 'Black 11': Bailed out in grid area 44821 after coming under fire from enemy fighters. Pilot missing.

133: 15.3.45   Heidrich, Lt. Waldemar; pilot 8./SG 1 (Rastatt/Baden, 11.5.24)

Fw 190 'Yellow 3': Shot down north of Woltin, east of Greifenhagen, presumably by enemy Flak. Pilot missing.

133: 5.4.45   Trenkel, Fw. Hans; pilot Stab III./SG 1 (Berlin,19.1.20)

Fw 190D: Failed to return from combat mission in area Zellin. Fate could not be established. Pilot missing, signed Schrepfer, Major and Gruppenkommandeur.